Certification Study Companion Series

The Apress Certification Study Companion Series offers guidance and hands-on practice to support technical and business professionals who are studying for an exam in the pursuit of an industry certification. Professionals worldwide seek to achieve certifications in order to advance in a career role, reinforce knowledge in a specific discipline, or to apply for or change jobs. This series focuses on the most widely taken certification exams in a given field. It is designed to be user friendly, tracking to topics as they appear in a given exam. Authors for this series are experts and instructors who not only possess a deep understanding of the content, but also have experience teaching the key concepts that support readers in the practical application of the skills learned in their day-to-day roles.

More information about this series at https://link.springer.com/bookseries/17100

CISSP Exam Certification Companion

1000+ Practice Questions
and Expert Strategies
for Passing the CISSP Exam

Mohamed Aly Bouke

Apress®

CISSP Exam Certification Companion: 1000+ Practice Questions and Expert Strategies for Passing the CISSP Exam

Mohamed Aly Bouke, PhD
Serdang, Selangor, Malaysia

ISBN-13 (pbk): 979-8-8688-0056-6   ISBN-13 (electronic): 979-8-8688-0057-3
https://doi.org/10.1007/979-8-8688-0057-3

Managing Director, Apress Media LLC: Welmoed Spahr
Acquisitions Editor: Susan McDermott
Development Editor: Laura Berendson
Coordinating Editor: Gryffin Winkler

Cover designed by eStudioCalamar

Distributed to the book trade worldwide by Apress Media, LLC, 1 New York Plaza, New York, NY 10004, U.S.A. Phone 1-800-SPRINGER, fax (201) 348-4505, e-mail orders-ny@springer-sbm.com, or visit www.springeronline.com. Apress Media, LLC is a California LLC and the sole member (owner) is Springer Science + Business Media Finance Inc (SSBM Finance Inc). SSBM Finance Inc is a **Delaware** corporation.

For information on translations, please e-mail booktranslations@springernature.com; for reprint, paperback, or audio rights, please e-mail bookpermissions@springernature.com.

Apress titles may be purchased in bulk for academic, corporate, or promotional use. eBook versions and licenses are also available for most titles. For more information, reference our Print and eBook Bulk Sales web page at http://www.apress.com/bulk-sales.

Any source code or other supplementary material referenced by the author in this book is available to readers on GitHub (https://github.com/Apress). For more detailed information, please visit https://www.apress.com/gp/services/source-code.

Paper in this product is recyclable

Table of Contents

TABLE OF CONTENTS

About the Author

Mohamed Aly Bouke, PhD, CISSP, is an acclaimed cybersecurity expert, educator, and IT certification specialist with over a decade of multifaceted experience. He currently holds dual roles: Cybersecurity Researcher at University of Putra Malaysia and Senior Instructor at Certangle, LLC. His scholarly contributions span cybersecurity, machine learning, and network security research. Renowned for his pedagogical prowess, Dr. Bouke has conducted numerous training sessions for IT certifications, including ISACA, ISC2, CompTIA, and Microsoft. Many students have successfully passed their certification exams under his guidance, cementing his reputation as an IT certification expert.

Aside from his rich academic background – which encompasses participating in many conferences and generating an extensive array of publications in cybersecurity and artificial intelligence – Dr. Bouke is also a respected reviewer for prestigious journals and publishers such as Packt Publishing, Elsevier, and IEEE.

On the corporate front, he has utilized his training expertise with well-regarded companies such as KnowledgeHut. His comprehensive consulting experience encompasses collaborations with international organizations focused on strengthening their cybersecurity infrastructure.

ABOUT THE AUTHOR

Holding multiple certifications, including CISSP, Dr. Bouke brings to this book not only a wealth of theoretical understanding but also practical, hands-on experience. Intended as a comprehensive guide, this book emerges as an indispensable resource for cybersecurity professionals at all stages of their careers. For additional learning resources and insightful tips, visit Dr. Bouke's website, www.bukacert.com.

About the Technical Reviewer

Trevor Chandler, CISSP No. 458840, CCSP, CCSK, CEH, CASP, has been a faculty member in higher education for more than 35 years. Trevor has also worked as a system administrator on UNIX (AIX, HP-UX, SunOS) and Linux (Red Hat) systems. As an educator, Trevor has delivered courses primarily in multiple levels of Linux system administration, Cisco networking (CCNA/CCNP R&S), and information systems security.

Acknowledgments

In pursuit of academic and professional excellence, the contributions of numerous individuals have been instrumental in shaping my journey. Foremost, I extend my heartfelt gratitude to my family, whose unwavering support has been the bedrock upon which I have built my aspirations. Their sacrifices and steadfast belief in my capabilities have been the driving forces behind my accomplishments. I am also deeply indebted to Dr. Azizol Abdullah, whose mentorship has been transformative in both my intellectual and ethical development. The credit he has generously attributed to me has served as a potent motivator in my scholarly endeavors. Additionally, I express my sincere thanks to Dr. Mike Chapple and Rob Witcher, from whom I have gleaned invaluable insights into this field. Their exceptional and distinctive content has significantly enriched my understanding and has been a source of continuous inspiration. To my students, your active engagement and constructive feedback have been invaluable in refining my teaching methodology and deepening my expertise. Your contributions have been pivotal in my professional growth. Lastly, I extend my appreciation to the editorial team, whose cooperation has been exemplary throughout the duration of this book project. Their meticulous attention to detail and unwavering commitment have been indispensable in bringing this work to fruition.

CHAPTER 1

Unlocking the CISSP Journey: An Introduction

Information security has become paramount in the digital age, where our lives are intricately intertwined with technology. As the world becomes progressively interconnected, the rate and sophistication of cyberattacks and data breaches are escalating at an alarming pace. This unstable environment has compelled organizations globally to prioritize and invest in a robust information security program. At the heart of this initiative lies the Certified Information Systems Security Professional (CISSP), a globally recognized cybersecurity certification governed by the International Information System Security Certification Consortium (ISC2).

For IT professionals, the CISSP certification serves as a golden standard, validating their broad and deep knowledge and expertise in the cybersecurity domain. It can be a career game-changer, opening doors to better job opportunities, career progression, and earning potential. For organizations, it provides a reliable benchmark to evaluate the competence of their IT professionals, ensuring they have a team capable of protecting their digital assets against ever-evolving threats.

© Mohamed Aly Bouke 2023

M. A. Bouke, *CISSP Exam Certification Companion*, Certification Study Companion Series, https://doi.org/10.1007/979-8-8688-0057-3_1

In this introductory chapter, we embark on a journey to explore the fascinating world of CISSP. We delve into its history, tracing its evolution and understanding its contemporary significance in the global cybersecurity landscape. We unravel the intricacies of the CISSP certification process, guiding you step by step from discerning if CISSP is the right choice for you, navigating through the rigorous exam requirements, to finally earning your membership with ISC2.

The CISSP certification exam encompasses eight diverse domains, each representing a specific aspect of information security. This chapter provides an overview of these domains, highlighting their relevance and importance in today's digital world. Moreover, we present a tailored study plan that caters to different experience levels, ensuring a focused and efficient preparation strategy.

Whether you are an experienced security practitioner looking to advance your career or a newcomer stepping into the field, this chapter serves as a compass, clarifying what the CISSP certification entails and how you can effectively embark on this journey.

By the end of this chapter, you will have a firm understanding of the significance of the CISSP certification, its certification process, and how to navigate through the subsequent chapters of this book to your advantage. Embarking on this journey will prepare you to pass the CISSP exam and equip you with the knowledge and skills required to excel in the dynamic field of information security. This chapter marks the start of your CISSP journey toward becoming an integral part of the global community of information security professionals.

Welcome to Chapter 1 – your first step toward becoming a CISSP.

ISC2: The Heart of Cybersecurity Certification

ISC2 is a nonprofit organization that is the global leader in cybersecurity certifications. Since its inception in 1989, it has been on a mission to empower cybersecurity and information security professionals, helping them validate their knowledge and expertise through a rigorous, standardized certification program.

The cornerstone of ISC2's certification programs is the Common Body of Knowledge (CBK), a comprehensive framework outlining the fundamental concepts, principles, and best practices in information security. Each of ISC2's certifications, including the coveted Certified Information Systems Security Professional (CISSP), Certified Cloud Security Professional (CCSP), and Certified Secure Software Lifecycle Professional (CSSLP), among others, is designed to assess a candidate's proficiency in specific areas of information security as detailed in the CBK.

As the digital landscape continues to evolve rapidly, so does the demand for certified cybersecurity professionals. The ISC2 certifications are recognized and respected globally as a benchmark for information security knowledge and competence. In industries where cybersecurity is a critical concern, employers and organizations value these certifications, often seeking out professionals who carry these credentials.

But ISC2 is not just about certifications. It is a vibrant community offering a host of resources to its members, aiding in continuous learning and professional development. From online courses and webinars to international conferences, ISC2 offers many opportunities for its members to stay updated with the latest in the field, share knowledge, and network with other professionals worldwide.

A fundamental aspect that sets ISC2 apart is its commitment to fostering ethical behavior and professionalism in information security. To this end, it has established a Code of Ethics that all certified professionals must abide by. This code encapsulates principles such as protecting society, acting with integrity, and advancing and protecting the profession. Adherence to this code is not just expected but also an obligation that underscores each member's responsibility in this critical field. We will discuss more about this code in Chapter 3.

The CISSP Exam: Your Gateway to Global Recognition

The CISSP certification stands as a beacon of excellence in the ever-evolving information security market. Recognized worldwide, this certification is a testament to a professional's in-depth technical and managerial understanding and experience in information security. CISSP-certified professionals showcase their prowess in designing, engineering, and managing the overall security posture of an organization, making them invaluable assets in their respective organizations.

The CISSP certification is anchored in the CBK, a comprehensive framework outlining key concepts, principles, and best practices in information security. The CBK's broad spectrum of topics ensures its relevance across all disciplines within the information security arena. Candidates who successfully achieve the CISSP certification demonstrate their competence in the following eight domains:

- **Security and Risk Management**: This domain establishes the bedrock of information security. It encompasses the development of policies, procedures, and guidelines to manage and mitigate risk effectively. The domain delves into concepts, principles, and structures that form the foundation of information security.

- **Asset Security:** This domain focuses on the protection of information and assets. It includes identifying and classifying information and assets and implementing appropriate controls to safeguard them.

- **Security Architecture and Engineering:** This domain covers the principles, concepts, and structures that underpin information security architecture and engineering. It includes designing, implementing, and managing secure systems and architectures.

- **Communication and Network Security:** This domain deals with secure network design, implementation, and management. It includes the use of cryptography and network segmentation to ensure secure communications.

- **Identity and Access Management (IAM):** This domain explores identity and access management concepts, principles, and structures. It delves into managing user access, authentication, authorization, and accountability, all vital aspects of a robust security framework.

- **Security Assessment and Testing:** This domain outlines the principles, concepts, and structures of security assessments and testing. It includes using various tools and techniques to evaluate the effectiveness of security controls and identify vulnerabilities. A thorough understanding of this domain is crucial for ensuring the effectiveness of security measures.

- **Security Operations**: This domain covers security operations' principles, concepts, and structures. It includes managing security operations centers, incident response, disaster recovery, and business continuity planning. Mastery of this domain ensures the ability to keep an organization's security operations running smoothly, even in unforeseen incidents or disasters.

- **Software Development Security**: This domain explores software development security concepts, principles, and structures. It includes implementing secure coding practices and integrating security into the Software Development Life Cycle. Understanding this domain is essential for ensuring the development of secure software products.

The CISSP CBK domains form a comprehensive outline of the information security field, ensuring that CISSP-certified professionals have a well-rounded and in-depth understanding of information security. The certification is not just about passing an exam; it's about understanding the bigger picture of information security and demonstrating competence in all its aspects.

Becoming CISSP certified is a significant achievement that requires commitment and preparation. The subsequent sections of this chapter will provide you with an overview of the certification process and offer a study plan tailored to your experience level. With the proper preparation and mindset, you can join the ranks of CISSP-certified professionals, opening up a world of opportunities for career advancement in cybersecurity.

Certification Process

The CISSP certification process (refer to Figure 1-1) is designed to ensure that individuals who earn the certification have the necessary knowledge and experience to effectively design, engineer, and manage the overall security posture of an organization. This section will provide an overview of the certification process, from determining if the CISSP is right for you to become an ISC2 member.

- **Step 1 - Determine if the CISSP is right for you**: The CISSP is ideal for experienced security practitioners, managers, and executives interested in proving their knowledge across various security practices and principles. Individuals in positions such as Chief Information Security Officer, Director of Security, IT Director/Manager, Security Analyst, Security Manager, Security Auditor, Security Architect, Security Consultant, and Network Architect are ideal candidates for the CISSP.

- **Step 2 - Register and prepare for the exam**: The CISSP exam is a rigorous exam that assesses an individual's knowledge of information security concepts, principles, and best practices. The exam covers eight domains representing the CBK. Therefore, it is crucial to thoroughly study all these domains to be fully prepared for the exam.

- **Step 3 - Meet the experience requirements**: To qualify for the CISSP certification, an individual must pass the exam and have at least five years of cumulative, paid work experience in two or more of the eight domains of the ISC2 CISSP CBK. If an individual holds a relevant four-year college degree or an approved credential, they may be able to satisfy one year of the required work experience. If an individual does not have enough experience, they can still pass the CISSP exam and become an Associate of ISC2 while earning the required work experience.

- **Step 4 – Complete the certification application process**: This process includes attesting that their assertions regarding professional experience are true, that they are in good standing within the cybersecurity industry, and agreeing to abide by the ISC2 Code of Ethics and privacy policy. In addition, all ISC2 members must commit to fully supporting ISC2 Code of Ethics Canons, which include protecting society, acting honorably and legally, providing diligent and competent service, and advancing and protecting the profession.

- **Step 5 – Pay the Annual Maintenance Fee (AMF)**: An individual must pay their first Annual Maintenance Fee (AMF) to become an ISC2 member. Certified members pay a single AMF of $125, which is due each year upon the anniversary of their certification date. Associates of ISC2 pay an AMF of $50, which is due each year upon the anniversary of achieving their associate status.

- *Please note that the AMF may be subject to change, and candidates should visit the ISC2 website for the latest updates on fees and other certification requirements.*

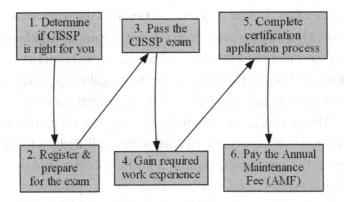

Figure 1-1. *CISSP Certification Process*

Experience Requirements

In the journey toward becoming a CISSP, the importance of practical experience cannot be overstated. Theoretical knowledge is a critical pillar, but applying this knowledge in real-world contexts truly shapes an effective information security professional.

The CISSP certification demands at least five years of cumulative, paid, full-time work experience in two or more of the eight domains of the CISSP CBK. This requirement underscores the value of hands-on professional experience in the diverse domains of information security.

However, ISC2 also acknowledges the value of formal education. Therefore, candidates can offset one year of the required experience with a four-year college degree (or regional equivalent) or an additional credential from the ISC2 approved list. It's important to note that this education credit can satisfy only one year of the required experience, emphasizing professional expertise.

But what if you're a recent graduate or a professional eager to take the CISSP exam but lacking the requisite experience? ISC2 offers a solution. By successfully passing the CISSP examination, you can earn the designation of an Associate of ISC2, even if you haven't yet met the work experience requirements. This designation is a testament to your knowledge of information security principles, even without practical experience.

Becoming an Associate of ISC2 sets you on a guided path toward CISSP. You're given a six-year window to earn five years of work experience. This period allows you to build a solid foundation in the field and gain the practical experience needed to be a full-fledged CISSP.

In essence, the experience requirements for CISSP ensure that certified professionals are well-versed in information security principles and have the hands-on experience to apply these principles effectively. Whether you're a seasoned professional or just starting in the field, the CISSP certification and its process are designed to guide you toward mastery of information security.

Book Goals

This book is crafted with one primary objective: to guide you on your journey to achieve the CISSP certification and help you do so on your first attempt. It is more than just a study guide; it is a comprehensive manual designed to provide a profound understanding of the CISSP exam's nuances, backed by expert strategies and beneficial tips.

To make the learning process more interactive and reinforce your understanding of the concepts, this book includes over 1000 practice questions. These questions are designed to simulate the actual exam's format and difficulty, allowing you to test your knowledge, identify your strengths and weaknesses, and ultimately build your confidence as you approach the exam.

However, the ambition of this book extends beyond just exam preparation. Its mission is also to equip you with the knowledge and skills necessary to excel in the field of information security, even after you pass the exam. It delves into the depths of all eight domains of the CISSP CBK, ensuring you understand the core principles, concepts, and best practices in the field.

In addition to being an excellent study aid, this book is an invaluable resource for information security professionals, irrespective of their career stage. It can be used as a reference guide to revisit critical concepts, refresh your knowledge, or stay updated with various topics in information security.

This book is your comprehensive companion on your journey toward CISSP certification and beyond. It's not just about helping you pass an exam; it's about equipping you with the knowledge and skills to become an effective and successful information security professional.

Whom This Book Is For?

This book primarily caters to information security professionals preparing to take the CISSP exam, encompassing individuals keen on obtaining the CISSP certification or those seeking to enhance their knowledge and skills in information security.

Designed to accommodate a diverse range of experience and knowledge levels, this book is equally suitable for novices seeking a comprehensive understanding of the CISSP exam as it is for seasoned professionals aiming to refresh their knowledge and skills. It is also ideal for those considering a career shift to information security, providing them with a thorough understanding of the concepts and best practices outlined in the CISSP CBK, indispensable for anyone aspiring to make their mark in this field.

Beyond the primary audience of information security professionals, this book extends its utility to

- **IT professionals**: This book is beneficial for their organization's information systems security. It offers an extensive understanding of information security concepts and best practices, empowering IT professionals to comprehend and implement adequate security measures within their organizations.

- **Students and educators**: This book serves as a valuable resource for those enrolled in information security programs or engaged in imparting knowledge in this field. It provides a comprehensive overview of the CISSP exam and the certification process and a detailed understanding of the information security concepts and best practices outlined in the CISSP CBK. This can aid students in their CISSP exam preparation or enhance their knowledge of the information security field.

- **Employers and HR professionals**: Those involved in hiring information security professionals or assessing the skills and knowledge of their existing security staff will find this book helpful. It provides a detailed understanding of information security concepts and best practices. It is a valuable tool to evaluate potential hires' or existing personnel's knowledge and skills.

In essence, this book serves as an essential guide to anyone interested in, or professional connection to, the field of information security. It doesn't just prepare you for the CISSP exam; it prepares you for a successful career in information security.

Benefits of Using This Book As a Study Resource

Using this book as a study resource offers several benefits to readers, including

- **Comprehensive coverage**: This book provides comprehensive coverage of the CISSP exam and the certification process, ensuring readers have all the information they need to prepare for the exam.

- **Expert strategies**: The book includes expert strategies for preparing for and passing the CISSP exam, helping readers develop an effective study plan and confidently approach the exam.

- **Practice questions**: With 1000+ practice questions, readers can test their knowledge and understanding of the CISSP CBK domains, identify areas where they need further study, and track their progress as they prepare for the exam.

- **Easy-to-understand language**: The book is written in an easy-to-understand language, making it accessible to readers with varying experiences and knowledge in information security.

- **Versatile resource**: This book can be used as a study resource by readers at different stages of their information security careers, making it a valuable investment for anyone interested in pursuing the CISSP certification or improving their knowledge and skills in information security.

Using this book as a study resource, readers can confidently prepare for the CISSP exam, enhance their knowledge of information security, and advance their careers in this rapidly growing field.

How to Use This Book

Crafted to serve as a comprehensive guide to help you ace the CISSP exam, this book has a road map to maximize its effectiveness. Here's how you can leverage this resource to your advantage:

- **Start with the introduction**: The book begins with an overview of the CISSP exam and the certification process. This section will help you understand the exam and the goals this book aims to achieve.

- **Understand the exam format and content**: Chapter 2 dives into the specifics of the exam format and content and shares insightful strategies to study effectively for the exam. Reviewing this chapter meticulously before embarking on your preparation journey is highly recommended.

- **Delve into the domains**: The book's structure aligns with the eight domains of the CISSP CBK, making it a comprehensive resource. Studying each domain thoroughly and attempting the practice questions at the end of each chapter to reinforce your understanding is crucial.

- **Try your hand at practice tests**: Two full-length practice tests await you at the end of the book. After studying all the domains, take these tests to gauge your exam readiness and identify areas that need more focus.

- **Examine test-taking strategies and tips**: Chapter 11 is a treasure trove of expert tips and strategies for passing the CISSP exam. Review this chapter thoroughly before you sit for the exam to equip yourself with invaluable tactics.

- **Complement with additional resources**: While this book provides a comprehensive guide to the CISSP exam, supplementing it with other resources can enrich your preparation. ISC2 offers official study materials and a wealth of online resources that can complement this book.

Remember, this book is not just about preparing for an exam; it's about building a solid foundation in information security. Use it as a springboard to dive deep into the fascinating world of cybersecurity and emerge as an expert in the field.

Charting Your Path: Crafting a Personalized Study

The journey to ace the CISSP exam begins with a well-crafted study plan. A customized study plan streamlines your preparation and optimizes your time and resources. Here are some steps to help you chart your path to success:

- **Take a knowledge inventory**: Kickstart your preparation by evaluating your current understanding of the CISSP domains. This self-assessment will help you identify your strengths and weaknesses, enabling you to allocate your study time effectively.

- **Set a goal with the exam date**: A target exam date is a beacon, keeping you motivated and focused on your preparation journey. Ensure ample time to cover and review all the material for better retention comprehensively.

- **Carve out your study schedule**: Based on your target exam date, carve out a study schedule that assigns time for each domain. Consider your daily routine, work commitments, and personal obligations when crafting this schedule.

- **Explore multiple study resources**: This book is a robust resource, but supplementing it with other materials, such as ISC2's official study materials, online resources, and study groups, can enhance your learning.

- **Monitor your progress**: Monitor your progress by regularly taking practice tests and quizzes. This allows you to spot improvement areas and adjust your study plan accordingly.

- **Invest time in revision**: As the exam date draws closer, reserve time to revise and review the studied material. Concentrate on areas where you need enhancement and ensure a thorough understanding of all concepts.

- **Keep the motivation high**: Sustained motivation is vital to successful exam preparation. Set achievable milestones, celebrate your progress, and constantly remind yourself of your goals.

Using these steps and tailoring a study plan that caters to your needs, you can optimize your CISSP exam preparation and significantly enhance your chances of success. Remember, this plan is not set in stone, and you should feel free to adjust it as you progress, ensuring it always aligns with your evolving learning style and pace:

- **Proposed study plan**

   The CISSP certification exam can be challenging, especially for those who are new to the cybersecurity field or do not have extensive experience in multiple domains. Therefore, creating a study plan that suits your experience level is essential, ensuring you allocate sufficient time to each domain and develop a thorough understanding of the material.

The following (see Table 1-1) proposed study plan is designed to cater to three different experience levels: experienced, intermediate, and beginner candidates. This plan spans 16 weeks, but it can be adjusted to accommodate your personal schedule, preferences, and pace of learning.

Table 1-1. *The Proposed Study Plan*

Week	Experienced Candidate	Intermediate Candidate	Beginner Candidate
1	Domain 1	Domain 1	Domain 1
2	Domain 2	Domain 1 (cont.)	Domain 1 (cont.)
3	Domain 3	Domain 2	Domain 1 (cont.)
4	Domain 4	Domain 2 (cont.)	Domain 2
5	Domain 5	Domain 3	Domain 3
6	Domain 6	Domain 3 (cont.)	Domain 3 (cont.)
7	Domain 7	Domain 4	Domain 4
8	Domain 8	Domain 4 (cont.)	Domain 4 (cont.)
9	Review and practice	Domain 5	Domain 5
10	Review and practice	Domain 6	Domain 6
11	Review and practice	Domain 7	Domain 7
12	Review and practice	Domain 8	Domain 7 (cont.)
13	–	Review and practice	Domain 8
14	–	Review and practice	Domain 8 (cont.)
15	–	–	Review and practice
16	–	–	Review and practice

For each experience level, the study plan outlines which domains to focus on each week, gradually progressing through the material. In the final weeks, the plan includes time for review and practice exams to consolidate your knowledge and assess your readiness for the actual CISSP exam.

- **Experienced candidate**: If you already have extensive knowledge and experience in the cybersecurity field, you may only need a quick review of each domain. The experienced student's plan allocates one week per domain and dedicates the last four weeks to reviewing and taking practice exams. This ensures that you have covered all the domains and have ample time to identify any weak areas that need further study.

- **Intermediate candidate**: As an intermediate candidate, you may have some experience and familiarity with the CISSP domains but need more time to study certain areas. This plan allocates one to two weeks per domain, depending on the complexity and the amount of material to cover. It allows you to focus on each domain in more depth, building a strong foundation before moving on to the next topic. The final two weeks are dedicated to reviewing and taking practice exams to solidify your knowledge and improve your test-taking skills.

- **Beginner candidate**: If you are new to cybersecurity or have limited experience, taking a more in-depth approach to study each domain is crucial. The beginner's plan allocates two to three weeks per domain, ensuring you have sufficient time to understand the material and develop a solid understanding of each topic. In the final weeks, you will cover Domain 7: Security Operations over two weeks (weeks 11 and 12) and then focus on Domain 8: Software Development Security during weeks 13 and 14. Weeks 15 and 16 are dedicated to reviewing and taking practice exams, allowing you to assess your readiness for the CISSP exam and identify areas requiring additional study.

Remember, this proposed study plan serves as a starting point and can be customized to fit your needs, schedule, and learning style. It is essential to regularly assess your progress and make adjustments to the plan as needed to ensure you are well prepared for the CISSP certification exam.

Overview of the Book Structure and Chapter Summaries

This book has been meticulously organized into 12 comprehensive chapters, each aimed at equipping you with the knowledge, skills, and strategies required to excel in the CISSP examination. Here's a detailed overview of what to anticipate from each chapter:

- **Chapter 2 – Decoding the CISSP Exam: Understanding Format and Content**: This chapter serves as your compass for navigating the CISSP exam. It illuminates the format and content of the exam, elucidates the most effective study methods, and includes pertinent practice questions to consolidate your understanding.

- **Chapter 3 – Security and Risk Management**: Immerse yourself in the domain of Security and Risk Management with this chapter. It thoroughly comprehends the fundamental concepts, spotlights best practices, and shares indispensable exam tips, concluded by relevant practice questions.

- **Chapter 4 – Asset Security**: This chapter delves into the heart of the Asset Security domain. It explains key concepts, outlines best practices, and provides exam tips, supplemented with practice questions to gauge your grasp on the subject.

- **Chapter 5 – Security Architecture and Engineering**: Familiarize yourself with the core concepts of the Security Architecture and Engineering domain in this chapter. It includes expert exam tips and practice questions to fortify your learning.

- **Chapter 6 – Communications and Network Security**: Traverse the Communications and Network Security domain with this chapter. It explores the key concepts, delineates best practices, offers exam tips, and includes practice questions for reinforcement.

- **Chapter 7 – Identity and Access Management**: This chapter empowers you with an in-depth understanding of the Identity and Access Management domain. It provides expert tips for exam success and practice questions for self-assessment.

- **Chapter 8 – Security Assessment and Testing**: Get acquainted with this chapter's critical concepts underpinning the Security Assessment and Testing domain. It offers valuable exam tips and practice questions to solidify your understanding.

- **Chapter 9 – Security Operations**: Dive into this chapter's fundamental concepts of the Security Operations domain. It is supplemented with expert exam tips and practice questions to ensure comprehensive coverage.

- **Chapter 10 – Software Development Security**: This chapter acquaints you with the essential concepts of the Software Development Security domain. It offers expert tips for exam preparedness and practice questions for review.

- **Chapter 11 – Tools and Strategies: Study Methods and Exam Techniques**: This chapter is your toolkit for exam success. It equips you with expert advice on strategically approaching the CISSP exam and offers indispensable tips for exam day.

- **Chapter 12 – Final Lap: Comprehensive Exam and Preparation Approach**: The concluding chapter ties together the main points covered throughout the book. It offers a reflective summary and guides you toward additional research resources.

As you progress through this book, each chapter is designed to build upon the last, ensuring a smooth and comprehensive learning journey toward your CISSP certification.

Summary and Key Takeaways

This chapter encapsulated a comprehensive overview of the CISSP certification, outlining its significance, the certification procedure, requisite experience, book objectives, and guidelines on making optimal use of this book. Moreover, it presented a versatile study plan, adaptable to different experience levels, to aid candidates in their CISSP exam preparation.

Key Takeaways

- The CISSP certification is a globally acknowledged standard in cybersecurity, serving as a testament to an individual's proficiency and expertise in information security. It is apt for seasoned security practitioners, managers, and executives seeking to validate their skills.

- The certification path involves discerning if the CISSP aligns with your career goals, enrolling for the exam, preparing for the exam through a thorough study of the eight domains, successfully passing the exam, and fulfilling the experience prerequisites. Upon completing these steps, candidates must pay the Annual Maintenance Fee and abide by the ISC2 Code of Ethics.

- CISSP aspirants must have at least five years of cumulative, paid work experience in two or more of the eight CISSP CBK domains to be eligible for the certification. Educational credits can substitute for one year of the necessary experience.

- This book is designed to be a comprehensive ally to candidates preparing for the CISSP exam, offering expert advice, more than 1000 practice questions, and an extensive guide to the exam. It encapsulates all eight domains of the CISSP CBK, ensuring a comprehensive understanding of foundational concepts and best practices.

- Effective usage of this book involves acquainting oneself with the introduction, understanding the exam format and content, studying each domain comprehensively, taking practice tests, reviewing exam strategies and tips, and integrating additional resources when necessary.

- The proposed study plan provides a structured pathway spanning over 16 weeks, catering to candidates with varying experience levels. The flexible plan can be modified to suit individual schedules, needs, and learning approaches.

Understanding the CISSP certification process and making effective use of the study plan and resources provided can enhance a candidate's readiness for the CISSP exam and boost their proficiency in the field of information security.

CHAPTER 2

Decoding the CISSP Exam: Understanding Format and Content

Welcome to Chapter 2, a crucial phase of your CISSP certification journey. This chapter is your road map to understanding the CISSP exam's intricacies, structure, and content, all essential for adequate preparation.

Our exploration begins with a detailed look at the CISSP exam format, which employs a unique methodology known as the Computerized Adaptive Testing (CAT) system. We will break down the mechanics of this testing format and shed light on how it personalizes your exam experience. This insight will demystify the exam process and help you confidently approach your test day.

In addition to understanding the exam format, knowing what content will be covered during the examination is imperative. Hence, we delve into the various domains of the CISSP exam and their corresponding weightings in both the CAT and linear exam formats. These insights will guide you to prioritize and allocate your study time effectively.

To further assist in your preparation, we will provide an initial assessment. This tool is designed to help you gauge your current knowledge level across the different domains and highlight areas that may

© Mohamed Aly Bouke 2023
M. A. Bouke, *CISSP Exam Certification Companion*, Certification Study Companion Series,
https://doi.org/10.1007/979-8-8688-0057-3_2

require more attention in your study plan. By identifying these areas early on, you can tailor your preparation strategy to address gaps and reinforce your understanding in areas where you're already strong.

This chapter aims to equip you with a clear understanding of the CISSP exam's structure and content and empower you with the knowledge to take control of your study plan. We aim to turn the daunting task of preparing for the CISSP exam into a manageable and rewarding process.

By the end of this chapter, you will have a comprehensive understanding of what the CISSP exam entails, and you'll be better prepared to tackle your CISSP certification journey head-on. So, let's dive into the world of CISSP and start turning your certification goal into a reality.

Before We Dive into the CISSP World

It's important to understand that the CISSP exam covers a vast range of topics and knowledge areas, as outlined in the CBK. However, the exam will not go into great depth in any particular area, except for domains 1 and 7, which may be covered in greater depth. The purpose of the exam is not to test your technical skills or make you an expert in every aspect of information security but to ensure that you have a baseline understanding of the various concepts and can apply them in the business context.

As such, it's essential to approach your studies with the mindset of understanding the core principles and how they relate to the overall security posture of an organization. While you may encounter questions requiring you to recall specific details or technical information, most of the exam will focus on your ability to apply concepts and make sound decisions based on the information presented.

Remember, the CISSP certification is meant to validate your experience and knowledge as a security professional, not to make you an expert in every area of information security. With this in mind, use this book to gain a broad understanding of the key concepts and best practices and apply them to make informed decisions supporting the business.

Exam Format

The CISSP exam uses CAT for all English exams. CISSP exams in all other languages are administered as linear, fixed-form exams. The exam lasts four hours, and the number of questions ranges from 125 to 175. The question format includes multiple choice and advanced innovative questions. The passing grade is 700 out of 1000 points.

Figure 2-1 provides a visual representation of the CISSP domain weights, showing the relative importance of each domain in the exam. It's important to note that while some domains have higher consequences than others, this should not intimidate you.

The CISSP exam is designed so that the domains compensate for each other.[1] It means that if a candidate performs exceptionally well in one domain, it can balance out their weaker performance in another domain. It is not required to pass all domains individually to succeed on the exam.

However, it is crucial to become familiar with the content in each domain and strive to achieve a solid understanding across all areas. This approach will ensure a well-rounded foundation in information security and increase your chances of passing the CISSP exam. Remember, the certification aims to validate your knowledge and experience as a security professional, so understanding the core principles and best practices in each domain will prepare you for success.

---

[1] www.isc2.org/Certifications/CISSP/CISSP-Cat (look at the question, "Does a candidate need to score 'Above Proficiency' in all domains in order to pass the exam?")

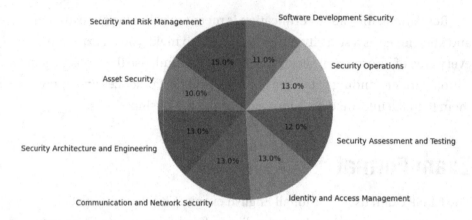

Figure 2-1. *CISSP Domain Weights*

For the CISSP Linear exam, the domains' average weights are the same as the CAT exam. The CISSP Linear exam is six hours long, and the number of items is 250. The question format includes multiple choice and advanced innovative questions, and the passing grade is 700 out of 1000 points. The CISSP CAT exam is available only in English, whereas the CISSP Linear exam is in Chinese, German, Japanese, Korean, and Spanish.

Computerized Adaptive Testing (CAT) Exam

As we already mentioned, the CISSP exam is now delivered using CAT for all English exams. This new testing format allows for a more personalized and efficient testing experience. In a CAT exam, the computer adapts the difficulty level of the questions based on the test-taker's performance. For example, the first question presented to the test-taker is of moderate difficulty. The computer will select the next question based on the answer to the first question. If the test-taker answers correctly, the next question will be slightly more difficult. If the test-taker answers incorrectly, the next question will be easier. This process continues until the computer determines the test-taker's ability level in each domain with a high degree of confidence. This means that the number of questions and the difficulty level of the questions presented to each test-taker will vary.

Figure 2-2 visually represents a simplified CAT exam process for a test-taker. Suppose the first question presented to the test-taker is about the Security and Risk Management domain. The difficulty level is set to moderate (indicated by the first point on the chart). If the test-taker answers correctly, the next question will be slightly more difficult (shown by an increase in the difficulty level on the y axis). If the test-taker answers incorrectly, the next question will be slightly easier (shown by a decrease in the difficulty level on the y axis).

As the test-taker continues to answer questions, the line on the chart moves up or down, representing the changes in the difficulty level of the questions. The line moves upward when the test-taker answers correctly, resulting in more difficult questions in the Security and Risk Management domain. Conversely, the line moves downward when the test-taker answers incorrectly, causing the computer to present easier questions in the domain.

This process continues until the computer determines the test-taker's ability level in the Security and Risk Management domain. The line chart visually demonstrates the adaptive nature of the CAT exam, ensuring that each test-taker is presented with a unique set of questions based on their ability level. This means that each test-taker will have a different testing experience, and the number of questions presented to each test-taker will vary, as represented by the length of the line on the chart.

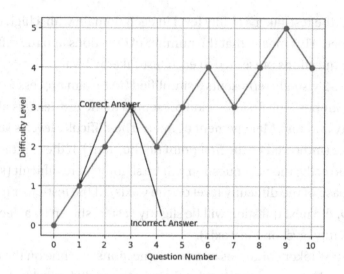

Figure 2-2. *Simple Example of CAT Exam Process*

Moreover, the CAT exam is more accurate than the linear model, as it adapts to each test-taker's knowledge and ability. After answering the 125th question, there are three possible outcomes based on the CAT algorithm's assessment:

- If the algorithm is confident that the candidate will pass the exam, the test will stop, and the candidate will pass.

- If the algorithm is confident that the candidate cannot pass the exam, the test will stop, and the candidate will fail.

- If the algorithm is still uncertain about the candidate's pass or fail status, the test will continue, presenting additional questions until a final decision is reached.

It is essential not to be discouraged if the exam continues after the 125th question. It indicates that you are close to success, and every additional question is an opportunity to demonstrate your knowledge and secure a passing score. Remember that if the exam continues after the 125th question, it can stop at any time once the algorithm reaches a conclusive decision. Stay focused and motivated, as each question you answer correctly may be the key to your success on the CISSP exam.

Summary and Key Takeaways

This chapter explored the CISSP exam format and content, focusing on the CAT model used for the English exam. We discussed how the CAT model adapts to each test-taker's knowledge and ability, ensuring a more accurate assessment of their skills. The chapter also provided an overview of the domain weights and emphasized the importance of becoming familiar with the content of each domain.

Key takeaways from this chapter include

- The CISSP exam covers a vast range of topics within the information security field, aiming to assess your overall understanding and ability to apply these concepts in a business context.

- The CAT model adjusts the difficulty level of questions based on your performance, providing a personalized and efficient testing experience.

- After the 125th question, the CAT algorithm may decide to stop the exam if it's confident in your pass or fail status. It may continue to present additional questions until a conclusive decision is reached.

- Don't be discouraged if the exam continues after the 125th question; stay focused and motivated, as every question is an opportunity to demonstrate your knowledge and secure a passing score.

- Familiarize yourself with the content of each domain and strive to gain a broad understanding of the key concepts and best practices.

- The initial assessment test helps you gauge your current knowledge level and identify areas to focus your study efforts. Correct answers and detailed explanations can be found at the end of this chapter.

Remember that by understanding the exam format, content, and best study practices, you can better prepare yourself for success on the CISSP exam.

Initial Assessment Test

The initial assessment is an important first step in preparing for the CISSP exam. It allows you to assess your current knowledge level and identify the areas that require more attention in your studies. In this section, we provide a set of practice questions that cover various exam-relevant topics. Take your time to answer each question and identify areas where you need more practice. This will help you create a targeted study plan that addresses your specific needs and prepares you for success on the CISSP exam. As you work through the initial assessment test, remember that the correct answers and detailed explanations can be found at the end of this chapter. Review these explanations to understand the concepts better and identify areas where you need further study or clarification.

1. Which of the following is NOT a component of the CIA triad?

   A. Confidentiality

   B. Integrity

   C. Availability

   D. Privacy

2. Which of the following is NOT a category of access control?

   A. Physical

   B. Administrative

   C. Technical

   D. Financial

3. What is the primary goal of a security risk assessment?

   A. To eliminate all risks

   B. To reduce risks to an acceptable level

   C. To identify all possible risks

   D. To transfer all risks to a third party

4. Which of the following is an example of symmetric key cryptography?

   A. RSA

   B. AES

   C. ElGamal

   D. Diffie-Hellman

5. Which of the following is NOT a common Software Development Life Cycle (SDLC) model?

    A. Waterfall

    B. Agile

    C. Spiral

    D. Sequential

6. What is the primary purpose of a firewall?

    A. To prevent unauthorized access to a network

    B. To detect and remove viruses from a network

    C. To provide secure remote access to a network

    D. To encrypt all network traffic

7. Which of the following is NOT an example of a physical security control?

    A. Security cameras

    B. Biometric scanners

    C. Firewalls

    D. Fences

8. Which of the following is NOT a type of encryption key?

    A. Public key

    B. Private key

    C. Session key

    D. Public-private key

9. Which of the following is an example of security control that falls under the security operations domain?

   A. Penetration testing

   B. Security awareness training

   C. Access control

   D. Application security testing

10. Which of the following is NOT a security incident response plan component?

   A. Preparation

   B. Detection

   C. Mitigation

   D. Penetration

11. Which of the following is an example of technical security control?

   A. Background checks

   B. Security awareness training

   C. Intrusion detection system

   D. Facility access controls

12. Which of the following is NOT an example of a common authentication factor?

   A. Something you know

   B. Something you have

   C. Something you are

   D. Something you want

13. Which of the following is a security control that falls under the security assessment and testing domain?

    A. Change management

    B. Vulnerability scanning

    C. Disaster recovery

    D. Incident response

14. Which of the following is NOT a common type of access control model?

    A. Discretionary access control (DAC)

    B. Mandatory access control (MAC)

    C. Role-based access control (RBAC)

    D. Access control list (ACL)

15. Which of the following is a key consideration when designing a secure network architecture?

    A. High availability

    B. Low cost

    C. Easy administration

    D. High bandwidth

16. What is the purpose of a security baseline?

    A. To establish the minimum-security requirements for a system or application

    B. To identify and prioritize security risks based on their potential impact

    C. To monitor and report on security events and incidents

    D. To test the effectiveness of security controls in a simulated attack environment

17.   Which of the following is NOT a common method of authentication?

   A. Password

   B. Certificate

   C. Token

   D. Proxy

18.   What is the primary goal of a security audit?

   A. To identify and assess security risks

   B. To monitor and report on security events and incidents

   C. To test the effectiveness of security controls

   D. To ensure compliance with security policies and standards

19.   Which of the following is a key principle of secure software development?

   A. Agile development

   B. Security by design

   C. Minimum viable product

   D. Continuous integration

20.   Which of the following is NOT a key component of an incident response plan?

   A. Preparation

   B. Detection and analysis

   C. Containment, eradication, and recovery

   D. Termination

21. Which of the following are NOT examples of a non-repudiation control?

    A. Digital signatures

    B. Audit trails

    C. Two-factor authentication

    D. Passwords

22. Which of the following is NOT an example of technical security control?

    A. Firewalls

    B. Biometric authentication

    C. Background checks

    D. Intrusion detection systems

23. Which of the following is crucial when designing a secure network topology?

    A. Network bandwidth

    B. Network latency

    C. Network availability

    D. Network throughput

24. Which of the following is a crucial principle of secure software development?

    A. Continuous delivery

    B. Code obfuscation

    C. Defense in depth

    D. Secure coding

25. Which of the following is NOT a type of access control?

    A. Identity verification

    B. Authorization

    C. Accountability

    D. Authentication

26. Which of the following is a crucial benefit of using cloud computing for security?

    A. Increased control over data security

    B. Improved physical security of data centers

    C. Reduced risk of insider threats

    D. Improved disaster recovery capabilities

27. Which of the following is crucial when designing secure Mobile Device Management?

    A. Protecting against insider threats

    B. Providing high-bandwidth connectivity

    C. Ensuring device compatibility with all apps

    D. Enforcing data encryption and access control policies

28. Which of the following is a key principle of secure password management?

    A. Requiring password changes every 90 days

    B. Using long, complex passwords

    C. Storing passwords in a centralized database

    D. Sharing passwords with trusted colleagues

29. Which of the following is NOT a common type of access control model?

A. Role-based access control (RBAC)

B. Mandatory access control (MAC)

C. Discretionary access control (DAC)

D. Hierarchical access control (HAC)

30. Which of the following is a key consideration when designing secure network segmentation?

A. Maximizing network throughput

B. Minimizing network latency

C. Isolating critical systems and resources

D. Providing open access to all users

31. Which of the following is a primary consideration when designing secure virtualization environments?

A. Providing unrestricted access to virtual resources

B. Ensuring compatibility with all virtualization platforms

C. Securing virtual machine images and snapshots

D. Maximizing virtual machine density

32. Which of the following is a critical principle of secure network design?

A. Maximizing network throughput

B. Minimizing network complexity

C. Providing unrestricted access to all network resources

D. Using open standards and protocols

33. Which of the following is NOT a type of vulnerability?

    A. Zero-day vulnerability

    B. Privilege escalation vulnerability

    C. Buffer overflow vulnerability

    D. Social engineering vulnerability

34. Which of the following is a crucial consideration when designing secure cloud architecture?

    A. Maximizing control over cloud infrastructure

    B. Using proprietary cloud technologies

    C. Ensuring compliance with applicable regulations and standards

    D. Avoiding the use of third-party cloud providers

35. Which of the following is a key principle of secure application development?

    A. Requiring all code to be written in-house

    B. Using open source libraries and frameworks

    C. Implementing secure coding practices

    D. Focusing on functionality over security

36. Which of the following is a primary consideration when implementing secure remote access?

    A. Providing unrestricted access to all network resources

    B. Using weak authentication mechanisms

    C. Minimizing network segmentation and access controls

    D. Enforcing strong encryption and access controls

37. Which of the following is an essential principle of secure data classification?

    A. Treating all data as sensitive and confidential

    B. Using open data standards and formats

    C. Applying consistent data classification criteria

    D. Allowing data to be stored on any device or platform

38. Which of the following is NOT a common type of encryption algorithm?

    A. AES

    B. RSA

    C. SHA-256

    D. HMAC

39. Which of the following is a key principle of secure incident response?

    A. Ignoring minor incidents to focus on major incidents

    B. Minimizing response time to all incidents

    C. Conducting thorough post-incident analysis and review

    D. Assigning blame and punishing those responsible

40. Which of the following is essential when implementing secure data storage?

    A. Maximizing data availability

    B. Using open data formats and standards

    C. Securing data at rest and in transit

    D. Storing all data on a single device or platform

41. Which of the following is a key concept of risk management?

    A. Avoid all risks

    B. Accept all risks

    C. Transfer all risks

    D. Risk decisions should be based on the impact on the business

42. What is the purpose of data classification?

    A. To ensure data privacy

    B. To ensure data integrity

    C. To ensure data availability

    D. To facilitate appropriate levels of protection based on value or sensitivity

43. What is the primary purpose of a firewall in network security?

    A. To facilitate network routing

    B. To control network traffic based on predetermined security rules

    C. To encrypt network traffic

    D. To store network data

44. Which of the following best describes "non-repudiation" in information security?

    A. Ensuring that a party in a dispute cannot deny the authenticity of their signature

    B. Ensuring that a party cannot deny receiving a message

    C. Ensuring that a party cannot deny sending a message

    D. All of the above

45. What is the primary aspect of security in the Software Development Life Cycle?

    A. Using a single programming language

    B. Testing the software only at the end of the development

    C. Integrating security throughout the life cycle, including design, development, and testing

    D. Ignoring security during development and adding it later

46. Which type of access control model uses labels and levels of protection to determine access?

    A. Role-based access control (RBAC)

    B. Discretionary access control (DAC)

    C. Mandatory access control (MAC)

    D. None of the above

47. What is the primary goal of a business continuity plan (BCP)?

    A. To provide a framework for building network infrastructure

    B. To establish steps to take for immediate response to a security incident

    C. To ensure the continuation of business processes during and after a disruption

    D. To provide a framework for prosecuting hackers

48. In the context of cryptography, what does "integrity" ensure?

    A. That the data is accessible when needed

    B. That the data has not been altered during transmission

    C. That the data is kept confidential

    D. That the sender of the data can be authenticated

49. What is the primary purpose of penetration testing?

    A. To gain unauthorized access to systems for malicious purposes

    B. To evaluate the effectiveness of security controls

    C. To troubleshoot network connectivity issues

    D. To monitor network traffic in real time

50. What is a key concept of identity and access management?

    A. Granting every user full access to all systems

    B. Granting users the minimum access necessary to perform their job function

    C. Not revoking access rights when a user changes roles

    D. Allowing shared accounts for convenience

51. Which one of the following is NOT a part of the CIA triad in information security?

    A. Confidentiality

    B. Integrity

    C. Availability

    D. Authenticity

52. What does the term "least privilege" mean in the context of information security?

A. Granting users only the permissions they need to perform their job functions

B. Giving all users the same level of access to information

C. Limiting access to information to the highest-ranking individuals in an organization

D. Granting all users full access to information but tracking their activities

53. Which of the following best describes "phishing"?

A. A method of securing a network by blocking certain websites

B. An attack that involves sending deceptive emails to trick individuals into revealing sensitive information

C. A physical security measure used to protect sensitive information

D. A type of malware that replicates itself across a network

54. What does "IDS" stand for in the context of information security?

A. Information Data System

B. Integrated Defense Strategy

C. Intrusion Detection System

D. Internal Domain Security

55. What type of security control is a biometric scanner?

A. Physical

B. Technical

C. Administrative

D. Operational

Answers

1. Answer: D. Privacy

   Explanation: The CIA triad consists of confidentiality, integrity, and availability. Privacy is an important security concept but not part of the CIA triad.

2. Answer: D. Financial

   Explanation: Access control has three categories: physical, administrative, and technical. Financial is not a category of access control.

3. Answer: B. To reduce risks to an acceptable level

   Explanation: The primary goal of a security risk assessment is to identify and analyze risks and then develop strategies to reduce them to an acceptable level.

4. Answer: B. AES

   Explanation: AES is a symmetric key algorithm, meaning the same key is used for encryption and decryption. RSA, Diffie-Hellman, and ElGamal are examples of asymmetric key algorithms.

5. Answer: D. Sequential

    Explanation: There is no SDLC model called
    sequential. The most common SDLC models are
    Waterfall, Agile, and Spiral.

6. Answer: A. To prevent unauthorized access to
    a network

    Explanation: The primary purpose of a firewall is
    to prevent unauthorized access to a network by
    blocking traffic that does not meet specific criteria.

7. Answer: C. Firewalls

    Explanation: Firewalls are an example of technical
    security control, not physical security. Physical
    security controls include security cameras,
    biometric scanners, and fences.

8. Answer: D. Public-private key

    Explanation: There is no such thing as a public-
    private key. Public key encryption uses a public and
    private key, while symmetric key encryption uses a
    session key.

9. Answer: B. Security awareness training

    Explanation: Security awareness training is a
    security control that falls under the security
    operations domain. It aims to educate employees
    about their responsibilities in maintaining the
    organization's security posture and helps them
    recognize and respond to potential threats.
    Penetration testing is not a correct answer because
    it falls under the Security Assessment and Testing

domain, which involves evaluating an organization's security posture by simulating real-world attacks. Access control is not a correct answer because it falls under the Identity and Access Management (IAM) domain, which deals with controlling who has access to resources and ensuring that only authorized individuals can access those resources. Application security testing is not a correct answer because it falls under the Software Development Security domain, which focuses on ensuring the security of applications throughout their development life cycle.

10.   Answer: D. Penetration

Explanation: Penetration is not a component of a security incident response plan. The three primary components of a security incident response plan are preparation, detection, and mitigation. Preparation involves developing policies, procedures, and controls to prevent security incidents from occurring. Detection consists of identifying and analyzing security incidents when they occur. Mitigation consists of responding to and containing the impact of security incidents and preventing similar incidents from occurring.

11.   Answer: C. Intrusion detection system

Explanation: Technical security controls use technology to prevent, detect, or respond to security threats. Examples include firewalls, antivirus software, and intrusion detection systems.

12. Answer: D. Something you want

Explanation: The three common authentication
factors are something you know (e.g., password),
something you have (e.g., token), and something
you are (e.g., biometric). Something you want is not
a recognized authentication factor.

13. Answer: B. Vulnerability scanning

Explanation: Vulnerability scanning is a security
control under the security assessment and testing
domain. It involves scanning a system for known
vulnerabilities and weaknesses.

14. Answer: D. Access control list (ACL)

Explanation: Access control lists (ACLs) are a
common implementation of access control but are
not themselves an access control model. The three
common access control models are discretionary
access control (DAC), mandatory access control
(MAC), and role-based access control (RBAC).

15. Answer: A. High availability

Explanation: A key consideration when designing
a secure network architecture is ensuring the
high availability of critical services and resources.
While cost, administration, and bandwidth are also
important, they are secondary to availability in the
context of security.

16. Answer: A. To establish the minimum-security
requirements for a system or application

Explanation: A security baseline is a set of minimum-security requirements that a system or application must meet to be considered secure. It serves as a starting point for security configuration and helps ensure security controls are implemented consistently across the organization.

17. Answer: D. Proxy

Explanation: Proxy is not a method of authentication. The three common methods of authentication are something you know (e.g., password), something you have (e.g., token), and something you are (e.g., biometric). The certificate is a type of token-based authentication.

18. Answer: D. To ensure compliance with security policies and standards

Explanation: A security audit systematically evaluates an organization's security policies, standards, and procedures to ensure compliance with established security requirements.

19. Answer: B. Security by design

Explanation: Security by design is a key principle of secure software development that involves considering security requirements throughout the entire Software Development Life Cycle rather than as an afterthought.

20. Answer: D. Termination

Explanation: Termination is not a key component of an incident response plan. The three primary components are preparation, detection and analysis, and containment, eradication, and recovery.

21.   Answer: C. Two-factor authentication and
      D. Passwords

      Explanation: Non-repudiation controls prevent
      the denial of an action or transaction. Digital
      signatures and audit trails are examples of non-
      repudiation controls, as they prove a transaction's
      origin and integrity. Two-factor authentication
      provides authentication and authorization but does
      not prevent repudiation. Passwords are not a non-
      repudiation control.

22.   Answer: C. Background checks

      Explanation: Background checks are a type of
      administrative security control, not a technical
      security control. Technical security controls involve
      using technology to prevent, detect, or respond to
      security threats.

23.   Answer: C. Network availability

      Explanation: Network availability is crucial when
      designing a secure network topology. The network
      must be designed to ensure that critical services
      and resources are available when needed while
      minimizing downtime and disruption in an attack
      or failure.

24.   Answer: D. Secure coding

      Explanation: Secure coding is a key principle of
      secure software development that involves writing
      code free from security vulnerabilities and exploits.
      This helps prevent the introduction of security
      weaknesses into the software and reduces the risk of
      a successful attack.

25. Answer: C. Accountability

Explanation: Accountability is not a type of access control but rather a concept related to responsibility and liability for actions taken. The three common types of access control are authentication, authorization, and audit/monitoring.

26. Answer: D. Improved disaster recovery capabilities

Explanation: Cloud computing can improve disaster recovery by providing redundant infrastructure and data backups in multiple locations. While cloud providers may also offer enhanced physical security and other benefits, improved disaster recovery is a key benefit for protection.

27. Answer: D. Enforcing data encryption and access control policies

Explanation: Enforcing data encryption and access control policies is a key consideration for secure Mobile Device Management. Mobile devices are highly portable and often contain sensitive data, making encryption and access control critical for protecting against unauthorized access or data loss.

28. Answer: B. Using long, complex passwords

Explanation: Using long, complex passwords is a key principle of secure password management. Requiring password changes too frequently can lead to weaker passwords while storing passwords in a centralized database or sharing passwords increases the risk of unauthorized access.

29. Answer: D. Hierarchical access control (HAC)

Explanation: Hierarchical access control (HAC) is not a recognized access control model. The three common access control models are role-based access control (RBAC), mandatory access control (MAC), and discretionary access control (DAC).

30. Answer: C. Isolating critical systems and resources

Explanation: Isolating critical systems and resources is a key consideration when designing secure network segmentation. Segmenting the network can help limit the impact of a security breach or failure, but it is important to ensure that critical systems and resources are properly isolated and protected.

31. Answer: C. Securing virtual machine images and snapshots

Explanation: Securing virtual machine images and snapshots is a key consideration when designing secure virtualization environments. Virtual machines can be easily copied or cloned, potentially exposing sensitive data or allowing unauthorized access. Proper security measures must be taken to secure virtual machine images and snapshots.

32. Answer: B. Minimizing network complexity

Explanation: Minimizing network complexity is a key principle of secure network design. Complex networks are more difficult to manage and secure and can increase the risk of security breaches or failures. Simplifying the network and reducing complexity can help improve security.

33. Answer: D. Social engineering vulnerability

    Explanation: Social engineering is a technique that manipulates people into divulging sensitive information or performing actions that compromise security. It is not a type of vulnerability. The three types of vulnerabilities listed are commonly found in software or systems.

34. Answer: C. Ensuring compliance with applicable regulations and standards

    Explanation: Ensuring compliance with applicable regulations and standards is a key consideration when designing secure cloud architecture. Cloud providers must comply with various regulations and standards, such as GDPR or HIPAA, depending on the industry and the data stored in the cloud.

35. Answer: C. Implementing secure coding practices

    Explanation: Implementing secure coding practices is a key principle of secure application development. Secure coding involves writing code free from security vulnerabilities and exploits and incorporating security considerations throughout the Software Development Life Cycle.

36. Answer: D. Enforcing strong encryption and access controls

    Explanation: Enforcing strong encryption and access controls is a key consideration when implementing secure remote access. Remote access can expose sensitive data and resources to

unauthorized access, so it is important to use strong
authentication mechanisms and enforce proper
access controls.

37. Answer: C. Applying consistent data classification
criteria

Explanation: Applying consistent data
classification criteria is a key principle of secure
data classification. Data classification involves
categorizing data based on its sensitivity and value
and applying appropriate security controls based
on the classification. Consistency in classification
criteria helps ensure that data is properly protected
across the organization.

38. Answer: D. HMAC

Explanation: HMAC (Hash-based Message
Authentication Code) is a cryptographic hash
function, not an encryption algorithm. The
three common encryption algorithms listed are
commonly used for encryption and decryption.

39. Answer: C. Conducting thorough post-incident
analysis and review

Explanation: Conducting thorough post-incident
analysis and review is a key principle of secure
incident response. Incident response involves
detecting, analyzing, and responding to security
incidents, and conducting a post-incident analysis
and review helps identify areas for improvement
and strengthen the organization's security posture.

40.   Answer: C. Securing data at rest and in transit

Explanation: Securing data at rest and in transit is a key consideration when implementing secure data storage. Data must be protected against unauthorized access or disclosure, whether stored on disk or transmitted across the network. Encryption and access controls are commonly used to secure data at rest and in transit.

41.   Answer: D. Risk decisions should be based on the impact on the business.

Explanation: Risk decisions should be made case by case, considering the unique context and potential impact on the business. A one-size-fits-all approach to risk management is not effective. Instead, an organization should evaluate each risk regarding its potential impact and decide the most appropriate risk response strategy: accept, avoid, transfer, or mitigate.

42.   Answer: D. To facilitate appropriate levels of protection based on value or sensitivity.

Explanation: Data classification is essential to an organization's information security strategy. By classifying data, organizations can apply appropriate levels of protection to sensitive information and ensure that resources are allocated efficiently.

43. Answer: B. To control network traffic based on predetermined security rules

Explanation: A firewall is a network security device that monitors incoming and outgoing network traffic and decides whether to allow or block specific traffic based on a defined set of security rules. It is a critical piece of a network security infrastructure and can help prevent unauthorized access to or from a network.

44. Answer: D. All of the above.

Explanation: Non-repudiation is a fundamental concept in information security and legal scenarios. It assures the origin or delivery of data, so the sender cannot deny sending a message, and the recipient cannot deny receiving it. This is often used in digital signatures and certificate authorities.

45. Answer: C. Integrating security throughout the life cycle, including design, development, and testing.

Explanation: Security should be a key consideration throughout the entire software development life cycle, not just at the end. This approach, often called "security by design," helps ensure that security is integrated into the software from the ground up and can help identify and mitigate vulnerabilities early in the development process.

46. Answer: C. Mandatory access control (MAC)

    Explanation: Mandatory access control (MAC) uses labels (often reflecting different sensitivity levels, such as confidential, secret, and top secret) to determine access. In a MAC model, users do not have the discretion to determine who has access to the information they own or control.

47. Answer: C. To ensure the continuation of business processes

    Explanation: The primary goal of a business continuity plan (BCP) is to ensure the continuation of business processes during and after a disruption. The BCP is a comprehensive plan to maintain or resume business during a disruption.

48. Answer: B. That the data has not been altered during transmission

    Explanation: In cryptography, "integrity" ensures that the data has not been altered during transmission. Alteration can be accidental, such as data corruption during transmission, or intentional, such as a malicious attack.

49. Answer: B. Evaluate the effectiveness of security controls

    Explanation: The primary purpose of penetration testing is to evaluate the effectiveness of security controls by simulating an attack. By identifying vulnerabilities and testing security measures, organizations can better understand their security posture and make informed decisions about risk management.

50. Answer: B. Granting users the minimum access necessary to perform their job function

    Explanation: A key principle of Identity and Access Management is granting users the minimum access necessary to perform their job functions. This principle, known as the principle of least privilege, is critical for reducing the risk of unauthorized access or actions.

51. Answer: D. Authenticity

    Explanation: The CIA triad in information security stands for confidentiality, integrity, and availability. While authenticity is an important concept in information security, it is not a part of the CIA triad.

52. Answer: A. Granting users only the permissions they need to perform their job functions

    Explanation: The principle of least privilege is a computer security concept in which users are given the minimum access necessary to complete their job functions. This helps to reduce the potential damage caused by errors or malicious actions.

53. Answer: B. An attack that involves sending deceptive emails to trick individuals into revealing sensitive information

    Explanation: Phishing is a cyberattack that targets individuals by email, telephone, or text message and tricks them into revealing sensitive information such as Personally Identifiable Information, banking and credit card details, and passwords.

54. Answer: C. Intrusion detection system

Explanation: In the context of information security, IDS stands for intrusion detection system. A device or software application monitors a network or systems for malicious activity or policy violations.

55. Answer: B. Technical

Explanation: A biometric scanner is technical security control. Technical controls are often hardware or software tools, such as firewalls, encryption, and authentication mechanisms, like biometric scanners, designed to protect systems and data.

CHAPTER 3

Security and Risk Management

In the ever-evolving landscape of information security, a solid grasp of Security and Risk Management principles is crucial for professionals in the field. This chapter, the third in our series, aims to explore this essential domain in depth.

Throughout this chapter, we will examine the concepts of risk, its components, and how understanding these elements can shape effective risk management strategies within an organization. We will discuss the importance of risk assessment methodologies and how qualitative and quantitative techniques can help estimate risks accurately and prioritize responses. We will explore the concept of risk treatment, discussing the four primary options: risk acceptance, avoidance, mitigation, and transfer. This will lead us to implement risk mitigation strategies, where we will examine the integration of technical, administrative, and physical controls to create a multifaceted approach to risk reduction.

Asset identification and valuation are critical aspects of risk management. We will discuss methodologies for appraising the worth of information assets within an organization. Next, we will examine risk management frameworks such as NIST SP 800-37, ISO/IEC 27005, FAIR, and COSO ERM. These structures provide consistent and repeatable methodologies for effective risk management. We will also discuss key

© Mohamed Aly Bouke 2023
M. A. Bouke, *CISSP Exam Certification Companion*, Certification Study Companion Series, https://doi.org/10.1007/979-8-8688-0057-3_3

elements of risk communication and reporting within an organization, emphasizing the importance of consistency, clarity, timeliness, relevance, and transparency.

Regular risk monitoring and review are vital in maintaining an effective risk management program. We will examine processes involved in tracking risk treatment progress, reviewing risk assessments, analyzing incident reports, and evaluating the overall risk management program. Another crucial aspect we will cover is integrating risk management with business processes. This includes aligning risk management objectives with business objectives, incorporating risk assessments in strategic planning, involving stakeholders in risk management activities, embedding risk management in project management, and establishing performance metrics.

Additionally, we will delve into compliance and regulatory considerations relevant to information security and risk management. We will highlight the importance of identifying applicable laws and regulations, developing appropriate policies and procedures, conducting compliance audits, maintaining documentation, and implementing incident response plans.

Finally, we will explore the integral components of business continuity and disaster recovery planning, discussing the steps needed to prepare for, respond to, and recover from disruptions or disasters.

Upon completing this chapter, you will have a comprehensive understanding of the Security and Risk Management domain, equipping you with the knowledge and insights necessary for the CISSP exam and your professional journey.

CIA and Fundamental Concepts

Confidentiality, integrity, and availability (CIA) are fundamental information security principles. Confidentiality ensures that information is only accessible to authorized individuals or entities. Integrity refers to the accuracy and consistency of data and that it has not been tampered with. Finally, availability ensures that information is accessible to authorized individuals when needed. For example, a healthcare organization must protect patient records by ensuring that only authorized healthcare professionals can access the records (confidentiality), the records have not been modified or tampered with (integrity), and the records are accessible to authorized healthcare professionals when needed (availability).

In addition to this, the following concepts are also important for the exam:

- Authentication is verifying or testing that a claimed identity is valid. Authentication requires information from the subject that corresponds to the identity indicated. For example, two-factor authentication involves verifying a user's identity using two different methods, such as a password and a biometric factor like a fingerprint.

- Authorization is granting access to an authenticated user to a resource or service based on their identity and permissions. For example, an employee can access specific files or databases based on their job role and security clearance.

- Auditing is the programmatic means by which subjects are held accountable for their actions while authenticated on a system by documenting or recording subject activities. For example, logging all user activity on a system to track who accessed what resources and when.

- Accountability is holding users responsible for their actions while using a system or accessing resources. Effective accountability relies on the capability to prove a subject's identity and track their activities. For example, if a data breach occurs, accountability measures can be used to determine who was responsible for the breach and take appropriate action.

- Non-repudiation is the assurance that the subject of an activity or event cannot deny that the event occurred. It prevents a subject from claiming not to have sent a message, not to have performed an action, or not to have been the cause of an event. For example, digital signatures provide non-repudiation by ensuring the signer's identity and the signed document's integrity.

- Defense in depth is the concept of using multiple layers of security controls to provide redundancy and increase security, for example, using firewalls, intrusion detection and prevention systems, and antivirus software to protect against different types of attacks.

- Abstraction is the process of grouping similar elements into groups, classes, or roles that are assigned security controls, restrictions, or permissions as a collective. It adds efficiency to carry out a security plan, for example, grouping users into roles based on their job functions and granting permissions and access control based on those roles.

- Data hiding is concealing data or code to prevent unauthorized access or modification, for example, hiding passwords or sensitive data using encryption or obfuscation techniques.

- Security boundaries refer to the line separating trusted and untrusted networks or systems. For example, a company's internal network is considered a trusted boundary, while the Internet is untrusted.

- Security perimeters refer to the physical or logical boundary that separates an organization's assets from the outside world. For example, a company's firewall is a security perimeter that separates its internal network from the Internet.

- Least privilege: This concept states that a user should only have the minimum level of access required to perform their job function. This helps to reduce the risk of accidental or intentional damage to systems or data. For example, a receptionist may only need access to schedule appointments, while an IT administrator may need access to install and configure software.

- Need to know: This concept states that a user should only have access to information necessary to perform their job function. This helps to protect sensitive information from unauthorized access or disclosure. For example, a human resources employee may need access to employee records, while a marketing employee may not.

Exam Tip: As a CISSP candidate, it is crucial to understand the importance of the CIA Triad and how it relates to the business needs of an organization. The CIA triad stands for confidentiality, integrity, and availability, which are the three essential components of information security. However, it is essential to understand that these three components are not equally important in all situations. Depending on the nature of the organization, certain components may need to be prioritized over others. For example, a financial institution may prioritize confidentiality and integrity over availability since they handle sensitive information that needs to be protected from unauthorized access and modification. On the other hand, an ecommerce website may prioritize availability since their revenue relies heavily on the website being accessible to customers at all times. As a CISSP candidate, it is important to understand the business needs of an organization and how they relate to the CIA Triad. Balancing the three components based on the business needs is critical to the success of an organization's information security program. It is also important to note that the CIA Triad is not the only factor to consider when developing an information security program. Other factors, such as legal and regulatory requirements, risk management, and cost, must also be considered.

These concepts are critical to information security and work together to create a comprehensive security architecture. The CISSP places a significant emphasis on defense in depth and assumes that security should be layered by default. CISSP candidates need to understand these concepts thoroughly and be able to apply them in practice to protect their organization's information assets.

Security Governance

Security governance is a crucial aspect of information security that involves the collection of practices aimed at supporting, defining, and directing an organization's security efforts. Understanding the concept of security governance for the CISSP exam as it relates to the overall management and control of an organization's security program is essential.

The following are some of the critical components of security governance:

- Policies are formal, written statements (high-level statements) that outline an organization's security objectives, principles, and guidelines. Policies serve as a foundation for the organization's security program and guide employees in handling security-related matters. For example, a policy might outline how to handle sensitive data, password requirements, or the acceptable use of company resources.

- Procedures are step-by-step instructions on how to carry out specific security-related tasks. They are often used with policies to provide more detailed guidance on implementing security measures. For example, a procedure might outline how to conduct a security audit or how to respond to a security incident.

- Guidelines are less formal than policies and procedures but provide recommendations for handling security matters. They are often used to address specific security concerns or provide advice on complying with security policies. For example, guidelines might be provided on transferring files or configuring a firewall securely.

- Risk management is critical to security governance, as it involves identifying and assessing potential security risks and developing mitigation strategies. A risk management framework can help organizations prioritize their security efforts and allocate resources accordingly. For example, an organization might identify that it faces a high risk of a data breach and develop a plan to implement additional security controls to reduce that risk.

- Compliance involves ensuring that the organization's security practices meet relevant laws, regulations, and industry standards. Compliance is an essential part of security governance, as failure to comply with legal or regulatory requirements can result in fines, legal action, or damage to the organization's reputation. For example, an organization might be required to comply with the General Data Protection Regulation (GDPR) and develop policies and procedures to protect personal data.

- Performance Monitoring involves regularly reviewing and assessing the organization's security program to ensure it is effective and meets its security objectives. It consists in measuring key performance indicators (KPIs) to track progress and identify areas where improvements can be made. For example, an organization might track the number of security incidents or the time to resolve security issues.

Essential Concepts for Effective Security Management Planning

Effective security management planning ensures that organizations are prepared to prevent, detect, and respond to security threats. Several key concepts must be understood and implemented to ensure adequate security management planning. These concepts include third-party governance; alignment of security functions to business strategy, goals, mission, and objectives; security management planning; and business case:

- Third-party governance refers to the oversight of external entities that law, regulation, industry standards, contractual obligation, or licensing requirements may mandate. To comply with these requirements, organizations must ensure that third-party entities follow appropriate security practices and appropriately secure the organization's data and systems. This may involve external investigators or auditors to review the third party's security practices and provide recommendations for improvement.

- Aligning security functions to business strategy, goals, mission, and objectives is essential for ensuring security efforts align with the organization's overall goals. This involves designing and implementing security measures based on business cases, budget restrictions, or scarcity of resources. It also ensures that security is integrated into the organization's overall strategic planning process so that security is considered at every stage.

- Security management planning is creating, implementing, and enforcing a security policy. This involves developing three types of plans: strategic, tactical, and operational. A strategic plan is a long-term plan that defines the organization's goals, mission, and objectives. A tactical plan is a mid-term plan that provides more details on accomplishing the goals outlined in the strategic plan. Operational plans are short-term and highly detailed plans based on strategic and tactical plans.

- A business case is a documented argument or stated position used to justify the need for a decision or action. In security management planning, a business case is often made to justify starting a new security project or initiative. A business case may include an analysis of the costs and benefits of a proposed security initiative and an assessment of the risks associated with not implementing the initiative.

Risk Management

Risk management is a critical aspect of any successful organization or project. It is the systematic process of identifying, assessing, prioritizing, and addressing potential risks to minimize their negative impact on an organization's objectives, operations, and overall success. Implementing effective risk management strategies ensures that organizations can better anticipate, prepare for, and mitigate the consequences of unforeseen events, ultimately leading to improved decision-making and greater resilience. This section will delve into the key concepts, methodologies, and best risk management practices, providing a comprehensive understanding of this essential organizational discipline.

Risk Analysis and Assessment

Understanding risk: Risk can be defined as the potential for loss, damage, or harm resulting from an event that exploits vulnerabilities and threatens assets. It comprises three components: threats, vulnerabilities, and potential impacts. For example, a threat could be a hacker attempting to gain unauthorized access to a company's network. A vulnerability could be weak security configurations on the network, and the potential impact might be data loss, financial damage, or reputational harm.

- **Risk assessment methodologies:** Two primary
  risk assessment methodologies are qualitative and
  quantitative. Qualitative risk assessments rely on
  subjective judgments and expert opinions to rank risks,
  while quantitative risk assessments use numerical
  values and calculations to estimate risks. For example,
  a qualitative risk assessment may categorize risks
  as low, medium, or high, whereas a quantitative
  risk assessment might calculate the monetary loss
  associated with each risk.

Whatever risk assessment methodologies will be used, either
qualitative or quantitative or both, the execution process should involve
five main steps:

- **Identify assets:** Determine the organization's critical
  assets, such as hardware, software, data, and personnel.

- **Identify threats:** Identify potential threats to each
  asset, including natural disasters, human errors, and
  malicious attacks.

- **Identify vulnerabilities:** Analyze the assets to identify
  potential weaknesses that threats could exploit.

- **Assess impact and likelihood:** Estimate each threat-
  vulnerability pair's potential impact and likelihood.

- **Prioritize risks:** Rank them based on their impact and
  likelihood, and prioritize them for treatment.

Moreover, Table 3-1 illustrates key metrics and formulas used in
quantitative risk analysis.

Table 3-1. *Quantitative Risk Analysis Metrics*

Metric/Formula	Description
Single Loss Expectancy (SLE) = Asset Value (AV) x Exposure Factor (EF)	SLE is the monetary loss or impact of each occurrence of a threat. It's calculated by multiplying the asset's value by the exposure factor (the proportion of asset loss caused by the identified threat)
Annualized Rate of Occurrence (ARO)	ARO estimates how often a specific threat event will occur within a year
Annualized Loss Expectancy (ALE) = SLE x ARO	ALE is the annual expected financial loss to an organization from a threat. It's computed by multiplying the SLE by the ARO
Return on Investment (ROI) = (Value of Benefit-Cost) / Cost	ROI is a performance measure used to evaluate the efficiency or profitability of an investment or compare the efficiency of several different investments
Total Cost of Ownership (TCO)	TCO is the purchase price of an asset plus the operation costs, representing the financial impact of acquiring, deploying, and maintaining the asset over its life cycle

Let's see an example for each formula:

- Single Loss Expectancy (SLE)

    Suppose you have a server valued at $10,000 (asset value, AV), and if a particular threat occurs, you estimate that 60% of its value would be lost (exposure factor, EF = 0.6). The SLE would be calculated as follows:

    SLE = AV * EF = $10,000 * 0.6 = $6000

- Annualized Rate of Occurrence (ARO)

  If you expect the threat to your server to occur twice a year, then the ARO is 2.

- Annualized Loss Expectancy (ALE)

  Given the SLE of $6000 from the previous example and an ARO of 2, the ALE would be calculated as follows:

  ALE = SLE * ARO = $6000 * 2 = $12,000

  This means you should expect to lose $12,000 annually due to this threat.

  Just note that calculating ARO is a bit confusing. For example, if I mention that a threat may occur twice every 30 years, in this case, the ARO is 2/30 (it is a probability metric).

- Return on Investment (ROI)

  Suppose you invest $2000 in a security measure that reduces the ARO of the threat to 1. The measure costs $2000, and the benefit (reduction in ALE) is $6000. The ROI would be

  ROI = (Benefit - Cost) / Cost = ($6000 - $2000) / $2000 = 2 or 200%

  This means the investment returns twice its cost.

- Total Cost of Ownership (TCO)

  To calculate the TCO of the server, you would add the purchase price to the operation costs. If the server costs $10,000 and the estimated operation costs over its life cycle are $5000 (including maintenance, energy, etc.), the TCO would be

TCO = Purchase Price + Operating Costs = $10,000 + $5000 = $15,000

These examples are simplified. In real scenarios, you would probably deal with more complex situations and potentially more detailed cost and benefit analyses.

Exam Tip: When preparing for the CISSP exam, it's important to remember that while you may come across a few questions related to the formulas mentioned earlier, this is not a math exam. These questions aim to test your understanding of risk assessment metrics and their application in real-world scenarios. You aren't expected to perform complex mathematical calculations. However, having a basic understanding of these formulas, what they represent, and how to apply them can certainly give you an edge. If calculations are required, remember that the exam will provide a standard function calculator on screen, so there's no need to worry about memorizing complex mathematical operations. Concentrate on understanding the concepts, as this is what the exam seeks to measure.

Risk Treatment

Upon completing our risk assessment, it's time to make informed decisions about risk treatment. However, these decisions should not be made in isolation. Senior management must be involved in this process as they are ultimately responsible for the organization's risk posture. As an information security professional, your role is to provide them with relevant and accurate information to guide their decision-making process.

There are four main risk treatment options:

- **Risk acceptance**: The organization acknowledges and tolerates the risk without implementing additional controls. For example, a company may accept the risk of a low-impact security breach due to the high cost of implementing more robust security measures.

- **Risk avoidance:** The organization eliminates the risk by discontinuing the activity or process that causes it. For example, a company may decide to stop storing sensitive customer data to avoid the risk of a data breach.

- **Risk mitigation:** The organization reduces the risk by implementing security controls, policies, or procedures. For example, a company may implement more robust password policies and multifactor authentication to mitigate the risk of unauthorized access.

- **Risk transfer:** The organization transfers the risk to a third party, such as an insurance company or a service provider. For example, a company may purchase cyber insurance to share the financial risk of a data breach.

Implementing Risk Mitigation Strategies

Risk mitigation strategies include technical, administrative, and physical controls. Technical controls involve the use of technology, such as firewalls and encryption. Administrative controls include policies, procedures, and training programs. Physical controls involve securing the physical environment, such as using locks, access control systems, and security cameras. Additionally, monitoring and reviewing risks are essential for ensuring the effectiveness and relevance of risk treatment plans.

Asset Valuation

A critical step in the risk management process is identifying and categorizing the information assets within an organization. An effective way to accomplish this is by creating a comprehensive inventory. This inventory should include all tangible and intangible assets, such as hardware, software, data, and personnel.

Categorizing assets within an organization hinges on understanding their sensitivity, criticality, and overall value. Sensitivity refers to an asset's potential impact on the organization if its confidentiality, integrity, or availability were compromised, examples of which might include trade secrets or sensitive personal data. Criticality, on the other hand, gauges the organization's dependency on the asset for normal operations. For instance, a key server running an ecommerce platform would be deemed a critical asset. Lastly, the value of an asset incorporates both its sensitivity and criticality while also taking into account its overall importance to the organization. This could be measured in terms of financial worth, contribution to strategic objectives, replacement cost, or potential impact of loss or compromise. Thus, when identifying and categorizing assets, these three aspects must be carefully evaluated to ensure a comprehensive understanding of the assets' significance within the organization.

Although not a tangible asset, personnel play a crucial role in the organization; their knowledge and skills can be considered valuable assets. Therefore, it's essential also to consider the potential impact of personnel-related incidents, such as errors, omissions, or malicious actions.

Following the identification and categorization, we must assign value to these assets. The value of an asset is a critical piece of information that informs various risk management decisions, such as determining the appropriate level of protection for each asset and prioritizing risk mitigation efforts.

There are several methods used to assign value to information assets, each with its advantages and limitations:

- **Financial value**: Estimate the direct monetary value of an asset, such as the cost of purchasing, maintaining, or replacing it.

- **Business impact**: Evaluate the potential impact on the organization's operations, reputation, or bottom line if the asset is compromised.

- **Market value:** Determine the asset's worth based on market demand or how much others are willing to pay.

- **Intangible value:** Consider the asset's intangible value, such as its contribution to the organization's intellectual property, customer trust, or competitive advantage.

Risk Management Frameworks

Risk management frameworks provide a structured approach to managing risks within an organization. They help organizations identify, assess, and treat risks consistently and repeatedly. Some common risk management frameworks include

- **NIST SP 800-37:** Developed by the National Institute of Standards and Technology, this framework provides guidelines for implementing a risk management process for federal information systems.

- **ISO/IEC 27005:** This international standard provides guidelines for organizations to implement an information security risk management process, which is part of the broader ISO/IEC 27000 family of standards.

- **FAIR (Factor Analysis of Information Risk):** This framework offers a quantitative approach to risk management, enabling organizations to measure and prioritize risks using financial terms.

- **COSO ERM (Committee of Sponsoring Organizations of the Treadway Commission Enterprise Risk Management):** This framework provides principles and guidance for organizations to develop a comprehensive enterprise risk management program.

Risk Communication and Reporting

Effective risk communication and reporting are critical to ensuring that decision-makers within an organization are informed about the risks they face and the steps taken to manage them. Some key elements of risk communication and reporting include

- **Clarity**: Present information in a clear, concise, and understandable manner, avoiding jargon and technical terms when possible.

- **Timeliness**: Communicate risks and risk management activities regularly and promptly, allowing for informed decision-making and timely response to emerging risks.

- **Relevance**: Tailor the content and format of risk reports to the needs and preferences of the intended audience, focusing on the most relevant risks and risk management activities.

- **Transparency**: Be open and honest about the organization's risk management processes and the assumptions, limitations, and uncertainties associated with risk assessments.

- **Consistency**: Ensure that risk communication and reporting are consistent across the organization, using standardized terms, definitions, and formats.

Risk Monitoring and Review

Regular risk monitoring and review are essential to ensure an organization's risk management processes remain practical and current. This involves

- **Tracking risk treatment progress**: Monitor the implementation of risk treatment plans and their effectiveness in reducing risks.

- **Reviewing risk assessments**: Conduct periodic assessments to identify new or changing risks and update risk treatment plans accordingly.

- **Analyzing incident reports**: Review and analyze incident reports to identify trends, lessons learned, and potential areas for improvement in risk management processes.

- **Evaluating the risk management program**: Assess the overall effectiveness of the organization's risk management program and identify areas for improvement or enhancement.

Risk Management Integration with Business Processes

Integrating risk management into an organization's business processes helps ensure that risk considerations are part of decision-making processes, resource allocation, and overall business strategy. To achieve this integration

- **Align risk management objectives with business objectives**: Ensure that risk management goals support the overall mission and objectives of the organization, such as increasing profitability, enhancing reputation, or achieving regulatory compliance.

- **Include risk assessments in strategic planning**: Incorporate risk assessment results into strategic planning processes, allowing decision-makers to consider potential risks when setting priorities, allocating resources, and selecting strategies.

- **Involve stakeholders**: Engage stakeholders from various departments and levels of the organization in risk management activities to promote a risk-aware culture and shared responsibility for risk management.

- **Embed risk management in project management**: Integrate risk management activities into project management processes, such as project initiation, planning, execution, and closure, to ensure that risks are identified and addressed throughout the project life cycle.

- **Establish performance metrics**: Develop performance indicators that measure the effectiveness of risk management activities and their alignment with business objectives. Use these metrics to inform decision-making and drive continuous improvement.

Risk Management Tools and Techniques

Various tools and techniques can help organizations manage risks more effectively. Some of these include

- **Risk registers**: A risk register is a centralized document or database that records identified risks, their assessments, and treatment plans. It helps track risks, assigns responsibility for risk management, and facilitates communication and reporting.

- **Risk matrices**: A risk matrix is a visual tool that helps organizations prioritize risks by plotting them based on their likelihood and impact. This can assist in decision-making and resource allocation for risk treatment.

- **Bowtie analysis**: A bowtie analysis is a graphical method for visualizing the relationship between hazards, potential events, and consequences. It helps organizations identify barriers and controls to prevent or mitigate the impacts of adverse events.

- **SWOT analysis**: A SWOT analysis evaluates an organization's strengths, weaknesses, opportunities, and threats to inform strategic planning and decision-making. It can also help identify risks and opportunities associated with internal and external factors.

- **Root cause analysis**: This technique investigates the underlying causes of incidents or problems to prevent a recurrence. It can help organizations identify vulnerabilities and implement targeted risk mitigation measures.

Developing a Risk-Aware Culture

A risk-aware culture is one in which every organization member understands the importance of risk management and actively participates in risk management activities. To develop a risk-aware culture

- **Leadership commitment**: Ensure top management demonstrates a solid commitment to risk management, setting the tone for the entire organization.

- **Clear communication**: Establish open communication channels for discussing risks and risk management activities, encouraging employees to share their concerns, ideas, and suggestions.

- **Education and training**: Provide regular education and training programs to enhance employees' understanding of risk management concepts, tools, and techniques and their role in managing risks.

- **Accountability and responsibility**: Clearly define roles and responsibilities for risk management and hold individuals accountable for fulfilling these responsibilities.

- **Continuous improvement**: Encourage continuous improvement by regularly reviewing and updating risk management processes and incorporating feedback from employees and stakeholders.

Compliance and Regulatory Considerations

Organizations must consider legal and regulatory information security and risk management requirements. Noncompliance can result in fines, legal actions, or reputational damage. Some key compliance considerations include the following:

- **Identify applicable laws and regulations**: Determine which laws and regulations apply to the organization's industry, location, and operations, such as data protection laws, industry-specific regulations, or international standards.

- **Develop policies and procedures**: Establish policies and procedures that address the organization's legal and regulatory requirements, and ensure that they are effectively communicated and enforced throughout the organization.

- **Conduct compliance audits**: Perform regular audits to assess the organization's compliance with relevant laws and regulations and to identify potential gaps or areas for improvement.

- **Maintain documentation**: Keep accurate and up-to-date records of risk management activities, compliance efforts, and incident responses to demonstrate due diligence and support regulatory reporting requirements.

- **Implement incident response plans**: Develop and maintain incident response plans that outline the organization's procedures for detecting, responding to, and recovering from security incidents, as well as reporting incidents to the relevant authorities, if required.

Vendor and Third-Party Risk Management

Organizations increasingly rely on vendors and third-party service providers for various aspects of their operations, such as data storage, processing, or software development. These relationships can introduce new risks that must be managed effectively. To address vendor and third-party risks

- **Conduct vendor risk assessments**: Evaluate potential vendors and service providers based on their security practices, reputation, and financial stability before entering a business relationship.

- **Establish clear contractual requirements**: Define security and compliance requirements in contracts with vendors and service providers, including data protection, incident response, and regulatory compliance obligations.

- **Monitor vendor performance**: Regularly review and assess vendors' and service providers' compliance with contractual requirements and overall security posture.

- **Implement vendor risk mitigation strategies**: Develop plans to address potential risks associated with vendor and third-party relationships, such as contingency plans for switching to alternate providers or implementing additional security controls.

- **Collaborate with vendors on incident response**: Establish processes for coordinating with vendors and service providers during security incidents, including communication, incident management, and recovery activities.

Risk Management Training and Awareness

Effective risk management requires a well-informed and risk-aware workforce. Effective risk management is not a task that can be solely delegated to a specific department within an organization; it's a collective responsibility that requires awareness and commitment at all levels. The term "well-informed and risk-aware workforce" encapsulates the concept that every individual within the organization needs to understand their role in managing risk and the potential impact of their actions on the organization's overall risk profile.

To achieve this, organizations should

- **Develop risk management training programs**: Design and deliver training programs that educate employees about the organization's risk management processes, policies, and procedures, as well as their roles and responsibilities in managing risks.

- **Promote a risk-aware culture**: Encourage employees to think about and consider risks in their day-to-day activities and decision-making processes and promptly report potential threats or incidents.

- **Provide targeted training for specific roles**: Offer specialized training for employees in key risk management roles, such as information security, compliance, or business continuity planning, to ensure they have the necessary skills and knowledge to manage risks effectively.

- **Evaluate training effectiveness**: Assess the impact of risk management training programs on employee knowledge, behavior, and the overall effectiveness of the organization's risk management processes, and use this information to refine training content and delivery methods.

Continuous Improvement in Risk Management

Continuous improvement is a concept that involves constantly analyzing and enhancing processes, systems, and strategies to adapt to changing circumstances and improve efficiency and effectiveness. In the context of risk management, continuous improvement is essential to ensure that risk management practices stay relevant and effective in the face of evolving risks, threats, and business environments.

- Establish a process for regularly reviewing and updating risk management policies, procedures, and practices to ensure they remain relevant and practical.

- Collect and analyze feedback from employees, stakeholders, and external sources, such as industry best practices or regulatory guidance, to identify potential areas for improvement.

- Measure and track the performance of risk management activities using key performance indicators (KPIs), and use this data to identify trends, gaps, and opportunities for improvement.

- Implement a formal change management process to guide the introduction of new risk management practices, tools, or technologies and to ensure that changes are effectively communicated and adopted across the organization.

- Continuously monitor and assess the organization's risk environment to identify emerging risks, changes in threat landscapes, or evolving regulatory requirements that may require risk management strategies or plan adjustments.

In conclusion, effective risk management is crucial for the success and resilience of any organization. By understanding the various components of risk, conducting regular risk assessments, implementing appropriate risk treatment strategies, and fostering a risk-aware culture, organizations can proactively manage risks, minimize their potential impacts, and seize opportunities for growth and innovation.

Legal and Regulatory Issues

Legal and regulatory landscape: Information security professionals must be familiar with various laws, regulations, and standards that impact information security. Examples include the General Data Protection Regulation (GDPR) for data privacy in the European Union, the Health Insurance Portability and Accountability Act (HIPAA) for healthcare data protection in the United States, and the Payment Card Industry Data Security Standard (PCI DSS) for the secure processing of payment card transactions.

Compliance with legal and regulatory requirements is crucial to avoid fines, penalties, and reputational damage. To develop and implement organizational compliance programs, identify relevant laws, regulations, and standards, and establish policies, procedures, and controls to meet their requirements. Regular audits, assessments, and training programs can help ensure ongoing compliance.

Intellectual property (IP) rights protect the ownership and use of intangible creations, such as ideas, inventions, artistic works, and symbols. IP rights include copyrights, patents, trademarks, and trade secrets. Understanding IP rights is essential for information security professionals to safeguard their organization's intellectual property and avoid legal disputes.

ISC2 Code of Ethics

A foundational aspect of the information security profession and a critical consideration for any CISSP candidate is adherence to ethical guidelines. ISC2, the organization that administers the CISSP certification, has developed a code of ethics that all its members, notably all CISSP-certified professionals, must uphold.

The ISC2 Code of Ethics outlines four obligatory canons that set the ethical standard for the security profession:

- Protect society, the common good, necessary public trust and confidence, and the infrastructure. This emphasizes the role of the security professional in safeguarding the public interest. The responsibility extends beyond the immediate scope of their work to include the wider societal context.

- Act honorably, honestly, justly, responsibly, and legally. The moral conduct of security professionals is underlined here. They must perform their duties fairly while always adhering to legal requirements.

- Provide diligent and competent service to principles. This canon stresses the need for professionals to perform their duties with diligence and competence, ensuring they provide the highest quality of service.

- Advance and protect the profession. Security professionals are expected to foster the growth and reputation of their field. They should contribute to developing their profession and safeguard it against any actions that could harm its standing.

The ISC2 Code of Ethics is vital in the CISSP exam and the profession. Candidates are expected to understand and agree to the code; it's not merely about passing the exam but also about acting as responsible and ethical professionals in the field of information security.

The CISSP exam may include questions related to the code of ethics, testing the candidate's understanding of ethical considerations in information security scenarios. Therefore, understanding and internalizing these principles is crucial for the exam and your ongoing professional practice.

In our dynamic field, where new threats and challenges constantly arise, adhering to this ethical code can guide professionals in making the right decisions, thereby preserving the digital world's trust, confidence, and security.

Ethics in Practice

Although understanding the principles of the ISC2 Code of Ethics is crucial, applying these principles in real-world situations is equally, if not more, important. This section will explore some case studies that exemplify these ethical principles in action.

- **Example 1 – Protecting society**: An information security professional discovers their company unknowingly hosts a child exploitation website on one of its servers. Although revealing this information might lead to negative publicity for the company, the professional decides to report it to law enforcement agencies, upholding the principle of protecting society.

- **Example 2 – Integrity**: A cybersecurity analyst finds a significant vulnerability in their organization's system. They report it promptly and accurately, even though it could reflect poorly on their department's work. This action displays integrity and honesty, which are vital to the ISC2 Code of Ethics.

- **Example 3 – Conflicts of interest**: An IT professional receives a lucrative offer from a software vendor to promote a particular security product within their organization. However, the professional rejects the offer to avoid a conflict of interest and ensures that their professional judgment remains unbiased and focused on the organization's best interest.

- **Example 4 – Enhancing the profession**: A seasoned security manager mentors junior security professionals, shares their knowledge at industry conferences, and contributes to open source projects. These actions demonstrate a commitment to enhancing the profession, one of the key principles of the ISC2 Code of Ethics.

These example studies illustrate the practical application of ethical principles in information security. By adhering to the ISC2 Code of Ethics, security professionals not only uphold their professional integrity but also contribute positively to the security of society and the advancement of their profession. As you prepare for the CISSP exam, it's important to understand and internalize these ethical principles, as they form the foundation of the professional conduct expected of a CISSP-certified professional.

Information Security Policies

Policy development: Information security policies provide the foundation for an organization's security program. They define the organization's objectives, principles, and requirements for protecting information assets. A well-structured policy includes a clear purpose, scope, roles and responsibilities, compliance requirements, and enforcement measures. Policies should be reviewed and updated regularly to reflect changes in the organization's environment, risk profile, and regulatory landscape.

Policy enforcement and monitoring: To enforce and monitor compliance with information security policies, organizations can use tools and techniques such as auditing, monitoring, and reporting. Auditing involves evaluating an organization's security controls, processes, and policies to identify gaps or weaknesses. Monitoring involves continuously observing the organization's systems and networks to detect policy violations or security incidents. Reporting includes documenting policy compliance status, audit findings, and incident reports to inform decision-making and improve security.

Business Continuity

The essence of risk management lies in the capability to anticipate, prepare for, and effectively respond to disruptions or disasters that could impact an organization's operations. Business continuity planning (BCP) and disaster recovery planning (DRP) are two vital components in this process.

BCP involves a comprehensive strategy that outlines the procedures for maintaining or restoring critical business processes during and after a disruption. The initial stage of developing a BCP is a business impact analysis (BIA), a process used to identify critical business processes, assess potential impacts of disruptions, and determine recovery priorities. This involves analyzing the potential consequences of disruptions to each process, estimating the maximum tolerable downtime, and identifying the resources required for recovery.

Upon understanding these critical elements, the organization can then develop recovery strategies. These could include alternative work locations, backup systems, and communication plans for emergency notifications and stakeholder updates. The final phase of a BCP includes testing and maintenance procedures such as regular plan reviews, updates, and exercises to ensure the plan's relevance and effectiveness.

On the other hand, DRP focuses primarily on the recovery of IT systems to resume normal operations following a disaster. This involves identifying critical systems and data, establishing recovery time objectives (RTOs) and recovery point objectives (RPOs), and defining recovery strategies like data backups and redundant systems. The plan also necessitates procedures for restoring systems and data.

BCP and DRP require regular testing and updating to align with the organization's changing needs and risk environment. Moreover, they are essential tools to mitigate potential disruptions, including natural disasters, power outages, or cyberattacks. By integrating these strategies, organizations can significantly enhance their resilience and maintain continuity despite unforeseen circumstances.

This section provides a general overview of BCP and DRP. We will delve deeper into these topics, exploring their intricacies and the methodologies to implement them in Chapter 9 effectively. The detailed exploration will equip you with the necessary understanding and skills required for both your CISSP examination and your professional journey beyond.

Personnel Security

One of the most crucial elements in information security is the human aspect. Organizations can implement the most advanced security measures, but the risk of breaches remains without proper employee training and understanding. This section, therefore, focuses on the importance of security awareness training, background checks and vetting, and the principles of separation of duties and least privilege.

Security awareness training is not merely a requirement but necessary in today's digital landscape. It serves as the first line of defense by educating employees about security risks, policies, and procedures. This is not a static but dynamic process, requiring constant updating and tailoring to address emerging threats and changing regulations. The objective of these programs is to make them engaging and relevant. Hence, online courses, workshops, simulations, or presentations cater to various learning styles and environments.

Regarding personnel security, background checks and vetting procedures take the forefront. These play a crucial role in ensuring that potential hires are qualified and trustworthy. Comprehensive checks may involve reviewing criminal records, verifying employment history, contacting references, and conducting interviews. Organizations should establish clear guidelines for these processes depending on the sensitivity of the roles being filled and the associated risks.

Another key aspect of personnel security is the implementation of the principles of separation of duties and least privilege. These principles are designed to prevent unauthorized access and reduce the risk of insider threats. Separation of duties involves distributing critical tasks among several individuals or teams, which helps to ensure that no single person has the power to compromise an organization's security. On the other hand, the least privilege principle stipulates that individuals should only have the minimum level of access required to perform their job functions. This can be achieved by creating access control policies, establishing role-based permissions, and regularly reviewing and updating access rights.

In sum, understanding and implementing these concepts can significantly aid organizations in managing risks, protecting assets, and ensuring compliance with legal and regulatory requirements. It emphasizes the importance of fostering a security culture through training, policy development, and continuous improvement, ultimately leading to a robust and resilient information security program.

Understanding Intellectual Property Rights

In the CISSP exam, intellectual property (IP) rights form a crucial component of the legal, regulations, investigations, and compliance domain. Understanding these rights is pivotal for ensuring the proper management and protection of data and resources, aligning with the CISSP's emphasis on high-level, holistic security management.

- **Copyrights:** Copyrights protect original works of authorship in a tangible form, including software programs and website content. For CISSP, it's crucial to understand that organizations must respect copyrights in their use of software, digital content, and other protected works. Any violation can lead to lawsuits and damage to the organization's reputation. Copyright laws, such as the Digital Millennium Copyright Act (DMCA), play a significant role in protecting against unauthorized access and duplication of protected works.

- **Patents:** Patents protect inventions for a specific period, typically 20 years, providing the owner with exclusive rights to the invention. CISSP candidates should be aware that patent infringement can result in significant financial penalties. Understanding patents can also guide IT security professionals in protecting their organization's innovative solutions.

- **Trademarks:** Trademarks are symbols, words, or phrases that distinguish a company's goods or services. Infringing on trademarks can lead to legal repercussions and can also lead to phishing or other fraudulent activities if not adequately secured. A CISSP professional should ensure systems are in place to protect the organization's trademarks and to avoid inadvertently infringing on others' trademarks.

- **Trade secrets**: Trade secrets are confidential and give a business a competitive edge. For a CISSP, it's essential to understand the role of nondisclosure agreements (NDAs), access controls, and other security measures in protecting trade secrets. Loss or theft of trade secrets can have severe consequences, including loss of business advantage and legal action by the affected party.

- **Industrial designs**: Industrial design rights protect the unique visual design of objects. The theft or unauthorized use of industrial designs can lead to legal repercussions. For a CISSP, it is crucial to ensure that proper measures are in place to safeguard such valuable assets.

In the CISSP exam, candidates might face questions related to these IP rights, their legal implications, and how they influence the development and implementation of security policies and procedures. Understanding these rights is also instrumental in incident response and investigation, ensuring that the organization's actions remain within the boundaries of law and ethics.

To effectively prepare for the exam, candidates should familiarize themselves with the laws and regulations relevant to IP rights in their jurisdiction and global conventions and treaties. This knowledge will equip candidates with the understanding needed to navigate the complex landscape of information security and legal compliance.

Regulations and Laws: Relevance for CISSP

The vast landscape of information security is significantly influenced by various laws, regulations, and standards, both on regional and international levels. For the CISSP exam, it's crucial to grasp the basics of these legalities, focusing not on the intricate details but on understanding when and why they apply in the context of information security. The following are some of the most relevant:

- **General Data Protection Regulation (GDPR):** A regulation enforced by the European Union, GDPR is centered around the protection of the personal data of EU citizens. As a CISSP candidate, you should understand GDPR's core principles, including data minimization, purpose limitation, and the rights of data subjects. This is particularly significant when dealing with international data transfers and ensuring cross-border data protection compliance.

- **Health Insurance Portability and Accountability Act (HIPAA):** This US law presides over the privacy and security of health information. HIPAA's understanding is crucial when dealing with healthcare data or designing systems for healthcare organizations.

- **Sarbanes-Oxley Act (SOX):** Enacted in the United States, SOX aims to shield shareholders and the public from fraudulent enterprise practices. This law has notable implications for IT governance and controls. As a CISSP professional, you might need to ensure SOX compliance in IT systems, particularly those related to financial reporting.

- **Payment Card Industry Data Security Standard (PCI DSS)**: Although not a law, PCI DSS is an industry standard adopted globally by organizations that handle branded credit cards. Grasping the basic requirements of PCI DSS is essential, especially when dealing with payment card data.

- **Children's Online Privacy Protection Act (COPPA)**: This US law safeguards the privacy of children under 13. Ensuring COPPA compliance is a must for professionals working on systems or applications targeting this age group.

- **Computer Fraud and Abuse Act (CFAA)**: This is a US federal law that was enacted in 1986 as an amendment to existing computer fraud law (18 U.S.C. § 1030). It was designed to combat hacking and other types of computer crimes. The law prohibits unauthorized access, or exceeding authorized access, to "protected computers" – a definition that has been extended to include virtually any computer connected to the Internet.

- **California Consumer Privacy Act (CCPA)**: A state law that bolsters privacy rights and consumer protection for residents of California. Understanding the CCPA is essential for CISSP candidates working in organizations that process the personal data of California residents.

- **Federal Information Security Management Act (FISMA)**: This US legislation aims to protect government information, operations, and assets against natural or man-made threats. FISMA's understanding is crucial for those in or with the government sector.

- **International Organization for Standardization (ISO) 27001/27002:** These are international standards outlining best practices for an information security management system (ISMS) and providing guidelines for implementing security controls. CISSP candidates should be familiar with these standards, especially when working globally.

- **Personal Information Protection and Electronic Documents Act (PIPEDA):** This Canadian law governs how private sector organizations collect, use, and disclose personal information in the course of commercial business. It also grants individuals the right to access and correct their personal information held by these organizations. Understanding PIPEDA is important when dealing with Canadian clients or organizations.

- **Gramm-Leach-Bliley Act (GLBA):** Also known as the Financial Services Modernization Act, this US law requires financial institutions to explain how they share and protect their customers' private information. If you are a CISSP professional working in the financial sector, understanding the requirements of the GLBA is crucial.

- **Family Educational Rights and Privacy Act (FERPA):** A federal law in the United States that protects the privacy of student education records. As a CISSP candidate, understanding FERPA becomes crucial when dealing with educational data or designing systems for educational institutions.

- **Computer Fraud and Abuse Act (CFAA):** This US
  law is designed to combat hacking by making it a
  federal crime to access a computer without proper
  authorization. CISSP professionals need to understand
  the CFAA, especially when designing systems and
  policies to prevent unauthorized access.

In your CISSP journey, you may encounter questions related to these laws, regulations, and standards, their implications for information security, and their influence on developing and implementing security policies and procedures. They are also crucial when handling incident responses and investigations, ensuring that an organization's actions remain within legal and ethical boundaries.

Table 3-2 summarizes each law/regulation/standard, its jurisdiction, applicability, and key points relevant to the CISSP exam. Remember, having a broad understanding of each is recommended rather than focusing on memorizing specific details. It's important to note for CISSP exam takers that while the table uses abbreviations for brevity, the actual CISSP exam is a high-level professional exam. Therefore, if an abbreviation is used in the exam, it will be spelled out or sufficiently explained in the question context. The intention is not to test the memorization of acronyms but rather the understanding of the relevant principles and implications of these laws, regulations, and standards. Hence, focusing on comprehending these concepts is more beneficial than memorizing the abbreviations.

Table 3-2. *Key Laws, Regulations, and Standards Relevant to CISSP Exam*

Law/ Regulation/ Standard	Area	Applicability	Key Points for CISSP
GDPR	EU	Personal data protection	Data minimization, purpose limitation, rights of data subjects. Requires breach notification to the supervisory within 72 hours
HIPAA	US	Health information privacy and security	Applies to healthcare data and systems
SOX	US	Corporate governance, financial transparency	Impacts IT governance and controls related to financial reporting
PCI DSS	Global	Payment card data security	Applies to systems handling payment card data
COPPA	US	Online privacy of children under 13	Applies to systems or applications aimed at children under 13
CCPA	US	Privacy rights and consumer protection	Applies to organizations processing personal data of California residents
PIPEDA	Canada	Personal information in commercial business	Applies to organizations dealing with Canadian clients or organizations

(continued)

Table 3-2. (*continued*)

Law/ Regulation/ Standard	Area	Applicability	Key Points for CISSP
GLBA	US	Financial institutions' customer data	Applies to systems and procedures within the financial sector
FERPA	US	Student education record privacy	Applies to systems dealing with educational data
CFAA	US	Combatting hacking, unauthorized access	Relevant in the design of systems and policies to prevent unauthorized access

To adequately prepare for the CISSP exam, familiarize yourself with these legalities, and understand their applicability and implications for information security. This foundational knowledge will serve as a stepping stone as you navigate the complex landscape of information security and legal compliance.

Summary and Key Takeaways

This chapter delved into the core concepts and exam tips for the Security and Risk Management domain of the CISSP CBK. It equipped readers to understand information security principles and best practices comprehensively. Key takeaways include

- **Understanding risk**: Comprehending risk components, such as threats, vulnerabilities, and potential impacts, is vital for effective risk management.

- **Risk assessment methodologies**: Mastering qualitative and quantitative risk assessment methods helps estimate and prioritize risks accurately.

- **Risk treatment options**: Recognizing risk acceptance, avoidance, mitigation, and transfer as crucial treatment options allows organizations to make informed decisions.

- **Implementing risk mitigation strategies**: Combining technical, administrative, and physical controls ensures a comprehensive approach to risk reduction.

- **Asset valuation**: Familiarity with different asset valuation methodologies aids in categorizing and prioritizing organizational assets.

- **Risk management frameworks**: Understanding common risk management frameworks, such as NIST SP 800-37, ISO/IEC 27005, FAIR, and COSO ERM, facilitates the structured management of risks.

- **Risk communication and reporting**: Emphasizing clarity, timeliness, relevance, transparency, and consistency ensures effective risk communication.

- **Risk monitoring and review**: Regular monitoring and reviewing of risks and risk management processes contribute to maintaining an up-to-date and effective program.

- **Integration with business processes**: Aligning risk management with business objectives and embedding it in all aspects of the organization promotes a risk-aware culture.

- **Compliance and regulatory considerations**:
  Addressing legal and regulatory requirements is crucial
  to avoid fines, legal actions, or reputational damage.

- **Business continuity and disaster recovery**:
  Developing comprehensive plans for business
  continuity and disaster recovery enhances an
  organization's resilience in disruptions or disasters.

Practice Questions

Before you start the practice questions, remember that one of the most
critical aspects of preparing for the CISSP exam is understanding the
context within which the questions are asked. Remember, your job is
to select the best answer from the provided options, not necessarily the
perfect answer in all circumstances.

The questions are designed to test your knowledge and application of
principles within a set context, not necessarily the real-world scenario you
may face in your day-to-day work. In the CISSP exam, you're expected to
think like a risk advisor, not a technician, and always consider the broader
organizational context.

Let's take an example. Suppose you encounter a question about
responding to a ransomware attack. The options might be

A. Pay the ransom.

B. Report the incident to law enforcement.

C. Try to decrypt the files yourself.

D. Ignore the ransom demand.

In a real-world scenario, your reaction might depend on various factors, such as the importance of the encrypted files, the likelihood of successful decryption, the organization's financial capacity, etc. However, in the context of the CISSP exam, "B. Report the incident to law enforcement" is the best answer. The CISSP principles discourage paying a ransom (option A) as it encourages criminal activity. Trying to decrypt the files yourself (option C) might cause further damage, and ignoring the ransom demand (option D) does not solve the problem.

The key is to stay within the context and scope of the question, apply the principles you have learned, and choose the best answer from the given options. Don't let your real-world experience override the principles that the CISSP exam is testing. Stick to the CISSP mindset, and remember that the "best" answer is the one that best aligns with CISSP principles and practices.

This book adopts a multilayered approach to practice questions, which I've found effective with all my students in training sessions. The first layer of questions appears at the end of each chapter, ensuring that you've grasped and understood the relevant concepts in the exam context. Once all chapters are completed, we move on to the second layer of questions, focusing on adopting the exam mindset. Remember, you don't need excessive practice questions to secure this mindset; instead, think like an advisor or consultant. While CISSP is a managerial exam rather than a technical one, comprehending the concepts can sometimes be challenging as it involves more than rote memorization. But remember, the CISSP exam is a high-level test, so there's no need to delve too deep to understand the "why questions." Know when and why we can utilize a particular security control or solution and the expected output.

1. What are the three primary components of risk?

    A. Threat, consequence, vulnerability

    B. Impact, threat, vulnerability

    C. Asset, threat, impact

    D. Asset, impact, consequence

2. Which risk treatment option involves an organization deciding to tolerate a risk without implementing additional controls?

    A. Risk avoidance

    B. Risk mitigation

    C. Risk transfer

    D. Risk acceptance

3. Which of the following is NOT a component of the ISC2 Code of Ethics?

    A. Protect society and the infrastructure

    B. Act honorably, honestly, and legally

    C. Provide diligent and competent service

    D. Prioritize personal gain over professional duties

4. Which of the following risk management frameworks is developed by the National Institute of Standards and Technology (NIST)?

    A. ISO/IEC 27005

    B. COSO ERM

    C. FAIR

    D. NIST SP 800-37

5. In the context of business continuity and disaster recovery planning, what does it mean to "identify critical business functions"?

    A. Determining the most essential functions and processes of the organization

B. Identifying potential disruptions to business functions

C. Implementing recovery plans for all business functions

D. Regularly testing business functions for potential disruptions

6. Which of the following best describes a qualitative risk assessment?

   A. It uses numerical values to estimate risk.

   B. It relies on subjective judgments to rank risk.

   C. It calculates the financial value of a risk.

   D. It identifies the vulnerabilities that might be exploited by threats.

7. What does the asset valuation method of "business impact" involve?

   A. Calculating the cost of maintaining or replacing an asset

   B. Determining the asset's worth based on market demand

   C. Evaluating the potential impact on operations if the asset is compromised

   D. Considering the asset's contribution to the organization's intellectual property

8. Which of the following is NOT a key element of effective risk communication and reporting?

   A. Clarity

   B. Timeliness

   C. Consistency

   D. Complexity

9. Which of the following activities is NOT involved in regular risk monitoring and review?

    A. Tracking risk treatment progress

    B. Reviewing risk assessments

    C. Analyzing incident reports

    D. Implementing risk treatment plans

10. In the context of compliance and regulatory considerations, what does it mean to "conduct compliance audits"?

    A. Determine which laws and regulations apply to the organization

    B. Establish policies and procedures that address legal and regulatory requirements

    C. Perform regular assessments of the organization's adherence to relevant laws and regulations

    D. Develop and maintain incident response plans

11. Which one of the following is not a risk treatment option?

    A. Risk acceptance

    B. Risk avoidance

    C. Risk mitigation

    D. Risk expansion

12. What does FAIR in the risk management framework stand for?

  A. Factual Analysis of Intrinsic Risk

  B. Factor Analysis of Information Risk

  C. Formal Assessment of Incident Response

  D. Functional Analysis of Infrastructure Resilience

13. What does the risk treatment option "risk transfer" involve?

  A. Eliminating the risk by discontinuing the activity that causes it

  B. Acknowledging the risk and deciding to tolerate it

  C. Implementing controls to reduce the risk

  D. Transferring the risk to a third party

14. Which of the following is not a type of control used in risk mitigation strategies?

  A. Technical controls

  B. Administrative controls

  C. Physical controls

  D. Emotional controls

15. Which of the following is not a part of the risk assessment process?

  A. Identify assets

  B. Identify threats

  C. Identify vulnerabilities

  D. Assess operational efficiency

16. What is the primary purpose of business continuity and disaster recovery planning?

    A. To prevent disasters from occurring

    B. To prepare for, respond to, and recover from disruptions or disasters

    C. To eliminate all risks associated with the organization

    D. To ensure all staff are trained in emergency procedures

17. Which asset valuation methodology considers the asset's contribution to the organization's intellectual property, customer trust, or competitive advantage?

    A. Financial value

    B. Business impact

    C. Market value

    D. Intangible value

18. What does the "canons" in the ISC2 Code of Ethics refer to?

    A. A list of security technologies

    B. A set of fundamental principles

    C. A set of regulatory laws

    D. A list of cybersecurity certifications

19. What is the primary difference between risk acceptance and risk avoidance?

    A. Risk acceptance eliminates the risk, while risk avoidance tolerates the risk.

    B. Risk acceptance tolerates the risk, while risk avoidance eliminates the risk.

    C. Risk acceptance transfers the risk, while risk avoidance mitigates the risk.

    D. Risk acceptance mitigates the risk, while risk avoidance transfers the risk.

20. Which of the following is not typically included in a comprehensive enterprise risk management program according to the COSO ERM framework?

    A. Risk governance and culture

    B. Risk strategy and objective setting

    C. Risk in execution and performance

    D. Risk in product design and marketing

21. In the context of risk management, what is the primary role of a quantitative risk assessment?

    A. To make subjective judgments about risks

    B. To rank risks based on expert opinion

    C. To use numerical values to estimate risks

    D. To categorize risks as low, medium, or high

22. Which of the following is not a primary component of risk, as defined in risk management?

    A. Threats

    B. Vulnerabilities

    C. Impacts

    D. Controls

23. What does the NIST SP 800-37 framework primarily provide guidelines for?

    A. Implementing an information security risk management process

    B. Implementing a risk management process for federal information systems

    C. Providing a quantitative approach to risk management

    D. Developing a comprehensive enterprise risk management program

24. What is one key element of effective risk communication and reporting?

    A. Using complex technical terms to explain risks

    B. Communicating risks as infrequently as possible

    C. Presenting information in a clear and understandable

    D. Presenting information in a clear and understandable manner

25. In the context of risk management, why is it important to integrate risk management into an organization's business processes?

   A. It helps to increase the number of risks the organization faces.

   B. It allows risk considerations to be part of decision-making processes and overall business strategy.

   C. It ensures that risks are only handled by the risk management department.

   D. It reduces the need for regular risk monitoring and review.

26. Which of the following best describes risk acceptance?

   A. The organization reduces the risk by implementing controls.

   B. The organization acknowledges the risk and decides to tolerate it.

   C. The organization transfers the risk to a third party.

   D. The organization eliminates the risk source.

27. What is the primary purpose of asset valuation in the context of risk management?

   A. To estimate the direct monetary value of an asset

   B. To identify potential threats to the asset

   C. To assess the potential impact and likelihood of threats to the asset

   D. To prioritize the asset for risk treatment

28. Which of the following is a key component of effective risk communication and reporting?

    A. Using complex technical terms and jargon

    B. Communicating risks and risk management activities irregularly

    C. Tailoring the content and format of risk reports to the needs of the intended audience

    D. Keeping risk communication and reporting inconsistent across the organization

29. What is the main goal of business continuity and disaster recovery planning?

    A. To eliminate all risks faced by the organization

    B. To ensure that the organization can continue operating during and after a disruption or disaster

    C. To prioritize risks for treatment

    D. To transfer the financial risk of a disruption or disaster to a third party

30. According to the ISC2 Code of Ethics, which of the following is a primary ethical obligation of a security professional?

    A. To advance one's own professional interests

    B. To provide diligent and competent service to principals

    C. To avoid service to the community

    D. To use their skills primarily for personal gain

31. Which of the following is not a type of control mentioned in the risk mitigation strategies?

    A. Technical

    B. Administrative

    C. Physical

    D. Spiritual

32. Which of the following is a key component of the risk monitoring and review process?

    A. Ignoring risk treatment progress

    B. Avoiding reviewing risk assessments

    C. Tracking risk treatment progress

    D. Omitting incident report analysis

33. How does integrating risk management into an organization's business processes benefit the organization?

    A. It decreases the organization's profitability.

    B. It ensures that risk considerations are part of decision-making processes.

    C. It eliminates all the risks faced by the organization.

    D. It restricts stakeholder involvement.

34. Which of the following activities is not a part of compliance and regulatory considerations?

    A. Identifying applicable laws and regulations

    B. Developing policies and procedures

    C. Ignoring compliance audits

    D. Implementing incident response plans

35. Which of the following is not a step in the risk assessment process?

    A. Identify assets

    B. Identify threats

    C. Ignore vulnerabilities

    D. Prioritize risks

36. Which of the following risk treatment options involves transferring the risk to a third party?

    A. Risk acceptance

    B. Risk avoidance

    C. Risk mitigation

    D. Risk transfer

37. What does the intangible value of an asset refer to in the context of asset valuation methodologies?

    A. The asset's direct monetary value

    B. The asset's market demand

    C. The asset's contribution to the organization's intellectual property or customer trust

    D. The asset's impact on the organization's operations

38. What is the most effective method to ascertain the value of an intangible asset?

   A. Calculate the physical storage costs and multiply by the company's projected lifespan

   B. Engage a financial or accounting expert to determine the asset's profit returns

   C. Examine the intangible asset's depreciation over the previous three years

   D. Refer to the historical cost of acquiring or developing the intangible asset

39. What is the key characteristic of qualitative risk assessment?

   A. It can be executed easily and by individuals with basic knowledge of the risk assessment process.

   B. It can be executed by individuals with basic knowledge of risk assessment and utilizes specific metrics for risk calculation.

   C. It uses specific metrics for risk calculation and can be easily implemented.

   D. It can be done by individuals with limited risk assessment knowledge and utilizes specific metrics for risk calculation.

40. How is Single Loss Expectancy (SLE) computed?

   A. By multiplying the asset value and the Annualized Rate of Occurrence (ARO)

   B. By using asset value, Local Annual Frequency Estimate (LAFE), and Standard Annual Frequency Estimate (SAFE)

C. By multiplying the asset value and exposure factor

D. By using the Local Annual Frequency Estimate and the Annualized Rate of Occurrence

41. What are the factors to consider when deciding on the type of risk assessment to perform?

A. Organizational culture, probability of exposure, and budget

B. Budget, resource capabilities, and probability of exposure

C. Resource capabilities, probability of exposure, and budget

D. Organizational culture, budget, and resource capabilities

42. What does security awareness training encompass?

A. Legal security compliance objectives

B. Security roles and responsibilities of staff

C. High-level results of vulnerability assessments

D. Specialized curriculum tasks, coursework, and an accredited institution

43. What is the purpose of a signed user acknowledgment of the corporate security policy?

A. To ensure that users have read the policy

B. To ensure that users understand the policy, as well as the consequences of not adhering to the policy

C. Can be waived if the organization is satisfied that users have a good understanding of the policy

D. To protect the organization if a user's behavior violates the policy

44. What does effective security management accomplish?

A. Achieves security at the lowest cost

B. Reduces risk to an acceptable level

C. Prioritizes security for new products

D. Implements patches in a timely manner

45. What threats does the principle of availability protect information from?

A. Denial-of-service attacks, fires, floods, hurricanes, and unauthorized transactions

B. Fires, floods, hurricanes, unauthorized transactions, and unreadable backup tapes

C. Unauthorized transactions, fires, floods, hurricanes, and unreadable backup tapes

D. Denial-of-service attacks, fires, floods, hurricanes, and unreadable backup tapes

46. To maintain impartiality, the security officer could report to which of the following?

A. CEO, application development, or CFO

B. Chief Information Officer, CFO, or application development

C. CFO, CEO, or Chief Information Officer

D. Application development, CFO, or CEO

47. What is the best use of tactical security plans?

   A. To establish high-level security policies

   B. To enable enterprise-wide security management

   C. To minimize downtime

   D. To deploy new security technology

48. Who is responsible for the implementation of information security?

   A. Everyone

   B. Senior management

   C. Security officer

   D. Data owners

49. In which phase is security likely to be the most costly?

   A. Design

   B. Rapid prototyping

   C. Testing

   D. Implementation

50. What attributes should a security policy have to remain relevant and meaningful over time?

   A. Directive words such as shall, must, or will, technical specifications, and should be short in length

   B. A defined policy development process, should be short in length, and contain directive words such as shall, must, or will

C. Short in length, contain technical specifications, and directive words such as shall, must, or will

D. Directive words such as shall, must, or will, a defined policy development process, and is short in length

51. Which among the following best describes an intangible asset's valuation process?

A. Multiplying the physical storage costs by the company's expected lifespan

B. Collaborating with finance or accounting professionals to ascertain the profit returned by the asset

C. Reviewing the intangible asset's depreciation over the past three years

D. Using the historical acquisition or development cost of the intangible asset

52. Which principle is violated if one individual in the finance department has the ability to add vendors to the vendor database and subsequently make payments to the vendor?

A. A well-formed transaction

B. Separation of duties

C. Least privilege

D. Data sensitivity level

53. What is the best way to mitigate collusion?

A. Job rotation

B. Data classification

C. Defining job sensitivity level

D. Least privilege

54. Who is best suited to make decisions about data access?

A. User managers

B. Data owners

C. Senior management

D. Application developers

55. What is the most significant source of cybercrime risk?

A. Outsiders

B. Nation-states

C. Insiders

D. Script kiddies

56. What is the primary obstacle in combating computer crime?

A. Computer criminals are generally smarter than computer investigators.

B. Adequate funding to stay ahead of the computer criminals.

C. Activity associated with computer crime is truly international.

D. There are so many more computer criminals than investigators that it is impossible to keep up.

57. What discipline does computer forensics combine
    with computer science, information technology,
    and engineering?

    A. Law

    B. Information systems

    C. Analytical thought

    D. The scientific method

58. Which principle allows an investigator to identify
    aspects of a person responsible for a crime, based
    on the residual traces left behind while stealing
    information?

    A. Meyer's principle of legal impunity

    B. Criminalistic principles

    C. IOCE/Group of 8 Nations principles for computer forensics

    D. Locard's principle of exchange

59. Which of the following is a part of the fundamental
    principles of evidence?

    A. Authenticity, redundancy, and admissibility

    B. Completeness, authenticity, and admissibility

    C. Completeness, redundancy, and authenticity

    D. Redundancy, admissibility, and completeness

60. Which of the following is not listed as a stage in
    incident response?

    A. Documentation

    B. Prosecution

C. Containment

D. Investigation

61. Which type of law primarily focuses on the abstract concepts and is greatly influenced by the writings of legal scholars and academics?

A. Criminal law

B. Civil law

C. Religious law

D. Administrative law

62. Which category of intellectual property protection covers the expression of ideas rather than the ideas themselves?

A. Trademark

B. Patent

C. Copyright

D. Trade secret

63. Which type of intellectual property safeguards the goodwill that a merchant or vendor invests in its products?

A. Trademark

B. Patent

C. Copyright

D. Trade secret

64. Which of the following represent types of software licensing?

    A. Freeware, open source, and commercial

    B. Commercial, academic, and open source

    C. Academic, freeware, and open source

    D. Freeware, commercial, and academic

65. What is most directly concerned with the rights and duties of individuals and organizations in relation to the gathering, usage, storage, and sharing of personal data?

    A. Privacy

    B. Secrecy

    C. Availability

    D. Reliability

66. Which of the following subphases are included in the triage process of incident response?

    A. Collection, transport, testimony

    B. Traceback, feedback, loopback

    C. Detection, identification, notification

    D. Confidentiality, integrity, availability

67. The integrity of a forensic bit stream image is verified by

    A. Comparing hash totals to the original source

    B. Keeping good notes

    C. Taking pictures

    D. Encrypted keys

68. In the context of digital evidence, the crime scene should

    A. Remain unaltered at all times

    B. Be fully replicable in a legal setting

    C. Be located in a single country

    D. Have the minimum possible level of contamination

69. In the context of outsourcing IT systems

    A. All regulatory and compliance requirements must be transferred to the provider.

    B. The outsourcing organization is relieved from compliance obligations.

    C. The outsourced IT systems are exempt from compliance obligations.

    D. The provider is exempt from compliance obligations.

70. How does the ISC2 Code of Ethics address conflicts between canons?

    A. There can never be conflicts between canons.

    B. Through a process of adjudication.

    C. Based on the order of the canons.

    D. By having all canon conflicts reviewed by the board of directors.

71. Which law in the United States requires federal agencies to develop, document, and implement an agency-wide program to provide security for the information systems that support its operations and assets?

   A. Health Insurance Portability and Accountability Act (HIPAA)

   B. Gramm-Leach-Bliley Act (GLBA)

   C. Federal Information Security Management Act (FISMA)

   D. Sarbanes-Oxley Act (SOX)

72. The General Data Protection Regulation (GDPR) is a regulation in EU law on data protection and privacy. Which of the following principles is NOT stated in GDPR?

   A. Data minimization

   B. Consent

   C. Data localization

   D. Accountability

73. The _____ provides guidance for the protection of electronically protected health information.

   A. HIPAA Security Rule

   B. Sarbanes-Oxley Act

   C. Computer Fraud and Abuse Act

   D. Federal Information Security Management Act

74. Which of the following laws mandates that organizations must have adequate security measures in place to protect customer data?

    A. Sarbanes-Oxley Act (SOX)

    B. Gramm-Leach-Bliley Act (GLBA)

    C. Data Protection Act (DPA)

    D. Federal Information Security Management Act (FISMA)

75. The purpose of the _____ is to ensure the accuracy, fairness, and privacy of the information in a consumer's credit reports.

    A. Fair Credit Reporting Act (FCRA)

    B. General Data Protection Regulation (GDPR)

    C. Gramm-Leach-Bliley Act (GLBA)

    D. Federal Information Security Management Act (FISMA)

76. What is the primary purpose of the Children's Online Privacy Protection Act (COPPA)?

    A. To regulate how websites collect data about children under 13

    B. To regulate how websites collect data about all users

    C. To protect children from inappropriate content online

    D. To protect the privacy of adults when they use websites

77. What is the primary purpose of the Payment Card Industry Data Security Standard (PCI DSS)?

    A. To protect customer data during online transactions

    B. To ensure the privacy of customer data

    C. To ensure the secure disposal of customer data

    D. To ensure the security of credit card transactions

78. The _____ outlines procedures to enhance the protection of critical infrastructure from cyber threats.

    A. Executive Order 13636

    B. HIPAA Security Rule

    C. Federal Information Security Management Act (FISMA)

    D. Computer Fraud and Abuse Act

79. Which law is designed to combat identity theft by requiring businesses to destroy sensitive information derived from consumer reports?

    A. Fair and Accurate Credit Transactions Act (FACTA)

    B. General Data Protection Regulation (GDPR)

    C. Sarbanes-Oxley Act (SOX)

    D. Federal Information Security Management Act (FISMA)

80. Which of the following laws makes it a crime to gain unauthorized access to protected computer systems?

    A. Computer Fraud and Abuse Act (CFAA)

    B. Fair Credit Reporting Act (FCRA)

C. Federal Information Security Management Act (FISMA)

D. Sarbanes-Oxley Act (SOX)

81. Imagine you are a cybersecurity analyst for a retail company. The company has assessed that the Single Loss Expectancy (SLE) for a data breach is $500,000. The exposure factor (EF) for such an event is estimated at 0.85, and the Annualized Rate of Occurrence (ARO) is 0.60. Additionally, the residual risk is calculated to be $200,000. Based on these metrics, what would be the resulting Annualized Loss Expectancy (ALE) for a data breach?

A. $255,000

B. $510,000

C. $300,000

D. $425,000

82. The correct sequence for the following formulas should be

A. ALE, residual risk, SLE, ARO

B. ALE, ARO, SLE, residual risk

C. ARO, SLE, ALE, residual risk

D. SLE, ARO, ALE, residual risk

83. What is the duration of copyright protection in both the United States and the European Union?

A. The author's life plus 20 years

B. The author's life plus 30 years

C. The author's life plus 70 years

D. The author's life plus 100 years

84. Which term refers to a flaw, loophole, oversight, or error that leaves an organization open to potential attack or harm?

    A. Risk

    B. Vulnerability

    C. Threat

    D. Exploit

85. Which of the following security documents is the broadest in scope?

    A. Procedures

    B. Standards

    C. Policies

    D. Baselines

86. Which role within an organization is responsible for assigning sensitivity labels to information assets?

    A. Management

    B. The auditor

    C. The user

    D. The owner

87. If the cost of implementing a countermeasure exceeds the value of the asset it's meant to protect, which approach should be preferred?

    A. Do nothing

    B. Transfer the risk

    C. Mitigate the risk

    D. Increase the cost of exposure

88. Which ISO document serves as a standard for information security management?

    A. ISO 27001

    B. ISO 27002

    C. ISO 27004

    D. ISO 27799

89. Which of the following accurately describes the risk management techniques?

    A. Risk acceptance, risk transference, risk avoidance, risk mitigation

    B. Risk acceptance, risk containment, risk avoidance, risk migration

    C. Risk acceptance, risk mitigation, risk containment, risk quantification

    D. Risk avoidance, risk migration, risk containment, risk quantification

90. Which of the following identifies a model that specifically targets security and not governance of an entire enterprise?

    A. The Zachman framework

    B. COBIT

    C. COSO

    D. SABSA

91. Which term allows the management to demonstrate that they took necessary steps to prevent negligence in lawsuits, even if their actions weren't flawless?

   A. Due care

   B. Prudency

   C. Due diligence

   D. Threat agent

92. Which term refers to the method of gathering information by interviewing individuals anonymously?

   A. ISO/IEC 27001

   B. Qualitative valuation

   C. The Delphi method

   D. Quantitative valuation

93. What is the suitable standard for governing third-party providers?

   A. A nondisclosure agreement (NDA)

   B. An acceptable use policy

   C. The same level as employees

   D. The same level as defined by the ISC2 Code of Ethics

94. Which term refers to the expected cost associated with a single loss event?

   A. Annualized loss expectancy (ALE)

   B. Exposure factor (EF)

   C. Asset value (AV)

   D. Single loss expectancy (SLE)

95. What is the rationale behind an enterprise reassessing the classification of its data files and records at least once a year?

   A. To adhere to the stipulations of the Internet Architecture Board

   B. Because the worth of data varies as time progresses

   C. Due to the necessity of mitigating new threats

   D. To safeguard the data's confidentiality

96. What should be the primary concern of management when establishing a governance framework?

   A. Enhancing profits

   B. Evading losses

   C. Catering to the needs of the business

   D. Ensuring safety

97. When it comes to forensically examining digital evidence, which is the most accurate description of the priorities?

   A. Carry out an analysis of a bit-level duplicate of the disk.

   B. Examine the log files on the duplicated disk.

   C. Perform steganographic analysis on the duplicated disk.

   D. Detect any harmful code present on the duplicated disk.

98. Which of the following illustrates an instance of self-regulation?

    A. Sarbanes-Oxley (SOX)

    B. Gramm-Leach-Bliley Act (GLBA)

    C. Payment Card Industry Data Security Standard (PCI DSS)

    D. Third-party governance

99. What are the possible actions that can be taken with residual risk?

    A. It can be either allocated or accepted.

    B. It can be either pinpointed or appraised.

    C. It can be either lessened or computed.

    D. It can be either unveiled or evaluated.

100. Which element does not constitute part of risk analysis?

    A. Assets

    B. Threats

    C. Vulnerabilities

    D. Countermeasures

101. What is it that security safeguards and controls are incapable of doing?

    A. Risk reduction

    B. Risk avoidance

    C. Risk transfer

    D. Risk analysis

102. Which of the following is most associated with risk acceptance?

    A. Risk detection

    B. Risk prevention

    C. Risk tolerance

    D. Risk correction

103. The quantity of risk an organization can endure should be based on what?

    A. Technological level

    B. Acceptable level

    C. Affordable level

    D. Measurable level

Answers

1. Answer: B. Impact, threat, vulnerability

    Explanation: Risk is typically composed of three components: threat (a potential cause of an incident that may result in harm), vulnerability (a weakness that can be exploited by a threat), and impact (the potential harm caused by a threat exploiting a vulnerability).

2. Answer: D. Risk acceptance

    Explanation: Risk acceptance is when an organization decides to acknowledge a risk but does not implement additional controls or measures to address it. The other options (avoidance, mitigation, and transfer) all involve taking some action to address the risk.

3. Answer: D. Prioritize personal gain over professional duties

    Explanation: The ISC2 Code of Ethics includes the principles of protecting society and the infrastructure; acting honorably, honestly, and legally; and providing diligent and competent service. Prioritizing personal gain over professional duties is contrary to the ethical principles outlined by ISC2.

4. Answer: D. NIST SP 800-37

    Explanation: NIST SP 800-37 is a risk management framework developed by the National Institute of Standards and Technology. ISO/IEC 27005 is an international standard, FAIR (Factor Analysis of Information Risk) is a quantitative risk management framework, and COSO ERM is a framework provided by the Committee of Sponsoring Organizations of the Treadway Commission.

5. Answer: A. Determining the most essential functions and processes of the organization

    Explanation: Identifying critical business functions involves determining the most essential functions and processes of the organization, which should be prioritized for recovery during an incident. This is a crucial first step in business continuity and disaster recovery planning. The other options are also part of the planning process, but they do not define what it means to "identify critical business functions."

6. Answer: B. It relies on subjective judgments to rank risk.

    Explanation: A qualitative risk assessment uses subjective judgments and expert opinions to rank risks, often categorizing them as low, medium, or high. In contrast, a quantitative risk assessment uses numerical values and calculations to estimate risks.

7. Answer: C. Evaluating the potential impact on operations if the asset is compromised

    Explanation: The "business impact" asset valuation method involves evaluating the potential impact on the organization's operations, reputation, or bottom line if the asset is compromised. The other options correspond to different asset valuation methods: "financial value," "market value," and "intangible value," respectively.

8. Answer: D. Complexity

    Explanation: Effective risk communication and reporting should be clear, timely, and consistent. Complexity, particularly in the form of jargon and technical terms, can actually hinder effective communication and should be avoided when possible.

9. Answer: D. Implementing risk treatment plans

   Explanation: Regular risk monitoring and review involves tracking risk treatment progress, reviewing risk assessments, and analyzing incident reports. Implementing risk treatment plans is part of risk treatment, not monitoring and review.

10. Answer: C. Perform regular assessments of the organization's adherence to relevant laws and regulations

    Explanation: Conducting compliance audits involves performing regular assessments to check if the organization is adhering to relevant laws and regulations. This process helps to identify any deviations or noncompliance issues, which can then be addressed to avoid legal penalties, reputational damage, and other negative consequences. Options A, B, and D are all important components of a compliance program but do not accurately define the term "conduct compliance audits."

11. Answer: D. Risk expansion

    Explanation: Risk expansion is not a recognized risk treatment option. The commonly accepted risk treatment options are risk acceptance, risk avoidance, risk mitigation, and risk transfer.

12. Answer: B. Factor Analysis of Information Risk

    Explanation: FAIR stands for Factor Analysis of Information Risk. It offers a quantitative approach to risk management, enabling organizations to measure and prioritize risks using financial terms.

13. Answer: D. Transferring the risk to a third party

    Explanation: Risk transfer involves shifting the risk to a third party, such as an insurance company or a service provider.

14. Answer: D. Emotional controls

    Explanation: Risk mitigation strategies involve technical, administrative, and physical controls. Emotional controls are not a recognized type of control in risk mitigation.

15. Answer: D. Assess operational efficiency

    Explanation: The risk assessment process involves identifying assets, threats, and vulnerabilities, assessing the potential impact and likelihood of each threat-vulnerability pair, and prioritizing risks. Assessing operational efficiency is not part of this process.

16. Answer: B. To prepare for, respond to, and recover from disruptions or disasters

    Explanation: The primary purpose of business continuity and disaster recovery planning is to prepare for, respond to, and recover from disruptions or disasters. While prevention is ideal, it is not always possible, hence the need for preparation, response, and recovery plans.

17. Answer: D. Intangible value

Explanation: Intangible value considers the asset's contribution to the organization's intellectual property, customer trust, or competitive advantage. These aspects may not have a direct monetary value but are critical to the organization's success.

18. Answer: B. A set of fundamental principles

Explanation: The "canons" in the ISC2 Code of Ethics refer to a set of fundamental principles that guide the ethical and professional behavior of information security professionals.

19. Answer: B. Risk acceptance tolerates the risk, while risk avoidance eliminates the risk.

Explanation: Risk acceptance involves acknowledging and deciding to tolerate the risk, whereas risk avoidance involves eliminating the risk by discontinuing the activity or process that causes it.

20. Answer: B. Risk in product design and marketing

Explanation: The COSO ERM framework includes principles and guidance focusing on risk governance and culture, strategy and objective setting, and risk in execution and performance. Risk in product design and marketing, while important, is not specifically mentioned in the framework.

21. Answer: C. To use numerical values to estimate risks

Explanation: Quantitative risk assessment uses numerical values and calculations to estimate potential risks, often in terms of potential financial impact.

22. Answer: D. Controls

    Explanation: Controls are not a component of risk
    but are measures taken to mitigate risk. The primary
    components of risk are threats, vulnerabilities, and
    potential impacts.

23. Answer: B. Implementing a risk management
    process for federal information systems

    Explanation: The NIST SP 800-37 framework
    primarily provides guidelines for implementing a risk
    management process for federal information systems.

24. Answer: D. Presenting information in a clear and
    understandable manner

    Explanation: Effective risk communication
    and reporting involve presenting risk-related
    information clearly, timely, and concisely. This
    allows stakeholders at all levels, regardless of their
    technical expertise, to comprehend the risks and
    make informed decisions. Option A is incorrect as
    complex technical terms can make the information
    harder to understand, especially for nontechnical
    stakeholders. Option B is also incorrect as frequent
    communication of risk-related information is crucial
    to keep all stakeholders informed and aware of the
    current risk landscape.

25. Answer: B. It allows risk considerations to be part
     of decision-making processes and overall business
     strategy.

     Explanation: Integrating risk management into an
     organization's business processes ensures that risk
     considerations are incorporated into all aspects of
     the business, including decision-making processes,
     resource allocation, and strategic planning. This
     approach promotes a risk-aware culture and allows
     the organization to proactively manage risks rather
     than reactively responding to them.

26. Answer: B. The organization acknowledges the risk
     and decides to tolerate it.

     Explanation: Risk acceptance involves
     acknowledging risk and deciding to tolerate it
     without implementing additional controls. This
     typically occurs when the cost of mitigating the risk
     exceeds the potential benefit or when the risk is
     deemed to have a low impact on the organization.

27. Answer: A. To estimate the direct monetary value of
     an asset

     Explanation: Asset valuation involves assigning a
     value to an organization's assets, such as hardware,
     software, data, or personnel. This value can be
     based on various factors, including the cost of
     purchasing, maintaining, or replacing the asset; its
     potential impact on the organization's operations or
     reputation; its market value; or its intangible value.

28. Answer: C. Tailoring the content and format of risk reports to the needs of the intended audience

   Explanation: Effective risk communication and reporting should be tailored to the needs and preferences of the intended audience. This includes presenting information in a clear, concise, and understandable manner; communicating risks and risk management activities regularly; and maintaining consistency in risk communication and reporting across the organization.

29. Answer: B. To ensure that the organization can continue operating during and after a disruption or disaster
   Explanation: Business continuity and disaster recovery planning aim to ensure that an organization can continue its critical operations during and after a disruption or disaster. This involves identifying critical business functions, assessing potential disruptions, developing recovery strategies, implementing recovery plans, and regularly testing and maintaining these plans.

30. Answer: B. To provide diligent and competent service to principals

   Explanation: According to the ISC2 Code of Ethics, a primary ethical obligation of a security professional is to provide diligent and competent service to principals. This means that security professionals should strive to serve their employers, clients, and other stakeholders with the highest level of professionalism.

31. Answer: D. Spiritual

Explanation: Risk mitigation strategies involve technical, administrative, and physical controls. Technical controls involve the use of technology, administrative controls involve policies and procedures, and physical controls involve securing the physical environment. Spiritual controls aren't a recognized category in risk management.

32. Answer: C. Tracking risk treatment progress

Explanation: Tracking risk treatment progress is a key component of the risk monitoring and review process. Other elements include reviewing risk assessments, analyzing incident reports, and evaluating the overall effectiveness of the risk management program.

33. Answer: B. It ensures that risk considerations are part of decision-making processes.

Explanation: Integrating risk management into an organization's business processes helps ensure that risk considerations are part of decision-making processes, resource allocation, and overall business strategy. This can help the organization make better-informed decisions and mitigate potential risks more effectively.

34. Answer: C. Ignoring compliance audits

Explanation: Ignoring compliance audits is not a part of compliance and regulatory considerations. Regular audits are important for assessing the organization's compliance with relevant laws and regulations and identifying potential gaps or areas for improvement.

35. Answer: C. Ignore vulnerabilities

Explanation: Ignoring vulnerabilities is not part of the risk assessment process. The steps involve identifying assets, threats, and vulnerabilities, assessing impact and likelihood, and prioritizing risks.

36. Answer: D. Risk transfer

Explanation: Risk transfer is a risk treatment option that involves transferring the risk to a third party, such as an insurance company or a service provider.

37. Answer: C. The asset's contribution to the organization's intellectual property or customer trust

Explanation: The intangible value of an asset refers to nonmonetary aspects such as its contribution to the organization's intellectual property, customer trust, or competitive advantage.

38. Answer: B. Engage a financial or accounting expert to determine the asset's profit returns

Explanation: The value of an intangible asset is best determined by assessing its economic benefits, such as the profits it generates. A financial or accounting professional would be most equipped to calculate this.

39. Answer: A. It can be executed easily and by
     individuals with basic knowledge of the risk
     assessment process.

     Explanation: Qualitative risk assessment is
     characterized by its simplicity and the ability
     to be performed by individuals with a basic
     understanding of the process. It does not rely
     heavily on specific metrics or calculations; rather,
     it uses descriptions or categories to assess and
     prioritize risks.

40. Answer: C. By multiplying the asset value and
     exposure factor

     Explanation: Single Loss Expectancy (SLE) is
     calculated by multiplying the asset value (how
     much the asset is worth) by the exposure factor (the
     proportion of the asset that is lost in the event of an
     incident).

41. Answer: D. Organizational culture, budget, and
     resource capabilities

     Explanation: The type of risk assessment to be performed
     in an organization is influenced by various factors. These
     include the organizational culture (which can determine
     the acceptance and understanding of the assessment
     process), the available budget (which can limit or extend
     the scope and depth of the assessment), and resource
     capabilities (which can impact the ability to perform
     certain types of assessments). While the probability of
     exposure is a factor in risk assessment, it is part of the
     assessment process itself rather than a determining
     factor in the type of risk assessment to be conducted.

42. Answer: B. Security roles and responsibilities of staff

Explanation: Security awareness training typically covers the roles and responsibilities of staff regarding security. It aims to equip them with the knowledge they need to recognize and respond appropriately to security threats.

43. Answer: D. To protect the organization if a user's behavior violates the policy

Explanation: While all options may have some relevance, a signed user acknowledgment of the corporate security policy primarily helps protect the organization if a user's behavior violates the policy. It serves as documented evidence that the user was aware of the policy and the associated consequences of noncompliance.

44. Answer: B. Reduces risk to an acceptable level

Explanation: Effective security management focuses on mitigating risk to a level that is acceptable to the organization, balancing the cost of risk mitigation with the potential impact of security incidents. While cost control, prioritization for new products, and timely patching are important, they are part of a broader strategy aimed at risk reduction.

45. Answer: D. Denial-of-service attacks, fires, floods, hurricanes, and unreadable backup tapes

Explanation: The principle of availability in information security is concerned with ensuring that authorized users have access to data and resources when needed. This involves protection against a variety of threats including denial-of-service attacks; natural disasters like fires, floods, and hurricanes; and technical issues such as unreadable backup tapes.

46.   Answer: C. CFO, CEO, or Chief Information Officer

Explanation: To avoid bias and ensure independence, a security officer could report directly to top-level management such as the Chief Financial Officer (CFO), Chief Executive Officer (CEO), or the Chief Information Officer (CIO). This arrangement helps to ensure that security concerns are addressed at the highest level of decision-making.

47.   Answer: D. To deploy new security technology

Explanation: Tactical security plans are typically used to guide the implementation of specific security measures, such as the deployment of new security technologies. These plans have a shorter time horizon than strategic security plans and are more detailed, focusing on the practical aspects of implementing security measures.

48.   Answer: A. Everyone

Explanation: While specific roles like the security officer, senior management, and data owners have key responsibilities, implementing information security is a shared responsibility. Everyone in an organization has a part to play in maintaining security, from following established policies to reporting potential security incidents.

49. Answer: D. Implementation

    Explanation: Implementing security measures often involves significant costs, including the purchase of security hardware or software, hiring or training staff, and potential disruptions to business operations. It's generally more cost-effective to consider security early in the design phase, where potential issues can be addressed before they become expensive problems during implementation.

50. Answer: D. Directive words such as shall, must, or will, a defined policy development process, and is short in length

    Explanation: A security policy that remains meaningful over time is one that is clear and concise, has a defined policy development and review process, and uses directive words to clearly communicate the requirements. It doesn't necessarily need to contain detailed technical specifications, as these may change over time and could make the policy less adaptable and more difficult to maintain.

51. Answer: B. Collaborating with finance or accounting professionals to ascertain the profit returned by the asset

    Explanation: The value of an intangible asset is often best determined by its ability to generate profit. Therefore, working with finance or accounting professionals to ascertain the profit returned by the asset is typically the most effective approach.

52. Answer: B. Separation of duties

Explanation: The separation of duties principle is designed to prevent errors and fraud that might be possible when only one person is in control of all parts of a process. Here, allowing one person to both add vendors and make payments could lead to fraudulent transactions. Hence, this scenario is a violation of the separation of duties principle.

53. Answer: A. Job rotation

Explanation: Collusion is the act of collaborating fraudulently within an organization to deceive or defraud. Job rotation, which involves moving employees between different roles, is a good way to prevent collusion because it reduces the opportunity for long-term manipulation in any single position.

54. Answer: B. Data owners

Explanation: Data owners, the individuals or entities responsible for the data's security and use, are best suited to make decisions about data access. They understand the data's sensitivity and the potential risks of unauthorized access. While other stakeholders may have input, the ultimate decision should lie with the data owner.

55. Answer: C. Insiders

Explanation: Although cybercrime can come from various sources, the greatest risk often comes from insiders. These are individuals who have legitimate access to the system and can misuse it for harmful activities. Insider threats are difficult to detect and can cause substantial damage.

56. Answer: C. Activity associated with computer crime is truly international.

    Explanation: The international nature of computer crime is a major hindrance to fighting it. Jurisdictional issues, differences in laws across countries, and the sheer scope of the Internet make it challenging to investigate and prosecute cybercrimes effectively.

57. Answer: A. Law

    Explanation: Computer forensics is a multidisciplinary field that combines computer science, information technology, and engineering with law. The goal is to gather and analyze data in a way that is legally admissible.

58. Answer: D. Locard's principle of exchange

    Explanation: Locard's exchange principle states that the perpetrator of a crime will bring something into the crime scene and leave with something from it and that both can be used as forensic evidence. This principle is applicable to cybercrimes, where digital traces can be left behind.

59. Answer: B. Completeness, authenticity, and admissibility

    Explanation: The five cardinal rules of evidence include completeness, authenticity, admissibility, accuracy, and reasonableness. Hence, option B is correct as it contains three of these principles.

60. Answer: B. Prosecution

Explanation: While prosecution may be a result
of an incident response, it is not a phase in
itself. The typical phases of incident response
include preparation, identification, containment,
eradication, recovery, and lessons learned/
documentation.

61. Answer: B. Civil law

Explanation: Civil law, also known as Roman law,
is primarily based on written codes, statutes, and
legal principles developed by legal scholars and
academics. It emphasizes abstract concepts of law.

62. Answer: C. Copyright

Explanation: Copyright law protects the expression
of an idea in a tangible medium, such as a book,
song, or software program, rather than the
idea itself.

63. Answer: A. Trademark

Explanation: Trademarks protect brand names,
logos, and other identifiers that signify the source of
goods or services. The value of a trademark lies in
the goodwill and brand recognition that a merchant
or vendor builds in its products or services.

64. Answer: D. Freeware, commercial, and academic

Explanation: These are all types of software
licensing. Freeware is software that is available
free of charge. Commercial software is typically
sold for profit. Academic licenses are special types

of software licenses designed for educational institutions. These licenses are often offered at a discounted rate and may come with specific terms and conditions that restrict usage to educational purposes only.

65. Answer: A. Privacy

    Explanation: Privacy deals with the rights and obligations of individuals and organizations with respect to the collection, use, retention, and disclosure of personal information.

66. Answer: C. Detection, identification, notification

    Explanation: The initial steps of triage in incident response typically include detection (discovering the incident), identification (understanding the nature of the incident), and notification (informing relevant parties about the incident).

67. Answer: A. Comparing hash totals to the original source

    Explanation: The integrity of a forensic bit stream image is typically verified by comparing the hash of the image to the hash of the original source. If the hashes match, it verifies that the image is an exact replica of the original.

68. Answer: D. Have the minimum possible level of contamination

    Explanation: The aim should always be to minimize contamination of the crime scene to maintain the integrity of the digital evidence. This aids in its admissibility and reliability in a court of law.

69. Answer: A. All regulatory and compliance requirements must be transferred to the provider.

Explanation: The responsibility for regulatory and compliance requirements lies with the organization, but when outsourcing IT systems, these requirements should be clearly communicated and agreed upon with the provider.

70. Answer: C. Based on the order of the canons

Explanation: If a conflict arises between the canons in the ISC2 Code of Ethics, they are resolved by giving precedence to the canon that appears earlier in the list.

71. Answer: C. Federal Information Security Management Act (FISMA)

Explanation: The FISMA requires federal agencies to develop, document, and implement an agency-wide program to provide information security for the information systems that support its operations and assets.

72. Answer: C. Data localization

Explanation: Data localization is not a principle stated in GDPR. GDPR principles include lawfulness, fairness, transparency, purpose limitation, data minimization, accuracy, storage limitation, integrity and confidentiality, and accountability.

73. Answer: A. HIPAA Security Rule
Explanation: The HIPAA Security Rule specifically focuses on the protection of electronic protected health information (ePHI).

74. Answer: B. Gramm-Leach-Bliley Act (GLBA)

Explanation: The GLBA requires financial institutions to explain their information-sharing practices to their customers and to safeguard sensitive data.

75. Answer: A. Fair Credit Reporting Act (FCRA)

Explanation: FCRA is designed to ensure the accuracy, fairness, and privacy of the information in a consumer's credit reports.

76. Answer: A. To regulate how websites collect data about children under 13

Explanation: COPPA imposes certain requirements on operators of websites or online services directed to children under 13 years of age and on operators of other websites or online services that have actual knowledge that they are collecting personal information online from a child under 13 years of age.

77. Answer: D. To ensure the security of credit card transactions
Explanation: PCI DSS is a set of security standards designed to ensure that all companies that accept, process, store, or transmit credit card information maintain a secure environment.

78. Answer: A. Executive Order 13636

Explanation: This executive order establishes a policy to enhance the security and resilience of the nation's critical infrastructure and to maintain a cyber environment that encourages efficiency, innovation, and economic prosperity.

79. Answer: A. Fair and Accurate Credit Transactions Act (FACTA)

Explanation: FACTA aims to help consumers protect their data from identity theft. It allows consumers to request and obtain a free credit report once every twelve months from each of the three nationwide consumer credit reporting companies.

80. Answer: A. Computer Fraud and Abuse Act (CFAA)

Explanation: The CFAA makes it illegal to intentionally access a computer without authorization or to exceed authorized access and thereby obtain protected information from any protected computer.

81. Answer: D. $425,000.

Explanation: The Annualized Loss Expectancy (ALE) is calculated by first determining the Single Loss Expectancy (SLE), which is the product of the asset value and the exposure factor (EF). In this case, the SLE would be $500,000 multiplied by 0.85, resulting in $425,000. The ALE is then calculated by multiplying the SLE by the Annualized Rate of Occurrence (ARO), which is 0.60. However, since the ALE is essentially an annualized version of the SLE in this specific scenario, the ALE would also be $425,000. The residual risk of $200,000 is a separate metric that indicates the remaining risk after security measures have been applied and does not directly factor into the ALE calculation for this question.

82. Answer: D. SLE, ARO, ALE, residual risk

Explanation: The correct order of these formulas in the context of risk assessment is as follows:

- **SLE (Single Loss Expectancy)**: This is calculated first as it represents the monetary loss expected from a single event.

- **ARO (Annualized Rate of Occurrence)**: This is the frequency with which a threat is expected to occur within a year.

- **ALE (Annualized Loss Expectancy)**: This is calculated by multiplying the SLE by the ARO; hence, it comes after SLE and ARO.

- **Residual risk**: This is the remaining risk after security controls have been applied and is typically assessed after understanding the potential losses (ALE).

Thus, the proper order is Single Loss Expectancy (SLE), Annualized Rate of Occurrence (ARO), Annualized Loss Expectancy (ALE), and then residual risk.

83.   Answer: C. The author's life plus 70 years

Explanation: In both the United States and the
European Union, copyright protection generally
lasts for the duration of the author's life plus 70
years. This time frame provides creators with a
substantial period of control over their works,
incentivizing further creation and innovation. It's
important to note that copyright laws can vary by
country and type of work, so always refer to specific
legislation for accurate information.

84.   Answer: B. Vulnerability

Explanation: In the context of information security,
a vulnerability refers to a flaw, loophole, oversight,
or error in a system that could be exploited
to cause harm. This could include software
bugs, misconfigurations, weak passwords, etc.
Vulnerabilities can be exploited by threats, such
as hackers or malware, to perform unauthorized
actions or gain unauthorized access. The process of
identifying and addressing these vulnerabilities is a
crucial part of any organization's risk management
and security strategy. The term "weakness" is quite
often used when defining vulnerability.

85.   Answer: C. Policies

Explanation: Policies are the most general type
of security document. They provide a high-level
overview of an organization's principles, rules,
and expectations regarding information security.
Policies set the foundation for all other security
documents and guide the development of standards,

procedures, and baselines, which are more specific and detail oriented. They are typically designed to guide decision-making and set the direction for an organization's information security program.

86. Answer: D. The owner

    Explanation: Within an organization, the owner of an information asset is typically responsible for assigning sensitivity labels. These labels represent the asset's classification level and help guide how the asset should be handled, stored, transmitted, and destroyed. The owner, having the best understanding of the data's value and sensitivity, is in the best position to assign these labels.

87. Answer: B. Transfer the risk

    Explanation: When the cost of the countermeasure is more than the value of the asset, the most appropriate approach is typically to transfer the risk. This could be through insurance or by using third-party services. In this way, the organization can balance the cost of protection with the value of the asset. This doesn't mean ignoring the risk (option A) or unnecessarily increasing costs (option D). Mitigating the risk (option C) might still be more expensive than the asset's value.

88. Answer: A. ISO 27001

    Explanation: ISO 27001 is the international standard for information security management. It establishes the requirements and best practices for an Information Security Management System (ISMS).

The other ISO standards listed here are also part of the ISO 27000 series, but they focus on different aspects of information security. For example, ISO 27002 provides a code of practice for information security controls, while ISO 27004 provides guidelines for the measurement of information security. ISO 27799 provides guidelines for health informatics – information security management in health using ISO/IEC 27002.

89. Answer: A. Risk acceptance, risk transference, risk avoidance, risk mitigation

Explanation: The four main risk management techniques are risk acceptance (accepting the potential loss and continuing operations), risk transference (shifting the potential loss to another party), risk avoidance (eliminating the risk by not engaging in a certain activity), and risk mitigation (reducing the impact of the risk). The other terms mentioned in the options, such as risk containment, risk migration, and risk quantification, are not standard risk management techniques.

90. Answer: D. SABSA

Explanation: The Sherwood Applied Business Security Architecture (SABSA) is a framework and methodology for enterprise security architecture and service management. It is specifically designed to focus on security, unlike other models like COBIT, COSO, or the Zachman framework, which are designed for broader governance of an entire enterprise. COBIT (Control Objectives for

Information and Related Technologies) and COSO (Committee of Sponsoring Organizations of the Treadway Commission) are used for IT governance and enterprise risk management, respectively. The Zachman framework is an enterprise architecture framework, which is not specifically focused on security.

91. Answer: A. Due care

Explanation: "Due care" refers to the effort made by an ordinarily prudent or reasonable party to prevent harm to another, taking the circumstances into account. It is the level of judgment, care, prudence, determination, and activity that a person would reasonably be expected to do under particular circumstances. In the context of lawsuits, demonstrating "due care" can help management show that they took all necessary precautions, even if the outcomes weren't perfect. The other options – "prudency," "due diligence," and "threat agent" – are not specifically related to this context.

92. Answer: C. The Delphi method

Explanation: The Delphi method is a structured communication technique, originally developed as a systematic, interactive forecasting method which relies on a panel of experts. The experts answer questionnaires in multiple rounds. After each round, a facilitator provides an anonymous summary of the experts' forecasts from the previous round as well as the reasons they provided for their judgments. Thus, the Delphi method involves anonymous interviews or surveys, and it's used to arrive at a group consensus. The other options – ISO/IEC 27001, qualitative valuation, and quantitative valuation – do not involve interviewing people anonymously.

93.   Answer: C. The same level as employees

Explanation: Third-party providers should be governed at the same level as employees. This is because they often have access to the same sensitive information and systems as employees and therefore pose a similar risk. They should be subject to the same policies, procedures, and controls as employees to ensure information security. The other options – an NDA, an acceptable use policy, and the ISC2 Code of Ethics – are components of a broader governance strategy, but they are not comprehensive standards for third-party governance on their own.

94.   Answer: D. Single loss expectancy (SLE)

Explanation: The Single Loss Expectancy (SLE) represents the monetary loss expected from the occurrence of a risk on an asset once. It is calculated by multiplying the asset's value (AV) by the exposure factor (EF), which represents the impact of the risk on the asset. The other terms – ALE, EF, and AV – are also important in risk assessment, but they do not directly represent the expected cost of a single loss event.

95. Answer: B. Because the worth of data varies as time progresses

Explanation: Data's value can change over time based on its relevance, accuracy, and usefulness to the organization. Therefore, it's essential to periodically reevaluate the classification of data files and records. While the other options may influence data management practices, they don't directly explain why data classification should be reevaluated annually.

96. Answer: C. Catering to the needs of the business

Explanation: A governance framework should be designed primarily to support the needs of the business. It should guide the organization in achieving its strategic objectives while managing risks and ensuring compliance. Although maximizing profits, avoiding losses, and ensuring safety are important, they are not the primary purpose of a governance framework.

97. Answer: A. Carry out an analysis of a bit-level duplicate of the disk.

Explanation: When forensically analyzing digital evidence, the first priority is to create and analyze a bit-level clone of the disk. This ensures that the original evidence remains unaltered and preserves its admissibility in court. After creating the clone, further analysis like reviewing log files, detecting malicious code, or performing a steganographic analysis can be done.

98.   Answer: C. Payment Card Industry Data Security Standard (PCI DSS)

Explanation: The Payment Card Industry Data Security Standard (PCI DSS) is an example of self-regulation. It's a standard created by the major credit card companies to protect cardholder data. The companies themselves enforce compliance with the standard, not a governmental or external regulatory body. In contrast, Sarbanes-Oxley (SOX) and the Gramm-Leach-Bliley Act (GLBA) are examples of governmental regulation, and third-party governance is a broader concept that includes various mechanisms of control over third-party relationships.

99.   Answer: A. It can be either allocated or accepted.

Explanation: Residual risk is the remaining risk after controls and mitigation efforts have been applied. This risk can either be accepted (if it's within the organization's risk tolerance) or it can be assigned/transferred to another entity, such as through insurance.

100.   Answer: D. Countermeasures

Explanation: Risk analysis involves the identification and assessment of assets, threats, and vulnerabilities. Countermeasures, however, are a response to the identified risk, applied after risk analysis to mitigate the risk. They are not a part of the analysis itself.

101.   Answer: D. Risk analysis

Explanation: Security safeguards and controls are used to reduce, avoid, or transfer risk. However, they do not perform risk analysis. Risk analysis is a separate process that identifies and assesses risk, which then informs the appropriate safeguards and controls.

102.   Answer: C. Risk tolerance

Explanation: Risk tolerance refers to the level of risk an organization is willing to accept. Therefore, it is most closely linked to risk acceptance.

103.   Answer: B. Acceptable level

Explanation: The amount of risk an organization can handle or tolerate is based on its acceptable level of risk. This level is determined by factors such as the organization's strategic goals, resources, and risk appetite. While affordability and measurability might influence the decision, the acceptable level is the determining factor.

CHAPTER 4

Asset Security

Asset Security is a pivotal domain within the CISSP examination, emphasizing the processes, principles, and techniques required to protect an organization's informational assets. As we delve into this chapter, we aim to equip you with a comprehensive understanding of the information security concepts and the best industry practices outlined in the CISSP CBK. But it's crucial to remember that the CISSP exam requires a holistic understanding of these principles, not mere rote memorization.

We aim to meticulously explore the core Asset Security concepts and provide you with strategic insights to ace this section in the CISSP exam. However, it is vital to understand why a particular strategy is used when appropriate and its potential implications. The exam is designed to assess your ability to make sound security decisions in various contexts, so always keep this practical application in mind as you study.

In keeping with this goal of practical understanding, this chapter extends beyond theoretical knowledge. We have included practice questions to reinforce the concepts and strategies discussed. Each question serves as a stepping stone, enhancing your grasp of the subject matter and instilling confidence in your preparation for the examination.

The field of asset security is complex and continually evolving, so stay abreast of the latest trends and technologies. This will help ensure your understanding reflects current best practices in the field. Remember, the CISSP certification aims to demonstrate that you are fully prepared to provide adequate security management and consulting in today's complex and challenging environment.

© Mohamed Aly Bouke 2023
M. A. Bouke, *CISSP Exam Certification Companion*, Certification Study Companion Series,
https://doi.org/10.1007/979-8-8688-0057-3_4

This strategic blend of theoretical understanding, real-world application, and practical exercises aims to provide you with a well-rounded preparation for the Asset Security domain of the CISSP exam. As you navigate this chapter, remember that the goal is to pass the exam and become a better, more knowledgeable security professional. Good luck with your studies!

Asset Security Concepts

To succeed in the CISSP exam, a strong grasp of asset security's foundational principles is vital. In this section, we'll succinctly cover asset types, their classifications, and the pivotal role of asset management in safeguarding an organization's valued resources. Let's dive into the key concepts crucial for acing the CISSP exam:

- Information classification is the process of categorizing data based on its sensitivity, value, and potential impact of unauthorized access or disclosure. Asset classification involves grouping an organization's assets, such as information systems, devices, and facilities, based on their importance and role in the operation.

- Data ownership refers to the responsibility for data accuracy, integrity, and protection. Data owners are typically responsible for classifying the information and ensuring proper access controls. On the other hand, data custodians are accountable for managing and maintaining data assets, including implementing and enforcing security controls defined by the data owner.

- Data retention refers to storing data for a predefined period, usually determined based on classification and legal or regulatory requirements. For instance, certain types of financial or health information may need to be retained for several years due to laws or industry standards. The key is that the data must be preserved securely during this period, ensuring its CIA is maintained.

- Data disposal is the end of the data life cycle. Once data is no longer needed or has reached the end of its retention period, it should be securely and permanently destroyed. This process, known as data disposal, is crucial in preventing unauthorized access or disclosure of the information. It involves methods like degaussing, overwriting, or physical destruction for hardware and secure deletion techniques for software. Proper data disposal practices are essential in safeguarding sensitive information, even at the end of its life cycle.

Furthermore, securing assets effectively necessitates adherence to asset security best practices, encompassing access control mechanisms, encryption techniques, secure storage solutions, and more. These best practices, applicable across various asset types, ensure protection from unauthorized access, misuse, and other threats. Let's delve into some of these prevalent best practices for securing assets:

- Maintaining a comprehensive asset inventory is crucial for adequate asset security. It should include physical and digital assets and be regularly updated to reflect organizational asset changes.

- Implementing robust access controls is essential to protect sensitive information and critical assets. Access control mechanisms should be based on the principles of least privilege and need to know, ensuring that users have access only to the information and resources necessary for their job function.

- Data leakage prevention (DLP) involves implementing measures to prevent unauthorized access, disclosure, or transfer of sensitive information. DLP solutions can include content filtering, data encryption, and monitoring user activities to detect and block potential data leakage incidents.

- An effective security awareness and training program is essential for reinforcing asset security policies and procedures. Regular training sessions should be conducted to educate employees on their responsibilities in protecting the organization's assets and the potential consequences of security breaches.

- Scoping and tailoring help organizations adapt security control frameworks to their needs and risk environment. Scoping involves determining the appropriate boundaries and scope of the security program, while tailoring involves customizing the security controls to fit the organization's requirements, risk appetite, and unique circumstances. Scoping and tailoring ensure that the implemented security controls are relevant and effective for the organization.

- Understanding the different states of data is essential for securing information assets. Data can exist in three states: at rest, in transit, and in use. Each state requires specific security measures to ensure the data's confidentiality, integrity, and availability.

- Data handling procedures define how an organization manages its information assets throughout their life cycle. These procedures should address data storage, access, modification, backup, retention, and disposal and be tailored to the specific data classification.

- Data encryption secures sensitive information by converting it into an unreadable format, which can only be decrypted with the correct key. Encryption should be employed for data at rest and in transit to protect it from unauthorized access and disclosure.

- Mobile devices such as smartphones, tablets, and laptops pose unique security challenges due to their portable nature and the potential for loss or theft. Organizations should implement security controls for mobile devices, including device encryption, remote wipe capabilities, and robust authentication methods.

- Data backup creates copies of critical data to ensure availability during data loss or system failure. A comprehensive data backup strategy should include regular backup schedules, off-site storage of backup copies, and periodic testing of backup and recovery procedures.

- Digital Rights Management (DRM) is a technology that controls access to and usage of digital content, such as software, documents, and multimedia files. DRM can help protect intellectual property and prevent unauthorized sharing or copying of sensitive information.

- Organizations must comply with various laws, regulations, and industry standards that dictate how personal and sensitive information should be collected, stored, processed, and shared. Implementing privacy controls and ensuring compliance with applicable regulations is essential for protecting the confidentiality of data and maintaining trust with customers and partners.

- Data collection limitation refers to the principle that organizations should only collect personal data necessary for their legitimate purposes and minimize the amount and types of data collected.

- Data remanence refers to the residual data traces that remain on a storage medium after deletion or formatting. This residual data can be recovered and pose a security risk if not properly sanitized.

- Memory is a computer system component that temporarily stores data and instructions for processing. Memory can be volatile, such as Random Access Memory (RAM), which loses its data when power is removed, or nonvolatile, like Read-Only Memory (ROM), which retains data without power. Memory security is vital to protect data from unauthorized access and ensure system integrity.

Classifying Data and Information Ownership

Data classification and information ownership play a pivotal role in asset security. In this section and the next section, we'll briefly delve into data classification processes, label assignments, clearances, and the roles of key stakeholders, such as data owners, system owners, and custodians. These insights will empower organizations to create robust data protection strategies that align with their unique needs and regulatory mandates. Key concepts underpinning this include

- Organizations must classify data based on its sensitivity, value, and potential impact of unauthorized access or disclosure to effectively protect data.

- Labels indicate data classification, often in the form of metadata or physical markings on documents or storage media. Labels help ensure that the appropriate security controls are applied to protect the data based on classification.

- Clearance is determining an individual's eligibility to access classified information. Clearance levels should correspond to the different data classification levels to ensure that users can only access the information they need to perform their duties.

- Formal access approval involves obtaining written authorization from the data owner or their designee to grant a user access to classified information. This process ensures that only authorized individuals are granted access to sensitive data.

- The need-to-know principle asserts that users should only have access to the specific information required to fulfill their job responsibilities. This principle helps minimize the risk of unauthorized access or disclosure of sensitive data.

- Organizations must implement security controls to protect sensitive information and media, both digital and physical. This includes access controls, encryption, secure storage, and disposal methods to ensure sensitive data's confidentiality, integrity, and availability.

Data Roles

Grasping the various data roles and their responsibilities is crucial for success in the CISSP exam. This section briefly breaks down the roles of data controllers, processors, and users, each with unique responsibilities in managing and processing data. Knowledge of these roles and associated duties is key in ensuring data is aptly managed, safeguarded, and used following organizational policies and regulations. The common data roles you encounter on the exam include

- Business or mission owners are responsible for the overall strategic goals and objectives of a specific business unit or mission within an organization.

- Data owners are responsible for data accuracy, integrity, and protection. They are typically accountable for classifying information and ensuring proper access controls.

- The system owner is responsible for the overall operation and security of a specific information system or application.

- Data custodians are responsible for the day-to-day management and maintenance of data assets, including implementing and enforcing security controls defined by the data owner.

- Users interact with an organization's information systems and data to perform their job functions.

- Data controllers determine the purposes and means of processing personal data, while data processors are responsible for processing personal data on behalf of the data controller. Both roles have specific responsibilities under various data protection regulations, such as the GDPR.

Data Destruction Methods

Data destruction or sanitization is removing or obliterating data from a storage medium to prevent it from being recovered. Various data destruction methods exist, each with its advantages and use cases. Selecting the appropriate method depends on the sensitivity of the data, the storage medium, and the organization's policies and regulatory requirements. For the exam, you need to understand the following data sanitization techniques:

- Physical destruction involves the destruction of the storage medium, rendering it unusable. This method is most suitable for highly sensitive data or when the storage medium has reached the end of its useful life. Standard physical destruction techniques include shredding, incineration, and crushing.

- Degaussing is a process that removes the magnetic field from a storage medium, such as a hard disk drive or magnetic tape, effectively erasing the data. This method is suitable for the destruction of data on magnetic storage media. However, it is inadequate for solid-state drives (SSDs) or other non-magnetic storage devices.

- Overwriting involves writing new data over the existing data on a storage medium, rendering the original data unrecoverable. This method can be used for magnetic and solid-state storage devices. Overwriting software often performs multiple passes, writing different data

177

patterns to ensure the original data is completely obliterated. Overwriting is suitable for most data destruction scenarios but may not be sufficient for sensitive data.

- Cryptographic erasure involves deleting the encryption keys to encrypt data stored on a device. Without the encryption keys, the data becomes unreadable and effectively unrecoverable. This method is suitable for encryption storage devices and allows quick data erasure without physically destroying the device.

- Secure Erase is a built-in function in many modern storage devices, such as hard disk drives and SSDs. This feature erases all data on the device by overwriting it with a predefined pattern or triggering the machine to perform an internal block erase. Secure Erase is an effective and efficient method for data destruction, provided that the storage device supports the feature.

When and Why to Use Each Method

The choice of data destruction method depends on various factors, as already mentioned, such as the sensitivity of the data, the storage medium, the organization's policies, and regulatory requirements. Organizations should consider the following when selecting a data destruction method:

- **Sensitivity of data**: Highly sensitive data may require more secure methods, such as physical destruction or degaussing, to ensure the data is completely unrecoverable.

- **Storage medium**: The type of storage medium dictates the appropriate destruction methods. For example, degaussing is suitable for magnetic storage devices but not SSDs.

- **Regulatory requirements**: Certain industries and regulations may mandate specific data destruction methods to ensure compliance.

- **Cost and environmental impact**: The cost and environmental impact of different data destruction methods should be considered when selecting the appropriate method for an organization.

- **Reusability of storage devices**: If the storage device is to be reused or repurposed, methods like overwriting, cryptographic erasure, or Secure Erase are more suitable than physical destruction.

- Organizations should develop clear policies and procedures for data destruction, including guidelines on when and how to apply the appropriate methods based on the abovementioned factors. This ensures that data is securely destroyed, minimizing the risk of unauthorized access or disclosure.

Different Data Types and Regulations

Chapter 3 touched upon the common laws, regulations, and standards pertinent to the CISSP exam. In this section, we'll revisit these topics, focusing on data-oriented laws and discussing various data types, such as PII and PHI. For the exam, it's important to note that you don't need to memorize these laws in detail, but it's crucial to understand their relevance, especially regarding compliance.

Personally Identifiable Information (PII)

Personally Identifiable Information (PII) is any information that can be used to identify, contact, or locate an individual, either by itself or when combined with other information. Examples of PII include names, addresses, social security numbers, email addresses, and phone numbers. Organizations that collect, store, or process PII must protect this sensitive data from unauthorized access, use, or disclosure.

Several regulations and standards govern the protection of PII:

- **General Data Protection Regulation (GDPR):** A comprehensive data protection regulation in the European Union that applies to organizations that process the personal data of EU residents. GDPR mandates strict data protection requirements, including obtaining consent, providing notice, and implementing appropriate security measures to protect personal data.

- **California Consumer Privacy Act (CCPA):** A data privacy law in California that grants consumers the right to know what personal information is being collected about them, the right to delete that information, and the right to opt out of the sale of their data.

- **Personal Information Protection and Electronic Documents Act (PIPEDA):** PIPEDA is a Canadian federal privacy law governing private sector organizations' collection, use, and disclosure of personal information during commercial activities. PIPEDA applies to organizations operating in Canada and those that collect, use, or disclose personal information about Canadian residents across provincial or national borders.

Protected Health Information (PHI)

Protected Health Information (PHI) is any information related to an individual's physical or mental health, the provision of healthcare, or payment for healthcare services that can be linked to a specific person. Examples of PHI include medical records, lab results, insurance information, and patient identifiers.

The primary regulation governing the protection of PHI is the Health Insurance Portability and Accountability Act (HIPAA) in the United States. HIPAA sets forth strict standards for the privacy and security of PHI, including

- **Privacy Rule**: Establishes standards for the use and disclosure of PHI by covered entities and their business associates. The Privacy Rule grants patients rights to their health information, including the right to access, amend, and control who can access their PHI.

- **Security Rule**: Requires covered entities and their business associates to implement technical, physical, and administrative safeguards to protect electronic PHI (ePHI). This includes access controls, data encryption, and regular risk assessments.

- **Health Insurance Portability and Accountability Act (HIPAA)**: While primarily focused on healthcare data, HIPAA also includes provisions related to PII in the context of healthcare providers, insurers, and their business associates.

Organizations that handle PII, PHI, or other sensitive data types must know their jurisdiction and the industry's applicable regulations and standards. Compliance with these regulations helps ensure that sensitive data is appropriately protected and managed, reducing the risk of data breaches and other security incidents.

181

Summary: Asset Security

In this chapter, we provided an in-depth exploration of asset security, focusing on the essential concepts and best practices required to protect an organization's valuable assets, including data, hardware, and software.

Key takeaways from this chapter include

- Asset security is vital for organizations to maintain their assets' confidentiality, integrity, and availability.

- Developing and maintaining a comprehensive asset inventory helps organizations understand their environment and apply appropriate security controls.

- Data classification and information ownership are crucial in determining the security controls to protect sensitive data.

- Data types, such as PII, PHI, and other sensitive information, are subject to various regulations and standards, including GDPR, CCPA, HIPAA, and PIPEDA.

- Implementing security measures for data in motion and data at rest, such as encryption and access controls, helps maintain the confidentiality and integrity of data.

- Certification and accreditation processes validate the effectiveness of an organization's security controls in protecting its assets.

- Adopting recognized standards and control frameworks, such as NIST Cybersecurity Framework or ISO/IEC 27001, can help organizations achieve higher security and compliance.

- Scoping and tailoring processes ensure that security controls are relevant and effective for an organization's specific needs and risk environment.

- Data roles, such as data owners, custodians, and users, define the responsibilities of individuals within an organization regarding data protection.

- Asset security tips include implementing a robust data classification policy, enforcing the principle of least privilege, using encryption for sensitive data, and regularly reviewing and updating asset security policies.

Understanding and implementing the concepts and best practices outlined in this chapter, readers can develop a strong foundation in asset security, an essential domain of the CISSP exam.

Practice Questions

1. In the context of IT management and governance, the Control Objectives for Information and Related Technology (COBIT) framework serves as a valuable tool. Who among the following roles would typically choose and utilize the COBIT framework to balance security controls and business requirements?

    A. Data owners

    B. Information stewards

    C. Enterprise owners

    D. Data custodians

2. An enterprise operates in a hybrid cloud environment, employing on-site and cloud-based systems. It has adequate on-site monitoring but needs to impose security policies on user activities and report exceptions in its increasing number of cloud services. What kind of tool would be most suitable for this requirement?

   A. A Next-Generation Firewall (NGFW)

   B. A Cloud Access Security Broker (CASB)

   C. An Intrusion Detection System (IDS)

   D. A Security Orchestration, Automation, and Response (SOAR) tool

3. In data handling, when media is tagged based on the classification of the data it houses, what principle is generally enforced about labels?

   A. The data is marked according to its integrity requisites.

   B. The media is tagged based on the highest classification tier of the data it accommodates.

   C. The media is tagged with all tiers of classification of the data it accommodates.

   D. The media is tagged with the lowest tier of classification of the data it accommodates.

4. Among the following administrative processes, which one aids organizations in allocating suitable security control levels to sensitive data?

   A. Data categorization

   B. Remanence

C. Data transmission

D. Clearing

5. What term refers to the kind of information kept about an individual that can be utilized to distinguish or trace their identity?

    A. Personally Identifiable Information (PII)

    B. Personal Health Information (PHI)

    C. Social Security Number (SSN)

    D. Secure Identity Information (SII)

6. Among the following information security risks to data at rest, which one would inflict the most substantial reputational damage to an organization?

    A. Incorrect classification

    B. Data breach

    C. Decryption

    D. A deliberate insider threat

7. Tools like Microsoft's BitLocker, which employs full disk encryption, are utilized to protect data in what state?

    A. Data in transit

    B. Data at rest

    C. Unlabeled data

    D. Labeled data

8. An employer issues mobile phones to its staff for work purposes and renews the devices every two years. How would you describe this practice if the phones are still operational and receiving system updates?

   A. End of Life (EOL)

   B. Planned obsolescence

   C. End of Support (EOS)

   D. Device risk management

9. What is the primary objective of data classification?

   A. It quantifies the cost of a data breach.

   B. It prioritizes IT expenditures.

   C. It enables compliance with breach notification laws.

   D. It identifies the value of the data to the organization.

10. What action is required to protect information and assets?

    A. Risk assessment

    B. Data categorization

    C. Asset identification

    D. Asset and information classification

11. What term refers to organizing data based on its sensitivity and the impact on the business if compromised?

    A. Data processing

    B. Data classification

    C. Data optimization

    D. Data indexing

12. What term refers to the process of identifying and categorizing an organization's resources?

    A. Resource classification

    B. Asset classification

    C. Asset allocation

    D. Resource allocation

13. What process involves setting the rules for how to deal with and manage information and assets within an organization?

    A. Establishing data retrieval protocol

    B. Setting information and asset handling guidelines

    C. Creating data backup plan

    D. Setting asset management policy

14. What process involves the secure allocation of resources, assigning ownership, and managing inventory of tangible and intangible assets?

    A. Asset management and secure provisioning

    B. Information security audit

    C. Network monitoring

    D. Data backup and restoration

15. What role in data management is responsible for the safe custody, transport, and storage of the data?

    A. Data controller

    B. Data processor

    C. Data owner

    D. Data custodian

16. Which term refers to the residual representation of data that remains even after attempts have been made to remove or erase the data?

    A. Data retention

    B. Data remanence

    C. Data collection

    D. Data location

17. What is the process of acquiring data for initial use?

    A. Data retention

    B. Data location

    C. Data collection

    D. Data destruction

18. Which term refers to the procedures that keep data for a predetermined period of time, after which it is discarded?

    A. Data remanence

    B. Data retention

    C. Data collection

    D. Data maintenance

19. What process ensures data is accurate, consistent, and reliable throughout its life cycle?

    A. Data collection

    B. Data maintenance

    C. Data retention

    D. Data destruction

20. Who decides who, what, when, where, and how data should be used or shared?

    A. Data custodian

    B. Data controller

    C. Data processor

    D. Data owner

21. Which term refers to the physical or virtual location where data is stored?

    A. Data collection

    B. Data location

    C. Data maintenance

    D. Data remanence

22. Who is responsible for processing personal data on behalf of the controller?

    A. Data custodian

    B. Data controller

    C. Data processor

    D. Data owner

23. Which term refers to eliminating data stored on memory devices, ensuring that the data is completely unreadable?

    A. Data collection

    B. Data retention

    C. Data destruction

    D. Data location

24. Who is the person that determines the purposes for which and how personal data is processed?

    A. Data owner

    B. Data custodian

    C. Data controller

    D. Data processor

25. What does the term "End-of-Life" (EOL) typically refer to in the context of asset retention?

    A. The period when an asset is fully depreciated

    B. The point at which the manufacturer no longer supports an asset

    C. The time when an asset is no longer useful for the organization and is disposed of

    D. The stage when an asset is upgraded or replaced with a newer model

26. What is the primary concern when a software asset reaches its End-of-Support (EOS) stage?

    A. The software will no longer function.

    B. The software may no longer receive security updates and patches.

    C. The software will be incompatible with newer systems.

    D. The software will automatically uninstall itself.

27. What is the primary purpose of establishing an asset retention policy in an organization?

    A. To ensure data is never deleted

    B. To prevent theft of organizational assets

    C. To ensure compliance with legal and regulatory requirements for data retention

    D. To ensure all assets are utilized to their fullest potential

28. In the context of data management, what is the main reason for properly managing an asset's End-of-Life (EOL) stage?

    A. To maximize the asset's value

    B. To ensure data contained on the asset is properly backed up

    C. To prevent unauthorized access or data breaches

    D. To ensure the asset can be reused

29. Which of the following is a best practice for managing assets that have reached their End-of-Support (EOS) stage?

    A. Continue using them as long as they still function

    B. Replace them with the latest models available

    C. Isolate them from the network and use them offline

    D. Evaluate risks associated with continued use and plan for their replacement or upgrade

30. What are the three states of data that need to be secured?

    A. Loaded, running, and unloaded

    B. In use, in transit, and at rest

    C. In motion, in storage, and processing

    D. Active, passive, and idle

31. What is the purpose of scoping and tailoring in the context of data security controls?

    A. To customize security controls to fit the specific needs of the organization

    B. To reduce the number of security controls applied to data

    C. To expand the range of security controls applied to data

    D. To standardize security controls across different types of data

32. What is the purpose of Digital Rights Management (DRM)?

    A. To prevent unauthorized access to digital media

    B. To facilitate the sharing of digital media

    C. To track the usage of digital media

    D. All of the above

33. How does a Cloud Access Security Broker (CASB) contribute to data security?

    A. By providing a security layer between users and cloud service providers

    B. By encrypting data stored in the cloud

    C. By monitoring user activity in the cloud

    D. All of the above

34. What is the primary goal of data loss prevention (DLP)?

    A. To prevent data breaches by detecting potential data breach/data ex-filtration transmissions

    B. To recover data that has been lost due to hardware failure

    C. To manage access rights to data

    D. To provide an audit trail of data access

35. What process involves analyzing retained data, determining its importance and value, and categorizing it accordingly?

    A. Implementing data security controls

    B. Setting data standards

    C. Acting as data custodians

    D. Conducting data classification

36. What term refers to the process of removing sensitive data from storage devices in a way that prevents its reconstruction through standard system functions or software file/data recovery utilities?

    A. Clearing

    B. Utilizing self-encrypting USB drives

    C. Purging

    D. Conducting data modeling

37. What provides more flexibility in applying encryption to specific files?

    A. File encryption software

    B. Categorization

    C. Self-encrypting USB drives

    D. Media encryption software

38. What term describes the pivotal point where a material's inherent magnetic alignment changes direction?

    A. Data remanence

    B. Clearing

C. Media encryption software

D. Curie temperature

39. What role ensures crucial datasets are developed, maintained, and accessible within their specified parameters?

A. Conducting data classification

B. Undertaking data modeling

C. Serving as data custodians

D. Implementing data security controls

40. In the context of US government document classifications, which signifies the least sensitive level?

A. Confidential

B. Top Secret

C. Top Secret

D. Secret

41. Which law in Europe is responsible for the protection of personal data privacy?

A. HIPAA

B. GLBA

C. GDPR

D. DPD

42. The TLS protocol is most effective for safeguarding which type of data?

    A. Data in motion

    B. Data in use

    C. Data at rest

    D. Data in an archived status

43. Which protocol should you opt for if you want to replace an old Telnet server with a secure alternative?

    A. SCP

    B. HTTPS

    C. SSH

    D. SFTP

44. Which of the following is considered the least secure method for removing data from magnetic media?

    A. Destruction

    B. Degaussing

    C. Purging

    D. Erasing

45. Which of the following locations exemplifies "data in use"?

    A. RAM

    B. Network transmission

    C. SSD

    D. Magnetic disk

46. When viewed independently, which data elements can be considered PII?

    A. Work ZIP code

    B. Home address

    C. Gender

    D. Age

47. Who updates the system security plan when a significant change occurs?

    A. Business owner

    B. Data processor

    C. Data owner

    D. System owner

48. What is the most important factor when determining a data classification level?

    A. Format of the data

    B. Value of the data

    C. Identity of the data owner

    D. Size of the data

49. Which encryption technology among the following is capable of protecting data within an email-attached file, ensuring it remains encrypted after being received?

    A. AES

    B. TLS

    C. SSL

    D. DES

50. What access control policy is being implemented when you set up and integrate a nondiscretionary system?

    A. Physical access control

    B. Mandatory access control

    C. Role-based access control

    D. Rule-based access control

51. You decide to use a passphrase instead of a password that can be found in the dictionary, aiming for enhanced security. In this case, the new password transforms into what?

    A. The strongest password

    B. A virtual password

    C. An unusual password

    D. A username

52. You want the highest security protection for your company, regardless of cost. Which of the following should you choose?

    A. Passwords

    B. Smart cards

    C. Palm vein scanner

    D. Fingerprint reader

53. What is the term for a control category that responds after an incident?

    A. Corrective control

    B. Directive control

C. Preventative control

D. Deterrent control

54. As a security manager, you are tasked with investigating a recent breach into the corporate network. Under what control category does this fall?

A. Retroactive control

B. Investigatory control

C. Preventative control

D. Detective control

55. How does an asset classification program enhance an organization's ability to fulfill its objectives and goals?

A. By meeting the audit function's requirements

B. By controlling changes to production environments

C. By reinforcing principles of ownership

D. By outlining controls to protect valuable assets

56. What is the correct sequence of the asset life cycle phases?

A. Create, use, share, store, archive, and destroy

B. Create, share, use, archive, store, and destroy

C. Create, store, use, share, archive, and destroy

D. Create, share, archive, use, store, and destroy

57. Which of the following is the BEST definition of defensible destruction?

   A. The destruction of assets using defense-approved methods

   B. The destruction of assets in a controlled, legally defensible, and compliant manner

   C. The destruction of assets without the possibility of recovering those assets

   D. The destruction of assets using a method that may not allow attackers to recover data

58. In a setting where asset classification has been implemented to meet privacy protection requirements, who is considered the owner and thus responsible for ensuring proper compliance and protection?

   A. Data processor

   B. Data subject

   C. Data controller

   D. Data steward

59. Which of the following is NOT a principle of privacy protection from the Organization for Economic Cooperation and Development (OECD)?

   A. Collection Limitation Principle

   B. Right to be Forgotten Principle

   C. Use Limitation Principle

   D. Accountability Principle

60. All of the following are necessary for effective retention requirements in organizations EXCEPT

A. Policy

B. Awareness, education, training

C. Understanding of compliance-related requirements

D. Data steward

61. Which of the following is not an objective of baseline security controls used in protecting assets?

A. Specific steps that must be executed

B. Minimum level of security controls

C. It may be associated with specific architectures and systems

D. A consistent reference point

62. Which of the following is the BEST definition of scoping?

A. Altering baselines to apply more specifically

B. Modifying assumptions based on previously learned behavior

C. Limiting general baseline recommendations by removing those that do not apply

D. Responsible protection of assets based on goals and objectives

63. How would you define "scoping" in the context of implementing new standards and frameworks in our organization?

   A. Implementing the complete standard or framework but setting higher standards in certain areas

   B. Selectively implementing parts of the standard or framework based on relevance

   C. Assessing the cost implications of the implementation

   D. Evaluating the suitability of the standard for the organization

64. What data destruction method would be most suitable for eliminating data remanence on devices like PROM, flash memory, and SSD drives?

   A. Degaussing

   B. Overwriting

   C. Shredding

   D. Formatting

65. In which of the three states of data is encryption protection unfeasible?

   A. Data at rest

   B. Data in motion

   C. Data in use

   D. Data on backup tapes

66. What type of memory is utilized in flash drives?

   A. SDRAM

   B. PROM

C. EEPROM

D. DRAM

67. What method should be employed to erase EPROM memory for a firmware upgrade?

   A. It's not possible to erase EPROM once it's written.

   B. Software programs can be used to erase content.

   C. Exposure to UV light.

   D. Degaussing the chip after removing it from the motherboard.

68. What are some methods for protecting data while an employee actively uses it?

   A. Encryption, clean desk policies, and view angle screens

   B. Clean desk policies, view angle screens, and automatic computer locking when not in use

   C. A need-to-know policy

   D. Clean desk policies, print policies, job rotation, mandatory vacations, and view angle screens

69. What is one way to protect data at rest?

   A. Clean desk policy

   B. Privacy screens for monitors

   C. Encryption

   D. Discretionary access control (DAC)

70. On what basis should the duration for keeping backups be decided?

    A. Permanently.

    B. For a month, as long as we have a full backup of everything.

    C. As long as it is useful or required, whichever is longer.

    D. All data is required to be kept for one year.

71. Which type of memory is considered volatile?

    A. DRAM

    B. PROM

    C. Flash Memory

    D. EEPROM

72. Which type of Read-Only Memory (ROM) can only be programmed once?

    A. EPROM

    B. EEPROM

    C. PROM

    D. APROM

73. Why would we opt to use multiple forms of data destruction on our sensitive information?

    A. Because it is easier than just a single type of data destruction

    B. To ensure there is no data remanence

    C. To ensure data is still accessible after the destruction

    D. To make sure we have the old drives available

74. What is a typical attack on our data at rest?

    A. Cryptanalysis

    B. Shoulder surfing

    C. Eavesdropping

    D. All of these

75. An attacker has stolen one of our backup tapes. What could prevent the data on the tape from being accessible?

    A. Proper data handling

    B. Proper data storage

    C. Proper data retention

    D. Proper data encryption

76. Looking at the data classification classes of the US government: data that, if disclosed, won't cause any harm to national security would be classified as?

    A. Unclassified

    B. Confidential

    C. Secret

    D. Top Secret

77. Which of these is a common attack against data at rest?

    A. Stealing unencrypted laptops

    B. MITM (man in the middle)

    C. Screen scrapers

    D. Keyloggers

78. In designing our data retention policy, which should not be considered?

    A. Which data do we keep?

    B. How long do we keep the data?

    C. Where do we keep the backup data?

    D. How to safely destroy the data after the retention has expired?

79. We have many policies we need to adhere to in our organization. Which of these would be part of our clean desk policy?

    A. Minimal use of paper copies and only used while at the desk and in use

    B. Cleaning your desk of all the clutter

    C. Shred all paper copies of everything

    D. Picking up anything you print as soon as you print it

80. What are we trying to eliminate with data disposal?

    A. Data remanence

    B. How long do we keep the data

    C. The data content

    D. The data in use

81. When assigning sensitivity to our data, which of these should not be a factor?

    A. Who will have access to the data

    B. What the data is worth

    C. How bad a data exposure would be

    D. How the data will be used

82. Which of these would be something we would consider for proper data disposal of SSD drives?

    A. Degaussing

    B. Formatting

    C. Deleting all files

    D. Shredding

83. Which of these would be something we can implement to protect our data in use better? (Select all that apply.)

    A. Clean desk policy

    B. Encryption

    C. View angle privacy screen for monitors

    D. Print policy

    E. Workstation locking

84. Which of these should we encrypt if we are dealing with sensitive data?

    A. Hard disks

    B. Backup tapes

    C. Data sent over the network

    D. All of these

85. What would be the role of the data custodian?

    A. Make the policies, procedures, and standards that govern our data security

    B. Perform the backups and restores

C. Be trained in the policies, procedures, and standards

D. Assign the sensitivity labels and backup frequency of the data

86. Which of these could be a common attack on our data in motion?

   A. Cryptanalysis

   B. Shoulder surfing

   C. Eavesdropping

   D. All of these

87. We've introduced logging on our backup servers to monitor employee data access. What does this demonstrate?

   A. Proper data handling

   B. Proper data storage

   C. Proper data retention

   D. Proper data encryption

88. We're discarding many hard drives in line with our hardware disposal and no data remanence policy. What method would we use to guarantee zero data remanence on damaged SSD drives?

   A. Degauss

   B. Overwrite

   C. Incinerate

   D. Format

89. Who bears the responsibility for our organization's day-to-day financial leadership?

    A. The CEO

    B. The CFO

    C. The CIO

    D. The CSO

90. Which activity would we perform during the e-discovery process?

    A. Discover all the electronic files we have in our organization

    B. Produce electronic information to internal or external attorneys or legal teams

    C. Make sure we keep data long enough in our retention policies for us to fulfill the legal requirements for our state and sector

    D. Delete data that has been requested if the retention period has expired

91. How is data classified in the US government's data classification scheme if its disclosure could cause serious damage to national security?

    A. Unclassified

    B. Confidential

    C. Secret

    D. Top Secret

92. For what type of data would we want to implement end-to-end encryption?

    A. Data at rest

    B. Data in use

    C. Data in motion

    D. All of these

93. What is the primary goal of information classification within an organization?

    A. To increase the workload of IT staff

    B. To facilitate communication between departments

    C. To protect the confidentiality, integrity, and availability of data

    D. To make data more accessible

94. Which one of the following is NOT a typical level of data classification in a private sector organization?

    A. Proprietary

    B. Confidential

    C. Top Secret

    D. Public

95. Who is typically responsible for data classification in an organization?

    A. IT department

    B. Data owner

    C. Security team

    D. All employees

96. What is the role of a data custodian in an organization?

   A. Define data classification levels

   B. Implement controls as defined by the data owner

   C. Determine how long data should be retained

   D. Create new datasets

97. Which of the following best describes data remanence?

   A. Data that remains on a storage medium after it has been deleted

   B. Data that is stored in the cloud

   C. Data that is currently in use

   D. Data that is being transmitted over a network

98. What is the purpose of a data retention policy?

   A. To define how long data should be kept before it is deleted

   B. To ensure data is accessible to all employees

   C. To classify data according to its sensitivity

   D. To protect data from malware attacks

99. Which one of the following is NOT a factor in determining data retention periods?

   A. Regulatory requirements

   B. Business needs

   C. The size of the data

   D. Legal considerations

100. What is the primary goal of privacy laws and regulations?

   A. To make data more accessible

   B. To protect the rights of individuals with respect to their personal data

   C. To classify data according to its sensitivity

   D. To ensure data is retained for the correct period of time

101. When considering the life cycle of information, what is typically the final stage?

   A. Creation

   B. Distribution

   C. Storage

   D. Destruction

102. What type of security control is data encryption?

   A. Preventative

   B. Detective

   C. Corrective

   D. Recovery

Answers

1. Answer: C. Enterprise owners

   Explanation: Enterprise or business owners are the most likely to select and apply the COBIT framework. COBIT allows them to govern and manage the IT environment to ensure that business needs, such as risk management, resource optimization, and value creation, are met effectively. While all roles may interact with COBIT somehow, the business owners are primarily responsible for aligning security controls with business requirements. Data processors, information stewards, and data custodians focus more on the operational aspects of data and may not be involved in strategic decision-making processes like selecting a governance framework.

2. Answer: B. A Cloud Access Security Broker (CASB)

    Explanation: A Cloud Access Security Broker (CASB) is a tool that sits between cloud service consumers and cloud service providers to enforce security, compliance, and governance policies for cloud applications. It can help monitor and secure the hybrid cloud environment.

3. Answer: B. The media is tagged based on the highest classification tier of the data it accommodates.

    Explanation: When labeling media based on the classification of the data it contains, the rule typically applied is to label it based on the highest classification level of the data. This ensures the most restrictive and appropriate controls are applied to protect the entire dataset.

4. Answer: A. Data categorization

   Explanation: Data classification, or categorization, is an administrative process that involves sorting data into categories based on its sensitivity level. This aids organizations in assigning appropriate levels of security controls to sensitive information, ensuring that each type of data is adequately protected according to its value and sensitivity.

5. Answer: A. Personally Identifiable Information (PII)

   Explanation: Personally Identifiable Information (PII) is any data that could identify a specific individual. It includes any information that can be used to distinguish or trace an individual's identity, such as name, social security number, date and place of birth, mother's maiden name, or biometric records.

6. Answer: B. Data breach

   Explanation: A data breach involving unauthorized access and retrieval of sensitive information often has the most significant reputational impact on an organization. It can lead to losing trust among customers and stakeholders, legal repercussions, and financial losses.

7. Answer: B. Data at rest

   Explanation: Full disk encryption tools like BitLocker are used to protect data at rest, that is, data that is stored on physical or virtual disk drives, storage devices, or other types of media.

8. Answer: B. Planned obsolescence

    Explanation: Planned obsolescence is a policy of planning or designing a product with an artificially limited useful life or a purposely frail design, so it becomes outdated or nonfunctional after a certain period. In this case, even though the phones are still operational and receiving updates, they are replaced every two years. This is a form of planned obsolescence, where the company ensures that the old devices are phased out and replaced, even though they might still be usable. EOL is when the device is no longer suitable for use and is discarded. EOS means that the manufacturer has stopped providing updates or fixes for the product. Device risk management is a process to identify, assess, and prioritize the risks associated with using devices in an organization. None of these options describes the scenario as accurately as planned obsolescence.

9. Answer: D. It identifies the value of the data to the organization.

    Explanation: The primary purpose of data classification is to identify the value of the data to the organization. This process involves categorizing data based on its sensitivity level and importance to the organization, which helps implement appropriate security controls and handling procedures.

10. Answer: D. Asset and information classification

   Explanation: Identifying and classifying information and assets is a key step in managing security risks. This process helps prioritize resources, apply appropriate protections, and comply with legal and regulatory requirements.

11. Answer: B. Data classification

   Explanation: Data classification categorizes data into types, forms, or other distinct classes. This classification may be based on data sensitivity such as private, confidential, public, or the data's importance to the organization.

12. Answer: B. Asset classification

   Explanation: Asset classification defines an organization's assets based on their criticality, sensitivity, and other factors. This helps organizations apply appropriate security measures and prioritize their resources.

13. Answer: B. Setting information and asset handling guidelines

   Explanation: Establishing information and asset handling requirements means setting up policies and procedures determining how data and assets should be managed, stored, transmitted, and disposed of. This is an essential part of an organization's information security strategy, helping to ensure that sensitive information and valuable assets are appropriately protected.

14. Answer: A. Asset management and secure provisioning

    Explanation: Asset management and secure provisioning encompass the secure allocation of resources, identifying and assigning ownership of information and assets, and maintaining a comprehensive inventory of tangible and intangible assets. This helps provide an organized view of the company's resources and assists in maintaining proper security controls.

15. Answer: D. Data custodian

    Explanation: A data custodian is responsible for the data's safe custody, transport, and storage. They maintain the integrity, confidentiality, and availability of the data.

16. Answer: B. Data remanence

    Explanation: Data remanence is the residual representation of data nominally erased or removed.

17. Answer: C. Data collection

    Explanation: Data collection is the process of gathering and measuring information on targeted variables in an established system, enabling one to answer relevant questions and evaluate outcomes.

18. Answer: B. Data retention

    Explanation: Data retention involves policies and strategies to keep data for compliance or business reasons. After the predetermined period, the data is discarded.

19. Answer: B. Data maintenance

Explanation: Data maintenance involves maintaining data assets by ensuring data accuracy, consistency, and reliability throughout its life cycle.

20. Answer: D. Data owner

Explanation: The data owner is typically a senior executive with legal authority and responsibility for a dataset.

21. Answer: B. Data location

Explanation: Data location refers to the physical or virtual place where data is stored, such as in-house servers, data centers, or cloud storage.

22. Answer: C. Data processor

Explanation: A data processor is responsible for processing personal data on behalf of the controller.

23. Answer: C. Data destruction

Explanation: Data destruction is destroying data stored on tapes, hard disks, and other electronic media so that it is completely unreadable and cannot be accessed or used for unauthorized purposes.

24. Answer: C. Data controller

Explanation: The data controller is the person (or business) who determines the purposes for which and how personal data is processed. They are responsible for establishing practices and policies in line with regulations to protect the data they are handling.

25. Answer: C. The time when an asset is no longer useful for the organization and is disposed of

    Explanation: EOL generally refers to a stage in the asset's life cycle when it is no longer beneficial or productive for the organization. This could be due to obsolescence, failure, or when it is more cost-effective to replace the asset than to continue maintaining it.

26. Answer: B. The software may no longer receive security updates and patches

    Explanation: When software reaches its EOS stage, the manufacturer or provider typically stops providing updates, patches, or fixes, including security-related ones. This can leave the software vulnerable to security threats and affect compliance with certain regulations.

27. Answer: C. To ensure compliance with legal and regulatory requirements for data retention

    Explanation: Asset retention policies are primarily designed to ensure that organizations comply with applicable legal and regulatory requirements. These requirements often specify how long certain data types must be retained and how they should be securely disposed of when no longer needed.

28. Answer: C. To prevent unauthorized access or data breaches
    Explanation: When an asset reaches its End-of-Life (EOL) stage, it's crucial to ensure that all data on the asset is either transferred or destroyed

appropriately. If not managed correctly, it can lead to unauthorized access or data breaches, which can have significant consequences for the organization.

29. Answer: D. Evaluate risks associated with continued use and plan for their replacement or upgrade

Explanation: When assets reach their EOS stage, evaluating the risks associated with their continued use is essential. These might include security vulnerabilities due to a lack of updates or incompatibility issues with other systems. Based on this evaluation, a plan should be made for replacing or upgrading the assets.

30. Answer: B. In use, in transit, and at rest

Explanation: The three states of data that need to be considered when securing data are "in use" (data being processed), "in transit" (data being moved from one location to another), and "at rest" (data that is stored).

31. Answer: A. To customize security controls to fit the specific needs of the organization

Explanation: Scoping and tailoring is adjusting a set of standard security controls to fit an organization's specific needs better. This may involve adding, modifying, or removing specific controls based on the organization's unique risk environment and business requirements.

32. Answer: D. All of the above

    Explanation: DRM is a technology used to
    protect digital media copyrights. It can prevent
    unauthorized access, track digital media usage, and
    control how digital media is shared.

33. Answer: D. All of the above

    Explanation: A CASB is a software tool or service
    between an organization's on-premises and cloud
    provider's infrastructure. A CASB can provide
    various services, including encrypting data,
    monitoring for malicious activity, and enforcing
    security compliance policies.

34. Answer: A. To prevent data breaches by
    detecting potential data breach/data ex-filtration
    transmissions

    Explanation: DLP ensures that end users do not
    send sensitive or critical information outside the
    corporate network. The term also describes software
    products that help a network administrator control
    what data end users can transfer.

35. Answer: D. Conducting data classification

    Explanation: Data classification involves analyzing
    an organization's data, determining its importance
    and value, and then categorizing it accordingly. This
    process is crucial for effective data management and
    protection.

36. Answer: C. Purging

    Explanation: Purging refers to securely removing sensitive data from storage devices so that it cannot be recovered using normal system functions or software file/data recovery utilities.

37. Answer: A. File encryption software

    Explanation: File encryption software allows for the encryption of specific files, providing flexibility in securing particular data elements.

38. Answer: D. Curie temperature

    Explanation: The Curie temperature is the critical point where a material's intrinsic magnetic alignment changes direction. This concept is relevant in data storage technologies that use magnetic storage media.

39. Answer: C. Serving as data custodians

    Explanation: Data custodians ensure that important datasets are developed, maintained, and accessible within their specifications. This role is crucial in an organization's overall data management and protection strategy.

40. Answer: A. Confidential

    Explanation: The US government ranks the sensitivity of information into several levels: Top Secret, Secret, and Confidential. Of these, Confidential is considered the lowest level of sensitivity.

41. Answer: C. GDPR

Explanation: The General Data Protection Regulation (GDPR) is the primary law in Europe regulating how companies protect EU citizens' personal data.

42. Answer: A. Data in motion

Explanation: The Transport Layer Security (TLS) protocol is primarily designed to provide privacy and data integrity between two or more communicating computer applications, making it suitable for securing data in motion.

43. Answer: C. SSH

Explanation: SSH (Secure Shell) is a secure protocol that can replace Telnet for secure server management.

44. Answer: D. Erasing

Explanation: Of the methods listed, erasing is generally the least secure method for data removal from magnetic media. It simply removes pointers to the data but doesn't physically erase them.

45. Answer: A. RAM

Explanation: RAM (Random Access Memory) is a type of computer memory used to read and write data that is being actively used or processed by the computer. Hence, it is an example of "data in use."

46.   Answer: B. Home address

Explanation: A home address can identify an individual even when seen in isolation. Hence, it is considered PII.

47.   Answer: D. System owner

Explanation: The system owner, or information system owner or information owner, is typically responsible for the overall procurement, development, integration, modification, or operation and maintenance of the information system. When there is a significant change in the system, they are primarily responsible for updating the system security plan (SSP). This includes documenting changes in the system environment, updating the system inventory, and reevaluating the security controls. The business owner, data processor, and data owner also have crucial roles in the organization but are not primarily responsible for the SSP. The business owner usually oversees the business process that the system supports. The data processor processes data on behalf of the data owner, who is responsible for the data's accuracy, privacy, and security.

48.   Answer: B. Value of the data

Explanation: The value of the data, in terms of its sensitivity and the impact if it were compromised, is the most important factor when determining a data classification level.

49. Answer: A. AES

Explanation: Advanced Encryption Standard (AES) is used for encrypting files, and it keeps the file encrypted even after it is received and detached from the email. While TLS and SSL secure communication channels, they do not encrypt the file, so it would not remain encrypted after receipt. Though it can encrypt files, DES is considered insecure due to its small key size.

50. Answer: B. Mandatory access control

Explanation: Mandatory access control (MAC) is a nondiscretionary access control policy regulated by a central authority. It's based on security labels attached to each information object, and access is granted or denied based on the security clearances assigned to users.

51. Answer: A. The strongest password

Explanation: When you use a passphrase instead of a standard dictionary word as your password, you are essentially creating a stronger password. Passphrases are typically longer than traditional passwords, making it more difficult for attackers to guess or crack using brute force. They can include spaces and be more mnemonic, making them easier for users to remember.

52. Answer: C. Palm vein scanner

Explanation: Biometric systems like palm vein scanners offer the highest level of security. These systems are unique to each individual and are more difficult to replicate or forge than passwords or smart cards.

53.   Answer: A. Corrective control

Explanation: Corrective controls are implemented in response to a security incident. They aim to limit the extent of any damage caused, recover the system's normal functions, and correct any system weaknesses identified during the incident.

54.   Answer: D. Detective control

Explanation: Detective controls are designed to discover and react to occurring incidents. In this case, investigating a breach is an example of a detective control, as you are identifying the cause and impact of the incident that has already taken place.

55.   Answer: D. By outlining controls to protect valuable assets

Explanation: Asset classification assists in identifying the most critical and valuable assets, enabling an organization to allocate resources and controls effectively to protect these assets. This leads to an improved ability to achieve its goals and objectives.

56.   Answer: A. Create, use, share, store, archive, and destroy

Explanation: The correct sequence of asset life cycle phases is create, use, share, store, archive, and destroy. This sequence reflects the typical progression of an asset's life.

57. Answer: B. The destruction of assets in a controlled, legally defensible, and compliant manner

Explanation: Defensible destruction refers to destroying assets in a way that complies with legal and regulatory requirements and can be defended if questioned.

58. Answer: C. Data controller

Explanation: In the context of data privacy, the data controller is the entity that determines the purposes and means of processing personal data. They are responsible for ensuring that the processing complies with relevant laws and regulations.

59. Answer: B. Right to be Forgotten Principle

Explanation: The Right to be Forgotten is not an OECD principle. It's a provision from the General Data Protection Regulation (GDPR) of the European Union. The OECD principles include the Collection Limitation, Use Limitation, and Accountability principles, among others.

60. Answer: D. Data steward

Explanation: While a data steward can help manage and enforce data policies, they're not a requirement for effective retention requirements. Policies, education, training, and an understanding of compliance requirements are all necessary.

61. Answer: A. Specific steps that must be executed

Explanation: Baseline security controls do provide a minimum level of security, can be associated with specific architectures and systems, and serve as a consistent reference point. However, they do not dictate specific steps that must be executed. While they set a base standard, the specific steps to achieve this standard can vary based on the organization's unique needs and circumstances.

62. Answer: C. Limiting general baseline recommendations by removing those that do not apply

Explanation: Scoping involves tailoring baseline security recommendations to fit the specific circumstances of an organization. This may involve removing recommendations that are not applicable, adding additional controls where necessary, or modifying existing recommendations to better suit the organization's needs.

63. Answer: B. Selectively implementing parts of the standard or framework based on relevance

Explanation: Scoping involves adapting a standard or framework to suit the specific circumstances of an organization, which might involve selecting only those parts that are relevant or useful to the organization.

64. Answer: B. Overwriting

Explanation: Overwriting is the process of replacing existing data with new data, which can be used to effectively eliminate data remanence on rewritable memory like PROM, flash memory, and SSD drives.

65. Answer: C. Data in use

Explanation: While data is in use, it is typically in an unencrypted state as it is being processed or accessed. Thus, it is difficult to apply encryption protection to data in this state.

66. Answer: C. EEPROM

Explanation: Flash drives use Electrically Erasable Programmable Read-Only Memory (EEPROM), which allows data to be electrically erased and reprogrammed.

67. Answer: C. Exposure to UV light

Explanation: Erasable Programmable Read-Only Memory (EPROM) can be erased by exposing it to strong UV light, allowing it to be rewritten.

68. Answer: D. Clean desk policies, print policies, job rotation, mandatory vacations, and view angle screens

Explanation: All these measures can contribute to protecting data in use. The need-to-know policy, while valuable, does not directly address the protection of data in use.

69. Answer: C. Encryption

Explanation: Encryption is a primary method for protecting data at rest. It renders the data unreadable without the correct decryption key, thereby protecting it even if physical security measures fail.

70. Answer: C. As long as it is useful or required, whichever is longer

Explanation: The duration for keeping backups should be based on both the utility of the data and any legal or regulatory requirements. Some data may need to be kept for a specific period due to regulations, while other data may be useful for business purposes for a certain length of time.

71. Answer: A. DRAM

Explanation: Dynamic Random Access Memory (DRAM) is a type of volatile memory. It retains data as long as it's powered on, but once the power is turned off, the data is lost.

72. Answer: C. PROM

Explanation: Programmable Read-Only Memory (PROM) can be programmed using a special device. This process can only happen once. Once the PROM has been programmed, the data written to it is permanent and cannot be erased or rewritten.

73. Answer: B. To ensure there is no data remanence

Explanation: Multiple forms of data destruction are used to ensure there is no data remanence, which means ensuring that no remnants of data remain that could be potentially recovered.

74. Answer: A. Cryptanalysis

Explanation: Cryptanalysis, or attempting to break encryption or cryptographic systems, is a common attack method targeting data at rest.

75. Answer: D. Proper data encryption

Explanation: Encryption is a process that transforms readable data into unreadable data. An attacker could not access the data without the decryption key if the backup tapes were adequately encrypted.

76. Answer: A. Unclassified

Explanation: In US government data classification, data that wouldn't harm national security if disclosed is typically classified as "Unclassified."

77. Answer: A. Stealing unencrypted laptops

Explanation: Stealing unencrypted laptops is a common attack against data at rest because the data on these devices is easy to access if not encrypted.

78. Answer: C. Where do we keep the backup data?

Explanation: While the location of the backup data is an important aspect of data management, it is not directly related to the data retention policy, which focuses on the duration and manner of data retention.

79. Answer: A. Minimal use of paper copies and only used while at the desk and in use

Explanation: A clean desk policy typically involves minimizing the use of paper copies and ensuring they are only in use while at the desk, to prevent unauthorized access to sensitive information.

80.   Answer: A. Data remanence

Explanation: The primary purpose of data disposal is to eliminate data remanence, or residual data that remains after data deletion or erasure, which could be potentially recovered and exploited.

81.   Answer: D. How the data will be used

Explanation: Although how the data is used can influence its sensitivity, the primary factors in determining sensitivity are who has access, its value, and the potential impact of its exposure.

82.   Answer: D. Shredding

Explanation: Shredding, or physically destroying the SSD, is one of solid-state drives' most secure data disposal methods.

83.   Answer: A, C, D, E. Clean desk policy, View angle privacy screen for monitors, Print policy, Workstation locking

Explanation: All of these, except encryption, are strategies that can be used to protect data. Encryption is typically used for data at rest or in motion.

84.   Answer: D. All of these

Explanation: When dealing with sensitive data, it is important to encrypt all these forms of data storage and transmission to ensure the security of the data.

85.   Answer: B. Perform the backups and restores

Explanation: A data custodian's primary role is to manage and handle the data, which includes performing backups and restorations.

86.   Answer: C. Eavesdropping

Explanation: Eavesdropping, or interception of information in transit, is a common type of attack on data in motion.

87.   Answer: A. Proper data handling

Explanation: Implementing logs to monitor who accesses what data on your backup servers is an example of proper data handling. This is a measure to ensure accountability and traceability in the event of any unauthorized or suspicious activities.

88.   Answer: C. Incinerate

Explanation: While all options can erase data, incineration is the most thorough method to ensure there is no data remanence on SSD drives. It physically destroys the drives, making data recovery impossible.

89.   Answer: B. The CFO

Explanation: The CFO, or Chief Financial Officer, is typically responsible for the day-to-day financial leadership of an organization.

90. Answer: B. Produce electronic information to internal or external attorneys or legal teams

    Explanation: The e-discovery process typically involves producing electronic information for internal or external legal teams in preparation for legal proceedings.

91. Answer: C. Secret

    Explanation: In the US government's data classification scheme, information is classified as Secret when its unauthorized disclosure could reasonably be expected to cause serious damage to national security.

92. Answer: C. Data in motion

    Explanation: End-to-end encryption is most relevant for data in motion. It's a secure communication method that prevents third parties from accessing data while it's transferred from one end system to another.

93. Answer: C. To protect the confidentiality, integrity, and availability of data

    Explanation: The primary goal of information classification is to protect the confidentiality, integrity, and availability of data by identifying the sensitivity of data and implementing suitable controls to protect it.

94. Answer: C. Top Secret

Explanation: The Top Secret classification is typically used within government organizations, not the private sector.

95. Answer: B. Data owner

Explanation: The data owner, who is usually someone with appropriate authority within the organization, is typically responsible for data classification.

96. Answer: B. Implement controls as defined by the data owner

Explanation: The data custodian is responsible for the implementation of the controls defined by the data owner, including storage, protection, and retrieval of datasets.

97. Answer: A. Data that remains on a storage medium after it has been deleted

Explanation: Data remanence refers to the residual representation of data that remains even after attempts have been made to remove or erase the data.

98. Answer: A. To define how long data should be kept before it is deleted

Explanation: A data retention policy outlines how long data should be stored based on regulatory requirements, business needs, and data value.

99.   Answer: C. The size of the data

Explanation: While the size of the data may affect storage requirements, it typically does not determine the length of data retention periods.

100.   Answer: B. To protect the rights of individuals with respect to their personal data

Explanation: The primary goal of privacy laws and regulations is to protect individuals' rights regarding their personal data, including how it is collected, stored, used, and shared.

101.   Answer: D. Destruction

Explanation: The final stage of the information life cycle is typically destruction, during which data is destroyed in a way that ensures it cannot be reconstructed or recovered.

102.   Answer: A. Preventative

Explanation: Encryption is a preventative control that protects data confidentiality and integrity by transforming plaintext into ciphertext that is unreadable without the decryption key.

CHAPTER 5

Security Architecture and Engineering

Security Architecture and Engineering is one of the eight domains of the CISSP Common Body of Knowledge. This domain focuses on designing, implementing, and maintaining secure systems and networks to protect an organization's information assets. This chapter will cover essential concepts and provide exam tips to help you effectively prepare for the CISSP exam. As you embark on this journey through Security Architecture and Engineering, you will uncover the principles underpinning modern information systems' security. You'll learn how to apply these principles in various contexts, from organizational security policies to the technical details of system design. By the end of this chapter, you will have a deeper understanding of how security models, system security architecture, and cryptography work together to create a robust defense against cyber threats. The following sections will delve into various aspects of security architecture, starting with the theoretical foundations provided by security models.

© Mohamed Aly Bouke 2023
M. A. Bouke, *CISSP Exam Certification Companion*, Certification Study Companion Series,
https://doi.org/10.1007/979-8-8688-0057-3_5

Security Models

Security models form the theoretical backbone of security architecture, providing a framework for implementing security policies and defining how a system enforces these policies. Understanding various security models is essential for designing and maintaining secure systems. This section will discuss some widely used security models and their features, including

- **Security clearance**: Security clearance is not a security model but a status granted to individuals, allowing them access to classified information or restricted areas within an organization. The clearance level is determined based on a person's need for specific information, background checks, and other factors. Different levels of clearance correspond to varying degrees of sensitivity of the information.

  Example: In a government agency, employees might be granted different clearance levels, such as Top Secret, Secret, and Confidential. A Top Secret clearance would allow access to the most sensitive national security information. In contrast, a Confidential clearance would permit access to information that, if disclosed, might cause damage to national security.

- **Reading down and writing up**: These concepts are associated with the Bell-LaPadula model (BLP), which focuses on data confidentiality. "Reading down" means a user with a higher security clearance can read data classified at a lower level, whereas "writing up" means a user can write data to a higher or equal security level. These principles prevent unauthorized access and data leaks.

Example: Imagine a military organization with different levels of security clearance: Top Secret, Secret, and Confidential. A general with Top Secret clearance can "read down" and access documents classified at all three levels. However, a sergeant with only Confidential clearance cannot access Secret or Top Secret documents. When writing data, the general can "write up" to Top Secret or any lower level, ensuring that sensitive information is not accidentally downgraded. Conversely, the sergeant can only write data at the Confidential level or higher, preventing them from potentially leaking information to a lower classification.

This structure ensures that individuals only have access to information that aligns with their security clearance, thereby maintaining the confidentiality and integrity of the data within the organization.

- **Bell-LaPadula model**: The Bell-LaPadula model is a confidentiality-centric security model that enforces the "no read up, no write down" principles using security labels and access control rules. The model helps to ensure that sensitive information is accessible only to users with appropriate security clearance.

- **Lattice-based access controls**: Lattice-based access control (LBAC) is a security model representing user permissions and object classifications in a lattice structure. LBAC enforces the "least upper bound" and "greatest lower bound" rules to manage resource access based on user security clearances and object classifications.

- **Integrity models**: Integrity models focus on maintaining data integrity by preventing unauthorized data modification. The Biba model and the Clark-Wilson model are examples of integrity models. The Biba model enforces the "no write up, no read down" principles, while the Clark-Wilson model enforces access controls and separation of duties to ensure data integrity.

- **Chinese Wall model**: The Chinese Wall model, the Brewer-Nash model, is designed to prevent conflicts of interest in commercial environments. This model restricts access to sensitive information based on a user's prior access to related data. The model helps to maintain data confidentiality and prevent the misuse of insider information.

- **Access control matrix**: An access control matrix is a table that represents the relationships between subjects (users or processes) and objects (resources). Each cell in the matrix contains a subject's permissions over an object. This model is useful for visualizing and managing access control policies but can be inefficient for large systems.

As you prepare for the CISSP exam, it's essential to grasp the underlying principles and practical applications of the security models discussed in this section and the specific contexts in which each model is the best option. The exam will likely focus on your ability to discern when and why to choose each model, such as selecting the Bell-LaPadula model for data confidentiality or the Chinese Wall model to prevent conflicts of interest. Familiarize yourself with real-world examples, and understand the unique features and applications of models like lattice-based access controls, integrity models, and access control matrix. The CISSP exam emphasizes comprehension and application of security principles, so a deep understanding of how and why these models are used in various scenarios will be vital for your success. Focus on the decision-making process behind selecting the appropriate model for different organizational needs, as this will help you navigate the complex scenarios you may encounter in the examination.

System Security Architecture

System security architecture is a comprehensive approach to designing and implementing secure systems that align with industry best practices and comply with relevant standards, such as ISO 27001 and NIST frameworks. It involves strategically integrating hardware, software, and policies to protect against potential threats. Key components of system security architecture include

- **Secure boot process**: This ensures the system boots securely using trusted hardware and software components. It verifies the integrity of the booting process, preventing unauthorized or malicious code from executing during startup.

- **Trusted computing base (TCB)**: TCB comprises the hardware, firmware, and software components forming a system's trusted foundation. It's the core of the system's security and is responsible for enforcing security policies and maintaining its integrity.

- **Security perimeter**: This is the boundary between the TCB and the rest of the system, where robust security controls should be in place. It acts as a barrier, controlling access and protecting the core components from potential threats.

Cryptography

In cybersecurity, encryption and hashing algorithms are pivotal in safeguarding data integrity, confidentiality, and authenticity. A comprehensive understanding of these algorithms is essential for professionals in the field and is a focal point in the CISSP exam. Table 5-1 summarizes the common encryption and hashing algorithms relevant to the CISSP exam. Cryptography is vital in ensuring data confidentiality, integrity, and authenticity. It's the science of encoding and decoding information to protect it from unauthorized access. Essential cryptographic concepts include

- **Symmetric cryptography**: Symmetric cryptography uses the same key for both encryption (converting plaintext into unreadable text) and decryption (converting unreadable text back into plaintext).

  Example: The Advanced Encryption Standard (AES) is a widely used symmetric encryption algorithm. Suppose you want to send a secure email to a friend. You both agree on a secret key, "12345." You use this key to encrypt the email, and your friend uses the same key to decrypt it. The challenge here is securely sharing the key, as anyone with access to it can decrypt the message.

  Symmetric cryptography is often used for bulk data encryption, such as encrypting entire hard drives or secure communication within a closed network.

- **Asymmetric cryptography**: Asymmetric cryptography, or public key cryptography, uses two different keys: a public key for encryption and a corresponding private key for decryption.

Example: RSA (Rivest–Shamir–Adleman) is a well-known asymmetric algorithm. If you want to send a secure email to a colleague, you encrypt it with their public key. Only their corresponding private key can decrypt it. Since the private key is never shared, this method is more secure for transmitting data over open networks. Asymmetric cryptography is commonly used in secure email communications, SSL/TLS for secure web browsing, and digital certificates.

- **Hash functions**: Hash functions take an input (or "message") and return a fixed-size string, which appears random. The same input will always produce the same output, but even a small change in the input produces a significant change in the output. **Example**: SHA-256 is a popular hash function used in Bitcoin's blockchain. When downloading a file, you can verify its integrity by comparing the file's SHA-256 hash with the expected hash value. If they match, the file is intact. Hash functions are used for data integrity verification, password storage, and digital signatures.

- **Digital signatures**: Digital signatures use cryptographic techniques to verify the authenticity of digital documents or messages, ensuring that the content has not been altered.

  Example: When signing a digital contract, a user's private key creates a digital signature. Others can verify the signature using the corresponding public key, confirming both the document's integrity and the signer's identity. Digital signatures are used in legal documents, software distribution (to verify that the software hasn't been tampered with), and secure email communication.

Table 5-1. *Summary of Common Encryption and Hashing Algorithms for the CISSP Exam*

Algorithm Type	Algorithm	Description	Common Usage
Symmetric Encryption	AES	Advanced Encryption Standard, known for strong security and performance	File encryption, Wi-Fi security (WPA2)
	DES	Data Encryption Standard, now considered less secure due to shorter key length	Legacy systems, replaced by AES
	3DES	Triple DES, an enhancement of DES with increased security	Financial services, secure data transmission
Asymmetric Encryption	RSA	Uses two different keys for encryption and decryption, widely used in digital signatures	Secure email, SSL/TLS certificates
	ECC	Elliptic curve cryptography, known for strong security with shorter key lengths	Mobile devices, smart cards
Hash Functions	SHA-256	Part of the SHA-2 family, widely used for data integrity verification	File integrity checks, digital signatures
	MD5	Message Digest Algorithm 5, now considered less secure due to vulnerabilities	Legacy systems, replaced by SHA-256
	SHA-1	Predecessor to SHA-2, also considered less secure now	Legacy systems, replaced by SHA-256
Digital Signatures	DSA	Digital Signature Algorithm, used to verify the authenticity of digital documents or messages	Document signing, code signing

Network Security

Network security has become a critical concern for organizations and individuals in our increasingly interconnected world. With the proliferation of devices, applications, and services relying on network connectivity, protecting data and ensuring its integrity is paramount. From online banking to remote work, virtually every aspect of modern life is facilitated by networks, making their security a vital component of our digital ecosystem.

For students preparing for the CISSP exam, understanding network security is not merely about memorizing terms and definitions. It requires a deep comprehension of how various security measures work together to defend against potential threats. The exam will likely test your ability to apply these concepts in real-world scenarios, evaluating how well you can design, implement, and maintain secure networks.

Adequate network security involves implementing layers of protection to defend against potential threats. This multifaceted approach ensures that if one defense line fails, others are in place to thwart an attack. Key network security concepts include

- **Firewalls**: Devices that control traffic between networks based on predefined rules. They act as barriers between trusted and untrusted networks, such as an internal corporate network and the Internet.

- **Intrusion detection systems (IDS) and intrusion prevention systems (IPS)**: Monitor network traffic and detect or prevent potential attacks. IDS alerts administrators of suspicious activities, while IPS takes active measures to mitigate threats.

- **Virtual Private Networks (VPNs)**: Secure communication channels that use encryption to protect data transmitted over the Internet. VPNs allow users to send and receive data as if their devices were directly connected to a private network.

- **Secure Socket Layer (SSL) and Transport Layer Security (TLS)**: Protocols used to secure communications between client and server systems. They encrypt the data transmitted, ensuring confidentiality and integrity.

Understanding these principles, from firewalls to secure protocols, is foundational to modern network security. Whether a professional in the field or a student preparing for the CISSP exam, this knowledge equips you to design, implement, and maintain secure networks in an ever-evolving digital landscape.

In addition to the key network security concepts discussed earlier, understanding common network protocols and their security considerations is essential. These protocols facilitate various network functions, from web browsing to email retrieval, and their security varies widely. Table 5-2 provides an overview of common network protocols, outlining their primary uses and whether they are considered secure. Recognizing the security implications of these protocols is vital for network security professionals and is likely to be a focus area on the CISSP exam.

Table 5-2. Common Network Protocols, Their Uses, and Security Considerations

Protocol	Use	Secure (Yes/No)
HTTP	Web browsing	No
HTTPS	Secure web browsing	Yes
FTP	File transfer	No
SFTP	Secure file transfer	Yes
SNMP	Network management	No
SNMPv3	Secure network management	Yes
POP3	Email retrieval	No
IMAP	Email retrieval with multiple device support	No
IMAPS	Secure email retrieval	Yes
SMTP	Sending email	No
SMTPS	Secure email sending	Yes
DNS	Domain name resolution	No
DNSSEC	Secure domain name resolution	Yes

Secure System Design Concepts

Secure system design is a critical component of Security Architecture and Engineering. It aims to create systems that are resilient to attacks and maintain their functionality even in adverse conditions. This section will discuss some essential secure system design concepts and their significance.

- **Layering**: A design principle organizes system components into separate, hierarchical layers. Each layer performs specific functions and interacts only with its adjacent layers. This approach enables better separation of concerns, limits the attack surface, and simplifies the management and maintenance of systems.

- **Abstraction**: Abstraction is a design concept that simplifies complex systems by hiding the details of lower-level components and providing a higher-level, more user-friendly interface. This approach allows developers and administrators to focus on the relevant aspects of a system while reducing complexity and potential vulnerabilities.

- **Security domains**: A security domain is a collection of resources that share a common security policy and are controlled by a single authority. Dividing systems into security domains helps enforce security policies and manage access controls more effectively. Security domains are often represented by trust boundaries, which define the level of trust between different domains and the rules governing data flow between them.

- **The ring model**: The ring model is a security architecture that organizes system components into hierarchical protection rings, each representing a different privilege level. The most privileged components, such as the operating system kernel, reside in the innermost ring (Ring 0). As the ring number increases, the level of privilege decreases. This model ensures that more sensitive components have higher levels of protection and limits the potential damage caused by security breaches.

- **Open and closed systems**: Open systems follow widely accepted standards and protocols, making it easier for components to interoperate with other systems. These systems often promote collaboration and innovation but may be more susceptible to security threats due to their transparency. On the other hand, closed systems use proprietary protocols and technologies, making it more difficult for external entities to interact with or compromise the system. While closed systems offer increased security, they can limit interoperability and hinder collaboration.

Understanding these secure system design concepts is essential for designing robust security architectures and engineering solutions. Incorporating these principles into your systems can enhance their security posture and minimize potential risks.

Other important secure design principles for the exam include

- **Threat modeling**: Threat modeling is a systematic process of identifying, prioritizing, and addressing potential threats and vulnerabilities in a system. It helps organizations proactively mitigate risks and improve the security posture of their systems.

- **Least privilege**: The principle of least privilege states that users, processes, and systems should have the minimum access rights necessary to perform their tasks. This approach limits the potential damage caused by security breaches and reduces the attack surface.

- **Defense in depth**: Defense in depth is a security strategy that employs multiple layers of protection to defend against potential threats. By implementing diverse security controls at various levels of a system, this approach ensures that even if one layer is compromised, other layers can still provide protection.

- **Secure defaults**: Secure defaults is a design principle that ensures systems are configured with secure settings by default. This approach reduces the likelihood of misconfigurations, which can lead to security vulnerabilities.

- **Fail securely**: Failing securely means that when a system encounters an error or failure, it should maintain its security posture and not expose sensitive data or resources. This approach helps to prevent data leaks and unauthorized access in case of system failures.

- **Separation of duties (SoD)**: Separation of duties is a principle that divides critical tasks among multiple individuals to prevent fraud and misuse of access privileges. By requiring more than one person to perform sensitive actions, SoD helps to ensure accountability and maintain data integrity.

- **Keep it simple**: The principle of simplicity emphasizes that systems should be designed with as little complexity as possible. Simpler systems are easier to manage, maintain, and secure, as they have fewer potential vulnerabilities and are less prone to errors.

- **Zero Trust**: Zero Trust is a security model that assumes all users, devices, and networks are untrustworthy by default. This model enforces strict access controls and continuous monitoring, requiring users to verify their identities and permissions for every access request.

- **Privacy by design**: Privacy by design is a framework that promotes the integration of privacy considerations into the design and development of systems and processes. This approach ensures that privacy is an integral part of a system's architecture rather than an afterthought.

- **Trust but verify**: Trust but verify is a security principle emphasizing the importance of validation and verification, even when dealing with trusted entities. By continuously monitoring and verifying the actions of users and systems, organizations can detect potential security issues and maintain a strong security posture.

- **Shared responsibility**: The shared responsibility model highlights the need for collaboration between stakeholders, such as service providers and customers, to ensure system security. All parties must implement and maintain security controls and practices in this model.

Overview of Different Computing Systems

A diverse range of computing systems exist, each designed to serve specific purposes and meet unique requirements. Understanding these computing systems is essential for security professionals as they design and implement secure solutions across various environments. This section will briefly discuss different types of computing systems and their primary characteristics, providing an essential foundation for recognizing the unique security considerations associated with each system type.

For the exam, make sure you understand the following concepts:

- **Client-based systems**: These are computing devices, such as desktops, laptops, or smartphones, that users interact with directly. They typically run end-user applications and rely on server-based systems for centralized data storage and processing.

- **Server-based systems**: Provide resources and services to client-based systems, such as file storage, application hosting, or data processing. They are often more powerful and have higher availability than client-based systems.

- **Database systems**: Database systems store, manage, and retrieve structured data. They support various data models, such as relational, NoSQL, or graph databases, and provide mechanisms for ensuring data consistency, integrity, and security.

- **Cryptographic systems**: These systems use cryptographic techniques, such as encryption, decryption, and digital signatures, to protect the confidentiality, integrity, and authenticity of data and communications.

- **Industrial control systems (ICS)**: ICS are used to monitor and control industrial processes, such as manufacturing, power generation, or water treatment. They include Supervisory Control and Data Acquisition (SCADA) systems and Distributed Control Systems (DCS).

- **Cloud-based systems**: Cloud-based systems offer computing resources and services over the Internet. Examples include Software as a Service (SaaS), Infrastructure as a Service (IaaS), and Platform as a Service (PaaS), which allow users to access applications, infrastructure, or development platforms on a subscription basis.

- **Distributed systems**: These systems consist of multiple computing nodes that collaborate to achieve a common goal, such as processing large datasets or providing high availability. Examples include peer-to-peer networks, distributed databases, and blockchain systems.

- **Internet of Things (IoT)**: IoT refers to the network of interconnected devices that collect and exchange data, often using sensors and actuators. These devices can range from smart home appliances to industrial equipment and wearables.

- **Microservices**: Microservices is an architectural pattern that breaks down applications into small, loosely coupled, and independently deployable services. This approach enables greater flexibility, scalability, and resilience than monolithic architectures.

- **Containerization**: Containerization is a virtualization method that packages applications and their dependencies into lightweight, portable containers. This approach allows faster deployment, improved resource efficiency, and greater application portability.

- **Serverless**: Serverless computing is a cloud-based execution model that automatically manages and scales the underlying infrastructure, allowing developers to focus on application logic rather than server management.

- **Embedded systems**: Embedded systems are specialized computing devices designed for a specific purpose, such as automotive control systems or smart appliances. They typically have limited resources and are optimized for their specific function.

- **High-performance computing (HPC) systems**: HPC systems are designed for processing complex and resource-intensive tasks, such as simulations, data analysis, or artificial intelligence. They often use parallel processing techniques and specialized hardware for high computational performance.

- **Edge computing systems**: Edge computing is a distributed computing paradigm that brings processing capabilities closer to the data sources, reducing latency and bandwidth consumption. This approach is beneficial for IoT and real-time applications.

- **Virtualized systems**: Virtualization allows multiple virtual machines (VMs) to run on a single physical host, sharing hardware resources. This approach improves resource utilization, reduces costs, and enables greater flexibility in managing and scaling computing environments.

Cloud Computing: Service Models and Deployment Models

Cloud computing has become integral to modern information technology, offering scalable, flexible, and cost-effective solutions. As part of the CISSP Common Body of Knowledge, understanding the various cloud service and deployment models is essential for real-world application and exam preparation.

Cloud Service Models

The cloud service models define the level of control and responsibility the customer has over the environment. These models are foundational to cloud computing:

- **Infrastructure as a Service (IaaS)** provides virtualized computing resources over the Internet. For example, Amazon EC2 allows businesses to run virtual servers and scale computing power based on needs. Users are responsible for managing the OS, applications, and data, offering flexibility but requiring a robust understanding of the underlying components.

- **Platform as a Service (PaaS)** takes this a step further by providing a platform for developers to build applications without worrying about the underlying infrastructure. For instance, Microsoft Azure's App Service offers a fully managed platform for building, deploying, and scaling web apps, abstracting the complexities and allowing developers to focus on creating applications.

- **Software as a Service (SaaS)** represents the most user-friendly model, delivering software applications over the Internet. Google Workspace, for example, provides access to productivity tools like Gmail, Docs, and Drive, all hosted and maintained by Google, making it an attractive option for end users without technical expertise.

Cloud Deployment Models

The deployment models describe how and where the cloud infrastructure is located and operated. Understanding these models is crucial for designing secure cloud environments:

- **Public clouds**: These are owned and operated by third-party providers and deliver resources over the Internet. Amazon Web Services (AWS) offers a wide range of cloud services publicly, available to anyone who wants to purchase them, offering scalability and flexibility.

- **Private clouds**: These are used exclusively by one organization. A large corporation might have its private cloud to ensure control and compliance with specific regulations. This model provides more control and is suitable for organizations with stringent security requirements.

- **Hybrid clouds**: These combine public and private clouds, allowing data and applications to be shared between them. A healthcare provider might use a private cloud for sensitive patient data and a public cloud for nonsensitive administrative information, offering greater flexibility and optimization of existing infrastructure.

- **Community clouds**: These are shared by several organizations with common concerns. Several government agencies might share a community cloud to collaborate on joint projects while maintaining regulatory compliance. This collaborative approach allows multiple entities to benefit from shared resources while maintaining aligned goals and requirements.

Cloud computing offers diverse models to suit various organizational needs and requirements. By aligning the right service and deployment models with organizational goals, businesses can harness the full potential of cloud computing. As you prepare for the CISSP exam, consider these concepts and examples, considering how they apply to different scenarios. Your mastery of cloud computing will serve you well in both the exam and your professional endeavors in the ever-evolving field of information security.

Cryptography and Key Management

Cryptography is crucial in securing data and communications in modern information systems. Information security professionals must understand cryptographic methods, key management practices, and associated concepts. This section will briefly discuss several key aspects of cryptography and key management, providing an essential foundation for implementing secure cryptographic solutions.

For the exam, bear in mind the following concepts:

- **Cryptographic life cycle**: The cryptographic life cycle includes the generation, distribution, usage, storage, and disposal of cryptographic keys. Proper management of the cryptographic life cycle helps ensure the security and integrity of encrypted data and communications.

- **Cryptographic methods**: Cryptographic methods include symmetric (e.g., AES), asymmetric (e.g., RSA), elliptic curve cryptography, and emerging quantum-resistant algorithms. Each method has its strengths, weaknesses, and use cases.

- **Public key infrastructure (PKI)**: PKI is a framework that enables the secure distribution and management of digital certificates and public keys. It provides a trusted environment for establishing secure communication and verifying identities.

- **Key management practices**: Key management practices involve securely generating, distributing, storing, using, and disposing of cryptographic keys. Proper key management is essential for maintaining the security of encrypted data and preventing unauthorized access.

- **Digital signatures and certificates**: Digital signatures use public key cryptography to authenticate the sender and ensure data integrity. Digital certificates issued by a certificate authority (CA) bind a public key to an entity's identity, enabling secure communication and identity verification.

- **Non-repudiation**: Non-repudiation ensures that a sender cannot deny having sent a message or performed an action. Cryptographic techniques, such as digital signatures, provide non-repudiation by authenticating the sender and verifying data integrity.

- **Integrity (e.g., hashing)**: Cryptographic hashing algorithms, such as SHA-256, maintain data integrity by creating a unique, fixed-size output (hash) from an input. A small change in the input data results in a significantly different hash, making it easy to detect alterations.

Understanding these cryptographic concepts and key management practices, information security professionals can effectively design and implement security solutions that protect sensitive data and maintain information systems' confidentiality, integrity, and availability.

Overview of Cryptanalysis Techniques and Common Cyberattacks

Introduction: In the ever-evolving cybersecurity landscape, various attack techniques and methods are employed by adversaries to exploit vulnerabilities and compromise systems. As information security professionals, it is crucial to be familiar with these attack methods to design and implement effective countermeasures. This section will briefly discuss various cryptanalysis techniques and common cyberattacks to provide a foundation for understanding and mitigating these threats.

Understanding the following concepts is crucial for the exam:

- **Brute force**: Brute-force attacks involve systematically attempting all possible combinations of keys or passwords until the correct one is found. These attacks can be resource-intensive but may succeed when weak encryption or passwords are used.

- **Ciphertext only**: In ciphertext-only attacks, an attacker attempts to decrypt a message using only the ciphertext without knowing the plaintext or encryption key.

- **Known plaintext**: In known plaintext attacks, the attacker possesses both the ciphertext and corresponding plaintext, which can be used to deduce the encryption key or reveal weaknesses in the encryption algorithm.

- **Frequency analysis**: Frequency analysis is a cryptanalysis technique that exploits the frequency of letters or patterns in the encrypted text to deduce the underlying plaintext or encryption key.

- **Chosen ciphertext**: In chosen ciphertext attacks, the attacker can choose ciphertexts and obtain their corresponding plaintexts, which can reveal weaknesses in the encryption scheme or deduce the encryption key.

- **Implementation attacks**: These attacks exploit weaknesses in how cryptographic algorithms or protocols are implemented in software or hardware rather than targeting the algorithms.

- **Side channel**: Side-channel attacks exploit information leaked through unintended channels, such as power consumption, electromagnetic emissions, or timing, to deduce sensitive data like encryption keys.

- **Fault injection**: These attacks intentionally induce errors in a system to exploit its behavior and reveal sensitive information or bypass security controls.

- **Timing**: Timing attacks exploit the time it takes for a system to perform cryptographic operations, allowing attackers to deduce sensitive information, such as encryption keys.

- **Man-in-the-middle (MITM)**: MITM attacks involve an attacker intercepting and potentially altering communications between two parties, allowing the attacker to eavesdrop or impersonate one of the parties.

- **Pass the hash**: These attacks exploit weaknesses in authentication protocols, allowing an attacker to use a stolen password hash to authenticate as a user without knowing the actual password.

- **Kerberos exploitation**: Exploitation attacks target the Kerberos authentication protocol, aiming to obtain or forge authentication tickets to gain unauthorized access to resources.

- **Ransomware**: This is a malware that encrypts a victim's files or systems, demanding a ransom payment for the decryption key. This attack can have severe consequences like data loss or business disruption.

By understanding these cryptanalysis techniques and common cyberattacks, information security professionals can better anticipate potential threats and design effective countermeasures to protect their systems and data.

Secure Facility Design and Environmental Considerations

Facilities' physical security and environmental design are critical aspects of an organization's overall security posture. Properly designed and maintained facilities can help prevent unauthorized access, protect sensitive data, and ensure the continuous operation of critical systems. This section will briefly discuss key concepts related to secure facility design and environmental considerations, providing a foundation for implementing effective physical security measures.

For the exam, understand these concepts:

- **Wiring closets/intermediate distribution facilities**: Wiring closets and intermediate distribution facilities house telecommunications and networking equipment. They should be secured to prevent unauthorized access and tampering and maintain the integrity and availability of the network infrastructure.

- **Server rooms/data centers**: Server rooms and data centers house critical computing and storage resources. These facilities should be designed with strict access controls, redundancy, and environmental controls to ensure the continuous operation and security of the housed systems.

- **Media storage facilities**: Media storage facilities store sensitive data on physical media, such as tapes or hard drives. They should be secured against unauthorized access, theft, and environmental hazards like fire, water damage, or electromagnetic interference.

- **Evidence storage**: Evidence storage facilities store physical evidence related to investigations or legal proceedings. They should be designed to maintain the stored evidence's integrity and chain of custody and protect against unauthorized access and tampering.

- **Restricted and work area security**: Restricted and work areas should have appropriate access controls, such as badge readers or biometric authentication, to ensure that only authorized personnel can access sensitive spaces and resources.

- **Utilities and heating, ventilation, and air conditioning (HVAC)**: Utilities and HVAC systems should be designed to maintain the proper environmental conditions for the equipment and personnel. This includes temperature, humidity, air quality control, and ensuring essential services like power and water availability.

- **Environmental issues**: Environmental issues, such as natural disasters, pollution, or climate change, can significantly impact the security and availability of facilities and systems. Organizations should assess and mitigate these risks through planning, design, and operational measures.

- **Fire prevention, detection, and suppression**: Fire prevention, detection, and suppression systems should be in place to minimize the risk of fire damage to facilities and equipment. This includes using fire-resistant materials, fire detection systems, and appropriate fire suppression systems, such as sprinklers or clean agent systems.

- **Power (e.g., redundant, backup)**: Power systems should be designed to ensure the continuous availability of critical systems. This includes redundant power sources, uninterruptible power supplies (UPS), and backup generators to maintain power during outages or other disruptions.

By understanding these secure facility design and environmental considerations, information security professionals can effectively implement physical security measures that protect sensitive resources and maintain the availability of critical systems.

Applying Security Principles to Site and Facility Design

The design of sites and facilities is crucial in ensuring the overall security of an organization's assets, data, and personnel. By applying security principles to the site and facility design, organizations can minimize risks, prevent unauthorized access, and maintain their critical resources' confidentiality, integrity, and availability. This section will discuss various aspects of incorporating security principles into site and facility design.

Moreover, when applying these concepts to system design, we should consider the following points:

- **Risk assessment and planning**: A thorough assessment helps organizations identify potential threats and vulnerabilities in their site and facility design. This information can be used to develop a comprehensive security plan that addresses identified risks and implements appropriate security measures.

- **Layered security**: Implementing a layered security approach ensures multiple security measures are in place to protect assets and personnel. This can include perimeter security, access controls, surveillance systems, and intrusion detection systems, which provide a robust and comprehensive security solution.

- **Secure access control**: Access control measures, such as card readers, biometric authentication, and security guards, should be implemented to restrict access to sensitive areas and resources. These controls help prevent unauthorized access and maintain the security of the site and facility.

- **Surveillance and monitoring**: Installing surveillance systems, such as CCTV cameras and intrusion detection systems, can help monitor and detect unauthorized access, theft, or vandalism. Monitoring systems should be strategically placed to cover critical areas and entry points, providing a clear view of the facility's premises.

- **Environmental controls**: Environmental controls, such as HVAC systems, fire detection and suppression systems, and backup power systems, should be implemented to maintain a safe and secure environment for personnel and equipment. These controls help ensure the continuous operation of critical systems and protect sensitive data from environmental hazards.

- **Segregation of duties and restricted areas**: Segregation of duties and restricted areas can help prevent unauthorized access to sensitive information or resources. By separating responsibilities and access to sensitive areas, organizations can minimize the risk of insider threats and maintain the security of their assets.

- **Physical security measures**: Implementing physical security measures, such as barriers, gates, locks, and lighting, can help deter unauthorized access and protect the site and facility from external threats. These measures should complement other security controls, providing a comprehensive security solution.

- **Emergency planning and response**: Developing emergency plans and response procedures can help organizations effectively manage incidents and minimize the impact of security breaches or other emergencies. These plans should include strategies for evacuating personnel, securing assets, and coordinating with emergency responders.

Organizations can create a secure environment that protects their assets, data, and personnel by applying these security principles to site and facility design. The effective site and facility design reduces the risk of security incidents and helps organizations respond to and recover from incidents more efficiently.

Summary and Key Takeaways

This chapter explored the Security Architecture and Engineering domain, an essential part of the CISSP CBK. This domain encompasses many concepts and best practices critical for designing, implementing, and maintaining secure information systems.

Key Takeaways

- **Secure system design concepts**: We discussed the importance of various design concepts, such as layering, abstraction, and security domains, and the ring model, open and closed systems, and their implications in creating secure information systems.

- **Security models**: We covered various security models, such as Bell-LaPadula, lattice-based access controls, integrity models, and the Chinese Wall model, which provide formal frameworks for designing and implementing secure systems.

- **Security principles**: We examined essential security principles, such as threat modeling, least privilege, defense in depth, secure defaults, fail securely, separation of duties, and Zero Trust, which guide the development of secure systems and applications.

- **Computing systems**: We provided an overview of different computing systems, such as client-based, server-based, database systems, cryptographic systems, cloud-based systems, IoT, and microservices, with unique security considerations.

- **Cryptography and key management:** We delved into the fundamentals of cryptography, including cryptographic life cycles, methods, public key infrastructure (PKI), key management practices, digital signatures, non-repudiation, and data integrity.

- **Cryptanalysis techniques and common cyberattacks:** We discussed various cryptanalysis techniques, such as brute force, ciphertext only, and frequency analysis, along with common cyberattacks like MITM, pass the hash, and ransomware, which pose significant threats to information systems.

- **Secure facility design and environmental considerations:** We explored the importance of physical security and environmental design in facilities, addressing aspects like wiring closets, server rooms, access control, surveillance, and fire prevention, among others.

- **Applying security principles to site and facility design:** We discussed using security principles in site and facility design, emphasizing the importance of risk assessment, layered security, access control, surveillance, environmental controls, segregation of duties, physical security measures, and emergency planning.

Through a comprehensive grasp of the essential principles and best practices in Security Architecture and Engineering, information security professionals are empowered to craft, deploy, and sustain robust systems. These systems safeguard sensitive information and uphold the fundamental pillars of information security: confidentiality, integrity, and availability.

Practice Questions

As you conclude your study of this chapter, focusing on the essential aspects of Security Architecture and Engineering, I invite you to challenge yourself with the practice questions in this section. These questions are meticulously designed to help you catch and fix information in your mind, reinforcing key concepts and preparing you for the real CISSP exam.

The practice questions are not merely a test of your knowledge but a vital part of your learning journey. By attempting all the questions and carefully reviewing the explanations, you will gain insights into areas where you excel and may need further study. Taking notes from the explanations will enable you to create a personalized study guide tailored to your unique needs and understanding.

These questions are crafted to emulate the style and complexity you will encounter in the full exam samples provided at the end of the book in Chapters 11 and 12. By engaging with these practice questions, you are taking a significant step toward acing those comprehensive exam samples and, ultimately, the real CISSP exam.

We encourage you to approach these questions with dedication and curiosity. Allow yourself to be challenged, learn from your mistakes, and celebrate your successes. Remember, these practice questions are more than a measure of what you know; they are a tool to deepen your understanding and sharpen your readiness for the real exam.

Take your time, think critically, and embrace this opportunity to solidify your Security Architecture and Engineering grasp. Your commitment to this practice will be a valuable asset as you continue your pursuit of the CISSP certification.

1. Which framework is recognized for its comprehensive life cycle approach to security architecture, from assessing business requirements to establishing a "chain of traceability" through strategy, concept, design, implementation, and metrics stages?

   A. Zachman

   B. SABSA

   C. ISO 27000

   D. TOGAF

2. Within ITIL's Service Portfolio, which component primarily focuses on transforming designs into operational services via a project management standard?

   A. Service strategy

   B. Service design

   C. Service transition

   D. Service operations

3. What is the BEST method to compile detailed security requirements?

   A. Threat modeling, covert channels, and data classification

   B. Data classification, risk assessments, and covert channels

   C. Risk assessments, covert channels, and threat modeling

   D. Threat modeling, data classification, and risk assessments

4. Which international security standard is renowned for codifying best security practices and standardizing an organization's Information Security Management System (ISMS) for certification purposes?

   A. ISO 15408

   B. ISO 27001

   C. ISO 9001

   D. ISO 9146

5. What describes the rules that must be put into place to ensure compliance with security requirements?

   A. Security kernel

   B. Security policy

   C. Security model

   D. Security reference monitor

6. What type of model is represented by a two-dimensional arrangement where individual subjects are grouped into roles, and access is granted to these groups for specific objects?

   A. Multilevel lattice

   B. State machine

   C. Non-interference

   D. Matrix-based

7. Which model ensures that a subject with a "Secret"
    clearance level can only write to objects classified as
    "Secret" or "Top Secret" and is barred from writing
    information classified as "Public"?

    A. Biba Integrity

    B. Clark-Wilson

    C. Brewer-Nash

    D. Bell-LaPadula

8. What feature is exclusive to the Biba
    Integrity Model?

    A. Simple property

    B. * (star) property

    C. Invocation property

    D. Strong * property

9. Which security model is best suited for a shared
    data hosting environment to ensure that one
    customer's data is not disclosed to a competitor or
    other customers sharing the same environment?

    A. Brewer-Nash

    B. Clark-Wilson

    C. Bell-LaPadula

    D. Lipner

10. Which security model is mainly concerned with how subjects and objects are created and how subjects are assigned rights or privileges?

    A. Bell-LaPadula

    B. Biba Integrity

    C. Chinese Wall

    D. Graham-Denning

11. In the context of information systems security, how would you describe a penetration?

    A. An attack followed by a breach

    B. A threat followed by an attack

    C. A breach resulting from a threat

    D. A countermeasure against a threat

12. Which of the following does not align with the fundamental goals of computer-based information systems security?

    A. Safeguarding system assets against loss, damage, and misuse

    B. Ensuring data accuracy and process reliability within applications

    C. Ensuring information and application processes are always accessible

    D. Managing data analysis

13. What is the main objective of a plan of action and milestones document?

    A. Eliminating or reducing known vulnerabilities

    B. Utilizing findings from security control assessments

C. Applying results from security impact analyses

D. Implementing findings from continuous monitoring activities

14. In terms of information systems security, how would you characterize an exposure?

A. An attack followed by a breach

B. A vulnerability combined with a threat

C. An attack following a threat

D. An attack combined with a vulnerability

15. Which type of technical security control is interrelated with other controls and consistently active for risk mitigation?

A. Supportive controls

B. Preventative controls

C. Detective controls

D. Recovery controls

16. What approach must information security follow?

A. Top-down process

B. Bottom-up process

C. Both top-down and bottom-up

D. Bottom-up initially, followed by top-down

17. Which feature or mode of IPSec conceals the actual IP addresses of the source and destination?

A. Transport mode

B. Tunnel mode

C. Internet Key Exchange (IKE)

D. Security Parameter Index (SPI)

18. Where should you look to verify if the issuer of an X.509 digital certificate has retracted its trust for the subject of the certificate?

A. The certificate revocation list (CRL)

B. Directory services registry

C. The organization's email server

D. The CRL distribution point (CDP)

19. Which of these does not pertain to the properties of the one-time pad?

A. The key is the same length as the message.

B. The key is not reused.

C. The key is tied to a certificate.

D. The key is highly random.

20. How would you describe an attack trying to produce a collision using a hashing algorithm?

A. A brute-force attack

B. A rainbow attack

C. A birthday attack

D. A ciphertext-only attack

21. What are the necessary components to create a signed and sealed message?

    A. Sender's public key, sender's private key, and a hashing algorithm

    B. Sender's private key, recipient's public key, and a hashing algorithm

    C. Sender's private key, recipient's private key, and a hashing algorithm

    D. Sender's private key, recipient's public key, and recipient's private key

22. Which type of attack is typically used to reveal a sender's symmetric key easily?

    A. Ciphertext only

    B. Known plaintext

    C. Chosen plaintext

    D. Chosen ciphertext

23. Which mode of symmetric key block ciphers is the fastest and most robust?

    A. Counter mode

    B. Output feedback mode

    C. Cipher feedback mode

    D. Cipher block chaining

24. What function is used in the S-box for modern symmetric key cryptosystems?

    A. Transposition

    B. Hashing

C. Pseudo-random number generation

D. Exclusive Or

25. How would you describe a superscalar processor?

A. Executes only one instruction at a time

B. Has two large input and output caches

C. Executes multiple instructions simultaneously

D. Has two large output caches

26. What term refers to shortcuts created by programmers during development, allowing bypass of normal processes, but are accidentally left in the software when shipped to customers?

A. Backdoors

B. Traps

C. Buffer overflows

D. Covert channels

27. You noticed a high level of TCP traffic and discovered malformed TCP ACK packets with unauthorized data. What type of attack did you discover?

A. Buffer overflow attack

B. Asynchronous attack

C. Covert channel attack

D. DoS attack

28. Which standard evaluates functionality and assurance separately?

    A. TCSEC

    B. TNI

    C. ITSEC

    D. CTCPEC

29. Which model was the first to focus on confidentiality?

    A. Bell-LaPadula

    B. Biba

    C. Clark-Wilson

    D. Take-Grant

30. Which model is based on integrity and was designed for commercial applications?

    A. Information flow

    B. Clark-Wilson

    C. Bell-LaPadula

    D. Brewer-Nash

31. What does the Biba model primarily address?

    A. Internal threats

    B. External threats

    C. Confidentiality

    D. Availability

32. Which model is also known as the Chinese Wall model?

   A. Biba

   B. Take-Grant

   C. Harrison-Ruzzo-Ullman

   D. Brewer-Nash

33. Which of the following evaluates both integrity and availability?

   A. Orange Book

   B. Brown Book

   C. Red Book

   D. Purple Book

34. What is the intent of the * property in the Bell-LaPadula model?

   A. No upward read

   B. No upward write

   C. No downward read

   D. No downward write

35. What is the aim of the simple integrity rule in the Biba model?

   A. No upward read

   B. No upward write

   C. No downward read

   D. No downward write

36. What can be used to bridge disparate mandatory access control (MAC) systems?

    A. Labels

    B. Reference monitor

    C. Controls

    D. Guards

37. Which security operating mode best describes when a user must have a legitimate need to know for all data?

    A. Dedicated

    B. System high

    C. Compartmented

    D. Multilevel

38. Which security model utilizes the "transformational procedures" (TLC) concept?

    A. Biba

    B. Clark-Wilson

    C. Bell-LaPadula

    D. Brewer-Nash

39. As a security manager for a bank with 100 employees, all required to encrypt data using DES encryption, how many keys would be necessary?

    A. 4950

    B. 49.5

    C. 99

    D. 4900

40. What is the best description of obtaining plaintext from ciphertext without a key?

    A. Frequency analysis

    B. Cryptanalysis

    C. Decryption

    D. Hacking

41. Which attack type involves an attacker intercepting session keys and reusing them later?

    A. Known plaintext attack

    B. Ciphertext-only attack

    C. Man-in-the-middle attack

    D. Replay attack

42. What is a drawback of symmetric encryption?

    A. Key size

    B. Speed

    C. Key management

    D. Key strength

43. Which of the following doesn't belong in the category of symmetric algorithms?

    A. DES

    B. RC5

    C. AES

    D. RSA

44. Which type of attack happens when an attacker can intercept session keys and use them at a later time?

    A. Known plaintext attack

    B. Ciphertext-only attack

    C. Man-in-the-middle attack

    D. Replay attack

45. Which is a drawback of symmetric encryption?

    A. Key size

    B. Speed

    C. Key management

    D. Key strength

46. Which of the following is not a symmetric algorithm?

    A. DES

    B. RC5

    C. AES

    D. RSA

47. In cryptography's physical security context, which modules are predominantly employed in encrypting routers' creation, implementation, and operation?

    A. Cryptographic modules with a single chip

    B. Stand-alone cryptographic modules with multiple chips

    C. Cryptographic modules in software

    D. Cryptographic modules in hardware

48. Concerning cryptographic modules, which attack targets the hardware module's operations without needing physical interaction with the module's internal components?

   A. Timing analysis attack

   B. Noninvasive attack

   C. Differential power analysis attack

   D. Simple power analysis attack

49. In terms of cryptography's physical security, which modules are most commonly used in the production, implementation, and operation of adapters and expansion boards?

   A. Single-chip cryptographic modules

   B. Stand-alone cryptographic modules with multiple chips

   C. Embedded cryptographic modules with multiple chips

   D. Hardware cryptographic modules

50. In cryptography, which of the following outwardly shows that a cryptographic module's physical security has been compromised?

   A. Tamper attempt

   B. Tamper evidence

   C. Tamper detection

   D. Tamper response

51. Which method studies the fluctuations in a cryptographic module's electrical power consumption to extract information about cryptographic keys?

A. Timing analysis attack

B. Differential power analysis attack

C. Simple power analysis attack

D. Electromagnetic emanation attack

52. Which of these physical security devices is approved for protecting nonsensitive and unclassified IT assets?

A. Smart cards

B. Memory cards

C. Hardware tokens

D. Physical tokens

53. From a cryptographic module's physical security perspective, tamper-evident seals or pick-resistant locks are placed on covers or doors to protect against unauthorized physical access to which of the following?

A. Environmental equipment

B. Critical security parameters

C. Configuration management system

D. Data center furniture

54. Which of these physical security devices possess integrated computing capabilities?

    A. Smart cards

    B. Memory cards

    C. Hardware tokens

    D. Physical tokens

55. Which physical security devices are suitable for safeguarding IT assets with a low risk and confidentiality level?

    A. Smart cards

    B. Memory cards

    C. Hardware tokens

    D. Physical tokens

56. Distributed system security services can be no stronger than the underlying

    A. Hardware components

    B. Firmware components

    C. Operating system

    D. Application system

57. What five aspects should a physical security plan focus on when deliberating on threats and the countermeasures to be implemented?

    A. Prevent, Identify, Respond, Sustain, and Preserve

    B. Discourage, Delay, Respond, Sustain, and Preserve

    C. Discourage, Delay, Identify, Evaluate, and Respond

    D. Identify, Delay, Evaluate, Respond, and Validate

58. What is the best definition of Faraday cage?

    A. A structure offering complex access control, including man traps

    B. A shield that prohibits any emanations from leaving or infiltrating the enclosed space

    C. A wired, cage-enclosed room that prohibits unauthorized access and has a single entry point

    D. Copper shielding around twisted-pair wiring that provides extra protection from emanations and adds strength

59. What two categories do uninterruptible power supplies (UPS) fall into?

    A. Inbuilt and external

    B. Continuous and disconnected

    C. Inbuilt and disconnected

    D. Continuous and standby

60. Can you name the four necessary elements for a fire?

    A. Fuel, oxygen, contaminants, and chemicals

    B. Fuel, chemical reaction, water, and temperature

    C. Oxygen, fuel, Halon, and temperature

    D. Fuel, oxygen, temperature, and chemical reaction

61. What are the five classes of fire?

    A. A, B, C, D, K

    B. A, B, C, D, E

C. A, B, C, D, F

D. L, M, N, O

62. What four main outcomes should a suppressant agent achieve either independently or in collaboration with another agent?

   A. Lower the temperature, reduce the smoke, minimize free radicals, disrupt chemical reactions

   B. Flood the environment, capture the smoke, control the flame, open doors in fail-safe mode

   C. Lower the temperature, decrease the oxygen supply, reduce the fuel supply, interfere with the chemical reaction

   D. Simply extinguish the fire

63. What purpose do security zones serve?

   A. Security zones differentiate varying security levels within a premise.

   B. Security zones are regions where tailgating is prohibited.

   C. Security zones necessitate armed guards at the entrance.

   D. Security zones refer to complete walls that segregate individuals into their respective departments.

64. Where should a data center ideally be situated within a facility?

   A. A data center should be in a separate facility and should not be merged with any other function of an organization.

   B. A data center should be situated in the basement of a facility, underground for added protection.

   C. A data center should be situated on the top floor of the building to ensure that intruders cannot access it from the ground.

   D. A data center should be situated in the center of the facility.

65. What element does not belong in a security domain?

   A. Adaptability

   B. Domain parameters

   C. Customized protections

   D. Domain interrelationships

66. What is external to the trusted computing base (TCB)?

   A. Memory channel

   B. Exploitable channel

   C. Communications channel

   D. Security-compliant channel

67. Which is not an example of a first line of defense?

   A. Physical security

   B. Network monitors

C. Software testing

D. Quality assurance

68. From a security perspective, what acts as a first line of defense?

    A. Remote server

    B. Web server

    C. Firewall

    D. Secure shell program

69. Within a fire suppression setting, how would you define a dry pipe?

    A. A sprinkler system where water is introduced into the pipes only when an automatic sensor detects a fire in the vicinity

    B. A sprinkler system with water inside the pipe, but the exterior of the pipe remains dry

    C. A Halon gas system incorporating a dry pipe

    D. A carbon dioxide (CO2) gas system that employs a dry chemical to quench a fire

70. Generally, what is the safest method to extract heat from a fire?

    A. Water

    B. Carbon dioxide

    C. Soda ash

    D. Halon gas

71. What is an electric power undervoltage referred to as?

A. Brownout

B. Blackout

C. Burnout

D. Dropout

72. Which type of fire is most prevalent?

A. Furniture fires

B. Electrical fires

C. Paper fires

D. Gasoline fires

73. Which stage of fire does not generate smoke?

A. Incipient stage

B. Smoldering stage

C. Flame stage

D. Heat stage

74. What component of a water sprinkler system comprises fire-triggered devices?

A. Water supply

B. Water heads

C. Water control valves

D. Alarm system

75. What is the initial action to take in the event of a fire?

    A. Report the fire.

    B. Extinguish the fire.

    C. Remain calm.

    D. Avoid using elevators.

76. Which term refers to an organization's certainty in its controls meeting security requirements?

    A. Trust

    B. Credentialing

    C. Verification

    D. Assurance

77. What kind of security weakness are developers most prone to introduce into their code when trying to simplify their access for testing purposes in their software?

    A. Maintenance hook

    B. Cross-site scripting

    C. SQL injection

    D. Buffer overflow

78. If Alice sends an encrypted message to Bob, what key does she use to encrypt the message?

    A. Alice's public key

    B. Alice's private key

    C. Bob's public key

    D. Bob's private key

79. When Bob receives the encrypted message from Alice, what key does he use to decrypt the message's plaintext content?

    A. Alice's public key

    B. Alice's private key

    C. Bob's public key

    D. Bob's private key

80. In this scenario, which key would Bob not have access to?

    A. Alice's public key

    B. Alice's private key

    C. Bob's public key

    D. Bob's private key

81. Bouke has discovered a SQL injection vulnerability in an application within his organization. Which of the following measures is not an appropriate response to this vulnerability?

    A. Upgrading the version of the database

    B. Utilizing parameterized queries

    C. Reengineering the web application

    D. Implementing stored procedures

82. Gina wants to send an encrypted message to her coworker, Eric, ensuring both confidentiality and authenticity. She plans to encrypt the message and append a digital signature to achieve this. What cryptographic goal does the digital signature fulfill?

A. Non-repudiation

B. Integrity

C. Confidentiality

D. Authentication

83. To create a secure message digest for a digital signature, which of the following cryptographic functions might Gina use?

A. SHA

B. AES

C. MD5

D. RSA

84. In a secure communication scenario, Bouke wants to send an encrypted message to Hayate and also provide a digital signature to ensure authenticity. They are using a public key infrastructure where each person has a pair of keys: a public key known to everyone and a private key known only to the individual. Consider the following questions based on this scenario:

To encrypt the message content, ensuring that only Hayate can decrypt it, which key should Bouke use?

A. Bouke's private key

B. Hayate's public key

C. Hayate's private key

D. Bouke's public key

85. To create the digital signature, allowing Hayate to verify that the message indeed came from Bouke, which key should Bouke use?

    A. Hayate's private key

    B. Hayate's public key

    C. Bouke's public key

    D. Bouke's private key

86. Which security model property dictates that an individual should not have read access to objects at a lower security level than their own?

    A. Integrity Property

    B. Security Property

    C. Simple Security Property

    D. Simple Integrity Property

87. Which ring houses the operating system kernel in systems that implement the ring protection model?

    A. Ring 3

    B. Ring 1

    C. Ring 2

    D. Ring 0

88. In the context of VM escape attacks, which component prevents such attacks?

    A. Guest operating system

    B. Hypervisor

    C. Virtual security module

    D. Host operating system

89. When a web browser verifies a website's digital certificate, which key does it use?

    A. Server's public key

    B. Certificate authority's (CA's) public key

    C. CA's private key

    D. Server's private key

90. Who are the stakeholders involved in the architecture of a secure network?

    A. Suppliers of the company

    B. Operators of the system

    C. Developers of the software

    D. All individuals invested in the system's functionality or usability

91. What is the term for computers utilizing multiple CPUs to enhance performance?

    A. Multiprocessing computers

    B. Computers with multiple CPUs

    C. Multithreaded computers

    D. Multiheaded computers

92. What loads the kernel when a computer is switched on and proceeds to boot the Linux operating system?

    A. BIOS

    B. MBR

    C. UEFI

    D. USER

93. What is the primary difference between a virtual machine and a container?

  A. Containers include an operating system, while virtual machines do not.

  B. Virtual machines are platform independent, while containers are not.

  C. Virtual machines include their own operating system, while containers share the host's operating system.

  D. Containers are less resource-intensive than virtual machines.

94. How does the Internet of Things (IoT) influence data management?

  A. It decreases the amount of data generated.

  B. It increases the need for real-time processing.

  C. It makes data management less complex.

  D. It reduces the need for data storage.

95. What is a key benefit of cloud computing?

  A. Increased infrastructure cost

  B. Limited scalability

  C. Lower maintenance responsibility

  D. Increased data security risk

96. What is a primary security concern when using containerization?

  A. Increased complexity of network configuration

  B. Difficulty in monitoring application performance

C. Vulnerabilities in the shared host operating system

D. Reduced data isolation compared to traditional virtualization

97. What does the term "elasticity" refer to in the context of cloud computing?

A. The ability to handle varying workloads by dynamically allocating and deallocating resources.

B. The ability to store large amounts of data.

C. The ability to operate without Internet connectivity.

D. The ability to recover quickly from hardware failures.

98. What is the primary function of a hypervisor in virtualization?

A. It provides a graphical interface for managing virtual machines.

B. It manages the virtual machines and allocates host system resources to them.

C. It encrypts the data stored on virtual machines.

D. It provides network connectivity for virtual machines.

99. What is the main advantage of containerization?

A. Containers use more resources than virtual machines.

B. Containers are more isolated than virtual machines.

C. Containers start up faster than virtual machines.

D. Containers are harder to manage than virtual machines.

100.   In IoT, what is the role of an edge device?

A. It serves as the central hub that connects all other devices.

B. It processes and analyzes data locally before sending it to the network.

C. It provides security for the IoT network.

D. It stores all the data generated by the IoT devices.

101.   What is the main reason to use a multi-cloud strategy?

A. To make applications run faster

B. To reduce the dependence on a single cloud provider

C. To simplify the management of cloud resources

D. To make the transition to the cloud easier

102.   What is "Docker" in the context of containerization?

A. A type of virtual machine

B. An operating system designed for containers

C. A platform used to develop and manage containers

D. A programming language used to create containerized applications

Answers

1. Answer: B. SABSA

   Explanation: The Sherwood Applied Business Security Architecture (SABSA) is a framework and methodology for enterprise security architecture and service management. It provides a holistic, business-driven approach to security architecture, encompassing everything from assessing business requirements to implementation and metrics.

2. Answer: C. Service transition

   Explanation: Service transition, as per ITIL's Service Portfolio, is primarily tasked with managing the transition of a service from design and development into operational status.

3. Answer: D. Threat modeling, data classification, and risk assessments

   Explanation: Threat modeling, data classification, and risk assessments effectively capture detailed security requirements. They help understand the threats, classify data based on sensitivity, and assess the risks associated with potential threats.

4. Answer: B. ISO 27001

   Explanation: ISO 27001 is an internationally recognized standard that provides guidelines for implementing an Information Security Management System (ISMS) in an organization. It is focused on standardization and certification of an organization's ISMS.

5. Answer: B. Security policy

Explanation: A security policy outlines the
rules, practices, and procedures that need to
be implemented to ensure that the security
requirements of an organization are met.

6. Answer: D. Matrix-based

Explanation: A matrix-based model allows for a
two-dimensional grouping of individual subjects
into roles, and the roles are then granted access to
objects.

7. Answer: D. Bell-LaPadula

Explanation: The Bell-LaPadula model is a
confidentiality model that provides a rule known
as the "no write down" policy (also known as the *
property), which prevents information flow from
a higher classification level to a lower one. In this
context, it ensures that a subject with 'Secret'
clearance can only write to 'Secret' or 'Top Secret'
classified objects but not to 'Public' classified ones.

8. Answer: D. Strong * property

Explanation: The Strong * property, which prevents
a subject from reading information at a lower
integrity level (no read down), is unique to the Biba
Integrity Model.

9. Answer: A. Brewer-Nash

Explanation: The Brewer-Nash or the "Chinese Wall"
model is designed to prevent conflict of interest by
prohibiting access to sensitive information beyond a

certain point. This makes it suitable for shared data hosting environments where data from different customers needs to be isolated.

10. Answer: D. Graham-Denning

Explanation: The Graham-Denning model is mainly concerned with how subjects and objects are created and deleted and how rights are assigned. It provides a set of basic operations that can be performed on a subject or an object, ensuring secure state transitions.

11. Answer: A. An attack followed by a breach

Explanation: A penetration in information systems security is typically defined as an attack that successfully breaches system defenses.

12. Answer: D. Managing data analysis

Explanation: The primary objectives of computer-based information systems security are to protect the system's assets, ensure the accuracy and reliability of data and processes, and guarantee system availability. Controlling data analysis, while important, does not directly align with these core objectives.

13. Answer: A. Eliminating or reducing known vulnerabilities

Explanation: A Plan of Action and Milestones (POA&M) document is primarily used to identify and track the progress of efforts to reduce or eliminate known vulnerabilities within a system.

14. Answer: B. A vulnerability combined with a threat

Explanation: Exposure in information systems security refers to the condition when a threat can potentially exploit a vulnerability.

15. Answer: A. Supportive controls

Explanation: Supportive controls are designed to be pervasive and interact with other controls in the system, providing a safety net that enhances other risk mitigation efforts.

16. Answer: A. Top-down process

Explanation: Information security should follow a top-down approach, where the initiative and direction come from the highest levels of management, ensuring organizational-wide commitment and alignment.

17. Answer: B. Tunnel mode

Explanation: Tunnel mode in IPSec protects the entire IP packet, including the source and destination IP addresses, by encapsulating it within a new IP packet.

18. Answer: A. The certificate revocation list (CRL)

Explanation: The certificate revocation list (CRL) is a list of certificates the certificate authority revoked before their scheduled expiration date. This is where to check if an issuer has retracted its trust for a given certificate.

19. Answer: C. The key is tied to a certificate.

    Explanation: The one-time pad is a type of encryption where a key, as long as the message and used only once, is combined with the plaintext message to produce the ciphertext. The key is not tied to a certificate in this type of encryption.

20. Answer: C. A birthday attack

    Explanation: A birthday attack is a cryptographic attack that exploits the mathematics behind the birthday problem in probability theory. The attacker attempts to find two inputs producing the same hash, known as a hash collision. This is significantly easier to achieve than breaking the hash function by brute force.

21. Answer: B. Sender's private key, recipient's public key, and a hashing algorithm

    Explanation: To create a signed and sealed message, the sender's private key is used for signing, the recipient's public key for encryption, and a hashing algorithm for generating a message digest.

22. Answer: D. Chosen ciphertext

    Explanation: A chosen ciphertext attack involves an attacker choosing ciphertexts to decrypt to reveal the sender's symmetric key or plaintext. By analyzing the decrypted results, the attacker may be able to deduce the key or the original plaintext.

23. Answer: A. Counter mode

Explanation: Counter mode (CTR) is considered the fastest and most secure mode of symmetric key block ciphers because it transforms the block cipher into a stream cipher, allowing for parallel processing and increased performance.

24. Answer: C. Pseudo-random number generation

Explanation: In modern symmetric key cryptosystems, the S-box (substitution box) uses pseudo-random number generation to create a nonlinear substitution function, increasing the cipher's complexity and security.

25. Answer: C. Executes multiple instructions simultaneously

Explanation: A superscalar processor can execute multiple instructions simultaneously by utilizing multiple execution units, improving performance and processing capabilities.

26. Answer: A. Backdoors

Explanation: Backdoors are intentionally created shortcuts or bypasses left in software by developers, often for debugging or testing purposes. However, when left in the released software, they can pose security risks.

27. Answer: C. Covert channel attack

Explanation: A covert channel attack involves using communication channels to transmit unauthorized data, often by hiding it within seemingly legitimate traffic, like malformed TCP ACK packets.

28. Answer: C. ITSEC

Explanation: The Information Technology Security Evaluation Criteria (ITSEC) evaluates functionality and assurance independently, providing a more flexible and comprehensive assessment framework.

29. Answer: A. Bell-LaPadula

Explanation: The Bell-LaPadula model was the first formal model focused on maintaining confidentiality. It's most known for its "no read up, no write down" (also called the * property) principle, which prevents data from being moved to less classified or trusted domains.

30. Answer: B. Clark-Wilson

Explanation: The Clark-Wilson model is an integrity-based model developed for commercial applications. It works on the principle of well-formed transactions and separation of duties to maintain data integrity.

31. Answer: C. Confidentiality

Explanation: The Biba model primarily addresses integrity, not confidentiality. It is best known for its "no write up, no read down" principle, which helps prevent data corruption.

32. Answer: D. Brewer-Nash

Explanation: The Brewer-Nash model is also known as the Chinese Wall model. It's designed to prevent conflicts of interest by restricting access to potentially compromising information.

33. Answer: B. Red Book

    Explanation: The Red Book, or the Trusted
    Network Interpretation (TNI), extends the Orange
    Book (TCSEC) concepts to networked systems,
    evaluating integrity and availability within the
    network environment. The Orange Book primarily
    focuses on confidentiality, while the Red Book
    considers additional factors, including integrity and
    availability.

34. Answer: D. No downward write

    Explanation: The * property, also known as the "no
    write down" or "star-property" rule, in the Bell-
    LaPadula model prevents the information from
    being written down to a lower security level, which
    could lead to unauthorized access.

35. Answer: B. No upward write

    Explanation: The simple integrity property in the
    Biba model, also known as the "no write up" rule,
    prevents a subject at a lower integrity level from
    modifying an object at a higher integrity level.

36. Answer: D. Guards

    Explanation: Guards are security mechanisms that
    can control and manage the flow of information
    between different mandatory access control (MAC)
    systems, especially when those systems operate
    under different security policies or classification
    levels. They ensure that the data being transferred
    complies with the security policies of both the
    sending and receiving systems, thus bridging
    disparate MAC systems.

37. Answer: A. Dedicated

Explanation: In the "Dedicated" security mode of operation, all users must have a valid clearance, formal access approval, and a valid need to know for all data processed in the system.

38. Answer: B. Clark-Wilson

Explanation: The Clark-Wilson model uses the concept of transformational procedures (TLC), certified programs that enforce the integrity policies of the system.

39. Answer: A. 4950

Explanation: DES is a symmetric encryption method, meaning each pair of users needs a unique key. The number of keys needed for n users in a symmetric system is n*(n-1)/2. So for 100 users, that would be 100*(100-1)/2 = 4950.

40. Answer: B. Cryptanalysis

Explanation: Cryptanalysis refers to the study of cryptographic systems to understand how they work and find a way to recover plaintext from ciphertext without necessarily knowing the key.

41. Answer: D. Replay attack

Explanation: A replay attack occurs when an attacker intercepts session keys and reuses them later to impersonate a user or gain unauthorized access to information.

42. Answer: C. Key management

    Explanation: While symmetric encryption methods such as AES, DES, or RC4 have many advantages like speed and efficiency, they also have a significant drawback – key management. This is because every pair of users who wish to communicate securely must have a unique key shared between them and only them. This leads to a rapid growth in the number of keys as the number of users increases.

43. Answer: D. RSA

    Explanation: RSA (Rivest-Shamir-Adleman) is not a symmetric algorithm. It's an asymmetric encryption algorithm. Asymmetric encryption uses two keys, a public key for encryption and a private key for decryption, while symmetric encryption uses the same key for both encryption and decryption.

44. Answer: D. Replay attack

    Explanation: In a replay attack, an attacker intercepts session keys and reuses them later, impersonating a user to gain unauthorized access to a system or network.

45. Answer: C. Key management

    Explanation: Key management is a significant challenge in symmetric encryption. Because each pair of users needs a unique key, the number of keys required grows quickly as the number of users increases. This can make the distribution and storage of keys difficult.

46. Answer: D. RSA

    Explanation: RSA is not a symmetric algorithm but an asymmetric one. Asymmetric algorithms, like RSA, use different keys for encryption and decryption, while symmetric algorithms use the same key.

47. Answer: A. Cryptographic modules with a single chip

    Explanation: Due to their compact size and integrated functionality, single-chip cryptographic modules are often used in devices such as encrypting routers. They provide robust security features while maintaining the efficiency of the device.

48. Answer: B. Noninvasive attack

    Explanation: Noninvasive attacks aim to exploit a cryptographic module's vulnerabilities without requiring physical contact with the module's internal components. These attacks often use power consumption analysis or electromagnetic emissions to extract sensitive data.

49. Answer: C. Embedded cryptographic modules with multiple chips

    Explanation: Multiple-chip embedded cryptographic modules are often used in adapters and expansion boards because they can be integrated into the existing hardware, providing robust security without requiring additional components.

50. Answer: B. Tamper evidence

Explanation: Tamper evidence refers to visible signs that someone has tried to interfere with the physical security of a cryptographic module. This could include broken seals or damage to the casing of the module.

51. Answer: B. Differential power analysis attack

Explanation: Differential power analysis attacks involve studying the variations in a cryptographic module's power consumption to infer information about the cryptographic keys being used. By examining how power usage changes when different keys are used, it is sometimes possible to deduce the keys themselves.

52. Answer: C. Hardware tokens

Explanation: Hardware tokens are physical devices that generate a unique code to authenticate a user's identity. They are typically used in addition to a password as part of two-factor authentication. While they can provide a high level of security, they are often used for protecting unclassified and nonsensitive IT assets because they don't require sophisticated infrastructure and are easy to use.

53. Answer: B. Critical security parameters

Explanation: Tamper-evident seals and pick-resistant locks typically protect critical security parameters within a cryptographic module. These parameters may include cryptographic keys and other sensitive information necessary for the module's operation. Unauthorized access to these parameters could compromise the module's security.

54. Answer: A. Smart cards

Explanation: Smart cards have integrated circuits (chips) to process data. This processing capability makes smart cards a versatile tool for security, as they can be programmed to perform various functions, such as authentication or data storage, securely.

55. Answer: D. Physical tokens

Explanation: While offering a certain level of security, physical tokens are generally more straightforward and less sophisticated than alternatives such as smart cards or hardware tokens. As such, they are often used in contexts where the level of risk and the need for confidentiality are relatively low.

56. Answer: C. Operating system

Explanation: The operating system plays a crucial role in enforcing security controls, as it manages hardware resources and provides services for the execution of applications. Therefore, the security of a distributed system is heavily reliant on the security of the underlying operating system. Despite having robust hardware or well-designed applications, the entire distributed system's security is at risk if the operating system is vulnerable.

57. Answer: C. Discourage, Delay, Identify, Evaluate, and Respond

    Explanation: A comprehensive physical security plan should aim to deter potential threats, delay any attempted breaches, detect any anomalies or breaches, assess the situation accurately, and respond effectively to mitigate the threat or damage.

58. Answer: B. A shield that prohibits any emanations from leaving or infiltrating the enclosed space

    Explanation: A Faraday cage is a protective enclosure that blocks electromagnetic fields. It distributes charges or radiation around the cage's exterior, thus providing a zone within the cage where the electromagnetic field does not penetrate.

59. Answer: B. Continuous and disconnected

    Explanation: An online (continuous) UPS maintains power to the system by continually supplying power from its inverter, while an offline (disconnected) UPS only comes into operation when it detects a loss of power from the primary source.

60. Answer: D. Fuel, oxygen, temperature, and chemical reaction

    Explanation: A fire requires four elements, often referred to as the fire tetrahedron: fuel (something to burn), oxygen (to sustain the combustion), heat (enough to make the fuel ignite), and a chemical reaction (between the fuel and oxygen).

61. Answer: A. A, B, C, D, K

    Explanation: Fires are classified into five categories based on the type of fuel involved. These categories are Class A (common combustibles), Class B (flammable liquids/gases), Class C (energized electrical equipment), Class D (combustible metals), and Class K (cooking oils and fats).

62. Answer: C. Lower the temperature, decrease the oxygen supply, reduce the fuel supply, and interfere with the chemical reaction

    Explanation: The primary goal of a fire suppressant agent is to extinguish the fire. This is achieved through various means, such as reducing the temperature (removing the heat source), decreasing the oxygen supply (releasing the oxygen), reducing the fuel supply (removing the fuel), and interfering with the chemical reaction (which sustains the fire).

63. Answer: A. Security zones differentiate varying security levels within a premise.

    Explanation: Security zones are defined areas within a facility that provide varying levels of security based on the sensitivity of the assets they contain. These zones allow for implementing specific security controls that are most appropriate for the assets within that zone.

64. Answer: D. A data center should be situated in the center of the facility.

    Explanation: Ideally, a data center should be located in the center of a building. This central location protects the most from external threats such as natural disasters or intrusion. It also ensures the shortest possible cable runs to the rest of the building, which can improve network performance.

65. Answer: A. Adaptability

    Explanation: A security domain is a grouping of systems and networks under a single security policy managed by a single authority. Key elements include domain parameters (the characteristics of the domain), tailored protections (specific security measures for the domain), and domain interrelationships (how this domain interacts with others). Flexibility or adaptability is not a key element, as the security policy should be strict, and compliance is mandatory.

66. Answer: B. Exploitable channel

    Explanation: The trusted computing base (TCB) is the set of all hardware, firmware, and software components critical to its security, namely, those that deal with control and enforcement of access. An exploitable channel, such as a covert channel or a channel vulnerable to attacks, exists outside the TCB.

67. Answer: D. Quality assurance

Explanation: Physical security, network monitors, and software testing all act as a first line of defense as they are proactive measures to prevent security incidents. Quality assurance, while important, is a broader concept that doesn't necessarily directly deal with security.

68. Answer: C. Firewall

Explanation: A firewall is the first line of defense in a network's security infrastructure. It filters incoming and outgoing traffic based on predetermined security rules, helping to block unauthorized access while permitting outward communication.

69. Answer: A. A sprinkler system where water is introduced into the pipes only when an automatic sensor detects a fire in the vicinity.

Explanation: A dry pipe sprinkler system is a type of fire suppression system that holds air or nitrogen under pressure in the pipes until a fire is detected. When a fire is detected, the pressure in the pipes is reduced, allowing water to flow through.

70. Answer: A. Water

Explanation: Water is typically the safest and most common substance to remove fire heat. It has a high heat capacity and, when applied correctly, can absorb and dissipate heat very effectively. The other options, including carbon dioxide, soda ash, and Halon gas, can pose potential safety and environmental risks.

71. Answer: A. Brownout

Explanation: A brownout is a temporary reduction in voltage within an electrical power supply system, and it is the correct term for an electric power undervoltage (option A). In contrast, a blackout (option B) refers to a total loss of electrical power in a particular area, resulting in a complete electrical service interruption. Burnout (option C) might refer to the failure of an electrical device due to overheating or other factors, but it doesn't describe the condition of the electrical power supply itself. Dropout (option D) doesn't specifically refer to an electric power undervoltage either; it might refer to a momentary signal or power loss in electrical engineering. However, it's not a standard term for describing a reduction in voltage like a brownout. Therefore, a brownout is a term that specifically refers to an electric power undervoltage.

72. Answer: B. Electrical fires

Explanation: Electrical fires are among the most common types of fires, often caused by faulty wiring, overloaded circuits or plugs, and malfunctioning electrical equipment or appliances.

73. Answer: C. Flame stage

Explanation: The flame stage of a fire, also known as the fully developed stage, is characterized by large flames that consume available fuel and oxygen. While this stage can produce gases and some smoke, it is not primarily characterized by smoke production as the other stages are.

74.   Answer: B. Water heads

Explanation: Water heads, also known as sprinkler heads, are the components of a sprinkler system that discharge water when a fire is detected. They are often heat-activated and designed to respond at a predetermined temperature.

75.   Answer: A. Report the fire.

Explanation: The first step in a fire situation is to ensure the fire is reported. This can mean activating the fire alarm, calling the fire department, or alerting others in the building. While the other responses are important, they should occur after the fire has been reported.

76.   Answer: D. Assurance
Explanation: Assurance refers to the level of confidence that an organization's controls (policies, procedures, and technology) adequately protect its information and systems. Trust, credentialing, and verification are all elements of building assurance, but they do not represent the overall confidence level in the security controls.

77.   Answer: A. Maintenance hook

Explanation: A maintenance hook is a type of software vulnerability that developers might inadvertently leave in the code, often to allow easier access for testing or debugging. While useful during development, these hooks can provide an avenue for unauthorized access if not removed before the software is released.

78. Answer: C. Bob's public key

Explanation: In public key cryptography, Alice would use Bob's public key to encrypt the message. This ensures that only Bob, who has the corresponding private key, can decrypt the message.

79. Answer: D. Bob's private key

Explanation: Bob would use his private key to decrypt the message. Since Alice used Bob's public key to encrypt the message, only Bob's private key can decrypt it.

80. Answer: B. Alice's private key

Explanation: In public key cryptography, each person has a pair of keys: a public key and a private key. The private key is kept secret and not shared, so Bob would not have access to Alice's private key. He would, however, have access to Alice's public key, as well as his own public and private keys.

81. Answer: A. Upgrading the version of the database

Explanation: While upgrading the database version may include patches and improvements, it doesn't necessarily fix SQL injection vulnerabilities. These vulnerabilities typically reside in the application layer (how the application interacts with the database), not in the database itself. Using parameterized queries, rewriting the application, or using stored procedures are more effective strategies for mitigating SQL injection vulnerabilities.

82. Answer: A. Non-repudiation

Explanation: Non-repudiation is a property that ensures an action, once done, cannot be denied by the party who did it. By appending a digital signature, Bouke ensures that the message cannot be denied as coming from her, fulfilling the goal of non-repudiation.

83. Answer: A. SHA

Explanation: SHA (Secure Hash Algorithm) is a family of cryptographic hash functions designed to create a message digest in the digital signature process. AES is a symmetric encryption algorithm, MD5 is a deprecated hash function, and RSA is an asymmetric encryption algorithm.

84. Answer: B. Hayate's public key

Explanation: By using Hayate's public key to encrypt the message, only Hayate, who possesses the corresponding private key, can decrypt it. This ensures that the message remains confidential and can only be read by the intended recipient.

85. Answer: D. Bouke's private key

Explanation: Bouke would use her private key to create a digital signature. Hayate can then use Bouke's public key to verify the signature, confirming that Bouke indeed signed the message and has not been altered in transit. This process ensures the authenticity and integrity of the message.

86. Answer: C. Simple Security Property

Explanation: The Simple Security Property, a component of the Bell-LaPadula model, states that a subject cannot read an object at a lower security level. This is often referred to as "no read down" policy.

87. Answer: D. Ring 0

Explanation: In the ring protection model, Ring 0 is the highest level of privilege and is where the operating system kernel resides.

88. Answer: B. Hypervisor

Explanation: A hypervisor, also known as a virtual machine monitor, is a type of software that creates and manages virtual machines. It is responsible for maintaining separation and isolation between VMs and preventing VM escape attacks where an attacker breaks out from a VM to attack the host system or other VMs.

89. Answer: B. Certificate authority's (CA's) public key

Explanation: The browser uses the public key of the certificate authority (CA) that issued the server's certificate to verify the digital signature on the certificate. This confirms that the certificate is valid and was indeed issued by the trusted CA.

90. Answer: D. All individuals invested in the system's functionality or usability

Explanation: A secure network architecture involves various stakeholders, including suppliers, system operators, software developers, and essentially anyone concerned with the functionality or usability of the system. All of these stakeholders play a role in maintaining the security and integrity of the network.

91.   Answer: A. Multiprocessing computers

Explanation: Multiprocessing computers are systems that use more than one CPU to perform tasks. This arrangement allows for the simultaneous processing of multiple tasks, thus enhancing overall performance.

92.   Answer: C. UEFI

Explanation: UEFI (Unified Extensible Firmware Interface) is a specification that defines a software interface between an operating system and platform firmware. In modern systems, UEFI replaces the BIOS (Basic Input/Output System) for initializing the system hardware and loading the kernel of the operating system during the boot process. The MBR (Master Boot Record) is a section of a system's hard drive that contains information about partitioning the hard drive and the boot loader program code. However, it doesn't directly load the kernel.

93.   Answer: C. Virtual machines include their own operating system, while containers share the host's operating system.

Explanation: Virtual machines (VMs) and containers are both methods to isolate applications and their dependencies into their own spaces. However, unlike VMs, which include a full copy of an operating system along with the application and its dependencies, containers share the host's operating system, which makes them more lightweight and faster to start than VMs.

94.   Answer: B. It increases the need for real-time processing.

Explanation: The Internet of Things (IoT) involves interconnected devices that generate a significant amount of data. This increase in data often requires real-time processing to extract valuable insights and make timely decisions.

95.   Answer: C. Lower maintenance responsibility

Explanation: One of the main benefits of cloud computing is that it lowers the maintenance responsibility for users. The cloud service provider handles much of the infrastructure maintenance, including hardware, software updates, and security measures.

96.   Answer: C. Vulnerabilities in the shared host operating system

Explanation: Because containers share the host's operating system, any vulnerabilities present in the host OS could potentially affect all containers running on it. Therefore, maintaining the security of the host OS is crucial when using containerization.

97.   Answer: A. The ability to handle varying workloads by dynamically allocating and deallocating resources.

Explanation: Elasticity in cloud computing refers to the ability to quickly scale computing resources up or down as demand changes, allowing for efficient resource utilization and cost savings.

98. Answer: B. It manages the virtual machines and allocates host system resources to them.

Explanation: The hypervisor, also known as a virtual machine monitor, is a key component of any virtualization effort. Its primary function is to manage the virtual machines running on a host and to allocate physical resources such as CPU, memory, and storage to these VMs.

99. Answer: C. Containers start up faster than virtual machines.

Explanation: Containers are designed to be lightweight and share the host system's operating system, which allows them to start up much faster than virtual machines. This makes containers ideal for applications that require rapid scaling.

100. Answer: B. It processes and analyzes data locally before sending it to the network.

Explanation: An edge device in IoT is a device that sits at the boundary between the local network and the broader Internet. It processes and analyzes data locally (at the "edge" of the network) before sending it to the network, reducing bandwidth usage and latency and often improving security.

101.   Answer: B. To reduce the dependence on a single cloud provider

Explanation: A multi-cloud strategy uses two or more cloud computing services from different cloud vendors. This approach helps to avoid the risk of a cloud service outage or a vendor lock-in situation, and it also allows businesses to leverage the unique and best features offered by different cloud providers.

102.   Answer: C. A platform used to develop and manage containers

Explanation: Docker is a popular open source platform for developing, shipping, and running container applications. It enables applications to be packaged with their dependencies into a standardized software development unit, which helps simplify the process of deploying and running applications across different environments.

CHAPTER 6

Communications and Network Security

In the ever-evolving landscape of information technology, Communications and Network Security is a vital domain in professional practice and a significant portion of the CISSP examination. This domain delves into the intricate design, implementation, and safeguarding of network systems, with an unwavering commitment to the triad of information security: confidentiality, integrity, and availability.

The importance of this domain cannot be overstated, as modern organizations increasingly rely on interconnected systems and networks. Network security, whether a multinational corporation or a small local business, is paramount. The threats are real and ever present, ranging from unauthorized access to sophisticated cyberattacks that can weaken an entire organization.

This chapter will equip you with the knowledge and skills to navigate this complex field. It will provide a comprehensive overview of essential concepts, including but not limited to network architecture, transmission methods, transport formats, and security measures. You'll explore various network devices, protocols, and security controls, understanding how they interact to form a secure and resilient network infrastructure.

Furthermore, this chapter will offer valuable insights and tips tailored to the CISSP exam. You'll find guidance on what to focus on, common pitfalls to avoid, and strategies to apply during the examination.

© Mohamed Aly Bouke 2023

M. A. Bouke, *CISSP Exam Certification Companion*, Certification Study Companion Series, https://doi.org/10.1007/979-8-8688-0057-3_6

Including practice questions with detailed explanations will reinforce your understanding and provide a practical application of the theoretical concepts.

As you progress through this chapter, you will cultivate a robust understanding of Communications and Network Security, aligning with the CISSP Common Body of Knowledge. Your mastery of this domain will set the stage for success in the examination and lay a strong foundation for your professional career in information security. The insights and practice questions provided herein are designed to reinforce key concepts and prepare you for the real-world challenges that await in the field of network security.

Network Architecture and Design

Network architecture and design are central to the effective operation of modern organizations, and they form a critical part of the CISSP examination. These concepts encompass the planning, configuring, and implementing of network components, protocols, and technologies. Let's explore the fundamental building blocks that underpin network architecture and design, as summarized in Table 6-1.

Table 6-1. *Fundamental Concepts in Network Architecture and Design*

Concept	Description	Examples or Details
Devices	Hardware that facilitates communication within or between networks	Routers (inter-network communication), switches (intra-network traffic), firewalls (security), servers (services)
Media	Physical or wireless connections used for communication	Physical: twisted pair, coaxial, fiber optic; wireless: radio frequency (RF) signals
Protocols	Rules and standards governing communication between devices	IP (addressing), TCP (reliable data delivery), UDP (connectionless protocol)
Topologies	Arrangements of devices in a network, affecting performance and scalability	Star (central hub), ring (closed loop), bus (single central cable), mesh (multiple connections)

- **Devices**: Network devices are essential for routing, managing, securing, and providing services within a network. For the CISSP exam, understanding the specific functions and applications of routers, switches, firewalls, and servers is crucial, as outlined in Table 6-1.

- **Media**: The choice of network media can significantly impact a network's speed, reliability, and security. Exam candidates should be familiar with physical and wireless media characteristics, as detailed in Table 6-1.

- **Protocols**: Protocols are the glue that holds networks together, defining how devices communicate and interact. Understanding protocols like IP, TCP, and UDP is vital for the exam, including their roles in addressing, error handling, and data delivery (see Table 6-1).

- **Topologies**: Network topologies shape the structure and behavior of a network. Knowledge of common topologies like star, ring, bus, and mesh, including their advantages and disadvantages, is essential for the exam, as described in Table 6-1.

As you delve into this chapter, you will cultivate a comprehensive understanding of these concepts, aligning with the CISSP Common Body of Knowledge. This mastery will prepare you for success in the examination and lay a strong foundation for your professional career in information security. The insights provided herein, including Table 6-1, are designed to reinforce key concepts and prepare you for the real-world challenges that await in the field of network security.

The OSI Model

The open systems interconnection (OSI) model is a seven-layer conceptual framework that standardizes network functions to enable interoperability between different systems and technologies. This model plays a vital role in understanding how data is processed and transmitted across a network. Table 6-2 provides an overview of the OSI model's layers.

Table 6-2. *Layers of the OSI Model*

Layer	Description	Examples or Details
Physical (Layer 1)	Deals with the physical transmission of data over network media	Signaling, encoding, synchronization
Data Link (Layer 2)	Responsible for error-free data transmission between devices	Data frames, MAC addresses, error detection
Network (Layer 3)	Manages data routing and forwarding between different networks	IP addressing, routing protocols (OSPF, BGP)
Transport (Layer 4)	Ensures reliable end-to-end data delivery and flow control	TCP (reliable), UDP (unreliable), segmentation, sequencing
Session (Layer 5)	Manages the establishment, maintenance, and termination of sessions	Authentication, authorization, synchronization
Presentation (Layer 6)	Translates and formats data for different applications and systems	Data compression, encryption, character encoding
Application (Layer 7)	Provides the interface between the network and user applications	Application-specific protocols (HTTP, FTP), services (DNS, DHCP)

- **Physical Layer (Layer 1)**: The Physical Layer, as described in Table 6-2, is concerned with transmitting raw data bits over the physical medium. This includes aspects such as signaling, encoding, and synchronization. For example, the choice of copper cables or fiber-optic connections would be determined at this layer.

- **Data Link Layer (Layer 2)**: The Data Link Layer ensures that data frames are transmitted without errors between devices on a network. It manages Media Access Control (MAC) addresses and error detection, as outlined in Table 6-2.

- **Network Layer (Layer 3)**: The Network Layer is responsible for routing data packets between different networks. It uses IP addressing and routing protocols like OSPF (Open Shortest Path First) and BGP (Border Gateway Protocol) to find the best path for data, as detailed in Table 6-2.

- **Transport Layer (Layer 4)**: The Transport Layer focuses on reliable data delivery, segmentation, and flow control. Protocols like TCP and UDP operate at this layer, ensuring that data is delivered in the correct sequence and without errors (see Table 6-2).

- **Session Layer (Layer 5)**: The Session Layer manages the connections between devices, including the establishment, maintenance, and termination of sessions. This layer handles authentication and synchronization, as summarized in Table 6-2.

- **Presentation Layer (Layer 6)**: The Presentation Layer translates and formats data for different applications and systems. It deals with data compression, encryption, and character encoding, as described in Table 6-2.

- **Application Layer (Layer 7)**: The Application Layer is the interface between the network and user applications. It supports specific protocols and services like HTTP, FTP, DNS, and DHCP, as detailed in Table 6-2.

Understanding the OSI model is essential for both network design and troubleshooting. It provides a common language and framework for network professionals and is a key concept for the CISSP exam. By studying Table 6-2 and the accompanying explanations, you will understand how the OSI model functions and its relevance in modern networking.

Moreover, Table 6-3 contains standard network devices, their functions, and the OSI model layer they primarily operate at.

Table 6-3. *Common Network Device Layers*

Device	Function	OSI Layer
Hub	Connects multiple devices on a network by repeating incoming data packets to all connected devices	Physical
Repeater	Regenerates and amplifies signal strength in a network segment to extend its reach	Physical
Switch	Connects multiple devices on a network and forwards data packets only to the intended recipient	Data Link

(continued)

Table 6-3. (*continued*)

Device	Function	OSI Layer
Bridge	Connects and filters traffic between two network segments at the Data Link Layer	Data Link
Network Interface Card (NIC)	Enables a device to connect to a network by providing a Physical and Data Link Layer connection	Physical, 2. Data Link
Router	Connects and routes traffic between different networks, often using the IP protocol	Network
Firewall	Monitors and filters incoming and outgoing network traffic based on predefined security rules	Network, 4. Transport and higher
Wireless Access Point (WAP)	Connects wireless devices to a wired network, converting between wired and wireless signals	Data Link
Load Balancer	Distributes network traffic across multiple servers to optimize resource utilization and performance	Transport, 7. Application
Proxy Server	Acts as an intermediary between a client and a server, forwarding client requests and server responses	Application

Additionally, Table 6-4 provides a general overview of some common protocols and their security status. Depending on the specific use case and configuration, some protocols may have additional security features or options that can be implemented.

Table 6-4. *Common Protocols and Security Status*

Protocol	OSI Layer	Secure/Insecure
HTTP	Application	Insecure
HTTPS	Application	Secure
FTP	Application	Insecure
SFTP	Application	Secure
Telnet	Application	Insecure
SSH	Application	Secure
SMTP	Application	Insecure
SMTPS	Application	Secure
POP3	Application	Insecure
POP3S	Application	Secure
IMAP	Application	Insecure
IMAPS	Application	Secure
SNMP	Application	Insecure
SNMPv3	Application	Secure
TCP	Transport	Insecure
UDP	Transport	Insecure
TLS	Transport	Secure
DTLS	Transport	Secure
IP	Network	Insecure
IPSec	Network	Secure
ICMP	Network	Insecure
ARP	Data Link	Insecure
RARP	Data Link	Insecure

- **Exam Tip**

  As a candidate preparing for the CISSP exam, it's
  essential to understand that this exam is not solely
  focused on the technical aspects of information
  security, nor is it a simple memorization test. The
  CISSP exam evaluates your understanding of security
  concepts, principles, and best practices across various
  domains. It emphasizes the importance of being
  familiar with the most popular protocols and their
  implications on security, as this is a security-oriented
  certification.

The exam assesses your ability to think critically and apply your
knowledge to real-world scenarios rather than simply recalling facts or
technical details. It's crucial to develop a strong foundation in information
security concepts and analyze the security implications of different
protocols and technologies. This holistic approach to learning will better
prepare you for the CISSP exam and help you excel in information security.

As you study for the exam, focus on understanding how popular
protocols contribute to or undermine security in various contexts.
Consider how different technologies and configurations can affect security
and the measures that can be taken to mitigate risks. Developing this
security-oriented mindset will be invaluable during the exam and your
career as an information security professional.

The TCP/IP Model

The TCP/IP model, also known as the Internet protocol suite, is a four-
layer model that simplifies and standardizes network communication. It
serves as the foundation for the Internet and aligns closely with the OSI
model. Table 6-5 provides an overview of the TCP/IP model's layers.

Table 6-5. *Layers of the TCP/IP Model*

Layer	Description	Corresponding OSI Layers	Examples or Details
Network Access Layer	Manages physical transmission of data and network access	Physical, Data Link	Framing, addressing, media access
Internet Layer	Handles routing and forwarding of data packets	Network	IP addressing, routing protocols (OSPF, BGP)
Transport Layer	Manages end-to-end data delivery and flow control	Transport	TCP (reliable), UDP (unreliable), segmentation, sequencing
Application Layer	Supports application-specific protocols and handles user applications	Session, presentation, application	Application-specific protocols (HTTP, FTP), services (DNS, DHCP)

- **Network Access Layer**: The Network Access Layer corresponds to the OSI model's Physical and Data Link layers, as described in Table 6-5. It is responsible for the physical transmission of data, including framing, addressing, and media access. This layer ensures data is appropriately formatted and transmitted over the chosen network medium.

- **Internet Layer**: The Internet Layer, equivalent to the OSI model's Network Layer, handles the routing and forwarding of data packets. It uses Internet Protocol (IP) addressing and routing protocols like OSPF and BGP, as detailed in Table 6-5. This layer is essential for directing data across interconnected networks.

- **Transport Layer**: The Transport Layer aligns with the OSI model's Transport Layer, managing end-to-end data delivery and flow control. As discussed in the previous section, it uses protocols such as TCP for reliable communication and UDP for connectionless communication. This layer ensures data segmentation, sequencing, and error recovery, as summarized in Table 6-5.

- **Application Layer**: The Application Layer in the TCP/IP model combines the functions of the OSI model's Session, Presentation, and Application Layers. It supports application-specific protocols like HTTP and FTP and handles user applications and high-level protocols, as described in Table 6-5.

The TCP/IP model provides a more streamlined approach to network communication than the OSI model. It is widely used in modern networking and forms the basis of the Internet. Understanding the TCP/IP model, as outlined in Table 6-5, is vital for network professionals and CISSP exam candidates. This knowledge will enable you to design, implement, and troubleshoot network systems effectively, building on the foundational concepts of TCP and the OSI model.

Communications and Network Security

This section delves into the intricate world of network technologies that form the backbone of modern communication systems. As part of the CISSP exam's core domains, understanding these technologies is a theoretical exercise and a practical necessity for aspiring information security professionals. This section will guide you through the various types of networks, including Local Area Networks (LANs), Wide Area Networks (WANs), and Wireless Local Area Networks (WLANs), among others. Each of these plays a unique role in facilitating communication, and understanding their operation, strengths, and vulnerabilities is essential for designing and protecting secure network systems. From the widely used Ethernet to the revolutionary Software-Defined Networking (SDN), this section offers a detailed exploration of the key concepts, illustrated with practical examples and contextualized for their relevance to the CISSP exam. Whether you are a seasoned network engineer or a newcomer, the insights provided here will enhance your comprehension of network security and prepare you for the challenges and opportunities in this ever-evolving domain.

- **Local Area Networks (LANs):** LAN technologies connect devices within a small geographical area, such as an office building. Ethernet, a widely used LAN technology, operates at the Data Link Layer, using MAC addresses for device identification. For example, switches manage network data traffic by directing frames to their intended destinations based on MAC addresses. Virtual LANs (VLANs) enhance security by logically separating devices within a network, allowing different departments in a company to communicate as if they were on separate physical networks.

- **Wide Area Networks (WANs):** WAN technologies connect devices across large geographical areas, such as between cities or countries. T1/E1 lines, specific to North America and Europe, are high-speed communication lines for voice and data transmission. Multiprotocol Label Switching (MPLS) efficiently routes data in large networks by using labels to direct data packets along predetermined paths. Asynchronous Transfer Mode (ATM) provides high-speed data transfer using fixed-size cells suitable for multimedia applications.

- **Wireless Local Area Networks (WLANs)**: WLANs enable wireless communication within a limited area. Wi-Fi, adhering to the IEEE 802.11 standard, operates in frequency bands like 2.4 and 5 GHz. Wireless access points (WAPs) bridge wired and wireless networks, allowing smartphones and laptops to connect to the network. Security techniques such as WEP and WPA2 encryption protect WLANs from unauthorized access.

- **Converged protocols**: Converged protocols integrate multiple communication methods. Voice over IP (VoIP) allows communication over IP networks, replacing traditional phone lines. IP Multimedia Subsystem (IMS) delivers multimedia services like video conferencing, and Unified Communications (UC) integrates tools like voice, video, and messaging for seamless collaboration.

- **Software-Defined Networking (SDN)**: SDN is a revolutionary network architecture that separates control from data, enabling dynamic networking. It simplifies deployment and management through software-based controllers, allowing network administrators to allocate, deallocate, and shift resources quickly.

- **Radio Frequency Identification (RFID)**: RFID uses electromagnetic fields to identify and track tags on objects. In retail, RFID tags on products enable automated inventory management. Security measures like encryption and authentication protect RFID systems from unauthorized access.

Essential Concepts in Network Security and Management

The integrity of a network is not only about its design but also about its continuous management and the security measures implemented. This section explores the essential network security and management concepts vital for maintaining a robust and reliable network infrastructure:

- **Operation of hardware**: Proper hardware operation is the cornerstone of network reliability. Implementing redundant power systems, such as uninterruptible power supplies (UPS) and backup generators, ensures continuous power and minimizes downtime. Warranty and support agreements with manufacturers safeguard the network's health and functionality.

- **Transmission media**: The choice of transmission media, including copper cables, fiber-optic cables, and wireless connections, significantly impacts the network's speed, distance capabilities, and reliability. Understanding different media properties helps select the right option for specific network requirements.

- **Network access control (NAC) devices**: NAC devices play a crucial role in network security by authenticating users, authorizing access based on roles, and continuously monitoring network activity. They form the first line of defense against unauthorized access and potential threats.

- **Endpoint security**: Protecting endpoint devices like desktops and laptops is vital as they can be entry points for attackers. Implementing antivirus software, firewalls, and regular updates helps maintain overall network security.

Secure Communication Channels in Modern Networking

Securing communication channels across various technologies and platforms is paramount in today's interconnected world. This section delves into the methods and technologies that ensure secure communication in different contexts:

- **Voice communication security**: Encrypting voice calls using protocols like Secure Real-time Transport Protocol (SRTP) prevents unauthorized access and interception, safeguarding privacy in voice communications.

- **Multimedia collaboration security**: Tools for video conferencing and instant messaging often employ end-to-end encryption, user authentication, and access control to secure data and prevent unauthorized access.

- **Remote access security**: Security measures for remote access, such as Virtual Private Networks (VPNs) and multifactor authentication (MFA), ensure that remote connections to the organization's network are secure and verified.

- **Data communications security**: Protocols like HTTPS and TLS are essential for securing data in transit, providing encrypted channels for sensitive information.

- **Virtualized network security**: The dynamic nature of virtualized networks like Software-Defined Networking (SDN) requires specialized security measures, including granular access control, micro-segmentation, and continuous monitoring.

- **Third-party connectivity security**: Integrating external services or partners requires robust security policies, regular assessments, and strict access control measures to ensure secure and compliant connectivity.

Understanding these comprehensive concepts and practices equips information security professionals with the tools to design, implement, and maintain secure systems. This knowledge is foundational for the Communications and Network Security domain of the CISSP exam. Mastery of these concepts positions you to safeguard sensitive data effectively and ensures information systems' confidentiality, integrity, and availability, reflecting the core principles of modern information security.

Summary

In this chapter, we have navigated the intricate landscape of Communications and Network Security, a domain that stands as a cornerstone for the CISSP exam. Our exploration began with the OSI and TCP/IP models, providing a structured understanding of how data travels through various network layers. We then ventured into the diverse world of networks and protocols, unravelling their roles in communication and the imperatives of securing them.

Key Takeaways

- **Understanding the OSI and TCP/IP models**: These frameworks are not merely theoretical constructs but vital tools for comprehending how data is transmitted and processed. They serve as a road map for network professionals, guiding them through the complex interactions within network layers.

- **Exploring network types and protocols**: The types of networks and protocols vary from LAN to WAN, from Ethernet to Wi-Fi. Recognizing their unique characteristics and security needs is paramount for safeguarding communication.

- **Network devices and their functions**: Devices like routers, switches, and firewalls are the building blocks of a network. Knowing how they operate and the OSI layer they primarily function at is essential for a robust network infrastructure.

- **Security implications of popular protocols**: The CISSP exam evaluates your grasp of how protocols can be both an asset and a vulnerability. Understanding the security aspects of protocols like HTTP, FTP, and VoIP is vital for a comprehensive security strategy.

- **Holistic approach to information security**: The CISSP exam transcends technical knowledge or rote memorization. It assesses your ability to think critically, apply real-world solutions, and establish a strong foundation in information security principles.

As you reflect on these key takeaways, consider them isolated facts and interconnected concepts shaping network security. Your preparation for the CISSP exam should be rooted in a deep understanding of these principles, coupled with an ability to apply them in various scenarios. This chapter aims to equip you with the knowledge and insights needed to confidently approach the Communications and Network Security domain, fostering a security-oriented mindset that will serve you well in both the exam and your professional career.

Practice Questions

As you conclude your exploration of the Communications and Network Security domain in this chapter, a new challenge awaits. This section presents a series of practice questions designed to reinforce key concepts, sharpen your analytical skills, and prepare you for the real CISSP exam.

These questions are not merely a test of your knowledge but an integral part of your learning journey. They emulate the style and complexity you will encounter in the full exam samples later in this book, reflecting the depth and breadth of understanding required for success. By attempting all the questions and carefully reviewing the explanations, you will gain insights into areas where you excel and identify those needing further study.

Approach these questions with dedication, curiosity, and a willingness to be challenged. Allow yourself to learn from your mistakes, celebrate your successes, and think critically. Remember, these practice questions are more than a measure of what you know; they are a tool to deepen your understanding and sharpen your readiness.

Your journey through the Communications and Network Security domain has been filled with complex models, diverse network types, essential protocols, and critical security considerations. Now, it's time to put that understanding to the test. Embrace this opportunity to solidify your grasp of this domain. Your commitment to this practice will be a valuable asset as you continue your pursuit of the CISSP certification.

Take your time, reflect on each question, and let these practice questions be a stepping stone toward your success in the CISSP exam and your continued growth as an information security professional.

1. Which device listed as follows does not function at the Data Link or Layer 2?

    A. Hub

    B. Switch

    C. Wireless access point

    D. Bridge

2. Who creates and publishes the OSI model from the following organizations?

    A. IEEE

    B. ISO

    C. IANA

    D. IETF

3. Which protocols work at the Transport Layer, or Layer 4, and offer a best-effort, connectionless method for delivering segments?

    A. ARP

    B. IGMP

    C. TCP

    D. UDP

4. What is the term for the data and header information processed at the Network Layer, or Layer 3, of the OSI model?

    A. Packet

    B. Data stream

C. Frame

D. Segment

5. Which of the following sequences accurately represents the order of the OSI model layers when processing incoming data from the network media?

A. Application, Presentation, Session, Transport, Network, Data Link, Physical

B. Physical, Transport, Network, Data Link, Presentation, Session, Application

C. Application, Session, Presentation, Transport, Network, Data Link, Physical

D. Physical, Data Link, Network, Transport, Session, Presentation, Application

6. Which of the following media types offers the highest protection against the detection of emanations?

A. Coax

B. Shielded twisted pair

C. Unshielded twisted pair

D. Fiber optic

7. Which of the following media access control methods is based on contention?

A. Token-passing bus

B. Carrier Sense Multiple Access with Collision Detection (CSMA/CD)

C. Token-passing ring

D. Polling

8. What filter is used in firewalls to block packets leaving a private network using a public source IP address?

   A. Ingress filter

   B. Content filter

   C. Egress filter

   D. Stateful filter

9. How is a bastion host best described?

   A. A system that has been hardened against attack

   B. A system that uses a default deny rule

   C. A system that performs FQDN-to-IP-address resolution

   D. A system that replaces private IP addresses with public IP addresses as the packet exits the private network

10. Which protocol places a tag in front of the Layer 2 header of a frame to help its transmission through the protocol-compliant cloud?

    A. Multiprotocol Label Switching (MPLS)

    B. Network Address Translation (NAT)

    C. Open Shortest Path First (OSPF)

    D. Dynamic Host Configuration Protocol (DHCP)

11. Which of the following options enables systems to utilize various existing and future mechanisms for authenticating user identities?

A. Zero-knowledge proof

B. Extensible Authentication Protocol (EAP)

C. Challenge Handshake Authentication Protocol (CHAP)

D. Synchronous Optical Network (SONET)

12. Which IEEE specification refers to a wireless access point employing multiple transmitters, receivers, and antenna?

A. 802.11h

B. 802.11j

C. 802.11b

D. 802.11n

13. Which attack from the following options utilizes a collection of compromised computers, known as zombies?

A. Ping of death

B. DDoS attack

C. LAND attack

D. SYN flood

14. On which layer of the OSI reference model is Ethernet (IEEE 802.3) positioned?

A. Layer 1 – Physical Layer

B. Layer 2 – Data Link Layer

C. Layer 3 – Network Layer

D. Layer 4 – Transport Layer

15. What would be considered the BEST proactive network defense strategy?

    A. Redundant firewalls

    B. Business continuity planning

    C. Disallowing P2P traffic

    D. Perimeter surveillance and intelligence gathering

16. In which scenario is the network not the direct target of the attack?

    A. A denial-of-service attack on servers on a network

    B. Hacking into a router

    C. A virus outbreak saturating network capacity

    D. A man-in-the-middle attack

17. What is the MOST effective countermeasure against a distributed denial-of-service (DDoS) attack?

    A. Secret fully qualified domain names (FQDNs)

    B. Redundant network layout

    C. Traffic filtering

    D. Network Address Translation (NAT)

18. Where is the optimal location for network-based intrusion detection systems (NIDS)?

    A. On the network perimeter, to alert the network administrator of all suspicious traffic

    B. On network segments with business-critical systems

C. At the network operations center (NOC)

D. At an external service provider

19. Which combination of endpoint devices would MOST likely be included in a converged IP network?

   A. File server, IP phone, security camera

   B. IP phone, thermostat, cypher lock

   C. Security camera, cypher lock, IP phone

   D. Thermostat, file server, cypher lock

20. What security advantage does fiber-optic cable offer over copper cables?

   A. Fiber optics provides higher bandwidth.

   B. Fiber optics are more difficult to wiretap.

   C. Fiber optics are immune to wiretap.

   D. None – the two are equivalent; network security is independent of the Physical Layer.

21. What devices are best to be included in a robust network perimeter defense strategy?

   A. A boundary router, a firewall, a proxy server

   B. A firewall, a proxy server, a host-based intrusion detection system (HIDS)

   C. A proxy server, a host-based intrusion detection system (HIDS), a firewall

   D. A host-based intrusion detection system (HIDS), a firewall, a boundary router

22. What is the principal security risk associated with wireless LANs?

   A. Lack of physical access control

   B. Demonstrably insecure standards

   C. Implementation weaknesses

   D. War driving

23. Which configuration related to a WLAN's SSID provides adequate security protection?

   A. Using an obscure SSID to confuse and distract an attacker

   B. Not using any SSID at all to prevent an attacker from connecting to the network

   C. Not broadcasting an SSID to make it harder to detect the WLAN

   D. An SSID does not provide protection

24. What is true about IPSec?

   A. It provides mechanisms for authentication and encryption.

   B. It provides mechanisms for non-repudiation.

   C. It will only be deployed with IPv6.

   D. It only authenticates clients against a server.

25. What is the function of a security event management (SEM) service?

   A. Gathers firewall logs for archiving

   B. Aggregates logs from security devices and application servers looking for suspicious activity

C. Reviews access control logs on servers and physical entry points to match user system authorization with physical access permissions

D. Coordination software for security conferences and seminars

26. What is the principal weakness of the Domain Name System (DNS)?

A. Lack of authentication of servers and thereby authenticity of records

B. Its latency, which enables insertion of records between the time when a record has expired and when it is refreshed

C. The fact that it is a simple, distributed, hierarchical database instead of a singular, relational one, thereby giving rise to the possibility of inconsistencies going undetected for a certain amount of time

D. The fact that addresses in email can be spoofed without checking their validity in DNS, caused by the fact that DNS addresses are not digitally signed

27. Which statement about open email relays is incorrect?

A. An open email relay is a server that forwards email from domains other than the ones it serves.

B. Open email relays are a principal tool for distribution of spam.

C. Using a denylist of open email relays provides a secure way for an email administrator to identify open mail relays and filter spam.

D. An open email relay is widely considered a sign of bad system administration.

351

28. How can a botnet be characterized?

    A. A network used solely for internal communications

    B. An automatic security alerting tool for corporate networks

    C. A group of dispersed, compromised machines controlled remotely for illicit reasons

    D. A type of virus

29. Why is a mesh network topology rarely implemented in modern networks?

    A. Cost

    B. Poor redundancy

    C. Throughput

    D. Optical fiber limits

30. What offers the strongest wireless encryption when installing an 801.11n wireless access point?

    A. WPA

    B. WEP

    C. PKI

    D. WPA2

31. What media is best suited in a heavy manufacturing area with substantial electromagnetic radiation and power fluctuations if little traffic degradation is tolerated?

A. Coax cable

B. Wireless

C. Shielded twisted pair

D. Fiber

32. What is true about multilayer protocols like Modbus used in industrial control systems?

A. Often have their own encryption and security like IPv6

B. Are used in modern routers as a routing interface control

C. Are often insecure by their very nature as they were not designed to natively operate over today's IP networks

D. Have largely been retired and replaced with newer protocols such as IPv6 and NetBIOS

33. For a security professional needing to administer a server remotely, assuming they can access the server from their location, what is the BEST approach for access?

A. TELNET

B. SSHv2

C. FTP

D. TFTP

34. As a security consultant for a company that
     requires a secure connection for online financial
     transactions, what Extensible Authentication
     Protocol would you recommend that's the most
     secure but also the most costly?

     A. EAP-LEAP

     B. EAP-MD5

     C. EAP-TLS

     D. EAP-SIM

35. If two people are discussing stealing electronic
     serial numbers (ESNs), what type of attack is being
     planned?

     A. Bank card hacking

     B. Modem hacking

     C. PBX hacking

     D. Cell phone hacking

36. What is the BEST protocol if a company needs link-
     to-link communications supporting encryption
     and authentication compatible with IPv6 and using
     L2TP at Layer 3 of the OSI model?

     A. IPSec Transport mode

     B. IPSec Tunnel mode

     C. PPTP

     D. L2F

37. Which mechanism converts internal IP addresses
     found in IP headers into public addresses for
     transmission over the Internet?

A. ARP

B. DNS

C. DHCP

D. NAT

38. If you need to implement IPv6 on an existing IPv4 network without a native connection to an IPv6 network, what technology should you use?

A. VRRP

B. Teredo

C. 802.1AE

D. 6to4

39. What is the term for a situation where a path is no longer available and shows an infinite hop count?

A. Loopback

B. Split horizon

C. Classless Inter-Domain Routing

D. Poison reverse

40. What is a current updated standard to the WEP protocol?

A. WPA2

B. SMLI

C. PGP

D. POP

41. What closely resembles a packet filtering device, making decisions based on addresses, ports, and protocols?

    A. Stateless firewall

    B. Circuit-level proxy

    C. Application proxy

    D. Stateful firewall

42. What protocol is a forerunner to Frame Relay and works over POTS lines?

    A. SMDS

    B. ATM

    C. X.25

    D. T-carriers

43. What does RADIUS provide?

    A. Authentication and accountability

    B. Authorization and accountability

    C. Authentication and authorization

    D. Authentication, authorization, and accountability

44. Which cell-switched WAN technology is the most suitable to use in rural areas considering that you don't want to use circuit-switched tech?

    A. DSL

    B. T1

    C. ISDN

    D. ATM

45. What is considered a third-generation firewall?

    A. Packet filter

    B. Circuit proxy

    C. Application proxy

    D. Stateful firewall

46. Identify the protocols corresponding to OSI Layers
    2, 6, 3, 4, and 7, respectively.

    A. ARP, SQL, ICMP, SMB, and SNMP

    B. L2TP, SMB, IP, SQL, and HTTP

    C. WEP, ASCII, IPX, TCP, and BootP

    D. PPP, ZIP, SPX, UDP, and TFTP

47. Which wireless standard operates in the frequency
    range of 5.15–5.35 GHz to 5.725–5.825 GHz and has
    a range of approximately 60 feet?

    A. 802.11a

    B. 802.11b

    C. 802.11g

    D. 802.11n

48. What is the BEST description of ISAKMP (Internet
    Security Association and Key Management
    Protocol)?

    A. Defines procedures for managing Security Associations,
       utilizes IKE, etc.

    B. Enables authentication of parties in a secure transition and
       contains certificate details

C. Manages private keys and certificates and follows X.509 standard

D. Defines protection of keys, establishes key lifetimes, and includes elements of business continuity

49. What is the OSI model in the context of network communication?

A. A seven-layer architecture for open systems interconnection

B. A five-layer architecture for closed systems interconnection

C. A protocol for data encryption

D. A type of firewall technology

50. Which of the following is NOT a method to handle collisions in network topologies?

A. Token-based collision avoidance

B. Polling

C. Carrier Sense Multiple Access (CSMA)

D. Data fragmentation

51. What is the primary function of the Address Resolution Protocol (ARP)?

A. Mapping IP addresses to MAC addresses

B. Encrypting data packets

C. Managing wireless signals

D. Detecting network intrusions

52. Which of the following is a security feature of the Open Shortest Path First (OSPF) routing protocol?

A. Data fragmentation

B. IP mapping

C. Encryption

D. Voice over IP

53. What is the purpose of a Virtual Local Area Network (VLAN)?

A. To increase the speed of data transmission

B. To create virtual tunnels through physical networks to connect devices

C. To detect and prevent network attacks

D. To encrypt wireless communication

54. Which of the following is a type of cable that utilizes light pulses to represent 0s and 1s?

A. Twisted pair

B. Coaxial

C. Fiber optic

D. Radio frequency

55. What is the primary purpose of the Internet Control Message Protocol (ICMP)?

A. Encrypting data

B. Providing feedback about problems in the network communication environment

C. Managing wireless signals

D. Handling collisions

56. Which of the following security solutions for the 802.11 wireless protocol family is the most updated?

    A. WEP

    B. WPA

    C. WPA2

    D. WPA3

57. What is the main difference between a denial-of-service (DoS) attack and a distributed denial-of-service (DDoS) attack?

    A. DoS involves multiple machines, while DDoS involves a single machine.

    B. DoS involves a single machine, while DDoS involves multiple machines.

    C. DoS encrypts data, while DDoS decrypts data.

    D. DoS and DDoS are the same and have no differences.

58. Which of the following is NOT a layer in the OSI model?

    A. Application

    B. Session

    C. Transport

    D. Fragmentation

59. Which of the following protocols is responsible for securely transmitting data over the Internet?

A. HTTPS

B. ICMP

C. ARP

D. OSPF

60. What is the primary function of the Data Link Layer in the OSI model?

   A. Routing data between networks

   B. Encrypting data

   C. Providing error detection and correction at the physical level

   D. Managing sessions between applications

61. Which of the following is a common method used to prevent unauthorized access to a wireless network?

   A. Data fragmentation

   B. MAC address filtering

   C. ICMP feedback

   D. OSPF routing

62. What type of attack involves intercepting and altering communications between two parties without their knowledge?

   A. Denial-of-service attack

   B. Man-in-the-middle attack

   C. Distributed denial-of-service attack

   D. Brute-force attack

63. Which of the following is NOT a characteristic of a Virtual Private Network (VPN)?

   A. Encrypts data transmission

   B. Creates a virtual tunnel through the public Internet

   C. Allows remote access to a private network

   D. Increases data transmission speed

64. What is the main purpose of the Simple Network Management Protocol (SNMP)?

   A. Encrypting data transmission

   B. Managing network devices

   C. Detecting network intrusions

   D. Routing data between networks

65. Which of the following is a characteristic of a stateful firewall?

   A. It monitors only the source and destination addresses.

   B. It monitors the state of active connections.

   C. It operates only at the Application Layer of the OSI model.

   D. It does not require any configuration.

66. What type of encryption is used by the Wired Equivalent Privacy (WEP) protocol?

   A. RSA

   B. AES

   C. RC4

   D. SHA-256

67. Which of the following best describes the function of a proxy server?

    A. It provides a direct connection between a client and a server.

    B. It acts as an intermediary between a client and a server.

    C. It manages network collisions.

    D. It encrypts all data on a local network.

68. What is the primary purpose of the Transport Layer in the OSI model?

    A. It provides physical connectivity between devices.

    B. It ensures reliable data transmission between devices.

    C. It translates data into a user-friendly format.

    D. It defines the network topology.

69. Which of the following protocols provides secure file transfer capabilities?

    A. FTP

    B. HTTP

    C. SFTP

    D. SNMP

70. What is the primary function of the Network Layer in the OSI model?

    A. It manages the physical connection between devices.

    B. It ensures reliable data transmission.

    C. It routes data between different networks.

    D. It translates data into a user-friendly format.

71. Which of the following is a common method used to authenticate users on a network?

A. Data fragmentation

B. MAC address filtering

C. Two-factor authentication

D. ICMP feedback

72. What type of attack involves overwhelming a system with traffic to make it unavailable to users?

A. Man-in-the-middle attack

B. Brute-force attack

C. Denial-of-service attack

D. Password cracking

73. Which of the following is NOT a characteristic of the Transmission Control Protocol (TCP)?

A. Connection oriented

B. Ensures reliable data transmission

C. Stateless

D. Provides error checking

74. What is the main function of the Presentation Layer in the OSI model?

A. It translates, encrypts, and compresses data.

B. It manages physical connections between devices.

C. It ensures reliable data transmission.

D. It routes data between different networks.

75. Which of the following is a security protocol designed to provide secure communication over an insecure network?

    A. SNMP

    B. ICMP

    C. SSL/TLS

    D. ARP

76. What type of network topology is characterized by devices connected in a closed loop?

    A. Star

    B. Mesh

    C. Ring

    D. Bus

77. Which of the following best describes the function of a demilitarized zone (DMZ) in network security?

    A. It encrypts all data on a local network.

    B. It acts as a buffer zone between the internal network and untrusted external networks.

    C. It manages network collisions.

    D. It provides a direct connection between a client and a server.

78. What is the primary purpose of a public key infrastructure (PKI)?

    A. To manage public and private keys for data encryption

    B. To increase data transmission speed

    C. To detect and prevent network attacks

    D. To route data between different networks

79. Which of the following best describes the function of a network intrusion detection system (NIDS)?

A. It encrypts data transmission.

B. It routes data between different networks.

C. It monitors network traffic for suspicious activities.

D. It manages physical connections between devices.

80. What is the main advantage of using a Virtual Private Network (VPN) for remote access?

A. It increases data transmission speed.

B. It provides a secure connection over the public Internet.

C. It manages network devices.

D. It routes data between different networks.

81. Which of the following is NOT a function of a firewall?

A. Filtering incoming and outgoing traffic

B. Encrypting data stored on a local network

C. Blocking unauthorized access

D. Monitoring connections

82. What type of network topology is characterized by each device being connected to every other device?

A. Star

B. Mesh

C. Ring

D. Bus

83. Which of the following protocols is used to send email securely?

A. HTTP

B. FTP

C. SNMP

D. SMTPS

84. Which of the following best describes the function of a honeypot in network security?

A. It acts as a decoy to attract attackers.

B. It encrypts data stored on a local network.

C. It increases data transmission speed.

D. It routes data between different networks.

85. What is the primary purpose of the Secure/Multipurpose Internet Mail Extensions (S/MIME) protocol?

A. To manage network devices

B. To encrypt email content

C. To detect and prevent network attacks

D. To increase data transmission speed

86. Which of the following is a characteristic of a stateless firewall?

A. It monitors the state of active connections.

B. It filters traffic based solely on source and destination addresses.

C. It requires extensive configuration.

D. It operates only at the Application Layer of the OSI model.

87. What type of network topology is characterized by a central hub or switch connecting all devices?

A. Star

B. Mesh

C. Ring

D. Bus

88. Which of the following is NOT a function of the Physical Layer in the OSI model?

A. It manages the physical connection between devices.

B. It translates data into a user-friendly format.

C. It defines the electrical and physical specifications.

D. It transmits raw bitstream over the physical medium.

89. Which of the following best describes the function of a security information and event management (SIEM) system?

A. It acts as a decoy to attract attackers.

B. It provides real-time analysis of security alerts.

C. It manages physical connections between devices.

D. It encrypts data stored on a local network.

90. What is the primary purpose of the Secure Hypertext Transfer Protocol (S-HTTP)?

A. To manage network devices

B. To encrypt web communication

C. To detect and prevent network attacks

D. To increase data transmission speed

91. Which of the following is NOT a characteristic of a Virtual LAN (VLAN)?

    A. It creates virtual tunnels through physical networks.

    B. It encrypts data transmission.

    C. It allows devices to be grouped logically.

    D. It enhances network management and security.

92. What type of network topology is characterized by a single central cable connecting all devices?

    A. Star

    B. Mesh

    C. Ring

    D. Bus

93. Which of the following is a common method used to secure data at rest?

    A. Firewall filtering

    B. Data encryption

    C. Network monitoring

    D. Traffic routing

94. Which of the following best describes the function of a security operations center (SOC)?

    A. It acts as a central hub for network devices.

    B. It provides real-time monitoring and analysis of security events.

    C. It encrypts web communication.

    D. It manages virtual tunnels through physical networks.

95. What is the primary purpose of the File Transfer Protocol (FTP)?

    A. To encrypt email content

    B. To transfer files over a network

    C. To detect and prevent network attacks

    D. To manage network devices

96. Which of the following is NOT a characteristic of the Secure Shell (SSH) protocol?

    A. It provides secure remote access.

    B. It encrypts data transmission.

    C. It increases data transmission speed.

    D. It uses public key cryptography.

97. What network topology is characterized by multiple connections between devices, providing redundancy?

    A. Star

    B. Mesh

    C. Ring

    D. Bus

98. Which of the following is a common method used to authenticate users based on something they have?

    A. Password

    B. Biometric scan

    C. Security token

    D. Security question

99. Which of the following best describes the function of a network access control (NAC) system?

    A. It encrypts data transmission.

    B. It manages network devices.

    C. It controls access to a network based on policies.

    D. It acts as a decoy to attract attackers.

100. What is the primary purpose of the Lightweight Directory Access Protocol (LDAP)?

    A. To encrypt web communication

    B. To provide a directory service for managing user information

    C. To increase data transmission speed

    D. To monitor and analyze security events

101. Which of the following is NOT a characteristic of the Internet Protocol Security (IPSec) protocol?

    A. It provides secure communication over IP networks.

    B. It encrypts data at the Transport Layer.

    C. It manages physical connections between devices.

    D. It uses authentication headers for integrity.

Answers

1. Answer: A. Hub

   Explanation: A hub operates at the OSI model's
   Physical Layer (Layer 1), simply forwarding
   incoming signals to all other ports without any
   filtering or decision-making process. In contrast, a
   switch, wireless access point (WAP), and bridge all
   have functionalities at the Data Link Layer (Layer
   2). A switch uses MAC addresses to determine
   the destination port for each incoming frame, a
   WAP allows Wi-Fi devices to connect to a wired
   network and can use MAC addresses for some
   decision-making processes, and a bridge is used
   to divide a network into segments, filtering traffic
   between them using MAC addresses. Therefore, the
   correct answer is A. Hub, as it is the only device not
   operating at the Data Link Layer.

2. Answer: B. ISO

   Explanation: The OSI model was developed by the
   International Organization for Standardization
   (ISO). The IEEE, IANA, and IETF are also involved
   in networking standards, but the OSI model is
   attributed explicitly to ISO.

3. Answer: D. UDP
   Explanation: The User Datagram Protocol (UDP)
   operates at the Transport Layer and is known for
   its best-effort, connectionless delivery. Unlike TCP,
   it does not provide error checking or guaranteed
   delivery, making it faster but less reliable. ARP and
   IGMP do not operate at this layer.

4. Answer: A. Packet

    Explanation: At Layer 3 of the OSI model, information is processed into units known as packets. This layer is responsible for logical addressing, routing, and path determination. The terms frame and segment refer to Layer 2 and 4 units, respectively, while "data stream" doesn't specifically refer to a Layer 3 structure.

5. Answer: D. Physical, Data Link, Network, Transport, Session, Presentation, Application

    Explanation: When processing inbound data from the network, the OSI model layers are traversed from the Physical Layer (Layer 1) to the Application Layer (Layer 7). Option D correctly lists the layers in this order.

6. Answer: D. Fiber optic

    Explanation: Fiber-optic cables use light signals to transmit data, making them less susceptible to electromagnetic interference (emanation detection). Therefore, fiber-optic cables provide the best protection against this type of detection compared to other listed media types.

7. Answer: B. Carrier Sense Multiple Access with Collision Detection (CSMA/CD)

    Explanation: Carrier Sense Multiple Access with Collision Detection (CSMA/CD) is based on contention among the media access control methods listed. In this method, devices listen to the network and transmit when they believe the channel is free. If a collision is detected, they stop and wait for a random time before trying again. This contrasts with other methods, such as the token-passing bus and token-passing ring, where devices must wait for a token to transmit data, ensuring orderly access, and polling, where a master device controls access without contention.

8. Answer: C. Egress filter

Explanation: An egress filter controls traffic flow as it leaves a network, blocking traffic that should not be exiting the network, such as packets with a public source IP address from a private network.

9. Answer: A. A system that has been hardened against attack

Explanation: A bastion host is best described as a system hardened against attack (option A). It is a special-purpose computer on a network specifically designed and configured to withstand attacks, serving as a critical part of a network's security system. While other options may describe various network functions, such as a default deny rule (option B), FQDN-to-IP-address resolution (option C, typically a DNS server), or replacing private IP addresses with public ones as the packet exits the private network (option D, describing Network Address Translation), they do not define the primary function of a bastion host.

10. Answer: A. Multiprotocol Label Switching (MPLS)

Explanation: Multiprotocol Label Switching (MPLS) is a protocol that uses labels to route packets quickly through a network. These labels are inserted before the Layer 2 header, allowing routers to forward the packets based on the labels without looking at the packet's actual content.

11. Answer: B. Extensible Authentication Protocol (EAP)

Explanation: Extensible Authentication Protocol (EAP) is a framework frequently used in network security and authentication. It supports multiple authentication methods, including token cards, smart cards, and public key authentication. It can also be extended to support new authentication mechanisms as they are developed, making it a fitting choice for the question.

12. Answer: D. 802.11n

Explanation: The IEEE 802.11n specification is designed to support multiple-input and multiple-output (MIMO) technology, which uses several transmitters and receivers to send and receive more data simultaneously. This technology increases the performance and range of wireless connections.

13. Answer: B. DDoS attack

Explanation: A distributed denial-of-service (DDoS) attack involves an "army" of compromised computers, often called zombies or bots, which an attacker controls. These computers flood a target system with traffic, rendering it inaccessible. Other options listed do not typically involve using multiple compromised computers in the same way as a DDoS attack.

14. Answer: B. Layer 2 – Data Link Layer

Explanation: Ethernet (IEEE 802.3) operates at the OSI model's Data Link Layer (Layer 2). It is responsible for the framing, addressing, and error detection of data packets.

15. Answer: D. Perimeter surveillance and intelligence gathering

Explanation: Among the options provided, the BEST proactive network defense strategy would be D. Perimeter surveillance and intelligence gathering. While redundant firewalls (option A) increase resilience, business continuity planning (option B) is more reactive, and disallowing P2P traffic (option C) is a specific measure not applicable to all organizations, perimeter surveillance and intelligence gathering (option D) represents a comprehensive and proactive approach. By monitoring the perimeter and gathering intelligence on potential threats, an organization can identify and mitigate risks before they materialize, making this strategy the most holistic and effective choice for proactive defense.

16. Answer: D. A man-in-the-middle attack

Explanation: A man-in-the-middle (MITM) attack primarily targets the communication between two parties rather than the network itself. The attacker intercepts, alters, or relays messages between two parties without them knowing that they are being manipulated.

17. Answer: C. Traffic filtering

Explanation: Among the options provided, the MOST effective countermeasure against a distributed denial-of-service (DDoS) attack is C. Traffic filtering. While keeping a fully qualified domain name's (FQDN's) secret (option A) may obscure targets and having a redundant network layout (option B) can increase resilience, neither approach directly addresses the nature of DDoS attacks. On the other hand, traffic filtering (option C) involves analyzing incoming traffic and filtering out malicious or unwanted requests. Via identifying and blocking the traffic associated with a DDoS attack, this method can prevent the attack from reaching its target, thereby maintaining the availability of the service, making it the most effective choice for mitigating such attacks.

18. Answer: A. On the network perimeter, to alert the network administrator of all suspicious traffic

Explanation: Placing NIDS on the network perimeter allows for early detection of suspicious activity and attacks, providing a critical line of defense.

19. Answer: A. File server, IP phone, security camera

Explanation: A converged IP network integrates various services such as voice, video, and data. Devices like IP phones, security cameras, and file servers are common in these environments.

20.   Answer: B. Fiber optics are more difficult to wiretap.

Explanation: Fiber-optic cables transmit data using light signals, making them more difficult to intercept or wiretap than copper cables that use electrical signals.

21.   Answer: A. A boundary router, a firewall, a proxy server

Explanation: A robust network perimeter defense typically includes boundary routers (to route data), firewalls (to filter traffic), and proxy servers (to act as intermediaries between internal and external networks).

22.   Answer: A. Lack of physical access control

Explanation: Wireless LANs are susceptible to risks from the lack of physical access control. Since the signals are transmitted through the air, unauthorized individuals can access the network without physical access to a network jack or cable.

23.   Answer: D. An SSID does not provide protection

Explanation: An SSID (Service Set Identifier) is simply a network name and does not provide any inherent security protection. While hiding or obscuring an SSID might make it slightly more difficult for casual users to find the network, it does not deter determined attackers. Tools that can discover hidden SSIDs are readily available, so relying on an SSID for security is not an effective strategy. Therefore, the correct answer is that an SSID does not provide protection, and other security measures, such as robust encryption and authentication methods, should be implemented to secure a WLAN.

24. Answer: A. It provides mechanisms for authentication and encryption.

    Explanation: IPSec (Internet Protocol Security) is a suite of protocols that secure Internet Protocol (IP) communications by authenticating and encrypting each IP packet in a data stream. The other options are not accurate descriptions of IPSec's primary function.

25. Answer: B. Aggregates logs from security devices and application servers looking for suspicious activity

    Explanation: Security event management (SEM) focuses on real-time monitoring, correlating events, notifications, and console views. It aggregates log data generated throughout the organization's technology infrastructure, looking for signs of malicious or otherwise suspicious activity.

26. Answer: A. Lack of authentication of servers and thereby authenticity of records

    Explanation: The principal weakness of DNS lies in its lack of authentication, which can allow malicious actors to perform attacks like DNS spoofing. This can lead to false DNS responses, redirecting users to fraudulent websites.

27. Answer: C. Using a denylist of open email relays
     provides a secure way for an email administrator to
     identify open mail relays and filter spam

     Explanation: Relying solely on a denylist of open
     email relays is not a secure way to filter spam.
     Open relays constantly change, and denylists may
     become outdated quickly, leading to false positives
     or negatives.

28. Answer: C. A group of dispersed, compromised
     machines controlled remotely for illicit reasons

     Explanation: A botnet is a network of compromised
     computers, known as "bots" or "zombies,"
     controlled remotely by an attacker. These machines
     can be commanded to perform malicious activities
     such as DDoS attacks, spam distribution, or other
     illicit actions.

29. Answer: A. Cost

     Explanation: Mesh networks provide high
     redundancy and resilience by creating multiple
     connections between devices, but the complexity
     and the need for more cabling or connections make
     them more expensive to implement and maintain.

30. Answer: D. WPA2

     Explanation: WPA2 (Wi-Fi Protected Access 2)
     provides stronger data protection by using the
     Advanced Encryption Standard (AES) protocol.
     It is considered more secure than the other
     options listed.

31. Answer: D. Fiber

    Explanation: Fiber-optic cables use light to transmit data, making thém immune to electromagnetic interference (EMI) and power fluctuations. They are the most suitable option in environments where such interference is prevalent.

32. Answer: C. Are often insecure by their very nature as they were not designed to natively operate over today's IP networks

    Explanation: Modbus and similar multilayer protocols used in industrial control systems were designed for closed, trusted environments. As they were not created with modern security challenges in mind, they often lack the necessary security features to protect against current threats, particularly when adapted to operate over the public Internet.

33. Answer: B. SSHv2

    Explanation: SSHv2 (Secure Shell version 2) is a network protocol providing secure remote server access. Unlike TELNET, FTP, and TFTP, which send information, including passwords, in clear text, SSHv2 encrypts the session, making it a far more secure option for remote administration.

34. Answer: C. EAP-TLS

    Explanation: EAP-TLS (Extensible Authentication Protocol–Transport Layer Security) provides strong security by using client and server authentication certificates. It's considered highly secure but costly and complex to implement due to the need for a public key infrastructure (PKI) to manage the certificates.

35. Answer: D. Cell phone hacking

Explanation: Stealing electronic serial numbers (ESNs) is associated with cell phone hacking. ESNs are unique identifiers for mobile devices, and unauthorized access can be used for fraudulent activities.

36. Answer: B. IPSec Tunnel mode

Explanation: IPSec Tunnel mode is suitable for encrypting traffic between different networks, and it supports both IPv4 and IPv6. It best fits this scenario, providing the required encryption and authentication for link-to-link communications.

37. Answer: D. NAT

Explanation: NAT (Network Address Translation) is the process of translating private IP addresses into public IP addresses for communication over the Internet. This enables multiple devices within a local network to share a single public IP address.

38. Answer: D. 6to4

Explanation: 6to4 is a transition mechanism for migrating from IPv4 to IPv6, allowing IPv6 packets to be transmitted over an IPv4 network. It's suitable for a scenario with no native connection to an IPv6 network.

39. Answer: D. Poison reverse

Explanation: Poison reverse is the term for a situation where a path is no longer available and shows an infinite hop count. Among the given options, loopback refers to a special IP address used for testing, split horizon is a method to prevent routing loops by restricting route advertisement, and Classless Inter-Domain Routing (CIDR) is a method for allocating IP addresses. In contrast, poison reverse is used in distance-vector routing protocols to prevent routing loops. When a router learns that a route is no longer available, it advertises the route with an infinite metric, effectively "poisoning" the route and informing other routers that it is no longer reachable, making it the correct answer for the described situation.

40. Answer: A. WPA2

Explanation: WPA2 (Wi-Fi Protected Access 2) enhances WEP (Wired Equivalent Privacy) and WPA, which provides more robust security. It has become the standard for securing wireless networks.

41. Answer: A. Stateless firewall

Explanation: A stateless firewall filters packets based solely on predefined rules concerning the source and destination IP addresses, ports, and protocols without keeping track of the state of active connections. It is the simplest type of firewall and closely resembles a packet filtering device.

42. Answer: C. X.25

Explanation: X.25 is a protocol suite widely used in the 1980s for packet-switched network services over public data networks (including over POTS lines). It's considered a forerunner to newer protocols like Frame Relay.

43. Answer: D. Authentication, authorization, and accountability

    Explanation: RADIUS (Remote Authentication Dial-In User Service) is a protocol that provides centralized authentication, authorization, and accounting (often called AAA) for network users. It is commonly used in ISP and corporate environments to manage access to network resources.

44. Answer: D. ATM

    Explanation: ATM (Asynchronous Transfer Mode) is a cell-switched technology that uses small, fixed-size cells to transmit data. It can be used in various applications, including WAN connections, making it suitable for the given scenario.

45. Answer: D. Stateful firewall

    Explanation: Third-generation firewalls are referred to as stateful firewalls. They monitor the state of active connections and make decisions based on the context of the traffic, such as TCP handshake completion and more.

46. Answer: D. PPP, ZIP, SPX, UDP, and TFTP

    Explanation: The question requires identifying protocols corresponding to OSI Layers 2, 6, 3, 4, and 7. The correct match for these layers would be protocols responsible for node-to-node communication (Layer 2), data translation including encryption and formatting (Layer 6), routing and forwarding (Layer 3), ensuring reliable data transfer (Layer 4), and interfacing with applications and end-user services (Layer 7). Analyzing the given options, the correct answer is D. PPP, ZIP, SPX, UDP, and TFTP, as these protocols correspond respectively to the functions of the specified OSI layers. Other options include protocols that do not typically align with the required OSI layers for this question.

47.   Answer: A. 802.11a

Explanation: The 802.11a standard operates in the 5 GHz bands, specifically in the 5.15–5.35 GHz and 5.725–5.825 GHz ranges, and typically has a shorter range, around 60 feet, depending on the environment and obstacles.

48.   Answer: A. Defines procedures for managing Security Associations, utilizes IKE, etc

Explanation: ISAKMP is a protocol that defines procedures and packet formats for the establishment, negotiation, modification, and deletion of Security Associations. It typically uses IKE (Internet Key Exchange) for key exchange but can implement other methods, making option A the correct description.

49. Answer: A. A seven-layer architecture for open systems interconnection

Explanation: The OSI (open systems interconnection) model is a structured, layered architecture comprising seven layers. It allows open systems to interconnect and communicate with each other using protocols.

50. Answer: D. Data fragmentation

Explanation: Data fragmentation is not a method to handle collisions. The methods mentioned in the content for handling collisions are token-based collision avoidance, polling, and Carrier Sense Multiple Access (CSMA).

51. Answer: A. Mapping IP addresses to MAC addresses

Explanation: ARP (Address Resolution Protocol) allows IP addresses to be mapped to physical MAC addresses. It facilitates communication between devices on a network.

52. Answer: C. Encryption

Explanation: OSPF (Open Shortest Path First) is a routing protocol routers use to manage and direct network traffic. It includes security features such as encryption, making it a more secure routing protocol.

53. Answer: B. To create virtual tunnels through physical networks to connect devices

Explanation: VLAN (Virtual Local Area Network) can be created using devices, technologies, and software. It reduces the need for physical rewiring by creating virtual tunnels through physical networks to connect devices, thereby enhancing network management and security.

54. Answer: C. Fiber optic

Explanation: Fiber-optic cable utilizes light pulses to represent 0s and 1s. It offers great advantages in speed and security compared to other types of cables like twisted pair and coaxial.

55. Answer: B. Providing feedback about problems in the network communication environment

Explanation: ICMP (Internet Control Message Protocol) is used for messaging and specifically provides feedback about problems in the network communication environment. Commands like Ping and traceroute utilize ICMP.

56. Answer: D. WPA3

Explanation: WPA3 (Wi-Fi Protected Access 3) is a security solution for the 802.11 wireless protocol family, released in 2018. It includes access control, authentication, encryption, and integrity protection.

57. Answer: B. DoS involves a single machine, while DDoS involves multiple machines.

Explanation: A denial-of-service (DoS) attack involves a single machine attempting to impede or deny functionality, while a distributed denial-of-service (DDoS) attack involves multiple devices acting in unison to achieve the same goal.

58. Answer: D. Fragmentation

Explanation: The OSI model consists of seven layers:
Application, Presentation, Session, Transport,
Network, Data Link, and Physical. Fragmentation is
not one of the layers in the OSI model.

59. Answer: A. HTTPS

Explanation: HTTPS (Hypertext Transfer Protocol
Secure) securely transmits data over the Internet.
It encrypts the client and server data, ensuring
confidentiality and integrity.

60. Answer: C. Providing error detection and correction
at the physical level

Explanation: The Data Link Layer in the OSI
model provides error detection and correction at
the physical level. It ensures that data frames are
transmitted without errors.

61. Answer: B. MAC address filtering

Explanation: MAC address filtering is a security
measure that controls access to a wireless network.
Allowing or denying specific MAC addresses
prevents unauthorized devices from connecting to
the network.

62. Answer: B. Man-in-the-middle attack

Explanation: A man-in-the-middle (MITM)
attack involves an attacker intercepting and
possibly altering communications between two
parties without their knowledge. It can lead to
eavesdropping or data manipulation.

63. Answer: D. Increases data transmission speed

    Explanation: A Virtual Private Network (VPN) encrypts data transmission, creates a virtual tunnel through the public Internet, and allows remote access to a private network. It does not inherently increase data transmission speed.

64. Answer: B. Managing network devices

    Explanation: SNMP (Simple Network Management Protocol) manages network devices. It allows administrators to monitor, configure, and control network devices such as routers and switches.

65. Answer: B. It monitors the state of active connections.

    Explanation: A stateful firewall monitors the state of active connections and makes decisions based on the context of the traffic, such as TCP handshake completion. It provides more advanced filtering compared to stateless firewalls.

66. Answer: C. RC4

    Explanation: WEP (Wired Equivalent Privacy) uses the RC4 encryption algorithm. It was an early security protocol for wireless networks but has been largely replaced due to its vulnerabilities.

67. Answer: B. It acts as an intermediary between a client and the server.

    Explanation: A proxy server is an intermediary between a client and a server. It can provide content filtering, privacy enhancement, and caching functions.

68. Answer: B. It ensures reliable data transmission between devices.

    Explanation: The Transport Layer in the OSI model is responsible for ensuring reliable data transmission between devices. It manages error recovery and data flow control and ensures that data packets are delivered in the correct sequence.

69. Answer: C. SFTP

    Explanation: SFTP (Secure File Transfer Protocol) provides secure file transfer capabilities by encrypting the data during transmission. It ensures the confidentiality and integrity of the files being transferred.

70. Answer: C. It routes data between different networks.

    Explanation: The Network Layer in the OSI model is responsible for routing data between different networks. It determines the best path for data to travel from the source to the destination.

71. Answer: C. Two-factor authentication

    Explanation: Two-factor authentication (2FA) is a common method used to authenticate users on a network. It requires two separate forms of identification, enhancing security by adding a layer of authentication.

72. Answer: C. Denial-of-service attack

Explanation: A denial-of-service (DoS) attack involves overwhelming a system with traffic to make it unavailable to users. It can be executed by sending excessive requests to a target, consuming its resources.

73. Answer: C. Stateless

Explanation: TCP (Transmission Control Protocol) is connection oriented and ensures reliable data transmission by providing error checking and acknowledgment of received packets. It is not stateless; rather, it maintains the state of the connection throughout the communication process.

74. Answer: A. It translates, encrypts, and compresses data.

Explanation: The Presentation Layer in the OSI model is responsible for translating, encrypting, and compressing data. It ensures that the data is in a format that both the sending and receiving devices can understand.

75. Answer: C. SSL/TLS

Explanation: SSL/TLS (Secure Sockets Layer/ Transport Layer Security) is a protocol designed to communicate securely over an insecure network. It encrypts the client and server data, ensuring confidentiality and integrity.

76. Answer: C. Ring

Explanation: In a Ring topology, devices are connected in a closed loop. Each device is connected to exactly two other devices, forming a circular structure.

77. Answer: B. It acts as a buffer zone between the internal network and untrusted external networks.

Explanation: A demilitarized zone (DMZ) acts as a buffer zone between internal and untrusted external networks, such as the Internet. It adds a layer of security by isolating public-facing servers from the internal network.

78. Answer: A. To manage public and private keys for data encryption

Explanation: Public key infrastructure (PKI) manages public and private keys for data encryption. It ensures secure communication by providing key management, certificate issuance, and authentication.

79. Answer: C. It monitors network traffic for suspicious activities.

Explanation: A network intrusion detection system (NIDS) monitors network traffic for suspicious activities and potential breaches. It can alert administrators to possible intrusions, allowing for a timely response.

80. Answer: B. It provides a secure connection over the public Internet.

Explanation: A Virtual Private Network (VPN) provides a secure connection over the public Internet by encrypting the data transmission. It allows remote access to a private network while maintaining confidentiality and integrity.

81. Answer: B. Encrypting data stored on a local network

Explanation: A firewall's primary functions include filtering incoming and outgoing traffic, blocking unauthorized access, and monitoring connections. It does not typically encrypt data stored on a local network.

82. Answer: B. Mesh

Explanation: In a Mesh topology, each device is connected to every other device. This provides multiple paths for data transmission and enhances redundancy and reliability.

83. Answer: D. SMTPS

Explanation: SMTPS (Secure Mail Transfer Protocol Secure) is used to send email securely. It encrypts the connection between the mail client and server, ensuring the email content is confidential.

84. Answer: A. It acts as a decoy to attract attackers.

Explanation: A honeypot in network security acts as a decoy to attract attackers. It is designed to be vulnerable to lure potential attackers, allowing security professionals to study their behaviors and techniques.

85. Answer: B. To encrypt email content

Explanation: S/MIME (Secure/Multipurpose Internet Mail Extensions) is a protocol to encrypt email content. It ensures the confidentiality and integrity of email messages by encrypting the data.

86. Answer: B. It filters traffic based solely on source and destination addresses.

Explanation: A stateless firewall filters traffic based solely on source and destination addresses without keeping track of the state of active connections. It provides basic filtering compared to stateful firewalls.

87. Answer: A. Star

Explanation: All devices are connected to a central hub or switch in a Star topology. This central connection point allows for easy addition and removal of devices but can create a single point of failure.

88. Answer: B. It translates data into a user-friendly format.

Explanation: The Physical Layer in the OSI model manages the physical connection between devices, defines the electrical and physical specifications, and transmits raw bitstream over the physical medium. It does not translate data into a user-friendly format.

89. Answer: B. It provides real-time analysis of security alerts.

Explanation: A security information and event management (SIEM) system provides real-time analysis of security alerts generated by various hardware and software entities in an organization. It helps in early detection and response to security incidents.

90. Answer: B. To encrypt web communication

Explanation: S-HTTP (Secure Hypertext Transfer Protocol) encrypts web communication. It ensures the confidentiality and integrity of data transmitted between the web browser and server.

91. Answer: B. It encrypts data transmission.

Explanation: A Virtual LAN (VLAN) creates virtual tunnels through physical networks, allows devices to be grouped logically, and enhances network management and security. It does not inherently encrypt data transmission.

92. Answer: D. Bus

Explanation: All devices are connected to a central cable in a bus topology. This central cable is a backbone for the network, and data is transmitted along this single pathway.

93. Answer: B. Data encryption

Explanation: Data encryption is commonly used to secure data at rest. Encrypting the data stored on a device or within a network prevents unauthorized access and potential breaches.

94. Answer: B. It provides real-time monitoring and analysis of security events.

Explanation: A security operations center (SOC) monitors and analyses security events within an organization. It coordinates security measures and responds to security incidents to protect against threats.

95. Answer: B. To transfer files over a network

Explanation: FTP (File Transfer Protocol) transfers files over a network. It allows users to upload and download files from servers, facilitating file sharing and management.

96. Answer: C. It increases data transmission speed.

Explanation: Secure Shell (SSH) provides secure remote access, encrypts data transmission, and uses public key cryptography to authenticate users. It does not inherently increase data transmission speed.

97. Answer: B. Mesh

Explanation: In a Mesh topology, devices are connected to multiple other devices, providing redundancy. This ensures that data can still be transmitted through alternative paths if one connection fails.

98. Answer: C. Security token

Explanation: Authenticating users based on something they have often involved using a security token. This can be a physical device or a digital token that generates a code, providing an additional layer of authentication.

99. Answer: C. It controls access to a network based on policies.

Explanation: A network access control (NAC) system controls access to a network based on policies. It evaluates the security posture of devices attempting to connect and enforces compliance with security policies.

100. Answer: B. To provide a directory service for managing user information

Explanation: LDAP (Lightweight Directory Access Protocol) provides a directory service for collecting user information. It allows organizations to store and retrieve user credentials, profiles, and other information in a structured manner.

101. Answer: C. It manages physical connections between devices.

Explanation: Internet Protocol Security (IPSec) provides secure communication over IP networks, encrypts data at the Transport Layer, and uses authentication headers for integrity. It does not manage physical connections between devices.

CHAPTER 7

Identity and Access Management (IAM)

Identity and Access Management (IAM) stands as a cornerstone in cybersecurity, orchestrating the intricate dance of user identities, permissions, and resources. It is a subject of paramount importance in the CISSP exam, reflecting its critical role in the real-world IT landscape.

IAM is not merely a set of technologies; it is a philosophy, a systematic approach that intertwines processes, technologies, and policies to manage user identities and control access to resources. Its mission is clear yet profound: to ensure that the right individuals are granted suitable access to the right resources precisely when they need it.

This chapter is more than a study guide; it is a journey into the heart of IAM. Here, you will find not only the concepts and best practices outlined in the CISSP Common Body of Knowledge but also insights, perspectives, and exam tips that will illuminate this domain in a way that transcends mere examination preparation.

Whether you are a seasoned professional or a newcomer, this chapter aims to provide a comprehensive understanding of IAM, equipping you with the knowledge and wisdom to navigate this complex domain with confidence and mastery. Welcome to a chapter that is not just about passing an exam but about understanding a critical aspect of the digital world that shapes our lives.

© Mohamed Aly Bouke 2023   399
M. A. Bouke, *CISSP Exam Certification Companion*, Certification Study Companion Series,
https://doi.org/10.1007/979-8-8688-0057-3_7

Effective Control of Physical and Logical Access to Assets

In today's interconnected technological landscape, safeguarding an organization's assets from unauthorized access has become a multifaceted challenge. Protecting information, systems, devices, facilities, and applications demands a comprehensive approach encompassing physical and logical dimensions. This section explores the principles and practices of controlling physical and logical access, providing insights and examples to illustrate these vital concepts. Let's discover these concepts:

Control of Physical Access to Assets

Physical access control represents the tangible layer of security, focusing on measures that restrict unauthorized access to an organization's facilities, equipment, and resources. The following areas of physical access control are key, each accompanied by practical examples:

- **Information:** Ensuring secure storage and handling of sensitive documents is paramount. Hospitals might use locked cabinets to store patient records, employing shredding protocols for no longer needed documents.

- **Systems:** Access to computers and servers can be restricted through locked rooms, cabinets, or cages. Data centers might employ biometric scanners, limiting entry solely to authorized personnel.

- **Devices:** Security measures for portable devices like laptops and mobile phones are essential. Corporations might use cable locks for laptops in shared spaces or store them in locked cabinets when not in use.

- **Facilities:** Implementing access control systems, such as card readers or security personnel, is vital. Research laboratories might utilize retina scanners, ensuring only authorized scientists can enter sensitive areas.

Control of Logical Access to Assets

Logical access control, in contrast, focuses on the virtual realm, securing digital assets by managing user access and permissions within IT systems. Here are the critical areas of logical access control, each illustrated with real-world examples:

- **Information**: Implementing access controls on databases and file systems is vital. Banks might limit access to customer financial data based on employee roles, ensuring that only authorized staff can view sensitive information.

- **Systems**: Employing security controls like firewalls and intrusion detection systems is essential. Ecommerce companies might deploy advanced firewalls, preventing unauthorized access to internal networks.

- **Devices**: Enforcing device security policies such as password protection and encryption is crucial. Government agencies might uphold strict encryption standards on mobile devices to protect classified information.

- **Applications**: Managing user access within applications ensures role-appropriate access. Universities might configure student information systems so that professors can access only the grades and attendance records relevant to their courses.

The synergy between physical barriers and logical safeguards forms a comprehensive defense against unauthorized access and potential security breaches. The examples provided herein serve as a guide, illuminating the path toward effective control of physical and logical access.

Moreover, in a world where threats are ever-evolving, implementing robust access control measures is a bulwark, maintaining a strong security posture and protecting an organization's most valuable treasures. The fusion of physical and logical controls creates a resilient security fabric that adapts to the changing landscape, ensuring that the right individuals have suitable access to the right resources at the right time.

Understanding Access Control Models

Access control models are the architectural blueprints for managing and securing access to an organization's resources. These models articulate the principles and mechanisms that define how permissions are granted, ensuring that users can only access the data and resources necessary for their job functions. For CISSP exam candidates, a profound understanding of these access control models is essential and foundational, as they are a vital component of the exam's objectives. We will explore various access control models, elucidating their characteristics, applications, and real-world examples.

Discretionary Access Controls (DAC)

Discretionary access controls empower resource owners to determine who has access to their resources and to what extent. In the DAC model, users can grant or revoke permissions for other users at their discretion.

Example: In a shared file system within a collaborative research project, a lead scientist with the necessary permissions can grant read or write access to specific files or folders to other team members, tailoring access based on individual responsibilities.

Mandatory Access Controls (MAC)

Mandatory access controls enforce access based on predefined security policies and classification levels. The MAC model is rigid, allowing access only to those with the appropriate security clearance and need-to-know basis.

Example: In a government agency handling classified information, a user with "Secret" clearance can access only "Secret" or lower documents. Access to "Top Secret" documents is restricted, maintaining the integrity of sensitive information.

Nondiscretionary Access Control (Role-Based Access Control or RBAC)

Nondiscretionary access control assigns permissions based on users' roles within an organization rather than their identities. The RBAC model grants access based on job responsibilities and functions.

Example: In a hospital's patient management system, nurses are granted access to patient medical records, while administrative staff members are granted access to billing information. Each role has specific permissions, aligning access with job functions.

Rule-Based Access Controls

Rule-based access controls enforce access permissions based on predefined rules or conditions, such as time of day, location, or network conditions.

Example: A financial institution might implement a rule-based access control policy that allows traders to access certain internal trading platforms only during market hours or from secure trading floors.

Content-Dependent and Context-Dependent Access Controls

Content-dependent access controls grant or deny access based on the content of the resources accessed. At the same time, context-dependent access controls consider the context in which the access request is made.

Example: A content-dependent policy in a law firm might restrict access to legal documents based on their confidentiality level. A context-dependent policy might grant access to specific resources only when a lawyer is connected to the firm's secure network using a firm-issued device.

The landscape of access control models is diverse and nuanced, reflecting the complexity of modern organizational structures and technological environments. Understanding these models is more than a theoretical exercise; it is a practical necessity for securing an organization's resources.

Each model offers unique strengths and applications, and their proper selection and implementation can be instrumental in maintaining a solid security posture. From the discretionary flexibility of DAC to the rigid enforcement of MAC, from the role-centric approach of RBAC to the condition-driven logic of rule-based controls, these models form the building blocks of a secure and resilient access control framework.

In a world where data is both an asset and a vulnerability, mastering access control models is a critical skill for cybersecurity professionals. It is a subject that transcends the boundaries of exams and reaches into the heart of protecting and empowering an organization in the digital age.

Identity Management and Authentication Techniques

Effective identification and authentication management for people, devices, and services stand as pillars in the edifice of information security. These processes form the gateways that ensure only authorized individuals and systems can access protected resources. For CISSP exam candidates, a deep and nuanced understanding of these concepts is vital and foundational, as they constitute a significant part of the exam's objectives. This guide will explore identification and authentication techniques, providing insights, examples, and practical applications.

Identity Management (IdM) Implementation

Identity Management involves creating, maintaining, and validating unique user identities across an organization. IdM implementation is the bedrock of access control, ensuring that users are accurately identified and authenticated.

Example: In a multinational corporation, IdM might include a centralized directory service that manages employee identities, roles, and permissions, ensuring consistency and security across global operations.

Single/Multifactor Authentication (MFA)

Authentication techniques can be categorized into single-factor and multifactor methods:

- **Single-factor authentication** relies on one method, such as a password or PIN. While simple, it can be vulnerable to attacks.

- **Multifactor authentication** combines two or more factors (e.g., something you know, something you have, and something you are) to provide a higher level of security. These factors are typically categorized into

  - **Something you know (knowledge-based factors):** These are pieces of information that the user must know to authenticate, such as passwords, PINs, or answers to security questions.

  - **Something you have (possession-based factors):** These are physical devices or objects the user must have to authenticate, such as a security token, smart card, or mobile phone with an authentication app.

  - **Something you are (inherence-based factors):** These are biometric characteristics unique to the individual, such as fingerprints, facial recognition, or voice patterns.

  - **Somewhere you are (location-based factors):** This newer category includes the user's location as a factor, such as a specific geographical location verified through GPS.

- **Something you do (behavior-based factors)**: This includes the unique ways in which a person interacts with a system, such as typing rhythm or mouse movement patterns.

The following table illustrates these types of authentication factors and examples of each:

Authentication Factor	Type	Example
Something you know	Knowledge-based	Password, PIN, and security questions
Something you have	Possession-based	Security token, mobile phone with SMS code
Something you are	Inherence-based	Fingerprint, facial recognition
Somewhere you are	Location-based	Geographical location via GPS
Something you do	Behavior-based	Typing rhythm, mouse movement patterns

The choice between single-factor and multifactor authentication, as well as the specific types of factors used, depends on the security requirements of a system or application. By understanding these different factors and how they can be combined, organizations can implement authentication methods that provide the appropriate level of security for their needs.

Accountability

Accountability in information security is the mechanism that ensures users are held responsible for their actions within a system. It is a multifaceted concept encompassing various measures:

- **Audit trails**: Audit trails are chronological records of user activities, providing evidence of system usage and helping trace unauthorized activities back to the responsible individual. **Example**: In a healthcare system, audit trails might record who accessed patient records, when, and what changes were made, ensuring compliance with privacy regulations.

- **Monitoring**: Continuous monitoring of user activities is essential for detecting potential security breaches, anomalies, and policy violations. **Example**: An ecommerce platform might employ real-time monitoring to detect and alert unusual purchasing patterns, potentially indicating fraudulent activity.

- **Access controls**: Enforcing strict access controls, such as the principle of least privilege, ensures that users have the minimum necessary access to perform their job functions. **Example**: In a manufacturing company, access controls might restrict engineers from designing files relevant to their projects, while managers have broader access to project management tools.

Additional Concepts

- **Federated Identity Management (FIM)**: FIM allows users to use the same Identity across different organizations or services. It's commonly used in collaborations between businesses.

- **Credential Management Systems**: These systems manage user credentials securely, often in conjunction with MFA.

- **Single Sign-On (SSO)**: SSO enables users to log in once and gain access to multiple related systems without reauthenticating.

- **Just-in-Time (JIT) provisioning**: JIT provisioning creates user accounts on the fly when needed, often used in cloud environments to enhance efficiency.

The landscape of identity management and authentication techniques is rich and complex, reflecting the multifaceted nature of modern information security. From the foundational principles of IdM to the nuanced layers of multifactor authentication, from the accountability mechanisms of audit trails and monitoring to the efficiency of SSO and JIT provisioning, these concepts form the building blocks of a secure and resilient information system.

In a world where Identity is both a key and a shield, mastering these techniques is a critical skill for cybersecurity professionals. It is a subject that reaches the core of protecting and empowering an organization in the digital age.

- **Exam Tip**

  Accountability is the cornerstone of information security. Ensuring that users are held responsible for their actions becomes challenging without proper accountability measures, which could lead to security breaches and compromised systems. For the CISSP exam, it is essential to understand that if there is no accountability, there is no security.

For example, consider an organization that does not enforce strict access controls or maintain audit trails. A malicious insider could exploit sensitive information or modify critical systems without detection in such an environment. In this scenario, the lack of accountability could lead to significant security breaches, ultimately jeopardizing the organization's reputation and operations.

Remember that accountability is essential for maintaining a solid security posture. Implementing audit trails, monitoring user activities, and enforcing access controls are vital to a comprehensive security strategy. By understanding the importance of accountability and its role in information security, you will be better prepared to tackle the CISSP exam and apply these principles in real-world scenarios.

Identity Management, Authentication Techniques, and Deployment Options

Accurately identifying and authenticating users, devices, and services is paramount in information security. As organizations become more interconnected and the boundaries between internal and external networks blur, the challenge of managing identities and controlling access to resources grows in complexity.

Identity management and authentication techniques encompass many methods, technologies, and practices designed to ensure that the right individuals can access the right resources at the right time. From creating digital identities to deploying sophisticated authentication mechanisms, these techniques form the foundation of a secure and resilient information system.

This section delves into various aspects of identity management and authentication, including session management, registration and proofing, credential management systems, Single Sign-On (SSO) deployment options, Federated Identity with third-party services, and Just-in-Time (JIT) provisioning. By exploring these concepts in detail, we will provide a comprehensive understanding of how organizations can safeguard their valuable assets and maintain a strong security posture.

Session Management

Session management is a multifaceted process that ensures a secure and continuous user experience within a system. It involves the creation of unique session identifiers, secure maintenance of session information, and proper termination to prevent unauthorized access:

- **Creation:** A unique session identifier is generated when users log in, allowing the system to track their activities and preferences.

- **Maintenance:** The system must securely maintain session information, such as session cookies and tokens, to ensure that the user's interaction remains seamless and secure.

- **Termination:** The session must be terminated adequately upon logout or timeout, and any session data must be invalidated to prevent unauthorized access.

Example: In an online healthcare portal, session management ensures patients can securely access their medical records, schedule appointments, and communicate with healthcare providers without interruption.

Registration, Proofing, and Establishment of Identity

Establishing a user's Identity is critical in ensuring only authorized individuals can access protected resources. It involves

- **Registration:** Users must provide personal information, such as name, email address, and phone number, to create an account.

- **Proofing:** The system verifies the user's Identity by validating the provided information, often through multi-step verification processes.

- **Establishment:** Once verified, a unique identifier and authentication credentials are assigned, forming the basis of the user's digital Identity within the system.

Example: A government service portal may require citizens to provide official identification and proof of residence during registration, followed by biometric verification, to ensure the authenticity of the user.

Credential Management Systems

Credential Management Systems are essential for securely storing and managing user authentication credentials. They include

- **Storage:** Credentials are stored in encrypted formats, often in secure hardware or virtual vaults, to prevent unauthorized access.

- **Management:** Regular updates, deactivation of obsolete credentials, and immediate revocation are managed systematically in case of suspected compromise.

Example: In a financial institution, credential management ensures that only authorized personnel can access sensitive financial data and that credentials are regularly rotated to mitigate the risk of unauthorized access.

Single Sign-On (SSO) Deployment Options

Single Sign-On (SSO) is a user-friendly authentication process that allows users to access multiple systems with a single set of credentials. Deployment options include

- **On-premise:** Managed within the organization's local data center, allowing complete control but requiring significant investment in infrastructure and maintenance

411

- **Cloud**: Leveraging third-party cloud services, reducing maintenance overhead and providing scalability

- **Hybrid**: Combining on-premise and cloud-based solutions, offering flexibility and a tailored approach to different systems or applications

Example: A multinational corporation may use a hybrid SSO solution to enable employees to access local intranet resources and global collaboration platforms with a single login.

Federated Identity with a Third-Party Service

Federated Identity Management (FIM) extends the principles of SSO across organizational boundaries. It can be implemented using

- **On-premise**: Complete control over the Federated Identity infrastructure, suitable for organizations with strict security requirements

- **Cloud**: Reduced maintenance overhead and scalability, suitable for organizations primarily using cloud-based services

- **Hybrid**: A combination of both, providing flexibility and a tailored approach

Example: Universities in a research consortium may use Federated Identity to allow researchers to access shared research databases and collaboration tools across institutions.

Just-in-Time (JIT) Provisioning

JIT provisioning is an agile approach to account management:

- **On-demand creation**: User accounts are created as needed rather than in advance, improving efficiency.

- **Dynamic permissions**: Permissions are assigned dynamically based on predefined rules, such as user roles or group memberships, ensuring that users have the appropriate level of access.

Example: A cloud-based project management tool might use JIT provisioning to create and manage user accounts for external contractors, granting them access only to relevant projects.

A comprehensive understanding of identity management, authentication techniques, and deployment options is vital in the modern information security landscape. These concepts are theoretical and practical building blocks of secure digital interactions.

From the nuanced layers of session management to the efficiencies of JIT provisioning, from the complexities of Federated Identity to the user-friendly nature of SSO, these techniques form a complex tapestry that cybersecurity professionals must master.

In a world where Identity is both a gateway and a barrier, these concepts are critical skills for anyone securing digital interactions. Mastery of these techniques will prepare candidates for exams like CISSP and equip them to navigate the ever-evolving challenges of cybersecurity in real-world scenarios.

Managing the Identity and Access Provisioning Life Cycle

Managing the Identity and access provisioning life cycle is critical to an organization's security posture. This process includes account access review, provisioning and deprovisioning, role definition, and privilege escalation. Like SSO and Federated Identity Management, the Identity and access provisioning life cycle can be managed using on-premise, cloud, or hybrid approaches:

- **On-premise:** Identity and access provisioning involves deploying and managing an organization's local data center infrastructure. This approach allows the organization to control its infrastructure and processes completely.

  Example: An organization may implement on-premise Identity and access management solutions, such as Microsoft Active Directory, to manage the provisioning life cycle, including user access review, role definition, and privilege escalation within its local network.

- **Cloud:** Cloud-based Identity and access provisioning leverages third-party cloud services to host and manage the infrastructure. This approach offers advantages such as reduced maintenance overhead, scalability, and access to resources from anywhere with an Internet connection.

  Example: An organization may use cloud-based Identity and access management services, such as Okta or AWS Identity and Access Management (IAM), to manage the provisioning life cycle for its cloud-based resources.

- **Hybrid:** A hybrid approach combines on-premise and cloud-based solutions, allowing organizations to choose the most appropriate solution for each system or application. This approach is useful for organizations with a mix of on-premise and cloud-based resources and those transitioning from on-premise to cloud-based infrastructure.

Example: An organization may use an on-premise solution like Microsoft Active Directory to manage the provisioning life cycle for local resources while integrating with a cloud-based identity and access management service like Azure Active Directory to manage cloud-based resources.

- **Account access review:** Reviewing user, system, and service accounts ensures only authorized users can access resources. This process includes verifying that accounts are still active, permissions are set correctly, and no unauthorized access has been granted. Depending on an organization's infrastructure, an account access review can be managed through on-premise, cloud, or hybrid tools.

- **Provisioning and deprovisioning:** Provisioning involves granting access rights to new users, systems, or services, while deprovisioning involves removing access rights when no longer needed (e.g., during off-boarding or transfers). Proper provisioning and deprovisioning help maintain a secure environment by ensuring access rights are only granted to authorized users. On-premise, cloud, and hybrid solutions can be used to manage these processes.

- **Role definition:** Defining roles within an organization helps streamline the provisioning process by assigning predefined permissions to users based on their job responsibilities. Role definition can be managed through on-premise, cloud, or hybrid Identity and access management tools, depending on the organization's infrastructure.

- **Privilege escalation**: Privilege escalation involves temporarily granting elevated permissions to users or services to perform specific tasks. This process should be carefully managed to minimize security risks associated with unauthorized access or misuse of elevated privileges. On-premise, cloud, and hybrid solutions can be used to manage privilege escalation, such as managed service accounts or using sudo in a Linux environment.

Understanding the critical components of managing the Identity and access provisioning life cycle and their implementation across on-premise, cloud, and hybrid environments is essential for CISSP exam candidates. By grasping the benefits and challenges of different deployment options, you can make informed decisions about implementing identity and access management solutions in various scenarios.

Implementing Authentication Systems Deployment Options

Various authentication systems are crucial for maintaining secure access to an organization's resources. The CISSP exam focuses on understanding different authentication protocols and their deployment options, including OpenID Connect (OIDC)/Open Authorization (OAuth), Security Assertion Markup Language (SAML), Kerberos, and Remote Authentication Dial-In User Service (RADIUS)/Terminal Access Controller Access Control System Plus (TACACS+). CISSP exam candidates should know the key features and benefits of various authentication protocols and their deployment across on-premise, cloud, and hybrid environments. These authentication protocols include

- **OpenID Connect (OIDC)/Open Authorization (OAuth)**: OIDC is an identity layer built on top of the OAuth 2.0 protocol, which allows users to authenticate and authorize applications to access resources on their behalf. OIDC and OAuth are often used in cloud and hybrid environments to provide secure authentication and authorization for web and mobile applications.

- **Security Assertion Markup Language (SAML)**: SAML is an XML-based standard for exchanging authentication and authorization data between parties, particularly between an identity provider (IdP) and a service provider (SP). SAML is commonly used in cloud and hybrid environments for Single Sign-On (SSO) and Federated Identity Management (FIM) implementations.

- **Kerberos**: Kerberos is a network authentication protocol that uses secret-key cryptography to securely authenticate users and services within a local network. Kerberos is typically implemented in on-premise environments, often as part of Microsoft Active Directory infrastructure, to provide secure authentication for internal resources.

- **Remote Authentication Dial-In User Service (RADIUS)/Terminal Access Controller Access Control System Plus (TACACS+)**: RADIUS and TACACS+ are authentication, authorization, and accounting (AAA) protocols commonly used for controlling access to network devices and services. RADIUS is often used in on-premise and hybrid

environments for remote access solutions like VPNs.
In contrast, TACACS+ is typically used for managing
access to network devices like routers and switches.

Understanding the key features and benefits of these authentication
protocols and their implementation across on-premise, cloud, and hybrid
environments is essential for CISSP exam candidates. By grasping the
advantages and challenges of different deployment options, you can make
informed decisions about implementing authentication systems in various
scenarios.

Summary

In this chapter, we delved into the vital concepts and exam tips related
to the Identity and Access Management domain of the CISSP exam.
Our exploration encompassed various facets of Identity and Access
Management, including diverse access control models; the intricate
process of managing the identification and authentication of people,
devices, and services; and the comprehensive management of the
identity and access provisioning life cycle. We also examined the practical
implementation of various authentication systems and their deployment
options across on-premise, cloud, and hybrid environments.

Key Takeaways

- **Access control models**: Understanding different access
  control models, such as discretionary, mandatory,
  and nondiscretionary access controls, is essential.
  Please familiarize yourself with their characteristics,
  advantages, and practical applications.

- **Identification and authentication**: Implementing and managing identification and authentication processes are central to securing asset access. Grasp the principles of identity management, multifactor authentication, and Federated Identity Management.

- **Accountability in security**: Accountability is a foundational component of information security. Recognizing and ensuring user accountability is vital for maintaining a secure environment.

- **Life cycle management**: Managing the identity and access provisioning life cycle involves nuanced tasks such as account access review, provisioning and deprovisioning, role definition, and privilege escalation. Comprehend the various deployment options along with their benefits and challenges.

- **Authentication protocols**: Familiarize yourself with diverse authentication protocols, including OIDC/OAuth, SAML, Kerberos, and RADIUS/TACACS+. Understand their implementation across different environments, such as on-premise, cloud, and hybrid.

With a thorough understanding of these key concepts and best practices within the Identity and Access Management domain, you are not only aligning yourself for success in the CISSP exam but also enhancing your capabilities to implement robust security controls in real-world scenarios.

Practice Questions

As you reach the culmination of your exploration of the Identity and Access Management domain in this chapter, a new phase of your preparation begins. This section introduces a series of practice questions meticulously crafted to reinforce the intricate concepts, enhance your analytical prowess, and align you with the demands of the real CISSP exam.

These questions are not merely an assessment of your retention but a vital extension of your learning process. They mirror the style and intricacy you will face in the full exam, encapsulating the profound understanding necessary for triumph. By engaging with each question and scrutinizing the explanations, you will unearth insights into your strengths and pinpoint areas that may require further refinement.

Approach these questions with earnestness, curiosity, and a readiness to be challenged. Embrace the learning from both success and error and engage in critical thinking. Remember, these practice questions are not just a gauge of your knowledge but an instrument to deepen your comprehension and hone your preparedness.

Your journey through the Identity and Access Management domain has been marked by complex concepts such as session management, Federated Identity, Just-in-Time provisioning, and various deployment options. Now, it's your moment to put that understanding under scrutiny. Seize this opportunity to cement your mastery of this domain. Your dedication to this practice will become an invaluable resource as you advance in your pursuit of the CISSP certification.

Take the time you need, ponder each question, and let these practice questions catalyze your success in the CISSP exam and your ongoing evolution as an information security expert.

1. If an attacker sees guard dogs and decides against attempting an attack, what kind of control does this illustrate?

   A. Physical deterrent

   B. Subject preventive

   C. Technical detective

   D. Physical corrective

2. Which of the following is a function included in the authentication aspect of AAA (authentication, authorization, accounting) services?

   A. One-time password

   B. Identification

   C. Integrity verification

   D. A transponder

3. What term describes a method where an individual convinces an authentication service that they know the password without actually revealing it?

   A. A Type I error

   B. SESAME

   C. A privilege attribute certificate (PAC)

   D. The zero-knowledge proof

4. What must be used to connect a network intrusion prevention system (IPS) sensor to a segment?

   A. TACACS

   B. A hybrid card

C. A supplicant

D. A span port

5. Which control relies on an attacker being unaware of the asset being protected or the existing vulnerability?

   A. Provisioning

   B. Subject deterrent

   C. Security through obscurity

   D. Separation of duties

6. When there is a worry that separation of duties may become less effective over time due to coworker familiarity, what should be implemented to manage fraud?

   A. Dual control

   B. The principle of least privilege

   C. Dynamic separation of duties

   D. Job rotation

7. Which authentication method uses only symmetric keys and tickets to provide its services?

   A. Biometrics

   B. Kerberos

   C. SESAME

   D. The Extensible Authentication Protocol (EAP)

8. Which access control model necessitates the use of unique identifiers for individual users?

   A. Discretionary access control (DAC)

   B. Mandatory access control (MAC)

   C. Role-based access control (RBAC)

   D. Rule-based access control

9. If you have doubts about the authenticity of a new employee's college diploma, what would be the most appropriate action for you to take to confirm their educational background?

   A. Examine the diploma's paper quality.

   B. Conduct a credit investigation.

   C. Reach out to the college's verification department.

   D. Get in touch with the employee's provided references.

10. What are two other types of access control mechanisms, besides technical controls, used to manage access within organizations?

   A. Physical

   B. Turnstile

   C. Firewall

   D. Administrative

11. Which method is the most robust form of authentication among the given options?

    A. Fingerprint scan

    B. Retinal scan

    C. Iris scan

    D. Password

12. Bouke, a security engineer, wants to enhance authentication by adding a smartphone authenticator that utilizes a time-based one-time password (TOTP) to the existing password system. What authentication method is he introducing?

    A. Two-factor authentication (2FA)

    B. Something you know

    C. Three-factor authentication (3FA)

    D. Multifactor authentication (MFA)

13. What term most accurately characterizes the utilization of a password for authentication?

    A. Something you know

    B. Somewhere you are

    C. Something you are

    D. Something you have

14. Aly fails to access a system using biometric authentication, along with his username and password. What kind of authentication event has taken place?

    A. True negative

    B. False positive

    C. False negative

    D. True positive

15. Which control offers the best defense against a rainbow table attack?

    A. Strong encryption

    B. Shadow file

    C. Hashing

    D. Salting

16. In the Kerberos authentication protocol, which component is tasked with issuing the Ticket Granting Ticket?

    A. Client

    B. Authentication Server

    C. Ticket Granting Server

    D. Service Server

17. What access control method is employed by the Windows NTFS file system in its standard configuration?

    A. Rule-based AC

    B. Role-based AC

    C. MAC (mandatory access control)

    D. DAC (discretionary access control)

18. Bouke and his supervisor must confirm a request to delete user data at their Internet service provider. What access control mechanism is being utilized?

    A. Separation of duties

    B. Least privilege

    C. Two-person control

    D. Security through obscurity

19. What access control flaw is most likely to occur in an organization where employees are frequently reassigned to new roles?

    A. False negative

    B. Man in the middle

    C. Privilege creep

    D. False positive

20. Which metric for an access control system is least likely to be manipulated by an administrator?

    A. Crossover error rate

    B. False rejection rate

    C. False positive rate

    D. False acceptance rate

21. In a public key infrastructure (PKI) system, what does a user send to someone else to securely provide the encryption key needed for encrypted communication?

    A. Private key

    B. Digital certificate

    C. Public key

    D. Digital signature

22. Which combination of controls exemplifies multifactor authentication?

    A. Token and access card

    B. Access card and PIN

    C. Eye scan and fingerprint reader

    D. Password and PIN

23. What is the correct definition of authentication?

    A. The declaration of a unique identity for an individual
       or system

    B. The procedure for confirming a user's Identity

    C. The process of outlining the specific resources a user requires
       and determining their access level

    D. The management's assertion that the user should have access
       to a system

24. The acronym IAAA represents the four stages of
    access control. Which option correctly defines and
    orders the IAAA terms?

    A. Integrity, authorization, auditing, and accounting

    B. Identity, authentication, authorization, and auditing

    C. Integrity, authorization, authentication, and auditing

    D. Identity, accounting, authorization, and auditing

25. What action should be taken when an employee
    moves to a different position within an
    organization?

    A. They must undergo a new security review.

    B. Their old system IDs must be disabled.

    C. All access permissions should be reviewed.

    D. They must surrender all access devices.

26. In a mandatory access control (MAC) system, what guides the assignment of data classifications?

    A. Analysis of the users in conjunction with the audit department

    B. Assessment by the information security department

    C. User's evaluation of a particular information element

    D. Organization's published security policy for data classification

27. Which security principle is at play in an access control system that grants users only the rights necessary to perform their work?

    A. Discretionary access

    B. Least privilege

    C. Mandatory access

    D. Separation of duties

28. The "state machine model" requires a system to be protected in all states, including startup, function, and shutdown. What security concept exemplifies this method of response?

    A. Open design

    B. Closed design

    C. Trusted recovery

    D. Least privilege

29. The Heartbleed virus exposed vulnerabilities in OpenSSL. Many believe that open design provides greater security than closed design. What consideration is typically required for open design to enhance security?

    A. Peer review

    B. Security through obscurity

    C. Complexity of design

    D. Trusted hierarchy

30. A key recovery agent may be used to mitigate the risk of losing a private key. However, this increases non-repudiation risk. What principle can be implemented to reduce this risk?

    A. Segregation of duties

    B. Principle of least privilege

    C. Dual control

    D. Need to know

31. During which phase of business continuity planning (BCP) development must senior management commit to support, fund, and assist in creating the BCP?

    A. Project initiation

    B. Planning

    C. Implementation

    D. Development

32. While training can reduce social engineering attacks, it doesn't eliminate the risk. What administrative policy is most likely to help mitigate this risk?

    A. Formal onboarding policies

    B. Job rotation

    C. Formal off-boarding policies

    D. Segregation of duties

33. The trust in a system reflects the trust in specific components. What are these components collectively called?

    A. Ring 1 elements

    B. Trusted computing base

    C. Operating system kernel

    D. Firmware

34. During access authorization, the conceptual ruleset is known as the _____, and the enforcement mechanism is referred to as the _____.

    A. Access control list, reference monitor

    B. Security enforcer, access control list

    C. Reference monitor, security kernel

    D. Security kernel, reference monitor

35. Why is the alignment of security controls with business objectives important?

   A. There is always a trade-off for security, so an organization has to weigh the cost vs. benefits.

   B. Security is cheap and easily implemented compared to potential loss.

   C. Security must be implemented as much as possible.

   D. Security is too costly for small organizations.

36. When evaluating a system's security categorization based on the potential impact of unauthorized disclosure (high), integrity breach (medium), and temporary unavailability (low), what is the overall categorization?

   A. High

   B. Medium

   C. Low

   D. Medium-high

37. While evaluating a system, trust and assurance are included in the scope. What best describes these two elements?

   A. Trust describes security; assurance describes performance.

   B. Assurance describes security; trust describes performance.

   C. Trust describes product function; assurance describes process reliability.

   D. Assurance describes product function; trust describes process reliability.

38. Which modern encryption technology is based on the ideas implemented in the Vernam Cipher, created in 1918?

    A. Asymmetric cryptography

    B. Digital signatures

    C. Handshake process used by IPSec

    D. Session keys

39. The Germans added a fourth rotor to the Enigma machine during World War II to increase the complexity of breaking the code. What modern relationship reflects this concept?

    A. AES and Kerberos

    B. DES/3DES

    C. RSA and DSA

    D. RSA and DES

40. Which security service would have indicated the spoofing if a user receives a spoofed email?

    A. Privacy

    B. Authorization

    C. Integrity

    D. Non-repudiation

41. How is non-repudiation achieved when using
     a combination of hashing and an asymmetric
     algorithm?

     A. Encrypt the document with the sender's private key,
        then hash the document

     B. Encrypt the document with the sender's public key,
        then hash the document

     C. Hash the document and then encrypt the hash with
        the sender's private key

     D. Hash the document, then encrypt the hash with the
        receiver's public key

42. What provides the secrecy in a hashing algorithm?

     A. A public key

     B. A private key

     C. One-way math

     D. A digital signature

43. What is a birthday attack?

     A. An attack on passwords based on users choosing weak
        passwords such as birthdays

     B. A logic bomb that triggers on the attacker's birthday

     C. An attack that attempts to find collisions in separate
        messages

     D. An attack that focuses on personnel databases to
        compromise personal information

44. If a network communication issue is caused by a Layer 1 problem, what is the most likely cause?

A. Cable

B. Router

C. Switch

D. Network Interface Card (NIC)

45. In an Ethernet environment using CSMA/CD (Carrier Sense Multiple Access with Collision Detection), what does CSMA/CD imply?

A. Ethernet environments avoid collisions by detecting their likelihood before transmitting.

B. Ethernet environments only allow an individual host to access the cable at any given time and are capable of detecting collisions as they happen.

C. Even though Ethernet traffic is prone to collisions, a hub can all but eliminate them.

D. Though multiple systems can access the media simultaneously, the result will be a collision, which should be immediately detected.

46. Which technique would be most appropriate if an enterprise wants to ensure that the cloud service provider can automatically provision and deprovision resources to match current demand?

A. Scalability

B. Elasticity

C. Availability

D. Reliability

47. What is the primary purpose of Identity and Access Management (IAM)?

   A. To ensure data integrity

   B. To control the way assets are accessed

   C. To ensure data availability

   D. To ensure data confidentiality

48. Which of the following is NOT a fundamental access control principle?

   A. Need to know

   B. Least privilege

   C. Separation of duties

   D. Maximum privilege

49. What does the acronym SAML stand for in the context of Federated Identity Management (FIM)?

   A. Security Assertion Markup Language

   B. Secure Access Management Language

   C. System Authentication Markup Language

   D. Secure Authorization Markup Language

50. What is the primary preventive measure for session hijacking?

   A. Frequent password changes

   B. Use of firewalls

   C. Frequent reauthentication

   D. Use of antivirus software

51. Which of the following is NOT a component of Access Control Services?

    A. Identification

    B. Authentication

    C. Authorization

    D. Encryption

52. What does the term "provisioning" refer to in the context of the identity life cycle?

    A. The process of confirming or establishing that somebody is who they claim to be

    B. The process of granting access to systems and data to a new employee or when an employee changes roles

    C. The process of terminating access when an employee leaves the organization

    D. The process of reviewing a user's access to assets and systems

53. What is the primary function of the Security Assertion Markup Language (SAML) in Federated Identity Management (FIM)?

    A. To provide encryption for data in transit

    B. To provide authentication and authorization

    C. To provide a secure communication channel

    D. To provide a firewall for network security

54. Which of the following is a potential risk relating to Identity as a Service (IDaaS)?

    A. Availability of the service

    B. Protection of critical identity data

    C. Entrusting a third party with sensitive or proprietary data

    D. All of the above

55. What is the purpose of the CAPTCHA security measure?

    A. To prevent automated account creation, spam, and brute-force password decryption attacks

    B. To encrypt data in transit

    C. To provide a firewall for network security

    D. To authenticate users

56. What does the term "Just-in-Time Access" refer to in the context of access control?

    A. The process of granting access to systems and data to a new employee

    B. The elevation of user privileges for a short period to complete necessary but infrequent tasks

    C. The process of terminating access when an employee leaves the organization

    D. The process of reviewing a user's access to assets and systems

57. What does the term "deprovisioning" refer to in the context of the identity life cycle?

   A. The process of granting access to systems and data to a new employee

   B. The process of confirming or establishing that somebody is who they claim to be

   C. The process of terminating access when an employee leaves the organization

   D. The process of reviewing a user's access to assets and systems

58. What is the primary purpose of the OAuth protocol in Federated Identity Management (FIM)?

   A. To provide a secure communication channel

   B. To provide encryption for data in transit

   C. To allow third-party services to access user data without needing to know the user's credentials

   D. To provide a firewall for network security

59. What is the main advantage of using a Single Sign-On (SSO) system?

   A. It reduces the number of passwords a user has to remember.

   B. It increases the complexity of the authentication process.

   C. It reduces the need for encryption.

   D. It increases the need for firewalls.

60. What is the purpose of the "need-to-know" principle in access control?

   A. To ensure that users have access to all the information they might need

   B. To ensure that users only have access to the information they need to perform their job functions

   C. To ensure that users know how to use the systems and data they have access to

   D. To ensure that users know the consequences of misusing their access rights

61. What does the term "federation" refer to in the context of Federated Identity Management (FIM)?

   A. The process of confirming or establishing that somebody is who they claim to be

   B. The process of granting access to systems and data to a new employee

   C. The process of allowing different organizations to share and manage identity information

   D. The process of terminating access when an employee leaves the organization

62. What is the primary purpose of the OpenID Connect protocol in Federated Identity Management (FIM)?

   A. To provide a secure communication channel

   B. To provide encryption for data in transit

   C. To allow third-party services to access user data without needing to know the user's credentials

   D. To provide a simple identity layer on top of the OAuth 2.0 protocol

63. What is the main disadvantage of using a Single
    Sign-On (SSO) system?

    A. It increases the number of passwords a user has to remember.

    B. If the SSO system is compromised, all services that
       use it are potentially at risk.

    C. It reduces the need for encryption.

    D. It increases the need for firewalls.

64. What is the purpose of the "separation of duties"
    principle in access control?

    A. To ensure that users have access to all the information
       they might need

    B. To ensure that users only have access to the
       information they need to perform their job functions

    C. To prevent any single individual from being able to
       complete a significant process or transaction on their own

    D. To ensure that users know the consequences of
       misusing their access rights

65. What does the term "authentication" refer to in the
    context of Access Control Services?

    A. The process of confirming or establishing that
       somebody is who they claim to be

    B. The process of granting access to systems and data to
       a new employee

    C. The process of allowing different organizations to
       share and manage identity information

    D. The process of terminating access when an employee
       leaves the organization

66. What does the term "accountability" refer to in the context of Access Control Services?

A. The process of confirming or establishing that somebody is who they claim to be

B. The process of granting access to systems and data to a new employee

C. The process of allowing different organizations to share and manage identity information

D. The ability to link actions to a specific user and hold them responsible for their actions

67. What does the term "authorization" refer to in the context of Access Control Services?

A. The process of confirming or establishing that somebody is who they claim to be

B. The process of determining what actions a user is allowed to perform

C. The process of allowing different organizations to share and manage identity information

D. The process of terminating access when an employee leaves the organization

68. What is the main advantage of using a Federated Identity Management (FIM) system?

A. It increases the number of passwords a user has to remember.

B. It allows users to use the same credentials to access services across multiple organizations.

C. It reduces the need for encryption.

D. It increases the need for firewalls.

69. What is the purpose of the "least privilege" principle in access control?

A. To ensure that users have access to all the information they might need

B. To ensure that users only have the minimum levels of access necessary to perform their job functions

C. To prevent any single individual from being able to complete a significant process or transaction on their own

D. To ensure that users know the consequences of misusing their access rights

70. What does the term "identification" refer to in the context of Access Control Services?

A. The process of a user claiming or professing an identity

B. The process of granting access to systems and data to a new employee

C. The process of allowing different organizations to share and manage identity information

D. The process of terminating access when an employee leaves the organization

71. What does the term "Identity as a Service (IDaaS)" refer to?

   A. The process of confirming or establishing that somebody is who they claim to be

   B. The process of granting access to systems and data to a new employee

   C. The process of allowing different organizations to share and manage identity information

   D. A cloud-based service that provides Identity and Access Management functions to an organization's systems that reside on-premises and/or in the cloud

72. What is the primary purpose of the Kerberos protocol in the context of authentication systems?

   A. To provide a secure communication channel

   B. To provide encryption for data in transit

   C. To allow third-party services to access user data without needing to know the user's credentials

   D. To provide a secure method for transmitting information and authenticating both the user and the server

73. What is the main disadvantage of using a Federated Identity Management (FIM) system?

   A. It increases the number of passwords a user has to remember.

   B. If the FIM system is compromised, all services that use it are potentially at risk.

   C. It reduces the need for encryption.

   D. It increases the need for firewalls.

74. What is the purpose of the "accountability" principle in access control?

    A. To ensure that users have access to all the information they might need

    B. To ensure that users only have the minimum levels of access necessary to perform their job functions

    C. To prevent any single individual from being able to complete a significant process or transaction on their own

    D. To ensure that actions can be traced back to the individual who performed them

75. What does the term "biometrics" refer to in the context of authentication systems?

    A. The process of a user claiming or professing an identity

    B. The use of physical or behavioral characteristics to verify a user's Identity

    C. The process of allowing different organizations to share and manage identity information

    D. The process of terminating access when an employee leaves the organization

76. What does the term "identity proofing" refer to in the context of Identity and Access Management (IAM)?

   A. The process of confirming or establishing that somebody is who they claim to be

   B. The process of granting access to systems and data to a new employee

   C. The process of verifying a user's claimed Identity by comparing it against one or more reliable sources

   D. The process of terminating access when an employee leaves the organization

77. What does the term "Identity Federation" refer to in the context of Identity and Access Management (IAM)?

   A. The process of confirming or establishing that somebody is who they claim to be

   B. The process of granting access to systems and data to a new employee

   C. The process of allowing different organizations to share and manage identity information

   D. The process of terminating access when an employee leaves the organization

78. What is the primary purpose of the RADIUS protocol in the context of authentication systems?

   A. To provide a secure communication channel

   B. To provide a networking protocol that offers centralized authentication, authorization, and accounting (AAA) management for users who connect and use a network service

  C. To allow third-party services to access user data without needing to know the user's credentials

  D. To provide encryption for data in transit

79. What is the main disadvantage of using biometric authentication systems?

  A. It increases the number of passwords a user has to remember.

  B. If the biometric data is compromised, it cannot be changed like a password.

  C. It reduces the need for encryption.

  D. It increases the need for firewalls.

80. What is the purpose of the "non-repudiation" principle in access control?

  A. To ensure that users have access to all the information they might need

  B. To ensure that users only have the minimum levels of access necessary to perform their job functions

  C. To prevent any single individual from being able to complete a significant process or transaction on their own

  D. To ensure that actions can be definitively traced back to the individual who performed them, and they cannot deny performing them

81. What does the term "multifactor authentication (MFA)" refer to in the context of authentication systems?

    A. The process of a user claiming or professing an identity

    B. The use of two or more independent credentials for verifying a user's Identity

    C. The process of allowing different organizations to share and manage identity information

    D. The process of terminating access when an employee leaves the organization

82. What does the term "identity life cycle" refer to in the context of Identity and Access Management (IAM)?

    A. The process of confirming or establishing that somebody is who they claim to be

    B. The stages a digital identity goes through from creation to deletion

    C. The process of allowing different organizations to share and manage identity information

    D. The process of terminating access when an employee leaves the organization

83. What is the primary purpose of the TACACS+ protocol in the context of authentication systems?

    A. To provide a secure communication channel

B. To provide a networking protocol that offers centralized authentication, authorization, and accounting (AAA) management for users who connect and use a network service

C. To allow third-party services to access user data without needing to know the user's credentials

D. To provide encryption for data in transit

84. What is the main disadvantage of using password-based authentication systems?

A. It increases the number of passwords a user has to remember.

B. Passwords can be easily forgotten, shared, or stolen.

C. It reduces the need for encryption.

D. It increases the need for firewalls.

85. What is the purpose of the "principle of least privilege" in access control?

A. To ensure that users have access to all the information they might need

B. To ensure that users only have the minimum levels of access necessary to perform their job functions

C. To prevent any single individual from being able to complete a significant process or transaction on their own

D. To ensure that actions can be definitively traced back to the individual who performed them, and they cannot deny performing them

86. What does the term "Single Sign-On (SSO)" refer to in the context of authentication systems?

   A. The process of a user claiming or professing an identity

   B. The use of a single set of credentials to access multiple applications or services

   C. The process of allowing different organizations to share and manage identity information

   D. The process of terminating access when an employee leaves the organization

87. What does the term "provisioning" refer to in the context of Identity and Access Management (IAM)?

   A. The process of confirming or establishing that somebody is who they claim to be

   B. The process of setting up a new user account with appropriate access rights

   C. The process of allowing different organizations to share and manage identity information

   D. The process of terminating access when an employee leaves the organization

88. What is the primary purpose of the SAML protocol in the context of authentication systems?

   A. To provide a secure communication channel

   B. To provide a standard for exchanging authentication and authorization data between parties

   C. To allow third-party services to access user data without needing to know the user's credentials

   D. To provide encryption for data in transit

89. What is the main disadvantage of using role-based access control systems?

    A. It increases the number of passwords a user has to remember.

    B. It can be difficult to manage if roles are not clearly defined or if users have multiple roles.

    C. It reduces the need for encryption.

    D. It increases the need for firewalls.

90. What is the purpose of the "mandatory access control" in access control?

    A. To ensure that users have access to all the information they might need

    B. To enforce access control policies based on the classification of information and the security clearance of users

    C. To prevent any single individual from being able to complete a significant process or transaction on their own

    D. To ensure that actions can be definitively traced back to the individual who performed them, and they cannot deny performing them

91. What does the term "attribute-based access control (ABAC)" refer to in the context of access control systems?

A. The process of a user claiming or professing an identity

B. A flexible access control method where access rights are granted to users through the use of policies which combine attributes together

C. The process of allowing different organizations to share and manage identity information

D. The process of terminating access when an employee leaves the organization

92. What does the term "deprovisioning" refer to in the context of Identity and Access Management (IAM)?

A. The process of confirming or establishing that somebody is who they claim to be

B. The process of removing an existing user account and its associated access rights

C. The process of allowing different organizations to share and manage identity information

D. The process of setting up a new user account with appropriate access rights

93. What is the primary purpose of the OAuth protocol in the context of authentication systems?

A. To provide a secure communication channel

B. To provide a standard for authorizing third-party applications to access user data without sharing passwords

    C. To allow third-party services to access user data without needing to know the user's credentials

    D. To provide encryption for data in transit

94. What is the main disadvantage of using discretionary access control systems?

    A. It increases the number of passwords a user has to remember.

    B. It can lead to "privilege creep" if access rights are not regularly reviewed and updated.

    C. It reduces the need for encryption.

    D. It increases the need for firewalls.

95. What is the purpose of "discretionary access control" in access control?

    A. To ensure that users have access to all the information they might need

    B. To allow the owners of information to control who can access their information

    C. To prevent any single individual from being able to complete a significant process or transaction on their own

    D. To ensure that actions can be definitively traced back to the individual who performed them, and they cannot deny performing them

96. What does the term "privilege escalation" refer to in the context of access control systems?

A. The process of a user claiming or professing an identity

B. The act of exploiting a bug, design flaw, or configuration oversight in an operating system or software application to gain elevated access to resources

C. The process of allowing different organizations to share and manage identity information

D. The process of terminating access when an employee leaves the organization

97. What is the primary function of the SESAME protocol in the context of Single Sign-On authentication?

A. To provide a secure communication channel

B. To provide accounting, authentication, and auditing services

C. To allow third-party services to access user data without needing to know the user's credentials

D. To support both symmetric and asymmetric cryptography

98. What is the primary purpose of the Authenticator Assurance Levels (AAL)?

A. To provide a secure communication channel

B. To rank the strength of authentication processes and systems

    C. To allow third-party services to access user data without needing to know the user's credentials

    D. To provide encryption for data in transit

99. What is the primary difference between discretionary access control (DAC) and mandatory access control (MAC)?

    A. DAC is determined by the owner of the asset, while MAC is determined by the system based on labels.

    B. DAC is determined by the system based on labels, while MAC is determined by the owner of the asset.

    C. DAC is a protocol for enabling Single Sign-On, while MAC is an improved version of DAC.

    D. DAC is an improved version of MAC, while MAC is a protocol for enabling Single Sign-On.

100. What does the term "Identity as a Service (IDaaS)" refer to?

    A. The process of confirming or establishing that somebody is who they claim to be

    B. The implementation or integration of identity services in a cloud-based environment

    C. The process of allowing different organizations to share and manage identity information

    D. The process of terminating access when an employee leaves the organization

101. What does the term "Just-in-Time Access" refer to in the context of access control?

   A. The process of confirming or establishing that somebody is who they claim to be

   B. The process of elevating user privileges for a short period to complete necessary but infrequent tasks

   C. The process of allowing different organizations to share and manage identity information

   D. The process of terminating access when an employee leaves the organization

Answers

1. Answer: A. Physical deterrent

   Explanation: A physical deterrent is a type of control used to discourage an attacker from proceeding with an attack. In this case, the presence of guard dogs serves as a visible obstacle, deterring the attacker from attempting to breach the premises.

2. Answer: B. Identification

   Explanation: Authentication is the process of verifying the Identity of a user, device, or other entities in a computer system, often using usernames and passwords. The identification step is crucial in this process, where the user claims an identity, typically using a username. Therefore, "identification" is the correct answer.

3. Answer: D. The zero-knowledge proof

   Explanation: A zero-knowledge proof is a method by which one party can prove to another party that they know a value (such as a password) without conveying any information about that value. In the context of authentication, it enables a party to prove they know the password without revealing it.

4. Answer: D. A span port

   Explanation: A span port, or Switched Port Analyzer port, is a designated port on a network switch used to monitor and analyze network traffic. It can be connected to an intrusion prevention system (IPS) sensor to provide the sensor with access to network data, allowing it to detect and prevent malicious activities.

5. Answer: C. Security through obscurity

   Explanation: Security through obscurity refers to a principle in security engineering where the details of a security mechanism, vulnerabilities, or the asset itself are kept secret and hidden. The belief is that if the attacker does not know the details, they will be less likely to find vulnerabilities or successfully attack the asset.

6. Answer: D. Job rotation

   Explanation: Job rotation is the practice of periodically moving employees between different roles or responsibilities. It is used to prevent fraud or collusion by ensuring that no single individual has control over all aspects of any critical transaction.

By rotating roles, it makes it more difficult for employees to engage in fraudulent activities, especially when they have worked together for an extended period.

7. Answer: B. Kerberos

   Explanation: Kerberos is a network authentication protocol that uses symmetric encryption and a ticketing system to authenticate users in a network. It relies on a trusted third party, known as the Key Distribution Center (KDC), to facilitate secure communication between entities.

8. Answer: A. Discretionary access control (DAC)

   Explanation: Discretionary access control (DAC) is an access control model where the owner of an object has complete control over who is allowed to access it. In DAC, access is typically controlled based on the Identity of the user or a group the user belongs to, so unique user identities are an essential part of this model.

9. Answer: C. Reach out to the college's verification department.

   Explanation: The most reliable way to verify the authenticity of a diploma is to contact the institution that supposedly issued it. In this case, reaching out to the college verification department would provide an official confirmation or denial of the diploma's authenticity. Other options are either irrelevant (such as running a credit check) or less reliable (such as inspecting the paper type or contacting references).

10. Answer: A. Physical, D. Administrative

    Explanation: Access controls can be broadly
    categorized into three types.
    Technical controls: These include firewalls,
    encryption, and other technology-based solutions
    to control access to systems and data.
    Physical controls: These are measures like locks,
    gates, and turnstiles that control physical access to
    facilities.
    Administrative controls: These include policies,
    procedures, and guidelines that define how access is
    granted, reviewed, and revoked.

11. Answer: C. Iris scan

    Explanation: Iris scans are considered one of the
    strongest forms of biometric authentication. They
    capture the unique patterns in the colored part
    of the eye, which are highly distinctive and stable
    over time. Retinal scans are also strong but are
    more intrusive, while fingerprint scans can be more
    easily spoofed. Passwords are generally considered
    the weakest option among these, as they can be
    guessed, hacked, or stolen.

12. Answer: A. Two-factor authentication (2FA)

    Explanation: Two-factor authentication (2FA)
    requires two separate forms of identification for
    access. In this case, Bouke is implementing a
    system that requires something the user knows
    (a password) and something the user has (a
    smartphone authenticator using TOTP). This
    combination of two factors enhances security by

requiring both something known and something possessed, making unauthorized access more difficult. Option D, MFA, is a broader term that includes 2FA but is not as specific to this scenario.

13. Answer: A. Something you know

Explanation: A password is something that a user knows and can recall. It's a knowledge-based form of authentication, as opposed to something physical (something you have), a location (somewhere you are), or a biometric characteristic (something you are).

14. Answer: C. False negative

Explanation: A false negative occurs when a legitimate user is incorrectly denied access. In this scenario, Aly is a valid user, but the system incorrectly rejects his authentication attempt.

15. Answer: D. Salting

Explanation: Salting involves adding random data (a "salt") to a password before hashing it. This ensures that even if two users have the same password, their hashes will be different due to the unique salts. Salting effectively defends against rainbow table attacks, which exploit precomputed tables to reverse cryptographic hash functions.

16. Answer: B. Authentication Server

Explanation: In Kerberos, the Authentication Server is responsible for authenticating the client and issuing a Ticket Granting Ticket (TGT), which is later used to obtain service tickets from the Ticket Granting Server.

17. Answer: D. DAC (discretionary access control)

    Explanation: Windows NTFS uses discretionary access control (DAC) by default. DAC allows the owner of the resource to determine who can access it and what permissions they have.

18. Answer: C. Two-person control

    Explanation: Two-person control requires two individuals to approve an action before it can be carried out. In this scenario, both Bouke and his supervisor must confirm the request, ensuring a higher level of scrutiny and reducing the risk of unauthorized or accidental deletions.

19. Answer: C. Privilege creep

    Explanation: Privilege creep occurs when individuals retain access rights after moving to a new position that does not require those rights. In an organization where reassignments are common, this can lead to employees accumulating unnecessary and potentially risky privileges.

20. Answer: A. Crossover error rate

    Explanation: The crossover error rate (CER) is a measure of the point where the false acceptance rate equals the false rejection rate. It's a fundamental characteristic of the system and is not something that can be easily adjusted by an administrator, unlike the other rates that might be influenced by system configuration.

21. Answer: C. Public key

Explanation: In PKI, the public key is used to encrypt messages, and only the corresponding private key can decrypt them. By sharing the public key, a user enables others to send them encrypted messages that only they can read.

22. Answer: B. Access card and PIN

Explanation: Multifactor authentication (MFA) requires the utilization of at least two distinct factors from different categories of authentication, such as something you know (knowledge), something you have (possession), and something you are (inherence). Analyzing the given options, the combination of an access card (something you have) and a PIN (something you know) represents two different categories of authentication factors. Therefore, option B, which combines an access card and a PIN, exemplifies multifactor authentication. The other options do not meet the criteria for MFA as they either combine two factors from the same category of something you have (option A), something you are (option C), or something you know (option D).

23. Answer: B. The procedure for confirming a user's Identity

Explanation: Authentication is the process of verifying the Identity of a user, system, or device. It ensures that the entity requesting access is who or what it claims to be.

24. Answer: B. Identity, authentication, authorization, and auditing

    Explanation: The IAAA model describes the four key components of access control.

    Identity: Establishing who the user is

    Authentication: Verifying the user's Identity

    Authorization: Determining what the user is allowed to do

    Auditing: Monitoring and recording user activities

25. Answer: C. All access permissions should be reviewed.

    Explanation: When an employee transfers within an organization, it's essential to review all access permissions to ensure that they align with the new role. This helps prevent privilege creep and ensures that the employee has the appropriate access for their new position.

26. Answer: D. Organization's published security policy for data classification

    Explanation: In a MAC system, data classifications are determined by the organization's formal security policy. This policy defines the rules for classifying, handling, and protecting information, ensuring that data is accessed only by authorized individuals.

27. **Answer: B. Least privilege**

Explanation: The principle of least privilege dictates that individuals should have only the permissions necessary to perform their job functions. This minimizes the potential damage from accidental mishaps or intentional malicious activities by limiting access rights to the bare minimum required to complete the task.

28. **Answer: C. Trusted recovery**

Explanation: Trusted recovery refers to the ability of a system to respond to failures or security breaches in a manner that prevents further compromises. It ensures that the system can recover to a secure state, even after a failure or attack.

29. **Answer: A. Peer review**

Explanation: Open design allows for transparency and collaboration, enabling peer review of the code. This collective examination can identify and fix vulnerabilities, making the system more secure.

30. **Answer: C. Dual control**

Explanation: Dual control requires two or more individuals to perform a task, ensuring that no single person has complete control over critical functions. This can mitigate the risk associated with a single individual having access to users' private keys.

31. Answer: A. Project initiation

    Explanation: The commitment from senior management is essential at the project initiation phase of BCP. This ensures that the project has the necessary support and resources to proceed.

32. Answer: D. Segregation of duties

    Explanation: Segregation of duties (SoD) ensures that no single individual has control over all aspects of any critical transaction. By dividing tasks and privileges, SoD reduces the risk of a single point of failure, which can be exploited through social engineering.

33. Answer: B. Trusted computing base

    Explanation: The trusted computing base (TCB) includes all the components of a system that are critical to its security, including hardware, firmware, and software. Trust in the TCB is essential for overall system security.

34. Answer: A. Access control list, reference monitor

    Explanation: During access authorization, the conceptual ruleset defining the access rights and permissions for users and objects within a system is commonly called the access control list (ACL). The enforcement mechanism that ensures that these access controls are properly implemented and adhered to is known as the reference monitor. Therefore, the correct answer to fill in the blanks is A. Access control list, reference monitor. The other options do not accurately represent the standard terminology used in access control and authorization within information security. The security kernel is a core component of a computer's operating system that deals with security-related functions, and the term "security enforcer" is not a standard term used in this context.

35. Answer: B. There is always a trade-off for security, so an organization has to weigh the cost vs. benefits.

Explanation: Aligning security controls with business objectives ensures that security measures are balanced with the organization's goals, resources, and risk tolerance. It helps in making informed decisions about where to invest in security.

36. Answer: A. High

Explanation: The overall categorization of a system is typically determined by the highest level of potential impact among the evaluated criteria. In this case, the high potential impact of unauthorized disclosure would define the overall categorization.

37. Answer: C. Trust describes product function; assurance describes process reliability.

Explanation: Trust refers to the functionality and security features of a product, while assurance relates to the confidence in the development process, ensuring that the product functions as intended.

38. Answer: D. Session keys

    Explanation: The Vernam Cipher is a symmetric key cipher using a one-time pad. Modern session keys, which are used for a single session and then discarded, are based on this concept of using a key only once.

39. Answer: B. DES/3DES

    Explanation: The relationship between DES and 3DES mirrors the concept of adding complexity to encryption. 3DES, which applies the DES algorithm three times to each data block, was developed to provide a simple method of increasing the key size of DES to protect against brute-force attacks.

40. Answer: D. Non-repudiation

    Explanation: Non-repudiation provides proof of the origin or delivery of data to protect against denial by the parties involved. In the context of email, it would provide evidence that the email was indeed sent by the claimed sender.

41. Answer: C. Hash the document and then encrypt the hash with the sender's private key

    Explanation: Non-repudiation is achieved by creating a hash of the message and then encrypting that hash with the sender's private key. This creates a digital signature that can be verified by anyone with the sender's public key, proving that the message came from the sender and has not been altered.

42. Answer: C. One-way math

Explanation: Hashing algorithms use one-way functions, meaning the output (the hash) cannot be reversed to reveal the original input. This provides the secrecy in a hashing algorithm.

43. Answer: C. An attack that attempts to find collisions in separate messages

Explanation: A birthday attack is a type of cryptographic attack that exploits the mathematics behind the birthday problem in probability theory. The attack depends on finding collisions, which are two inputs producing the same hash output.

44. Answer: A. Cable

Explanation: Layer 1 of the OSI model, the Physical Layer, deals with the physical characteristics of the network, such as the network cable. Therefore, if there's a Layer 1 issue, it's most likely related to the physical connection, such as the cable.

45. Answer: D. Though multiple systems can access the media simultaneously, the result will be a collision, which should be immediately detected.

Explanation: CSMA/CD is a network protocol for carrier transmission in Ethernet networks. It allows multiple hosts to access the media simultaneously, but if a collision occurs (two devices transmit at the same time), it is detected and the transmissions are stopped to avoid corrupting data.

46. Answer: B. Elasticity

    Explanation: Elasticity in cloud computing is the
    ability to quickly expand or decrease computer
    processing, memory, and storage resources to meet
    changing demands without worrying about capacity
    planning and engineering for peak loads. It allows
    resources to be provisioned and deprovisioned
    automatically as the demand changes.

47. Answer: B. To control the way assets are accessed

    Explanation: IAM is primarily concerned with
    controlling how assets are accessed within an
    organization. It involves managing digital identities
    and implementing the necessary technology to
    improve user experience, cost control, and risk
    mitigation.

48. Answer: D. Maximum privilege

    Explanation: The fundamental principles of access
    control are "need to know," "least privilege," and
    "separation of duties." The principle of "maximum
    privilege" does not exist in access control; it
    contradicts the principle of "least privilege," which
    states that a user should have the minimum levels of
    access necessary to perform their job functions.

49. Answer: A. Security Assertion Markup Language

    Explanation: SAML stands for Security Assertion
    Markup Language. It is a key protocol used in
    Federated Identity Management (FIM) solutions,
    providing both authentication and authorization.

50. Answer: C. Frequent reauthentication

Explanation: The primary and best way to prevent session hijacking is through frequent reauthentication. This means that a user is continually reauthenticated by the system in a manner that is transparent to the user, making it much more difficult for an attacker to compromise a user's active session.

51. Answer: D. Encryption

Explanation: Access Control Services consist of identification, authentication, authorization, and accountability. Encryption, while a crucial aspect of security, is not a component of Access Control Services as defined in this context.

52. Answer: B. The process of granting access to systems and data to a new employee or when an employee changes roles

Explanation: Provisioning in the identity life cycle refers to the process of granting access to systems and data to a new employee or when an employee changes roles. This includes activities such as background checks, confirming skills, and Identity proofing.

53. Answer: B. To provide authentication and authorization

Explanation: SAML is a key protocol used in Federated Identity Management (FIM) solutions, providing both authentication and authorization.

54. Answer: D. All of the above

    Explanation: All the options listed are potential risks relating to IDaaS. These include the availability of the service, protection of critical identity data, and entrusting a third party with sensitive or proprietary data.

55. Answer: A. To prevent automated account creation, spam, and brute-force password decryption attacks

    Explanation: CAPTCHA is a security measure that works by asking a user to complete a simple test to prove they're human and not a robot or automated program. It is used to prevent automated account creation, spam, and brute-force password decryption attacks.

56. Answer: B. The elevation of user privileges for a short period to complete necessary but infrequent tasks

    Explanation: Just-in-Time Access refers to the elevation of user privileges to an authorized user for a short period, so a user may complete necessary but infrequent tasks. It mitigates the need for long-term elevation of privileges, which minimizes potential security risks.

57. Answer: C. The process of terminating access when an employee leaves the organization

    Explanation: Deprovisioning in the identity life cycle refers to the process of terminating access when an employee leaves the organization. This includes activities such as revoking access rights, returning equipment, and archiving user data.

58. Answer: C. To allow third-party services to access user data without needing to know the user's credentials

Explanation: OAuth is a protocol used in Federated Identity Management (FIM) that allows third-party services to access user data without needing to know the user's credentials.

59. Answer: A. It reduces the number of passwords a user has to remember.

Explanation: The main advantage of using a Single Sign-On (SSO) system is that it reduces the number of passwords a user has to remember. This not only improves user convenience but also reduces the risk of password-related security issues.

60. Answer: B. To ensure that users only have access to the information they need to perform their job functions

Explanation: The "need-to-know" principle in access control is designed to ensure that users only have access to the information they need to perform their job functions. This minimizes the risk of unauthorized access and data breaches.

61. Answer: C. The process of allowing different organizations to share and manage identity information

Explanation: Federation in the context of Federated Identity Management (FIM) refers to the process of allowing different organizations to share and manage identity information. This allows users to use the same credentials to access services across multiple organizations.

62. Answer: D. To provide a simple identity layer on top of the OAuth 2.0 protocol

    Explanation: OpenID Connect is a protocol used in Federated Identity Management (FIM) that provides a simple identity layer on top of the OAuth 2.0 protocol. It allows clients to verify the Identity of the end user based on the authentication performed by an authorization server.

63. Answer: B. If the SSO system is compromised, all services that use it are potentially at risk.

    Explanation: The main disadvantage of using a Single Sign-On (SSO) system is that if the SSO system is compromised, all services that use it are potentially at risk. This is because the attacker would have access to all the systems the user can access through the SSO system.

64. Answer: C. To prevent any single individual from being able to complete a significant process or transaction on their own

    Explanation: The "separation of duties" principle in access control is designed to prevent any single individual from being able to complete a significant process or transaction on their own. This reduces the risk of fraud and error.

65. Answer: A. The process of confirming or establishing that somebody is who they claim to be

    Explanation: Authentication in the context of Access Control Services refers to the process of confirming or establishing that somebody is who they claim to be. This is typically done through the use of passwords, biometrics, or other forms of identification.

66. Answer: D. The ability to link actions to a specific user and hold them responsible for their actions

    Explanation: Accountability in the context of Access Control Services refers to the ability to link actions to a specific user and hold them responsible for their actions. This is typically done through the use of audit logs and other tracking mechanisms.

67. Answer: B. The process of determining what actions a user is allowed to perform

    Explanation: Authorization in the context of Access Control Services refers to the process of determining what actions a user is allowed to perform. This is typically based on the user's role, responsibilities, and the principle of least privilege.

68. Answer: B. It allows users to use the same credentials to access services across multiple organizations.

    Explanation: The main advantage of using a Federated Identity Management (FIM) system is that it allows users to use the same credentials to access services across multiple organizations. This not only improves user convenience but also reduces the risk of password-related security issues.

69. Answer: B. To ensure that users only have the minimum levels of access necessary to perform their job functions

Explanation: The "least privilege" principle in access control is designed to ensure that users only have the minimum levels of access necessary to perform their job functions. This minimizes the risk of unauthorized access and data breaches.

70. Answer: A. The process of a user claiming or professing an identity

Explanation: Identification in the context of Access Control Services refers to the process of a user claiming or professing an identity. This is typically the first step in the authentication process.

71. Answer: D. A cloud-based service that provides Identity and Access Management functions to an organization's systems that reside on-premises and/ or in the cloud

Explanation: Identity as a Service (IDaaS) refers to a cloud-based service that provides Identity and Access Management functions to an organization's systems that reside on-premises and/or in the cloud. It is typically used by organizations that want to outsource their identity services to a third-party provider.

72. Answer: D. To provide a secure method for transmitting information and authenticating both the user and the server

Explanation: Kerberos is a network authentication protocol that provides a secure method for transmitting information and authenticating both the user and the server. It uses secret-key cryptography to prevent eavesdropping and replay attacks.

73. Answer: B. If the FIM system is compromised, all services that use it are potentially at risk.

Explanation: The main disadvantage of using a Federated Identity Management (FIM) system is that if the FIM system is compromised, all services that use it are potentially at risk. This is because the attacker would have access to all the systems the user can access through the FIM system.

74. Answer: D. To ensure that actions can be traced back to the individual who performed them

Explanation: The "accountability" principle in access control is designed to ensure that actions can be traced back to the individual who performed them. This is typically done through the use of audit logs and other tracking mechanisms.

75. Answer: B. The use of physical or behavioral characteristics to verify a user's Identity

Explanation: Biometrics in the context of authentication systems refers to the use of physical or behavioral characteristics to verify a user's

Identity. This can include fingerprints, facial recognition, voice recognition, and other unique characteristics.

76. Answer: C. The process of verifying a user's claimed Identity by comparing it against one or more reliable sources

    Explanation: Identity proofing in the context of IAM refers to the process of verifying a user's claimed Identity by comparing it against one or more reliable sources. This is typically done as part of the onboarding process when a new account is created.

77. Answer: C. The process of allowing different organizations to share and manage identity information

    Explanation: Identity Federation in the context of IAM refers to the process of allowing different organizations to share and manage identity information. This allows users to use the same credentials to access services across multiple organizations.

78. Answer: B. To provide a networking protocol that offers centralized authentication, authorization, and accounting (AAA) management for users who connect and use a network service

    Explanation: RADIUS (Remote Authentication Dial-In User Service) is a networking protocol that offers centralized authentication, authorization, and accounting (AAA) management for users who connect and use a network service.

79. Answer: B. If the biometric data is compromised, it cannot be changed like a password.

    Explanation: The main disadvantage of using biometric authentication systems is that if the biometric data is compromised, it cannot be changed like a password. This can lead to serious security issues.

80. Answer: D. To ensure that actions can be definitively traced back to the individual who performed them, and they cannot deny performing them

    Explanation: The "non-repudiation" principle in access control is designed to ensure that actions can be definitively traced back to the individual who performed them, and they cannot deny performing them. This is typically important in legal contexts where proof of action is required.

81. Answer: B. The use of two or more independent credentials for verifying a user's Identity

    Explanation: Multifactor authentication (MFA) in the context of authentication systems refers to the use of two or more independent credentials for verifying a user's Identity. This typically involves a combination of something the user knows (like a password), something the user has (like a smart card), and something the user is (like a biometric trait).

82. Answer: B. The stages a digital identity goes through from creation to deletion

Explanation: The identity life cycle in the context of IAM refers to the stages a digital identity goes through from creation to deletion. This includes processes such as provisioning, managing, and deprovisioning identities.

83. Answer: B. To provide a networking protocol that offers centralized authentication, authorization, and accounting (AAA) management for users who connect and use a network service

Explanation: TACACS+ (Terminal Access Controller Access Control System Plus) is a networking protocol that offers centralized authentication, authorization, and accounting (AAA) management for users who connect and use a network service.

84. Answer: B. Passwords can be easily forgotten, shared, or stolen

Explanation: The main disadvantage of using password-based authentication systems is that passwords can be easily forgotten, shared, or stolen. This can lead to unauthorized access and other security issues.

85. Answer: B. To ensure that users only have the minimum levels of access necessary to perform their job functions

Explanation: The "principle of least privilege" in access control is designed to ensure that users only have the minimum levels of access necessary to perform their job functions. This minimizes the risk of unauthorized access and data breaches.

86. Answer: B. The use of a single set of credentials to access multiple applications or services

Explanation: Single Sign-On (SSO) in the context of authentication systems refers to the use of a single set of credentials to access multiple applications or services. This simplifies the user experience and reduces the risk of password-related security issues.

87. Answer: B. The process of setting up a new user account with appropriate access rights

Explanation: Provisioning in the context of IAM refers to the process of setting up a new user account with appropriate access rights. This includes activities such as creating the user's account, assigning roles, and granting access to resources.

88. Answer: B. To provide a standard for exchanging authentication and authorization data between parties

Explanation: SAML (Security Assertion Markup Language) is a standard for exchanging authentication and authorization data between parties. It is commonly used in Single Sign-On (SSO) and Federated Identity Management (FIM) systems.

89. Answer: B. It can be difficult to manage if roles are not clearly defined or if users have multiple roles.

Explanation: The main disadvantage of using role-based access control systems is that it can be difficult to manage if roles are not clearly defined or if users have multiple roles. This can lead to users having more access rights than they need, which can increase the risk of unauthorized access and data breaches.

90. Answer: B. To enforce access control policies based on the classification of information and the security clearance of users

    Explanation: Mandatory access control is a type of access control that enforces access control policies based on the classification of information and the security clearance of users. It is commonly used in government and military environments where information must be classified and access must be strictly controlled.

91. Answer: B. A flexible access control method where access rights are granted to users through the use of policies which combine attributes together

    Explanation: Attribute-based access control (ABAC) in the context of access control systems refers to a flexible access control method where access rights are granted to users through the use of policies which combine attributes together. These attributes can be associated with the user, the object to be accessed, or the environment.

92. Answer: B. The process of removing an existing user account and its associated access rights

    Explanation: Deprovisioning in the context of IAM refers to the process of removing an existing user account and its associated access rights. This is typically done when an employee leaves an organization or changes roles.

93. Answer: B. To provide a standard for authorizing third-party applications to access user data without sharing passwords

Explanation: OAuth (Open Authorization) is a standard for authorizing third-party applications to access user data without sharing passwords. It is commonly used in scenarios where you want to give an application access to your data without giving it your password.

94. Answer: B. It can lead to "privilege creep" if access rights are not regularly reviewed and updated.

Explanation: The main disadvantage of using discretionary access control systems is that it can lead to "privilege creep" if access rights are not regularly reviewed and updated. Privilege creep occurs when users accumulate more privileges than they need to perform their job functions, which can increase the risk of unauthorized access and data breaches.

95. Answer: B. To allow the owners of information to control who can access their information

Explanation: Discretionary access control is a type of access control that allows the owners of information to control who can access their information. It is commonly used in environments where information sharing is encouraged, but control is still required.

96. Answer: B. The act of exploiting a bug, design flaw, or configuration oversight in an operating system or software application to gain elevated access to resources

Explanation: Privilege escalation in the context of access control systems refers to the act of exploiting a bug, design flaw, or configuration oversight in an operating system or software application to gain elevated access to resources. This is a common technique used in cyberattacks to gain unauthorized access to systems.

97. Answer: D. To support both symmetric and asymmetric cryptography

    Explanation: The Secure European System for Applications in a Multivendor Environment, better known as SESAME, is an improved version of Kerberos. One of the big advantages of SESAME over Kerberos is that it supports both symmetric and asymmetric cryptography.

98. Answer: B. To rank the strength of authentication processes and systems

    Explanation: Authenticator Assurance Levels (AAL) refer to the strength of authentication processes and systems. AAL levels rank from AAL1 (least robust) to AAL3 (most robust).

99. Answer: A. DAC is determined by the owner of the asset, while MAC is determined by the system based on labels.

    Explanation: Discretionary access control (DAC) means an asset owner determines who can access the asset; access is given at the discretion of the owner. Mandatory access control (MAC) determines access based upon the clearance level of the subject and classification, or sensitivity, of the object.

100. Answer: B. The implementation or integration of identity services in a cloud-based environment

Explanation: Identity as a Service (IDaaS) refers to the implementation or integration of identity services in a cloud-based environment. It has a variety of capabilities, including provisioning, administration, Single Sign-On (SSO), multifactor authentication (MFA), and directory services.

101. Answer: B. The process of elevating user privileges for a short period to complete necessary but infrequent tasks

Explanation: Just-in-Time Access refers to the elevation of user privileges to an authorized user for a short period, so a user may complete necessary but infrequent tasks. It mitigates the need for long-term elevation of privileges, which minimizes potential security risks.

CHAPTER 8

Security Assessment and Testing

Security Assessment and Testing represent a vital domain within the CISSP certification, emphasizing the intricate methodologies and practices employed to scrutinize an organization's information security stance. This chapter delves into the foundational principles that govern this domain, offering a comprehensive exploration of the subject matter.

The chapter is structured to examine the various techniques and tools used in Security Assessment and Testing. It commences with an overview of the importance of evaluating security measures within an organization, highlighting the necessity of continuous monitoring and assessment to ensure optimal protection.

Subsequently, the chapter explores the different types of assessments, including vulnerability assessments, penetration testing, and security audits. These are explained in detail, with examples and case studies illustrating their practical applications.

Furthermore, the chapter includes practice questions to facilitate hands-on learning. These practice questions reinforce the theoretical concepts presented, enabling readers to apply their knowledge in simulated environments.

© Mohamed Aly Bouke 2023
M. A. Bouke, *CISSP Exam Certification Companion*, Certification Study Companion Series,
https://doi.org/10.1007/979-8-8688-0057-3_8

Security Assessment Strategies

A well-rounded security assessment strategy is vital for organizations to identify vulnerabilities, manage risks, and uphold a strong security posture. Incorporating internal, external, and third-party assessments enables organizations to address potential security issues from multiple angles. Developing and continuously refining assessment strategies are essential in safeguarding an organization's security infrastructure, ensuring robustness and resilience against potential threats. Effective assessment strategies must encompass various approaches, including internal, external, and third-party assessments. Each of these plays an indispensable role in the discovery of vulnerabilities, adherence to industry regulations, and sustaining the organization's overall security integrity. This section will delve into each of these assessment approaches, offering insights and examples that highlight their importance and practical applications:

- **Internal assessments**: Internal assessments are carried out within an organization, utilizing the in-depth knowledge of the company's personnel regarding its systems, processes, and infrastructure. Leveraging this expertise allows organizations to conduct regular, cost-effective evaluations of their security posture. Such assessments facilitate the swift identification and remediation of vulnerabilities, ultimately fortifying the organization's security. For example, a corporation's IT department might undertake a network vulnerability assessment to uncover outdated software and security gaps that have not been patched. The organization then has the opportunity to prioritize and address these vulnerabilities, taking action to prevent potential exploitation from malicious actors.

- **External assessments**: External assessments are conducted by independent security specialists or companies without affiliation to the assessed organization. The impartial perspective provided by external assessments is valuable for identifying weaknesses in an organization's security infrastructure that internal personnel may overlook due to familiarity with the systems and processes. For example, a financial institution might hire a third-party firm to perform a penetration test. This involves simulating real-world attacks to identify weaknesses in the organization's security controls. The financial institution can gain an unbiased view of its security posture and implement necessary improvements to safeguard against potential threats.

- **Third-party assessments**: Third-party assessments involve evaluating the security posture of an organization's vendors, suppliers, or partners, who may have access to sensitive information or systems. These assessments help organizations manage the risks of sharing sensitive data and ensure their partners maintain a strong security posture. Consider a company that plans to use a cloud service provider to store sensitive customer data. Before entrusting the provider with this critical information, the company should conduct a thorough security assessment to ensure that the provider has robust security measures in place to protect the data. By doing so, the company can minimize the risk of data breaches and maintain the trust of its customers.

In addition, in the context of security assessments, organizations often employ a combination of internal, external, and third-party assessments. Each approach serves a unique purpose and is more suitable for specific scenarios. Table 8-1 compares these approaches, delineating their key characteristics and highlighting when each is more suitable. Understanding the distinctions and applications of these assessment methods allows organizations to employ them, thus fortifying their security posture strategically.

Table 8-1. *Comparison of Security Assessment Strategies*

Approach	Description	When More Suitable
Internal Assessments	Conducted by an organization's own personnel, leveraging in-depth knowledge of systems, processes, and infrastructure. Allow for regular, cost-effective evaluations and swift identification and remediation of vulnerabilities	When an organization needs to perform regular security checks, identify internal vulnerabilities, and prioritize remediation efforts
External Assessments	Executed by independent security specialists or companies without affiliation to the assessed organization. Provide an unbiased perspective and identify weaknesses that internal personnel may overlook	When an unbiased view is required, such as compliance audits, or when specialized expertise is needed to identify hidden vulnerabilities
Third-Party Assessments	Involve evaluating the security posture of vendors, suppliers, or partners. Help manage the risks of sharing sensitive data and ensure that partners maintain a strong security posture	When an organization needs to assess the security of external entities like vendors or partners, especially when sensitive data is shared

Understanding the significance and practical applications of internal, external, and third-party assessments empowers organizations to craft comprehensive and potent security assessment strategies. Integrating a blend of these approaches guarantees that organizations have the tools to identify vulnerabilities, reduce risks, and uphold a robust security posture against constantly changing threats. As your exploration of the realm of information security deepens, keep in mind each assessment approaches distinct advantages and applications, as this awareness will guide you in constructing a balanced and resilient security assessment strategy.

Security Control Testing Approaches

Effective security control testing is fundamental for organizations to identify vulnerabilities, validate their security controls, and maintain a strong security posture. Employing various security control testing methods helps organizations detect potential weaknesses from multiple angles, ensuring a comprehensive evaluation of their security infrastructure. This guide will delve into various security control testing approaches, providing insights and examples to illustrate their significance and real-world applications.

To understand an organization's security posture comprehensively, it is essential to utilize a diverse range of security control testing methods. Each approach plays a crucial role in identifying vulnerabilities, validating the effectiveness of security controls, and ensuring overall security. The following are some common security control testing approaches:

- **Vulnerability assessment**: A vulnerability assessment is a systematic process of identifying, analyzing, and prioritizing vulnerabilities within an organization's systems, networks, and applications. Conducting vulnerability assessments allows organizations to discover potential security gaps and prioritize remediation efforts based on the severity of the vulnerabilities.

- **Penetration testing**: Penetration testing, often referred to as ethical hacking, involves simulating real-world cyberattacks to identify potential weaknesses in an organization's security controls. This proactive approach helps organizations uncover vulnerabilities that might be exploited by malicious actors and address them before they can be used in a real attack.

- **Log reviews**: Log reviews involve the examination of system, network, and application logs to identify unusual activity or security events. Regularly reviewing logs enables organizations to detect potential security incidents early and initiate appropriate response measures.

- **Synthetic transactions**: Synthetic transactions involve automated tests to simulate user interactions with applications or systems, mimicking real-world usage patterns. This approach helps organizations monitor the performance and availability of their services and detect potential security issues that may arise during normal operations.

- **Code review and testing**: Code review involves examining source code to identify potential security flaws, such as injection vulnerabilities, insecure configurations, and weak cryptographic implementations. Both manual and automated code review methods can be employed to ensure that an application's code adheres to secure coding practices and industry standards.

- **Misuse case testing**: Misuse case testing focuses on how a malicious user can abuse or exploit an application or system. Creating and testing misuse cases allows organizations to identify potential attack vectors and implement appropriate security measures to mitigate risks.

- **Test coverage analysis**: Test coverage analysis involves measuring how much an organization's testing efforts cover its systems, networks, and applications. Conducting test coverage analysis enables organizations to identify gaps in their testing efforts and prioritize areas that require additional attention.

- **Interface testing**: Interface testing validates the interactions between various system components, such as APIs, network connections, and user interfaces. This testing method helps organizations ensure that data is exchanged correctly between components and identify and address potential security issues.

- **Breach attack simulations**: Breach attack simulations use automated tools to emulate cyberattacks on an organization's systems and networks. This approach enables organizations to evaluate the effectiveness of their security controls and incident response plans in a controlled environment.

- **Compliance checks**: Compliance checks involve evaluating an organization's adherence to industry regulations, standards, and best practices. Conducting compliance checks enables organizations to ensure that they meet their legal and contractual obligations and maintain a strong security posture.

Moreover, Table 8-2 summarizes these security control testing approaches, delineating their key characteristics and highlighting when each is more suitable. Organizations must utilize diverse security control testing approaches to identify vulnerabilities, validate their security controls, and maintain a strong security posture.

Table 8-2. *Comparison of Security Control Testing Approaches*

Approach	Description	When More Suitable
Vulnerability Assessment	Systematic process of identifying, analyzing, and prioritizing vulnerabilities within systems, networks, and applications	For regular monitoring of security gaps and prioritizing remediation efforts
Penetration Testing	Simulating real-world cyberattacks to identify potential weaknesses in security controls	To uncover vulnerabilities that might be exploited by malicious actors
Log Reviews	Examination of system, network, and application logs to identify unusual activity or security events	For early detection of potential security incidents and initiating response measures
Synthetic Transactions	Automated tests to simulate user interactions with applications or systems, mimicking real-world usage patterns	To monitor performance and availability of services and detect potential security issues
Code Review and Testing	Examining source code to identify potential security flaws, such as injection vulnerabilities, insecure configurations, and weak cryptographic implementations	To ensure adherence to secure coding practices and industry standards

(continued)

Table 8-2. (*continued*)

Approach	Description	When More Suitable
Misuse Case Testing	Focuses on how a malicious user can abuse or exploit an application or system	To identify potential attack vectors and implement appropriate security measures
Test Coverage Analysis	Measuring how much testing efforts cover systems, networks, and applications	To identify gaps in testing efforts and prioritize areas that require additional attention
Interface Testing	Validates the interactions between various system components, such as APIs, network connections, and user interfaces	To ensure correct data exchange between components and identify potential security issues
Breach Attack Simulations	Using automated tools to emulate cyberattacks on systems and networks	To evaluate the effectiveness of security controls and incident response plans in a controlled environment
Compliance Checks	Evaluating adherence to industry regulations, standards, and best practices	To ensure legal and contractual obligations are met and maintain a strong security posture

Organizations must utilize diverse security control testing approaches to identify vulnerabilities, validate their security controls, and maintain a strong security posture. Understanding and employing these various methods allows organizations to detect potential weaknesses from multiple angles and comprehensively evaluate their security infrastructure.

Gathering Security Process Data

Collecting security process data is vital to maintaining an organization's security posture, ensuring both technical and administrative aspects are addressed effectively. Gathering this data enables organizations to make informed decisions, optimize security processes, and demonstrate adherence to industry standards and regulations. This guide will explore various types of security process data collection, providing insights and examples to illustrate their significance and real-world applications. To maintain a strong security posture and ensure effective risk management, organizations must gather diverse security process data. This data helps organizations make informed decisions, identify areas for improvement, and measure the effectiveness of their security controls. The following are some common types of security process data that organizations should consider collecting:

- **Account management**: Account management data includes user account creation, modification, and termination information. Collecting this data ensures that access to sensitive information and systems is granted only to authorized users and that access rights are revoked when no longer needed.

- **Management review and approval**: Management review and approval data encompass records of management decisions related to security policies, procedures, and controls. This data demonstrates an organization's commitment to security and ensures that key stakeholders are involved in critical security decisions.

- **Key performance and risk indicators**: Key performance indicators (KPIs) and key risk indicators (KRIs) are metrics used to evaluate the effectiveness of an organization's security controls and processes. Tracking KPIs and KRIs allows organizations to identify trends, measure progress, and make data-driven decisions to enhance their security posture.

- **Backup verification data**: Backup verification data consists of records confirming that an organization's data backups have been completed and are recoverable. Collecting this data ensures that critical data can be restored during data loss, system failure, or a security incident.

- **Training and awareness**: Training and awareness data includes records of security awareness and training programs employees attend. Collecting this data ensures that employees have the knowledge and skills to protect sensitive information and maintain a strong security posture.

- **Disaster recovery (DR) and business continuity (BC)**: Disaster recovery and business continuity data consist of records related to an organization's DR and BC plans, including testing results, updates, and revisions. Gathering this data helps organizations ensure that their DR and BC plans are effective and up to date, enabling them to minimize downtime and continue operations in the event of a disaster or security incident.

Collecting security process data is essential for organizations to maintain a strong security posture and make informed decisions about their security processes and controls. Gathering and analyzing diverse types of security process data allows organizations to identify areas for improvement, optimize security processes, and demonstrate adherence to industry standards and regulations. As you continue to build and enhance your organization's security posture, remember to consider the various types of security process data and their unique benefits in strengthening your organization's overall security.

Analyzing Test Output and Facilitating Security Audits

Analyzing test output and generating reports are crucial to maintaining and improving an organization's security posture. Conducting thorough analyses and facilitating security audits enable organizations to identify vulnerabilities, implement remediation measures, and maintain compliance with industry regulations. In this guide, we will explore the process of analyzing test output, generating reports, and facilitating security audits, providing insights and examples to illustrate their significance and real-world applications.

Test Output Analysis and Report Generation

- **Remediation**: Remediation involves the process of addressing identified vulnerabilities or security weaknesses. After analyzing test output and generating a report, organizations should prioritize and implement remediation measures to mitigate risks and enhance their security posture. These measures may include patching software, updating configurations, or implementing new security controls.

- **Exception handling**: Exception handling involves managing deviations or noncompliance instances identified during security testing or audits. Organizations must have a well-defined exception handling process to address these issues, including documenting exceptions, evaluating risks, and implementing compensating controls when necessary.

- **Ethical disclosure**: Ethical disclosure responsibly reports security vulnerabilities or weaknesses discovered during testing or audits. Organizations should have a clear ethical disclosure policy, including notifying affected parties, coordinating with vendors, or reporting vulnerabilities to industry organizations.

The process of analyzing test output and generating reports is a vital component of an organization's security strategy. It not only helps in identifying and addressing vulnerabilities but also ensures that the organization's security measures are in line with industry standards and regulations. Through remediation, exception handling, and ethical disclosure, organizations can create a robust security framework that is responsive to the ever-changing landscape of threats and challenges. This comprehensive approach fosters a culture of continuous improvement and vigilance, contributing to the overall strength and resilience of the organization's security posture.

Conducting and Facilitating Security Audits

Security audits help organizations evaluate their security posture, identify vulnerabilities, and maintain compliance with industry standards and regulations. Conducting or facilitating security audits is essential to ensuring the effectiveness of an organization's security controls. Security audits can be internal, external, or third party:

- **Internal audits**: Internal audits are conducted within an organization, utilizing the in-depth knowledge of the company's personnel regarding its systems, processes, and infrastructure. Organizations can identify vulnerabilities and inefficiencies through internal audits, enabling them to implement improvements and maintain a strong security posture.

- **External audits**: External audits are performed through independent security specialists or companies without affiliation to the organization being audited. The impartial perspective provided through external audits is valuable for identifying weaknesses in an organization's security infrastructure that internal personnel may overlook due to familiarity with the systems and processes.

- **Third-party audits**: Third-party audits involve the evaluation of an organization's vendors, suppliers, or partners, who may have access to sensitive information or systems. These audits help organizations manage the risks of sharing sensitive data and ensure their partners maintain a strong security posture.

Analyzing test output, generating reports, and conducting or facilitating security audits enable organizations to pinpoint vulnerabilities, implement remediation measures, and uphold compliance with industry regulations. As efforts to fortify your organization's security posture continue, remember the vital role these processes play in augmenting the overall security of your systems, networks, and applications. With a meticulous approach to test output analysis and a diverse strategy for security audits, your organization can sustain a robust and resilient security stance against the constant flux of emerging threats.

Common Frameworks and Standards for Security Control Assessment

Security control assessment is a critical process that helps organizations identify, evaluate, and manage their security controls. Various frameworks and standards guide this process, providing a structured approach to assessing the effectiveness of security controls. The following are some of the widely recognized frameworks and standards used for security control assessment:

- **ISO/IEC 27001** is a globally recognized standard that outlines the requirements for an Information Security Management System (ISMS). It emphasizes the importance of risk management and continuous improvement in implementing security controls. For example, a multinational corporation operating in various countries might adopt ISO/IEC 27001 to ensure its security practices are consistent across all regions. This standard is particularly suitable for international organizations that want to demonstrate their commitment to information security to stakeholders, clients, and regulators.

- **NIST Special Publication 800-53** is a comprehensive set of security controls developed by the National Institute of Standards and Technology (NIST) in the United States. It is specifically designed for federal information systems. A US government agency, for instance, must adhere to these controls to ensure the security and integrity of its information systems. This framework is most suitable for US federal organizations or those working closely with the US government, as it aligns with federal regulations and standards.

- **Center for Internet Security (CIS):** CIS Controls, developed by the CIS, is a set of prioritized best practices to improve cybersecurity defenses. Small- to medium-sized businesses might find CIS Controls particularly beneficial as a practical and cost-effective way to identify and mitigate common cybersecurity threats. This framework is ideal for organizations looking for a hands-on, actionable approach to cybersecurity, especially those with limited resources.

- **Control Objectives for Information and Related Technologies (COBIT):** COBIT is a framework that integrates governance and management practices for information technology (IT). It helps organizations align their IT processes with business goals and governance requirements. A financial institution, for example, might use COBIT to ensure that its IT operations comply with regulatory requirements and support its business objectives. COBIT is suitable for organizations that must tightly align IT processes with business strategies and regulatory compliance.

- **Factor Analysis of Information Risk (FAIR):** FAIR is a unique framework providing a quantitative risk management approach. It helps organizations understand, analyze, and quantify information risk in financial terms. An insurance company might use FAIR to assess cybersecurity risk in monetary terms, providing a clear financial perspective on potential risks. FAIR is ideal for organizations that require a quantitative, financially oriented approach to risk management, especially in industries like finance and insurance.

- **System and Organization Controls (SOC):** SOC reports are vital for service providers needing to demonstrate control effectiveness to clients or regulatory bodies. These reports ensure control environments related to data retrieval, storage, processing, and transfer. There are different types of SOC reports, each serving a specific purpose:

  - **SOC 1:** Focuses on controls related to financial reporting. It is often used by financial service providers or organizations that must comply with financial regulations.

  - **SOC 2:** This type is particularly relevant to the CISSP exam and focuses on controls related to security, availability, processing integrity, confidentiality, and customer data privacy. SOC 2 suits technology and cloud computing companies that handle sensitive customer information.

  - **SOC 3:** Similar to SOC 2 but with a public-facing report, SOC 3 is used when an organization wants to demonstrate its commitment to security controls without disclosing the details of the controls. For example, a cloud service provider might undergo a SOC 2 assessment to assure clients that robust controls are in place for data security and privacy. SOC assessments suit service providers in various industries, particularly those handling sensitive client data.

Choosing the right framework or standard for security control assessment is a decision that aligns with an organization's specific needs, industry, regulatory environment, and security objectives. Understanding each framework's unique characteristics and real-world applications enables organizations to adopt the most appropriate approach, ensuring a robust and resilient security posture. The continuous evolution of threats and regulations calls for a thoughtful selection of frameworks that can adapt to an ever-changing security landscape. For those preparing for the CISSP exam, special attention to SOC 2 and its focus on data security controls will be beneficial in understanding the practical application of security control assessments.

Summary

This chapter explored the importance of analyzing test output, generating reports, and conducting security audits to strengthen an organization's security posture. We discussed various aspects of test output analysis, including remediation, exception handling, and ethical disclosure. Additionally, we examined the different types of security audits, such as internal, external, and third-party audits, emphasizing their significance in identifying vulnerabilities and maintaining compliance with industry regulations.

Key Takeaways

- **Analyzing test output and generating reports** are essential in identifying vulnerabilities, prioritizing remediation measures, and enhancing an organization's security posture.

- **Remediation** involves addressing identified vulnerabilities or security weaknesses to mitigate risks and improve security.

- **Exception handling** is crucial for managing deviations or noncompliance instances identified during security testing or audits.

- **Ethical disclosure** is the responsible practice of reporting discovered security vulnerabilities or weaknesses.

- **Security audits** help organizations evaluate their security posture, identify vulnerabilities, and maintain compliance with industry standards and regulations.

- **Internal, external, and third-party security audits** each provide unique benefits in strengthening an organization's overall security infrastructure.

As you continue to build and improve your organization's security posture, keep in mind the significance of analyzing test output, generating reports, and conducting security audits. These processes play a vital role in ensuring the effectiveness of your security controls, enabling you to maintain a robust and resilient security posture in the face of evolving threats.

Practice Questions

As you conclude your study of the intricate processes of analyzing test output, generating reports, conducting security audits, and understanding security control assessment frameworks in this chapter, a pivotal stage of your CISSP exam preparation unfolds. This section presents a collection of practice questions meticulously designed to solidify your grasp of these multifaceted concepts, sharpen your analytical skills, and align you with the real-world demands of the CISSP exam.

These questions are more than a mere test of your memory; they are an essential continuation of your learning journey. They reflect the complexity and depth you will encounter in the exam, encapsulating the profound insights needed for success. Engaging with each question and delving into the explanations will reveal your strengths and highlight areas needing further attention.

Approach these questions with determination, curiosity, and a willingness to be challenged. Embrace the lessons from both correct answers and mistakes, and immerse yourself in critical thinking. Remember, these practice questions are not just a measure of your knowledge but a tool to deepen your understanding and fine-tune your readiness.

Your exploration of this chapter has been characterized by essential aspects such as remediation, exception handling, ethical disclosure, security audits, and security control assessment frameworks like SOC. Now is the time to scrutinize your comprehension of these elements. Seize this chance to solidify your expertise in this domain. Your commitment to this practice will be a priceless asset as you progress in your quest for the CISSP certification.

Take the time you need, reflect on each question, and allow these practice questions to fuel your success in the CISSP exam and your continued growth as an information security professional.

1. Which of the following is the primary purpose of a vulnerability assessment?

   A. To exploit vulnerabilities in a system

   B. To determine the effectiveness of security controls

   C. To identify weaknesses in a system without exploiting them

   D. To test the organization's incident response capability

2. What is the primary difference between a white box and a black box test?

   A. The tools used for testing

   B. Knowledge of the system's architecture and design

   C. The time taken to complete the test

   D. The outcome of the test

3. Which phase of the penetration testing process involves gathering as much information as possible about the target system before launching an attack?

    A. Exploitation

    B. Post-exploitation

    C. Reconnaissance

    D. Scanning

4. During a security assessment, a tester identifies a vulnerability but does not have a tool or an exploit to take advantage of it. What should the tester do next?

    A. Ignore the vulnerability.

    B. Manually attempt to exploit the vulnerability.

    C. Report the vulnerability to the organization.

    D. Wait for a tool to become available.

5. Which of the following best describes a false positive in the context of security testing?

    A. A vulnerability that is correctly identified but cannot be exploited

    B. A vulnerability that is misclassified by the testing tool

    C. An identified vulnerability that does not actually exist

    D. A vulnerability that is missed by the testing tool

6. For which attack type is IP spoofing most frequently utilized?

    A. Salami

    B. Keystroke logging

    C. Denial of service (DoS)

    D. Data diddling

7. Which statement accurately characterizes session hijacking?

   A. Session hijacking initially undermines the DNS process, allowing an attacker to exploit an existing TCP connection.

   B. Session hijacking manipulates the UDP protocol, enabling an attacker to leverage an ongoing connection.

   C. Session hijacking focuses on the TCP connection between the client and the server. If an attacker discerns the initial sequence, they can potentially take over the connection.

   D. Session hijacking begins by compromising the DNS process, subsequently allowing an attacker to exploit an established UDP connection.

8. Following a series of email scams targeting your company's employees, which solution would most effectively address these attacks?

   A. Enforce a stringent password policy mandating complex passwords.

   B. Initiate an employee training and awareness campaign.

   C. Enhance the company's email filtering capabilities.

   D. Implement a policy limiting email to strictly official purposes.

9. Which statement is part of the ISC2 Code of Ethics?

    A. One must not use a computer to harm others.

    B. Violating user privacy is deemed unethical.

    C. All information should be universally accessible.

    D. Conduct oneself with honor, honesty, justice, responsibility, and within the bounds of the law.

10. Which group poses the most significant threat to your organization?

    A. Internal employees

    B. Corporate espionage agents

    C. State-sponsored agents

    D. Novice hackers

11. What does Locard's exchange principle assert?

    A. The continuity of evidence must remain unbroken.

    B. Trace evidence always exists.

    C. A crime necessitates means, motive, and opportunity.

    D. Authenticating evidence requires checksums.

12. Which global entity was founded to standardize the treatment of forensic evidence?

    A. The Global Forensic Analysis Organization

    B. The European Union's Criminal Evidence Policy Council

    C. The United Nations Computer Evidence Committee

    D. The International Organization on Computer Evidence

13. For evidence to be admissible in court, it must not be?

    A. Pertinent

    B. Preserved correctly

    C. Recognizable

    D. Justified

14. How is hearsay evidence best defined?

    A. Admissible in civil proceedings

    B. Inadmissible in court

    C. Regarded as third-tier information

    D. Used to corroborate evidence presented as the best evidence

15. In what fundamental way do ethical hackers differ from malicious hackers?

    A. They are authorized to dismantle networks.

    B. Their primary objective is to avoid causing harm.

    C. They are immune to legal repercussions for damages.

    D. They are exempt from legal prosecution.

16. In the realm of computer forensics, which component should be prioritized for examination?

    A. Hard disk drives

    B. DVD media

    C. Random Access Memory (RAM) content

    D. Printed outputs from the computer

17. How is the tool SATAN best characterized?

    A. A utility for password decryption

    B. A tool for analyzing audit logs

    C. A software for system exploitation

    D. A scanner for system vulnerabilities

18. What should an investigator ensure during the duplication in computer forensics?

    A. Create an exact duplicate.

    B. Generate a bit-by-bit copy.

    C. Produce a logical copy.

    D. Format the destination drive to erase any existing data before duplication.

19. Which type of penetration testing evaluates the access capabilities of internal users?

    A. White box testing

    B. Gray box testing

    C. Black box testing

    D. Blue box testing

20. Which group of individuals is notorious for targeting PBX and telecommunication infrastructures?

    A. Novice hackers

    B. Phreakers

    C. System breakers

    D. Ethical hackers

21. What is the difference between validation and verification in the context of security assessment and testing?

   A. Validation checks if the right product is being built, while verification checks if the product is being built correctly.

   B. Validation checks if the product is being built correctly, while verification checks if the right product is being built.

   C. Validation and verification both check if the right product is being built.

   D. Validation and verification both check if the product is being built correctly.

22. What is the purpose of fuzz testing?

   A. To check if the application responds correctly to normal inputs

   B. To check if the application responds correctly to erroneous inputs

   C. To throw randomness at an application to see how it responds and where it might "break"

   D. To check if the application responds correctly to both normal and erroneous inputs

23. What is the difference between a vulnerability assessment and a penetration testing?

   A. A vulnerability assessment identifies potential vulnerabilities and attempts to exploit them, while a penetration test only identifies potential vulnerabilities.

B. A vulnerability assessment only identifies potential vulnerabilities, while a penetration test identifies potential vulnerabilities and attempts to exploit them.

C. Both vulnerability assessment and penetration test identify potential vulnerabilities and attempt to exploit them.

D. Both vulnerability assessment and penetration test only identify potential vulnerabilities.

24. What are the two primary types of vulnerability scans?

A. Credentialed/authenticated scans and uncredentialed/unauthenticated scans

B. Internal scans and external scans

C. Manual scans and automated scans

D. Static scans and dynamic scans

25. What is the purpose of security assessment and testing in the context of an organization's security strategy?

A. To ensure that security requirements/controls are defined, tested, and operating effectively

B. To ensure that the organization's security strategy is aligned with its business goals

C. To ensure that the organization's security strategy is compliant with regulatory requirements

D. To ensure that the organization's security strategy is cost-effective

26. What is the difference between a SOC 1 report and a SOC 2 report?

A. SOC 1 reports focus on financial reporting risks, while SOC 2 reports focus on the controls related to the five trust principles: security, availability, confidentiality, processing integrity, and privacy.

B. SOC 1 reports focus on the controls related to the five trust principles – security, availability, confidentiality, processing integrity, and privacy – while SOC 2 reports focus on financial reporting risks.

C. Both SOC 1 and SOC 2 reports focus on financial reporting risks.

D. Both SOC 1 and SOC 2 reports focus on the controls related to the five trust principles: security, availability, confidentiality, processing integrity, and privacy.

27. What is the difference between positive testing, negative testing, and misuse testing?

A. Positive testing checks if the system is working as expected and designed, negative testing checks the system's response to normal errors, and misuse testing applies the perspective of someone trying to break or attack the system.

B. Positive testing checks the system's response to normal errors, negative testing checks if the system is working as expected and designed, and misuse testing applies the perspective of someone trying to break or attack the system.

C. Positive testing applies the perspective of someone trying to break or attack the system, negative testing checks if the system is working as expected and designed, and misuse testing checks the system's response to normal errors.

D. All three types of testing check if the system is working as expected and designed.

28. What is the purpose of regression testing?

A. To verify that previously tested and functional software still works after updates have been made

B. To verify that the software works as expected under heavy load

C. To verify that the software works as expected in different operating systems

D. To verify that the software works as expected with different types of inputs

29. What does the term "test coverage" refer to in the context of security assessment and testing?

A. The number of test cases executed divided by the total number of test cases

B. The number of test cases passed divided by the total number of test cases

C. The amount of code covered divided by the total amount of code in the application

D. The amount of code tested divided by the total amount of code in the application

30. What are the two well-known and often-used threat modeling methodologies mentioned in the content?

    A. STRIDE and PASTA

    B. DREAD and PASTA

    C. STRIDE and DREAD

    D. DREAD and OCTAVE

31. What is the difference between Static Application Security Testing (SAST) and Dynamic Application Security Testing (DAST)?

    A. SAST tests an application while it's running, while DAST tests the underlying source code of an application.

    B. SAST tests the underlying source code of an application, while DAST tests an application while it's running.

    C. Both SAST and DAST test an application while it's running.

    D. Both SAST and DAST test the underlying source code of an application.

32. What are the two types of alerts that often show up in any type of monitoring system?

    A. False positives and false negatives

    B. True positives and true negatives

    C. False positives and true negatives

    D. True positives and false negatives

33. What is the purpose of log review and analysis in an organization's security strategy?

   A. To identify potential vulnerabilities in the system

   B. To identify potential threats to the system

   C. To identify errors and anomalies that point to problems, modifications, or breaches

   D. To identify the effectiveness of the system's security controls

34. What is the difference between a Type 1 and a Type 2 SOC report?

   A. A Type 1 report focuses on the design of controls at a point in time, while a Type 2 report examines the design of a control and its operating effectiveness over a period of time.

   B. A Type 1 report examines the design of a control and its operating effectiveness over a period of time, while a Type 2 report focuses on the design of controls at a point in time.

   C. Both Type 1 and Type 2 reports focus on the design of controls at a point in time.

   D. Both Type 1 and Type 2 reports examine the design of a control and its operating effectiveness over a period of time.

35. What is the purpose of a security audit in the context of an organization's security strategy?

A. To identify potential vulnerabilities in the system

B. To ensure that security controls are operating effectively and as designed

C. To identify potential threats to the system

D. To identify the effectiveness of the system's security controls

36. What is the difference between a white box test and a black box test?

A. In a white box test, the tester has full knowledge of the system being tested, while in a black box test, the tester has no knowledge of the system.

B. In a white box test, the tester has no knowledge of the system being tested, while in a black box test, the tester has full knowledge of the system.

C. Both white box and black box tests require the tester to have full knowledge of the system being tested.

D. Both white box and black box tests require the tester to have no knowledge of the system being tested.

37. What is the purpose of a code review in the context of security assessment and testing?

A. To identify potential vulnerabilities in the code

B. To identify potential threats to the system

C. To identify errors and anomalies that point to problems, modifications, or breaches

D. To identify the effectiveness of the system's security controls

38. What is the difference between a credentialed scan and an uncredentialed scan?

    A. A credentialed scan is performed with system-level access, while an uncredentialed scan is performed without system-level access.

    B. A credentialed scan is performed without system-level access, while an uncredentialed scan is performed with system-level access.

    C. Both credentialed and uncredentialed scans are performed with system-level access.

    D. Both credentialed and uncredentialed scans are performed without system-level access.

39. What is the purpose of a security control self-assessment?

    A. To identify potential vulnerabilities in the system

    B. To ensure that security controls are operating effectively and as designed

    C. To identify potential threats to the system

    D. To identify the effectiveness of the system's security controls

40. What is the purpose of a risk-based approach to security testing?

    A. To focus testing efforts on areas of greatest risk

    B. To identify potential vulnerabilities in the system

    C. To identify potential threats to the system

    D. To identify the effectiveness of the system's security controls

41. What is the purpose of a security control in the context of an organization's security strategy?

    A. To identify potential vulnerabilities in the system

    B. To protect the system against potential threats

    C. To identify potential threats to the system

    D. To identify the effectiveness of the system's security controls

42. What is the difference between a false positive and a false negative in the context of security monitoring?

    A. A false positive is when the system claims a vulnerability exists, but there is none, while a false negative is when the system says everything is fine, but a vulnerability exists.

    B. A false positive is when the system says everything is fine, but a vulnerability exists, while a false negative is when the system claims a vulnerability exists, but there is none.

    C. Both false positives and false negatives are when the system claims a vulnerability exists, but there is none.

    D. Both false positives and false negatives are when the system says everything is fine, but a vulnerability exists.

43. What is the purpose of a security control baseline in the context of an organization's security strategy?

    A. To identify potential vulnerabilities in the system

    B. To provide a starting point for the implementation of security controls

C. To identify potential threats to the system

D. To identify the effectiveness of the system's security controls

44. What is the purpose of the "Process for Attack Simulation and Threat Analysis" (PASTA) methodology in threat modeling?

A. To identify potential vulnerabilities in the system

B. To simulate potential attack scenarios and analyze threats

C. To identify potential threats to the system

D. To identify the effectiveness of the system's security controls

45. What is the difference between a Type 1 SOC report and a Type 3 SOC report?

A. A Type 1 report focuses on the design of controls at a point in time, while a Type 3 report examines the design of a control and its operating effectiveness over a period of time.

B. A Type 1 report examines the design of a control and its operating effectiveness over a period of time, while a Type 3 report focuses on the design of controls at a point in time.

C. Both Type 1 and Type 3 reports focus on the design of controls at a point in time.

D. Both Type 1 and Type 3 reports examine the design of a control and its operating effectiveness over a period of time.

46. What is the purpose of the "Spoofing, Tampering, Repudiation, Information disclosure, Denial-of-Service, Elevation of privilege" (STRIDE) methodology in threat modeling?

    A. To identify potential vulnerabilities in the system

    B. To categorize potential threats to the system

    C. To simulate potential attack scenarios

    D. To identify the effectiveness of the system's security controls

47. What is the difference between a Type 2 SOC report and a Type 3 SOC report?

    A. A Type 2 report examines the design of a control and its operating effectiveness over a period of time, while a Type 3 report focuses on the design of controls at a point in time.

    B. A Type 2 report focuses on the design of controls at a point in time, while a Type 3 report examines the design of a control and its operating effectiveness over a period of time.

    C. Both Type 2 and Type 3 reports focus on the design of controls at a point in time.

    D. Both Type 2 and Type 3 reports examine the design of a control and its operating effectiveness over a period of time.

48. What is the purpose of Real User Monitoring (RUM) in operational testing?

   A. RUM is a passive monitoring technique that monitors user interactions and activity with a website or application.

   B. RUM is an active monitoring technique that monitors user interactions and activity with a website or application.

   C. RUM is a passive monitoring technique that monitors the performance of a website or application under load.

   D. RUM is an active monitoring technique that monitors the performance of a website or application under load.

49. What is the purpose of the Common Vulnerability Scoring System (CVSS)?

   A. CVSS reflects a method to characterize a vulnerability through a scoring system considering various characteristics.

   B. CVSS is a list of records for publicly known cybersecurity vulnerabilities.

   C. CVSS is a method to identify the unique characteristics of a system through an examination of how packets and other system-level information are formed.

   D. CVSS is a method to identify a system's operating system, applications, and versions.

50. What is the purpose of Synthetic Performance Monitoring
     in operational testing?

A. Synthetic Performance Monitoring is a passive
    monitoring technique that monitors user interactions
    and activity with a website or application.

B. Synthetic Performance Monitoring examines
    functionality as well as functionality and performance
    under load.

C. Synthetic Performance Monitoring is a passive
    monitoring technique that monitors the performance
    of a website or application under load.

D. Synthetic Performance Monitoring is an active
    monitoring technique that monitors the performance
    of a website or application under load.

51. What is the purpose of the Common Vulnerabilities
     and Exposures (CVE) dictionary in the context of
     interpreting and understanding results from activities
     like vulnerability scanning, banner grabbing, and
     fingerprinting?

A. CVE is a list of records for publicly known
    cybersecurity vulnerabilities.

B. CVE reflects a method to characterize a vulnerability
    through a scoring system considering various
    characteristics.

C. CVE is a method to identify the unique characteristics
    of a system through an examination of how packets
    and other system-level information are formed.

D. CVE is a method to identify a system's operating
    system, applications, and versions.

52. What is the difference between Static Application Security Testing (SAST) and Dynamic Application Security Testing (DAST) in the context of runtime testing?

   A. SAST involves examining the underlying source code when an application is not running, while DAST involves focusing on the application and system as the underlying code executes when an application is running.

   B. SAST involves focusing on the application and system as the underlying code executes when an application is running, while DAST involves examining the underlying source code when an application is not running.

   C. Both SAST and DAST involve examining the underlying source code when an application is not running.

   D. Both SAST and DAST involve focusing on the application and system as the underlying code executes when an application is running.

53. What is the difference between blind testing and double-blind testing in the context of vulnerability assessment and penetration testing?

   A. Blind testing involves the assessor being given little to no information about the target being tested, while double-blind testing involves the assessor and the IT and Security Operations teams being given little to no information about the upcoming tests.

B. Blind testing involves the assessor and the IT and Security Operations teams being given little to no information about the upcoming tests, while double-blind testing involves the assessor being given little to no information about the target being tested.

C. Both blind testing and double-blind testing involve the assessor being given little to no information about the target being tested.

D. Both blind testing and double-blind testing involve the assessor and the IT and Security Operations teams being given little to no information about the upcoming tests.

54. What is the difference between circular overwrite and clipping levels in the context of log file management?

A. Circular overwrite limits the maximum size of a log file by overwriting entries, starting from the earliest, while clipping levels focus on when to log a given event based upon threshold settings.

B. Circular overwrite focuses on when to log a given event based upon threshold settings, while clipping levels limit the maximum size of a log file by overwriting entries, starting from the earliest.

C. Both circular overwrite and clipping levels limit the maximum size of a log file by overwriting entries, starting from the earliest.

D. Both circular overwrite and clipping levels focus on when to log a given event based upon threshold settings.

55. What are the three types of audit strategies mentioned in the context of organizational audit strategies?

    A. Internal, external, and fourth party

    B. Internal, external, and third party

    C. First party, second party, and third party

    D. Internal, external, and inter-party

56. What are the different types of coverage testing you need to explain for the CISSP exam?

    A. Black box, white box, dynamic, static, manual, automated, structural, functional, negative

    B. Black box, white box, dynamic, static, manual, automated, structural, positive, negative

    C. Black box, white box, dynamic, static, manual, automated, structural, functional, positive

    D. Black box, white box, dynamic, static, manual, automated, structural, functional, neutral

57. What is the difference between awareness, training, and education in the context of security process data collection?

    A. Awareness refers to the "what" of an organization's policy or procedure, training refers to the "how," and education refers to the "why."

    B. Awareness refers to the "how" of an organization's policy or procedure, training refers to the "why," and education refers to the "what."

C. Awareness refers to the "why" of an organization's policy or procedure, training refers to the "what," and education refers to the "how."

D. Awareness, training, and education all refer to the "what" of an organization's policy or procedure.

58. What is the purpose of breach attack simulations in the context of security controls?

A. Breach attack simulations are where you simulate real-world attacks across your whole environment, typically both automatic and always running.

B. Breach attack simulations are where you simulate real-world attacks in a controlled environment, typically both manual and occasionally running.

C. Breach attack simulations are where you simulate hypothetical attacks across your whole environment, typically both automatic and always running.

D. Breach attack simulations are where you simulate hypothetical attacks in a controlled environment, typically both manual and occasionally running.

59. What is the role of security control compliance checks?

A. Security control compliance checks are regularly performed to assess whether the organization is currently following their controls.

B. Security control compliance checks are occasionally performed to assess whether the organization is currently following their controls.

C. Security control compliance checks are regularly performed to assess whether the organization is currently violating their controls.

D. Security control compliance checks are occasionally performed to assess whether the organization is currently violating their controls.

60. What is the main difference between internal, external, and third-party audit strategies?

A. Internal audits are closely aligned to the organization, external audits ensure procedures/compliance are being followed with regular checks, and third-party audits provide a more in-depth, neutral audit.

B. Internal audits ensure procedures/compliance are being followed with regular checks, external audits are closely aligned to the organization, and third-party audits provide a more in-depth, neutral audit.

C. Internal audits provide a more in-depth, neutral audit, external audits ensure procedures/compliance are being followed with regular checks, and third-party audits are closely aligned to the organization.

D. All three types of audits are closely aligned to the organization.

61. What is the main objective of breach attack simulations?

A. To simulate real-world attacks across the whole environment, typically both automatic and always running

   B. To simulate hypothetical attacks across the whole environment, typically both automatic and always running

   C. To simulate real-world attacks in a controlled environment, typically both automatic and always running

   D. To simulate hypothetical attacks in a controlled environment, typically both automatic and always running

62. What is the main purpose of security control compliance checks?

   A. To assess whether the organization is currently following their controls

   B. To assess whether the organization is currently violating their controls

   C. To assess whether the organization is currently updating their controls

   D. To assess whether the organization is currently implementing their controls

63. What is the main purpose of analyzing test output and generating reports in the context of security audits?

   A. To handle test results and report any results of concern to management immediately so they can be aware of potential risks and alerts

   B. To handle test results and report any results of concern to the IT department immediately so they can be aware of potential risks and alerts

C. To handle test results and report any results of concern to the security team immediately so they can be aware of potential risks and alerts

D. To handle test results and report any results of concern to the stakeholders immediately so they can be aware of potential risks and alerts.

64. What are the two primary categories of assessments that you need to be aware of for the CISSP exam?

A. Formal assessments and informal assessments

B. Formal assessments and no-notice assessments

C. Informal assessments and no-notice assessments

D. Internal assessments and external assessments

65. What are the key elements of an audit report?

A. Purpose, scope, results of the audit, audit events

B. Purpose, scope, results of the audit, audit strategies

C. Purpose, scope, results of the audit, audit techniques

D. Purpose, scope, results of the audit, audit procedures

66. What are the four types of SOC reports?

A. SOC 1 Type 1, SOC 1 Type 2, SOC 2, SOC 3

B. SOC 1, SOC 2 Type 1, SOC 2 Type 2, SOC 3

C. SOC 1, SOC 2, SOC 3 Type 1, SOC 3 Type 2

D. SOC 1 Type 1, SOC 2 Type 1, SOC 3 Type 1, SOC 4

67. What are the two phases in preparing for the SOC audit?

   A. Preparations phase and Audit phase

   B. Preparations phase and Reporting phase

   C. Audit phase and Reporting phase

   D. Preparations phase and Review phase

68. What is the main purpose of analyzing test output and generating reports in the context of security audits?

   A. To present the data in a meaningful way for most people who need the data

   B. To present the data in a raw format for most people who need the data

   C. To present the data in a meaningful way for a few gifted people who can draw salient conclusions

   D. To present the data in a raw format for a few gifted people who can draw salient conclusions

69. What is the main purpose of "no-notice" assessments?

   A. To evaluate the situation without any forewarning of the evaluation

   B. To evaluate the situation with prior notice of the evaluation

   C. To evaluate the situation with occasional notice of the evaluation

   D. To evaluate the situation with frequent notice of the evaluation

70. What is the main purpose of internal assessments?

   A. To see if controls meet risk expectations or to see if there are ways to improve efficiency of operations

   B. To see if controls exceed risk expectations or to see if there are ways to improve efficiency of operations

   C. To see if controls meet risk expectations or to see if there are ways to reduce efficiency of operations

   D. To see if controls exceed risk expectations or to see if there are ways to reduce the efficiency of operations

71. Among the following tools, which is predominantly designed to conduct network discovery scans to identify active hosts and open ports?

   A. Nmap

   B. OpenVAS

   C. Metasploit Framework

   D. lsof

72. After executing a network port scan from an external network on an internal web server to simulate an attacker's viewpoint, which scan results should be of utmost concern and warrant immediate attention?

   A. Port 80 is open.

   B. Port 22 is filtered.

   C. Port 443 is open.

   D. Port 1433 is open.

73. When devising a schedule for security testing of a specific system, which of the following factors should be excluded from your considerations?

    A. The sensitivity level of the data stored on the system

    B. The complexity involved in executing the test

    C. The inclination to experiment with novel testing tools

    D. The system's attractiveness as a target for attackers

74. For whom is a security assessment report primarily intended?

    A. Organizational management

    B. The individual conducting the security audit

    C. Security professionals within the organization

    D. The organization's customer base

75. Which port number is customarily designated for establishing administrative connections via the Secure Shell (SSH) protocol?

    A. 20

    B. 22

    C. 25

    D. 80

76. Among the listed testing methodologies, which one furnishes the most comprehensive and precise insights into a server's security posture?

A. Unauthenticated scan

B. Port scan

C. Half-open scan

D. Authenticated scan

77. Which variant of network discovery scan employs only the initial two steps of the TCP three-way handshake and does not complete the connection?

A. TCP connect scan

B. Xmas scan

C. TCP SYN scan

D. TCP ACK scan

78. Which tool from the following options is most suitable for SQL injection vulnerability detection?

A. Port scanner

B. Network vulnerability scanner

C. Network discovery scanner

D. Web vulnerability scanner

79. On a system operating an HTTP server without encryption, which port is generally left open to facilitate communication?

A. 22

B. 80

C. 143

D. 443

80. Following a recent cyberattack that led to an extended service outage within your organization, you are tasked with inspecting systems for known vulnerabilities that could be exploited in future attacks. Which of the following options would be the most effective for identifying such vulnerabilities?

A. Versioning tracker

B. Vulnerability scanner

C. Security audit

D. Security review

81. Among the listed processes, which one is most likely to provide a comprehensive inventory of all security risks present within a system?

A. Configuration management

B. Patch management

C. Hardware inventory

D. Vulnerability scan

82. A newly appointed Chief Information Officer (CIO) discovers that the organization lacks a formal change management program and mandates its immediate implementation. What would be a primary objective of instituting such a program?

A. Ensuring the safety of personnel

B. Facilitating the rollback of changes

C. Ensuring that implemented changes do not compromise security

D. Auditing privileged access

83. Among the following cloud service models, which affords an organization the highest degree of administrative control while also necessitating that the organization assume full responsibility for maintaining operating systems and applications?

A. Infrastructure as a Service (IaaS)

B. Platform as a Service (PaaS)

C. Software as a Service (SaaS)

D. Public Cloud Service

84. Among the following elements, which one is typically not a component of a comprehensive security assessment?

A. Conducting a vulnerability scan

B. Performing a risk assessment

C. Implementing vulnerability mitigation measures

D. Carrying out a threat assessment

85. For whom is a security assessment report primarily intended?

A. Organizational management

B. The individual conducting the security audit

C. Security professionals within the organization

D. The organization's customer base

86. Which of the following steps is executed first?

    A. Response

    B. Mitigation

    C. Remediation

    D. Lessons learned

87. Security administrators are in the process of reviewing the entire set of data collected through event logging. What is the most accurate term to describe this collection of data?

    A. Identification

    B. Audit trails

    C. Authorization

    D. Confidentiality

88. Which network device is most likely to be connected to this mirrored port?

    A. An intrusion prevention system (IPS)

    B. An intrusion detection system (IDS)

    C. A honeypot

    D. A sandbox

89. A network is equipped with a network-based intrusion detection system (NIDS). Security administrators later discover that an attack penetrated the network without triggering an alarm from the NIDS. What is this scenario best described as?

    A. A false positive

    B. A false negative

    C. A Fraggle attack

    D. A Smurf attack

90. Among the following actions, which one is most likely to be indicative of a terrorist attack, as opposed to other forms of cyberattacks?

    A. Tampering with sensitive trade secret documents

    B. Disrupting communication capabilities in preparation for a physical attack

    C. Exfiltrating unclassified information

    D. Illicitly transferring funds to foreign countries

91. Which of the following actions would not align with the primary objectives typically associated with a grudge attack?

    A. Publicly disclosing embarrassing personal information

    B. Deploying a virus on the target organization's systems

    C. Sending emails with inappropriate content from a spoofed address of the victim organization

    D. Utilizing automated tools to scan for vulnerable ports on the organization's systems

92. What is the paramount rule to adhere to during the process of evidence collection in a cyber investigation?

    A. Refrain from shutting down the computer until the screen is photographed

    B. Document the names of all individuals present during the collection

    C. Avoid altering the evidence during the collection process

    D. Transport all collected equipment to a secure storage facility

93. What category of evidence encompasses written documents presented in court to substantiate a particular fact?

    A. Best evidence

    B. Parol evidence

    C. Documentary evidence

    D. Testimonial evidence

94. Among the following types of investigations, which one necessitates the highest standard of evidence for prosecution?

    A. Administrative

    B. Civil

    C. Criminal

    D. Regulatory

95. What is the expected conduct for CISSP holders?

    A. Act honestly, diligently, responsibly, and legally

    B. Act honorably, honestly, justly, responsibly, and legally

    C. Uphold the security policy and protect the organization

    D. Act in a trustworthy, loyal, friendly, and courteous manner

96. Which kind of identity platform would be most suitable for ensuring the continuous availability of authentication services?

    A. On-site

    B. Cloud based

    C. Hybrid

    D. Outsourced

97. Which technology should you consider implementing to facilitate sharing identity information with a business partner?

    A. Single Sign-On

    B. Multifactor authentication

    C. Federation

    D. Identity as a Service (IDaaS)

98. Which guiding principle mandates that an individual exerts every effort to fulfill their responsibilities accurately and within a reasonable time frame?

    A. Least privilege

    B. Separation of duties

    C. Due care

    D. Due diligence

99. Which metric would provide crucial information regarding the maximum duration the organization can afford without a particular service before incurring irreparable damage?

    A. Maximum tolerable downtime (MTD)

    B. Annualized loss expectancy (ALE)

    C. Recovery point objective (RPO)

    D. Recovery time objective (RTO)

Answers

1. Answer: C. To identify weaknesses in a system without exploiting them

   Explanation: A vulnerability assessment aims to identify vulnerabilities in a system, application, or network without actually exploiting them. This is different from a penetration test, which attempts to exploit the vulnerabilities.

2. Answer: B. Knowledge of the system's architecture and design

    Explanation: In a white box test, the tester has knowledge of the system's architecture and design, whereas in a black box test, the tester has no such knowledge and tests the system from an outsider's perspective.

3. Answer: C. Reconnaissance

    Explanation: The reconnaissance phase of penetration testing involves collecting information about the target system, often without directly interacting with it. This phase helps the tester understand the system and identify potential vulnerabilities.

4. Answer: C. Report the vulnerability to the organization.

    Explanation: Even if the tester cannot exploit a vulnerability, it's essential to report it to the organization. This allows the organization to take corrective measures and ensure that potential attackers cannot exploit the vulnerability in the future.

5. Answer: C. An identified vulnerability that does not actually exist

    Explanation: A false positive refers to a situation where a security testing tool or process identifies a vulnerability that, upon further investigation, does not actually exist. It's an erroneous alert that can lead to wasted resources if not correctly identified.

6.   Answer: C. Denial of service (DoS)

Explanation: IP spoofing is a technique where an attacker sends IP packets from a false source address. This is often used in denial-of-service (DoS) attacks to mask the true origin of the attack and to amplify the attack by involving innocent third-party systems.

7.   Answer: C. Session hijacking focuses on the TCP connection between the client and the server. If an attacker discerns the initial sequence, they can potentially take over the connection.

Explanation: Session hijacking, also known as session takeover, involves an attacker taking over a user's session. The primary target is the TCP connection. By predicting or intercepting the session token, an attacker can impersonate the victim and hijack their session.

8.   Answer: B. Initiate an employee training and awareness campaign.

Explanation: While all the options have their merits, the most effective way to combat email scams, such as phishing, is through user education. Training employees to recognize and avoid suspicious emails can significantly reduce the risk of successful attacks.

9.   Answer: D. Conduct oneself with honor, honesty, justice, responsibility, and within the bounds of the law.

Explanation: The ISC2 Code of Ethics emphasizes professional and ethical behavior. The mentioned statement aligns with the principles set forth by ISC2 for its members.

10. Answer: A. Internal employees

Explanation: Insiders, or internal employees, often have access to sensitive information and systems. Their familiarity with the organization's infrastructure and potential grievances can make them a significant threat.

11. Answer: B. Trace evidence always exists.

Explanation: Locard's exchange principle posits that every contact leaves a trace. This means that whenever two objects come into contact, there will always be an exchange of material. .

12. Answer: D. The International Organization on Computer Evidence

Explanation: The International Organization on Computer Evidence (IOCE) was established to provide international standards for digital evidence handling and processing.

13. Answer: D. Justified

Explanation: Evidence must be relevant, properly preserved, and identifiable to be admissible in court. "Justified" is not a criterion for evidence admissibility.

14. Answer: B. Inadmissible in court

Explanation: Hearsay evidence refers to statements made outside of court that are presented as evidence for the truth of the matter asserted in the statement. Generally, hearsay is not admissible in court unless it falls under specific exceptions.

15. Answer: B. Their primary objective is to avoid causing harm.

Explanation: Ethical hackers, also known as "white hat" hackers, are professionals who test systems for vulnerabilities with the intent of identifying and fixing them, not exploiting them. They operate with permission and aim to improve security without causing harm.

16. Answer: C. Random Access Memory (RAM) content

Explanation: The contents of RAM are volatile, meaning they are lost when the power is turned off. RAM can contain valuable information such as encryption keys, running processes, and other transient data. Therefore, it's crucial to capture this information first before it's lost.

17. Answer: D. A scanner for system vulnerabilities

Explanation: SATAN (Security Administrator Tool for Analyzing Networks) is a tool designed to detect vulnerabilities in computer networks. It helps administrators identify potential security risks in their systems.

18. Answer: B. Generate a bit-by-bit copy.

    Explanation: In computer forensics, it's essential to make a bit-level copy (or bit-by-bit copy) of the original evidence to ensure that all data, including deleted files and slack space, is captured. This ensures the integrity of the evidence and allows for a thorough investigation.

19. Answer: A. White box testing

    Explanation: White box testing, also known as clear box testing, is a method where the tester has complete knowledge of the system's internals. In the context of penetration testing, it simulates what insiders with knowledge of the system can access and potentially exploit.

20. Answer: B. Phreakers

    Explanation: Phreakers are individuals who manipulate telecommunication systems, especially to make free calls. They have historically been associated with exploring and exploiting the vulnerabilities of PBX (Private Branch Exchange) systems and other telecommunication platforms.

21. Answer: A. Validation checks if the right product is being built, while verification checks if the product is being built correctly.

    Explanation: Validation is concerned with answering the question: Is the right product being built? Verification follows validation and is the process that confirms an application or product is being built correctly.

22.   Answer: C. To throw randomness at an application to see how it responds and where it might "break"

Explanation: Fuzz testing involves throwing randomness at an application to see how it responds and where it might "break." It is a form of dynamic testing.

23.   Answer: B. A vulnerability assessment only identifies potential vulnerabilities, while a penetration test identifies potential vulnerabilities and attempts to exploit them.

Explanation: Both processes start the same way as they seek to identify potential vulnerabilities. However, with a vulnerability assessment, once vulnerabilities are noted, no further action is taken apart from producing a report of findings. A penetration test goes an essential step further: after identifying vulnerabilities, an attempt is made to exploit each vulnerability.

24.   Answer: A. Credentialed/authenticated scans and uncredentialed/unauthenticated scans

Explanation: There are two primary types of vulnerability scans: credentialed/authenticated scans and uncredentialed/unauthenticated scans.

25.   Answer: A. To ensure that security requirements/ controls are defined, tested, and operating effectively

Explanation: Security assessment and testing ensure that security requirements/controls are defined, tested, and operating effectively. It applies to the development of new applications and systems as well as the ongoing operations, including end of life, related to assets.

26. Answer: A. SOC 1 reports focus on financial reporting risks, while SOC 2 reports focus on the controls related to the five trust principles: security, availability, confidentiality, processing integrity, and privacy.

Explanation: SOC 1 reports are quite basic and focus on financial reporting risks. SOC 2 reports are much more involved and focus on the controls related to the five trust principles: security, availability, confidentiality, processing integrity, and privacy.

27. Answer: A. Positive testing checks if the system is working as expected and designed, negative testing checks the system's response to normal errors, and misuse testing applies the perspective of someone trying to break or attack the system.

Explanation: Positive testing focuses on the response of a system based on normal usage and expectations, checking if the system is working as expected and designed. Negative testing focuses on the response of a system when normal errors are introduced. Misuse testing applies the perspective of someone trying to break or attack the system.

28.   Answer: A. To verify that previously tested and functional software still works after updates have been made

Explanation: Regression testing is the process of verifying that previously tested and functional software still works after updates have been made. It should be performed after enhancements have been made or after patches to address vulnerabilities or problems have been issued.

29.   Answer: C. The amount of code covered divided by the total amount of code in the application

Explanation: Test coverage refers to the relationship between the amount of source code in a given application and the percentage of code that has been covered by the completed tests. It is a simple mathematical formula: amount of code covered/ total amount of code in application = test coverage percent.

30.   Answer: A. STRIDE and PASTA

Explanation: Two well-known and often-used threat modeling methodologies are STRIDE (Spoofing, Tampering, Repudiation, Information disclosure, Denial-of-Service, Elevation of privilege) and PASTA (Process for Attack Simulation and Threat Analysis).

31.   Answer: B. SAST tests the underlying source code of an application, while DAST tests an application while it's running.

Explanation: With Static Application Security Testing (SAST), an application is not running, and it's the underlying source code that is being examined. With Dynamic Application Security Testing (DAST), an application is running, and the focus is on the application and system as the underlying code executes.

32. Answer: A. False positives and false negatives

Explanation: With any type of monitoring system, two types of alerts often show up: false positives, where the system claims a vulnerability exists, but there is none, and false negatives, where the system says everything is fine, but a vulnerability exists.

33. Answer: C. To identify errors and anomalies that point to problems, modifications, or breaches

Explanation: Log review and analysis is a best practice that should be used in every organization. Logs should include what is relevant, be proactively reviewed, and be especially scrutinized for errors and anomalies that point to problems, modifications, or breaches.

34. Answer: A. A Type 1 report focuses on the design of controls at a point in time, while a Type 2 report examines the design of a control and its operating effectiveness over a period of time.

Explanation: A Type 1 report focuses on the design of controls at a point in time. A Type 2 report examines not only the design of a control but, more importantly, the operating effectiveness over a period of time, typically a year.

35. Answer: B. To ensure that security controls are operating effectively and as designed

Explanation: A security audit is a systematic, measurable technical assessment of how the organization's security policy is employed. It is used to ensure that security controls are operating effectively and as designed.

36. Answer: A. In a white box test, the tester has full knowledge of the system being tested, while in a black box test, the tester has no knowledge of the system.

Explanation: In a white box test, the tester has full knowledge of the system being tested, including source code, architecture, and both the software and hardware involved. In a black box test, the tester has no knowledge of the system being tested.

37. Answer: A. To identify potential vulnerabilities in the code

Explanation: A code review is a systematic examination of computer source code intended to find and fix mistakes overlooked in the initial development phase, improving both the overall quality of software and the developers' skills. In the context of security, it is used to identify potential vulnerabilities in the code.

38. Answer: A. A credentialed scan is performed with system-level access, while an uncredentialed scan is performed without system-level access.

Explanation: A credentialed scan is performed with system-level access, and it can see everything that is happening on a given host. An uncredentialed scan is performed without system-level access, and it can only see what is visible on the network.

39. Answer: B. To ensure that security controls are operating effectively and as designed

Explanation: A security control self-assessment is a process where an organization evaluates its own security controls to ensure they are operating effectively and as designed. It is a proactive measure to identify any potential issues before they become problems.

40. Answer: A. To focus testing efforts on areas of greatest risk

Explanation: A risk-based approach to security testing allows an organization to focus its testing efforts on the areas of greatest risk. This approach ensures that resources are used effectively and that high-risk areas receive the attention they require.

41. Answer: B. To protect the system against potential threats

Explanation: A security control is a safeguard or countermeasure designed to avoid, counteract, or minimize security risks. In the context of an organization's security strategy, the purpose of a security control is to protect the system against potential threats.

42. Answer: A. A false positive is when the system claims a vulnerability exists, but there is none, while a false negative is when the system says everything is fine, but a vulnerability exists.

Explanation: A false positive is when the system claims a vulnerability exists, but there is none. This can lead to wasted resources as teams investigate nonexistent issues. A false negative is when the system says everything is fine, but a vulnerability exists. This can lead to undetected breaches and significant damage.

43. Answer: B. To provide a starting point for the implementation of security controls

Explanation: A security control baseline provides a set of basic controls that an organization can use as a starting point for their security strategy. It provides a foundation upon which additional, more specific controls can be built based on the organization's unique risks and requirements.

44. Answer: B. To simulate potential attack scenarios and analyze threats

Explanation: The Process for Attack Simulation and Threat Analysis (PASTA) is a threat modeling methodology that aims to provide a dynamic threat identification, enumeration, and scoring process. It simulates potential attack scenarios and analyzes threats in a structured and methodical way.

45.   Answer: A. A Type 1 report focuses on the design of controls at a point in time, while a Type 3 report examines the design of a control and its operating effectiveness over a period of time.

Explanation: A Type 1 SOC report focuses on the design of controls at a point in time. A Type 3 SOC report, on the other hand, examines not only the design of a control but also its operating effectiveness over a period of time.

46.   Answer: B. To categorize potential threats to the system

Explanation: The STRIDE methodology is a threat modeling technique used to categorize potential threats to a system. It stands for Spoofing, Tampering, Repudiation, Information disclosure, Denial-of-Service, and Elevation of privilege.

47.   Answer: A. A Type 2 report examines the design of a control and its operating effectiveness over a period of time, while a Type 3 report focuses on the design of controls at a point in time.

Explanation: A Type 2 SOC report examines not only the design of a control but also its operating effectiveness over a period of time. A Type 3 SOC report, on the other hand, focuses on the design of controls at a point in time.

48. Answer: A. RUM is a passive monitoring technique that monitors user interactions and activity with a website or application.

    Explanation: Real User Monitoring (RUM) is a passive monitoring technique that monitors user interactions and activity with a website or application. It provides insights into how users are interacting with the system in real time.

49. Answer: A. CVSS reflects a method to characterize a vulnerability through a scoring system considering various characteristics.

    Explanation: The Common Vulnerability Scoring System (CVSS) reflects a method to characterize a vulnerability through a scoring system considering various characteristics. It provides a way to capture the principal characteristics of a vulnerability and produce a numerical score reflecting its severity.

50. Answer: B. Synthetic Performance Monitoring examines functionality as well as functionality and performance under load.

    Explanation: Synthetic Performance Monitoring examines functionality as well as functionality and performance under load. Test scripts for each type of functionality can be created and then run at any time.

51. Answer: A. CVE is a list of records for publicly known cybersecurity vulnerabilities.

Explanation: CVE, also known as Common Vulnerabilities and Exposures dictionary, is "a list of records – each containing an identification number, a description, and at least one public reference – for publicly known cybersecurity vulnerabilities."

52. Answer: A. SAST involves examining the underlying source code when an application is not running, while DAST involves focusing on the application and system as the underlying code executes when an application is running.

Explanation: Static Application Security Testing (SAST) involves examining the underlying source code when an application is not running. This is a form of white box testing. Dynamic Application Security Testing (DAST), on the other hand, involves focusing on the application and system as the underlying code executes when an application is running. This is a form of black box testing.

53. Answer: A. Blind testing involves the assessor being given little to no information about the target being tested, while double-blind testing involves the assessor and the IT and Security Operations teams being given little to no information about the upcoming tests.

Explanation: In blind testing, the assessor is given little to no information about the target being tested. In double-blind testing, not only is the assessor given little to no information about the target, but the IT and Security Operations teams are also not informed about the upcoming tests.

54.   Answer: A. Circular overwrite limits the maximum
size of a log file by overwriting entries, starting from
the earliest, while clipping levels focus on when to
log a given event based upon threshold settings.

Explanation: Circular overwrite is a method of log
file management that limits the maximum size of
a log file by overwriting entries, starting from the
earliest. Clipping levels, on the other hand, focus
on when to log a given event based upon threshold
settings, which can also help limit log file sizes.

55.   Answer: B. Internal, external, and third party

Explanation: The three types of audit strategies
mentioned are internal, external, and third party.
Each of these strategies has a different focus and is
used in different contexts within an organization's
overall audit strategy.

56.   Answer: A. Black box, white box, dynamic, static,
manual, automated, structural, functional, negative

Explanation: The types of coverage testing that you
need to explain for the CISSP exam are black box,
white box, dynamic, static, manual, automated,
structural, functional, and negative.

57.   Answer: A. Awareness refers to the "what" of an
organization's policy or procedure, training refers to
the "how," and education refers to the "why."

Explanation: Awareness refers to the "what" of
an organization's policy or procedure, aiming at
knowledge retention. Training focuses on the "how,"
enabling the ability to complete a task and apply
problem-solving at the application level. Education

focuses on the "why," providing an understanding of the big picture and enabling design-level problem-solving with architectural exercises.

58. Answer: A. Breach attack simulations are where you simulate real-world attacks across your whole environment, typically both automatic and always running.

Explanation: Breach attack simulations simulate real-world attacks across the entire environment. They are typically automatic and always running, using tools that are constantly updated and provide remediation steps and documentation.

59. Answer: A. Security control compliance checks are regularly performed to assess whether the organization is currently following their controls.

Explanation: Security control compliance checks are regularly performed to assess whether the organization is currently following their controls. These checks can be automated and may use either in-house or third-party tools. Failed compliance checks typically result in the organization investigating and remediating the issues found.

60. Answer: A. Internal audits are closely aligned to the organization, external audits ensure procedures/compliance are being followed with regular checks, and third-party audits provide a more in-depth, neutral audit.

Explanation: Internal audits should be closely aligned to the organization. The external strategy needs to ensure procedures/compliance are being followed with regular checks and complement the internal strategy. The third-party strategy is an objective, neutral approach that reviews the overall strategy for auditing the organization's environment, methods of testing, and can also ensure that both internal and external audits are following defined policies and procedures.

61. Answer: A. To simulate real-world attacks across the whole environment, typically both automatic and always running

Explanation: Breach attack simulations are where you simulate real-world attacks. It is simulated across your whole environment and typically are both automatic and always running. Red and blue teams use tools that are constantly updated and provide remediation steps and documentation.

62. Answer: A. To assess whether the organization is currently following their controls

Explanation: Security control compliance checks are regularly performed to assess whether the organization is currently following their controls. This may be automated and use either in-house or third-party tools. Failed compliance checks normally end up in the organization investigating and remediating the issues it found.

63. Answer: A. To handle test results and report any results of concern to management immediately so they can be aware of potential risks and alerts

Explanation: Those that analyze the security of organization apps and services need to know how to handle test results. Any results of concern need to be reported to management immediately so they can be aware of potential risks and alerts. The detail in reporting to management may be on a "need-to-know" basis.

64. Answer: A. Formal assessments and informal assessments

Explanation: The two primary categories of assessments are formal assessments and informal assessments. Formal assessments are evaluations against a compliance standard, which includes regulatory and other legal requirements.

65. Answer: A. Purpose, scope, results of the audit, audit events

Explanation: The key elements of an audit report are the purpose, scope, results of the audit, and audit events. The purpose outlines the reason for the audit, the scope defines the boundaries of the audit, the results of the audit provide the findings, and the audit events detail the specific instances or activities audited.

66. Answer: A. SOC 1 Type 1, SOC 1 Type 2, SOC 2, SOC 3

Explanation: The four types of SOC reports are SOC 1 Type 1, SOC 1 Type 2, SOC 2, and SOC 3. Each type of report has a different focus and is used for different purposes within an organization's overall audit strategy.

67.   Answer: A. Preparations phase and Audit phase

Explanation: There are two phases in preparing for the SOC audit: the Preparations phase and the Audit phase. The Preparations phase involves scheduling, defining the scope, inventorying controls, conducting a readiness review, and resolving discrepancies. The Audit phase involves creating a detailed project plan, gathering artifacts, providing physical access and workspace, conducting meetings, testing, off-site analysis, issue resolution, providing audit reports, and conducting a lessons learned review.

68.   Answer: A. To present the data in a meaningful way for most people who need the data

Explanation: Security controls, vulnerability scans, penetration tests, and audits – all these activities generate a significant amount of data. Perhaps a few gifted people can review the raw data and draw salient conclusions, but most people need the data presented to them in a meaningful way.

69.   Answer: A. To evaluate the situation without any forewarning of the evaluation

Explanation: "No-notice" assessments, which simply means that the situation being evaluated has no forewarning of the evaluation (e.g., spot check, desk audit). A no-notice assessment isn't really a "type" of assessment, it's basically a surprise audit or an informal assessment where notice isn't given. It can likely fit into a subcategory or type of informal assessment.

70. Answer: A. To see if controls meet risk expectations or to see if there are ways to improve efficiency of operations

Explanation: Internal assessments are done for the purpose of seeing if controls meet risk expectations or to see if there are ways to improve efficiency of operations and how well an organization is prepared for an external or formal audit. An internal assessment might follow a formal process, but is most likely considered informal by nature.

71. Answer: A. Nmap

Explanation: Nmap (Network Mapper) is primarily used for network discovery and port scanning. It is a versatile tool that allows for the identification of active hosts and open ports within a network.

72. Answer: D. Port 1433 is open.

Explanation: Port 1433 is commonly associated with Microsoft SQL Server. An open SQL Server port exposed to an external network is a significant security risk and should be addressed immediately.

73. Answer: C. The inclination to experiment with novel testing tools

Explanation: The desire to experiment with new testing tools should not be a factor when planning a security testing schedule. The focus should be on the system's security posture and potential risks.

74. Answer: A. Organizational management

Explanation: A security assessment report is primarily intended for organizational management. It provides them with an overview of the security posture of the system or network, allowing them to make informed decisions regarding security policies and resource allocation.

75. Answer: B. 22

Explanation: Port 22 is the standard port used for SSH connections, commonly employed for secure server access.

76. Answer: D. Authenticated scan

Explanation: An authenticated scan provides the most detailed information about the security state of a server. It allows for a deeper system inspection by using valid credentials to access it.

77. Answer: C. TCP SYN scan

Explanation: A TCP SYN scan, also known as a "half-open" scan, utilizes only the first two steps of the TCP three-way handshake. It sends a SYN packet and waits for a SYN-ACK response but does not send the final ACK packet to complete the handshake.

78. Answer: D. Web vulnerability scanner

Explanation: A web vulnerability scanner is specifically designed to identify vulnerabilities in web applications, including SQL injection flaws.

79. Answer: B. 80

Explanation: Port 80 is the standard port for
unencrypted HTTP traffic. Servers running
unencrypted HTTP services typically listen on
this port.

80. Answer: B. Vulnerability scanner

Explanation: A vulnerability scanner is specifically
designed to automatically identify known
vulnerabilities in systems and networks, making it
the most effective choice for this scenario.

81. Answer: D. Vulnerability scan

Explanation: A vulnerability scan is designed to
identify known security risks in a system by probing
for its configuration, software, and hardware
weaknesses.

82. Answer: C. Ensuring that implemented changes do
not compromise security

Explanation: One of the primary goals of a change
management program is to ensure that any changes
made to systems or processes do not adversely affect
the organization's security posture.

83. Answer: A. Infrastructure as a Service (IaaS)

Explanation: Infrastructure as a Service (IaaS)
provides an organization with the most control over
its cloud resources, including virtual machines,
storage, and networking. However, this level of
control comes with the responsibility of managing
and maintaining the operating systems and
applications.

84. Answer: C. Implementing vulnerability mitigation
     measures

     Explanation: A security assessment focuses on
     identifying vulnerabilities, assessing risks, and
     evaluating threats. The actual mitigation of
     vulnerabilities is usually a separate process that
     follows the assessment.

85. Answer: A. Organizational management

     Explanation: A security assessment report is
     primarily intended for organizational management.
     It provides them with an overview of the security
     posture of the system or network, allowing them to
     make informed decisions regarding security policies
     and resource allocation.

86. Answer: A. Response

     Explanation: In the (ISC)² framework for incident
     management, the first step is usually the "Response"
     phase, where the incident is initially addressed and
     contained.

87. Answer: B. Audit trails

     Explanation: The term "audit trails" best describes
     the body of data collected through event logging.
     Audit trails are records that provide documentary
     evidence of sequences of activities that have affected
     at any time a specific operation, procedure, or event.

88. Answer: B. An intrusion detection system (IDS)

    Explanation: A mirrored port is often used to connect an intrusion detection system (IDS) for monitoring network traffic.

89. Answer: B. A false negative

    Explanation: A false negative occurs when an intrusion detection system fails to detect an actual attack, allowing it to penetrate the network without raising an alarm.

90. Answer: B. Disrupting communication capabilities in preparation for a physical attack

    Explanation: Disrupting an organization's ability to communicate and respond to a physical attack is most indicative of a terrorist attack, as it aims to cause widespread harm and panic.

91. Answer: D. Utilizing automated tools to scan for vulnerable ports on the organization's systems

    Explanation: Grudge attacks are usually motivated by personal vendettas and aim to cause embarrassment or harm to the target. Scanning for vulnerable ports is more indicative of a broader cyberattack rather than a grudge attack.

92. Answer: C. Avoid altering the evidence during the collection process

    Explanation: The integrity of evidence is crucial in any investigation. Therefore, avoiding any modification to the evidence during its collection is paramount.

93. Answer: C. Documentary evidence

Explanation: Documentary evidence refers to written documents that are used in court to prove a fact.

94. Answer: C. Criminal

Explanation: Criminal investigations require the highest standard of evidence, often "beyond a reasonable doubt," due to the severe consequences involved, such as imprisonment.

95. Answer: B. Act honorably, honestly, justly, responsibly, and legally

Explanation: The (ISC)² Code of Ethics outlines that CISSPs are expected to act honorably, honestly, justly, responsibly, and legally.

96. Answer: B. Cloud based

Explanation: A cloud-based identity platform typically offers high availability and redundancy, making it a suitable choice when availability is the organization's biggest priority.

97. Answer: C. Federation

Explanation: The Federation allows for sharing identity information across different organizations and systems, making it the most appropriate choice for sharing identity information with a business partner.

98. Answer: C. Due care

Explanation: The principle of "due care" requires that an individual should act responsibly and take the necessary steps to complete their responsibilities accurately and in a timely manner.

99. Answer: A. Maximum tolerable downtime (MTD)

Explanation: Maximum tolerable downtime (MTD) is the metric that indicates the longest period of time a business process can be inoperative before causing irreparable harm to the organization.

CHAPTER 9

Security Operations

In the multifaceted world of information security, the domain of Security Operations stands as a critical pillar, holding a central position in the CISSP examination. This chapter delves into the intricate daily operations that are instrumental in safeguarding the confidentiality, integrity, and availability of information within an organization, a task paramount in today's digitally connected era.

The objective of this chapter is not merely to prepare you for the CISSP examination but to equip you with a profound and holistic understanding of the principles, concepts, methodologies, and best practices that govern the field of Security Operations. We aim to provide a comprehensive guide that transcends the boundaries of exam preparation by exploring real-world scenarios, case study analysis, and underlying theory dissection.

We recognize that the mastery of Security Operations requires theoretical knowledge and practical insight. Therefore, this chapter is meticulously structured to offer a balanced blend of theoretical explanations, practical examples, and expert insights. From the fundamental aspects of security administration to the complex mechanisms of incident response, we will navigate through the various facets of Security Operations, elucidating the essential components that form the backbone of modern information security.

To further enhance your learning experience and gauge your readiness for the CISSP exam, we have included a series of practice questions at the end of this chapter. These questions, carefully crafted with the guidance

© Mohamed Aly Bouke 2023

M. A. Bouke, *CISSP Exam Certification Companion*, Certification Study Companion Series, https://doi.org/10.1007/979-8-8688-0057-3_9

of industry experts, are designed to test your comprehension, analytical skills, and application of the concepts discussed in this chapter. They are a valuable tool to reinforce your understanding and provide a simulated exam experience, fostering confidence as you approach the examination.

Essential Concepts

The first step in any successful security investigation is understanding the rules and regulations that govern the process. It's crucial to comply with all applicable laws, such as privacy and organizational policies. Noncompliance can lead to legal complications, jeopardize the investigation, and potentially compromise the organization's reputation. Compliance includes maintaining the investigation's confidentiality, preserving the evidence's integrity, and ensuring the investigation is conducted ethically and responsibly. Some important concepts here include

- **Evidence collection and handling**: Evidence collection and handling are vital to any investigation. It's essential to preserve the original state of the evidence to maintain its admissibility in any potential legal proceedings. It would be best to use forensically sound methods during the collection, such as making bit-by-bit copies of digital evidence. Proper documentation, including chain-of-custody forms, should always accompany evidence to maintain its integrity and prove its authenticity.

- **Reporting and documentation**: Accurate reporting and documentation are integral to the investigation process. Reports should include a detailed account of the incident, the steps taken during the investigation, the evidence found, and any actions taken in response to the incident. Documentation provides a historical record, aids decision-making, and is vital if legal action is required. Ensure that all documentation is clear, accurate, and securely stored.

- **Investigative techniques**: Various investigative techniques can be used in a security investigation. These may include network traffic analysis, log analysis, malware analysis, and social engineering identification. The choice of technique depends on the nature of the incident. Staying current with the latest investigative techniques as technology and threats evolve is important.

- **Digital forensics tools, tactics, and procedures**: Digital forensics involves using specialized tools and procedures to identify, collect, examine, and preserve digital evidence. Tools may include disk imaging software, file recovery tools, network forensics tools, and more. Tactics could involve live system forensics, memory forensics, and timeline analysis. Standard procedures should be established and followed to maintain the integrity of the investigation and the collected evidence.

- **Artifacts**: Artifacts refer to data left behind on a digital device that can provide valuable insight during an investigation. These can include log files, browser history, deleted files, and more. Depending on the type of incident, artifacts may be found on various devices, such as computers, network servers, or mobile devices. Knowing where to look for artifacts and how to extract and interpret them correctly is essential to ensure a successful investigation.

571

Remember that these concepts are integral to your understanding of the Security Operations domain of the CISSP exam. Take the time to digest this information and familiarize yourself with the real-world application of these principles.

Conduct Logging and Monitoring Activities

Logging and monitoring are crucial to maintaining a secure environment, each serving unique yet interconnected roles. Logging is the systematic process of recording specific events or activities within a system or application, creating a historical record that can be used for future reference, analysis, compliance, incident response, and forensic investigations. Monitoring, on the other hand, refers to the continuous observation and analysis of those recorded logs or other system activities. While logging focuses on data collection and creating detailed and timestamped records of events, monitoring emphasizes interpretation, analysis, and response to those recorded events. Monitoring involves real-time or near-real-time analysis to detect abnormal or suspicious behavior, trigger alerts, track system performance, and identify long-term trends. Logging provides the raw data and historical context, and monitoring adds the analytical layer, transforming that data into actionable insights. Together, they form a robust security posture, with logging offering valuable information during incident response and forensic investigations and monitoring, enabling real-time threat detection and proactive security measures. For the CISSP exam, be familiar with the following techniques and tools for logging and monitoring:

- **Intrusion detection and prevention**: Intrusion detection systems (IDS) and intrusion prevention systems (IPS) are essential for identifying and preventing potential security threats. IDS systems monitor network traffic for suspicious activity and send alerts when they detect potential attacks. IPS systems go a step further by actively blocking or mitigating detected threats.

- **Security information and event management (SIEM)**: SIEM solutions provide real-time analysis of security alerts generated by applications and network hardware. They collect and aggregate log data, identify abnormal activity, and provide reporting capabilities. SIEM systems are integral to an organization's security strategy, providing a centralized view of its security landscape.

- **Continuous monitoring**: Continuous monitoring is an ongoing process that ensures the effectiveness of an organization's security controls. It involves regularly reviewing and updating security measures, assessing system vulnerabilities, and promptly addressing identified security gaps. This approach allows organizations to maintain an up-to-date understanding of their security posture and respond quickly to changing threat environments.

- **Egress monitoring**: Egress monitoring involves overseeing the data leaving a network. This type of monitoring can help detect data exfiltration attempts, identify malware communicating with external servers, and ensure compliance with data privacy regulations. Egress monitoring is a critical component of a comprehensive security monitoring strategy.

- **Log management**: Log management involves the collection, storage, analysis, and disposal of log data from various sources within an organization.

Effective log management can aid in detecting security incidents, troubleshooting system issues, and complying with data retention policies. It ensures that logs are securely stored and only accessible to authorized individuals.

- **Threat intelligence:** Threat intelligence involves gathering and analyzing information about potential or current attacks threatening an organization. Threat feeds provide real-time or near-real-time information about current threats from various sources, while threat hunting proactively searches for advanced persistent threats that evade existing security solutions. This intelligence can help organizations anticipate, prepare for, and respond to attacks.

- **User and entity behavior analytics (UEBA):** UEBA uses machine learning, algorithms, and statistical analyses to understand the normal behavior of users and entities within an organization. It can then identify any abnormal behavior or anomalies indicating a potential threat. UEBA can help detect insider threats, compromised credentials, and sophisticated external attacks.

Understanding these concepts is vital for the Security Operations domain of the CISSP exam. These principles play a significant role in maintaining a secure environment within an organization. In the next section, we'll provide practice questions to help you further understand these concepts and evaluate your readiness for the exam.

Apply Foundational Security Operations Concepts

Understanding and applying foundational security operations concepts are paramount in maintaining a secure environment within any organization. These concepts, which form the bedrock of security practices, encompass many principles and strategies that protect digital and physical assets. In the following, we explore these essential concepts in detail:

- **Need-to-know/least privilege principle:** This principle restricts access rights for users, limiting them to the bare minimum permissions required to perform their work. It serves as a fundamental safeguard against unauthorized access and potential breaches.

- **Separation of duties (SoD) and responsibilities:** SoD is a method that discourages fraud and prevents conflicts of interest. Critical functions are divided among staff members, creating a system of checks and balances that enhances security.

- **Privileged account management:** This concept involves the application of special restrictions and monitoring of accounts with elevated access to secure information. It ensures that privileged access is controlled and audited, reducing the risk of misuse.

- **Job rotation:** A strategy that involves moving employees between jobs, job rotation helps to prevent fraud or detect errors. It fosters a culture of transparency and accountability, enhancing the overall security posture.

- **Service-Level Agreements (SLAs)**: SLAs are contracts between a service provider and a customer that detail the expected level of service. They play a vital role in defining and maintaining the quality and reliability of services.

In addition to these principles, the protection of resources, both digital and physical, is vital to an organization's security posture. This includes media management and media protection techniques:

- **Media management**: Strategies for securely handling, storing, and disposing of media, such as hard drives, removable storage devices, and paper records. These strategies ensure that sensitive information is protected throughout its life cycle.

- **Media protection techniques**: Methods for securing media, including encryption, physical locks, and secure disposal methods. These techniques provide multiple layers of defense against unauthorized access and potential breaches.

- **Configuration management (CM)**: A systems engineering process for establishing and maintaining consistency in a product's performance and functional attributes. It involves provisioning (establishing system resources), baselining (setting a standard for comparing future measurements), and automation (using software to manage configurations to improve efficiency and reduce human error).

Understanding and implementing these foundational concepts is crucial for managing a secure environment's day-to-day operations and forming the cornerstone of a robust security posture. They are essential knowledge for the CISSP exam and anyone involved in information security.

Conduct Incident Management

Incident management is a critical process in security operations that involves identifying, analyzing, and correcting disruptions to prevent future recurrence. It comprises the following steps:

- **Detection**: The first step in incident management is detection, which involves identifying potential security incidents. This could involve various methods, from automated alerts from security systems to reports from users or third parties.

- **Response**: Once an incident is detected, the next step is the response. This involves assessing the incident, escalating it to the appropriate parties, and limiting its impact. This might involve isolating affected systems, implementing additional monitoring, or activating a response team.

- **Mitigation**: Mitigation involves taking actions to limit the impact of an incident. This could include patching software, blocking malicious IP addresses, changing user credentials, or other actions depending on the nature of the incident.

- **Reporting**: Incident reporting documents all incident details, actions taken, and decisions made. This is crucial for communicating with stakeholders, supporting forensic analysis, meeting regulatory requirements, and planning preventative measures.

- **Recovery**: Recovery involves restoring systems and processes to normal operations. This could involve removing malware, restoring systems from backups, validating the recovery with testing, and confirming systems function normally.

- **Remediation**: Remediation involves addressing the incident's root cause to prevent future recurrence. This could involve patching software, updating firewall rules, educating users, or improving detection and response processes.

- **Lessons learned**: The final step in incident management is conducting a lessons learned session. This involves reviewing what happened, what was done, what worked well, what didn't, and what can be improved for future incidents. This continuous improvement process is critical to maturing an organization's incident response capability.

Mastering these concepts is vital to your success in the CISSP exam and your future role as a security professional. The next section will provide practice questions to reinforce these concepts and evaluate your readiness for the exam.

Operate and Maintain Detective and Preventative Measures

Operating and maintaining detective and preventative measures is a key aspect of managing security operations. This involves various tools and techniques to prevent, detect, and respond to security threats.

- **Firewalls**: Firewalls act as a barrier between trusted and untrusted networks, monitoring and controlling incoming and outgoing network traffic based on predetermined security rules. Next-generation firewalls (NGFWs) offer more advanced features like intrusion prevention, SSL and SSH inspection, deep-packet inspection, and reputation-based malware detection.

- **Intrusion detection systems (IDS) and intrusion prevention systems (IPS)**: IDS and IPS are used to detect and prevent potential security threats. IDS monitors network traffic for suspicious activity and sends alerts, while IPS goes further by actively preventing or mitigating detected threats.

- **Allowlisting/blocklisting**: Allowlisting and blocklisting control access to a network or system. Allowlisting allows access to only pre-approved entities, while blocklisting blocks access from known malicious entities.

- **Third-party provided security services**: These services can include security-as-a-service solutions, managed security services, and consulting services. These can offer specialized expertise, 24/7 coverage, and cost savings for organizations.

- **Sandboxing**: Sandboxing is a security technique that isolates potentially unsafe programs in a restricted environment (the "sandbox") to prevent them from affecting other parts of the system.

- **Honeypots/honeynets**: Honeypots are decoy systems designed to attract and distract attackers, allowing organizations to detect and study attack methods. Honeynets are networks of honeypots, providing a higher level of interaction for the attacker.

- **Anti-malware**: Anti-malware tools detect, prevent, and remove malicious software, such as viruses, ransomware, and spyware.

- **Machine learning and artificial intelligence (AI) based tools**: These tools use algorithms to learn from data and make predictions or decisions without being explicitly programmed. In security, machine learning and AI can help detect unusual behavior, identify new threats, and automate responses.

Mastering these concepts is crucial to maintaining a robust security posture and succeeding in the CISSP exam. The next section will provide practice questions to reinforce these concepts further and assess your readiness for the exam.

Patch Management, Recovery, and System Availability

Patch and vulnerability management involves identifying, classifying, remediating, and mitigating vulnerabilities. This includes regularly applying patches (updates) to software and systems to address known vulnerabilities and reduce the potential for exploitation.

- **Change management processes**: Change management is a structured approach to transitioning individuals, teams, and organizations from a current state to a desired future state. In the context of IT, change management involves controlling and managing changes to the system in an orderly and predictable manner to minimize disruptions and unintended consequences.

- **Implement recovery strategies**: Recovery strategies are plans for responding to and recovering from an event that impacts business operations. This could include a variety of approaches, depending on the nature and impact of the incident, such as restoring systems from backups, switching to a redundant system, or activating a disaster recovery site.

- **Backup storage strategies**: Backup storage strategies involve making copies of data so that these additional copies may be used to restore the original data in the event of data loss. Strategies can vary widely depending on the organization's needs but may include full, incremental, or differential backups and on-site or off-site storage.

- **Recovery site strategies**: Recovery site strategies are plans for recovering IT infrastructure at an alternate location during a disaster. This could include hot sites (fully equipped data centers ready to take over operations), warm sites (partially equipped data centers that can be ready to take over operations within a short period), or cold sites (locations where equipment, data, and personnel can be moved to if necessary).

- **Multiple processing sites**: Multiple processing sites are used to distribute IT processes and data across different locations. This helps ensure business continuity in a disaster or other events that make one site unavailable.

Additionally, system resilience is the ability of a system to prepare for, respond to, and recover from a disruption. High availability (HA) involves designing systems to be available and operational for a high percentage of the time. Quality of service (QoS) refers to the performance level of a service or a system. Fault tolerance is the ability of a system to continue operating without interruption when one or more of its components fail.

Mastering these concepts is essential to maintaining a secure and reliable IT environment and is key to success in the CISSP exam. The next section will provide practice questions to reinforce these concepts further and assess your readiness for the exam.

Implement Disaster Recovery

Disaster recovery (DR) is a set of policies and procedures that protect an organization from significant negative events. DR allows an organization to maintain or quickly resume mission-critical functions following a disaster. Here are the main steps:

- **Response**: This is the immediate reaction once a disaster has been identified. It often involves invoking the disaster recovery plan, alerting the disaster recovery team, and implementing the initial steps of the plan.

- **Personnel**: Personnel management during disaster recovery includes assigning roles and responsibilities to the team and ensuring all individuals understand their tasks. It may also involve coordinating with external parties such as emergency responders, suppliers, or customers.

- **Communications**: Effective communication is crucial in a disaster recovery situation. This may involve communicating with employees, stakeholders, and possibly the public, depending on the nature and extent of the disaster. It's important to share accurate information about the situation and the organization's response plan.

- **Assessment**: Assessment involves understanding the nature and extent of the disaster and its impact on critical systems and processes. This step determines which parts of the disaster recovery plan to implement.

- **Restoration**: Restoration involves getting the affected systems back up and running. Depending on the disaster, this could involve repairing physical systems, restoring backup data, or implementing alternate systems.

- **Training and awareness**: All personnel involved in disaster recovery need to be trained on the disaster recovery plan and their specific roles within it. Additionally, broader training and awareness programs can help all employees understand what to do in a disaster.

- **Lessons learned**: After the disaster recovery process has been executed, it's important to conduct a "lessons learned" review to identify what worked well, what didn't, and how the process can be improved for the future.

Moreover, testing disaster recovery plans is crucial to ensure they will function as intended during a real disaster. There are several methods to test a DRP:

- **Read-through/tabletop**: This is a discussion-based exercise where team members review the plan and discuss their roles and responses to disaster scenarios.

- **Walk-through**: In a walk-through, the disaster recovery team physically performs their roles according to the plan but without actually implementing any recovery measures.

- **Simulation**: The team responds to a simulated disaster scenario in a simulation. This test is more realistic than a walk-through but doesn't involve any disruption to normal operations.

- **Parallel**: A parallel test involves recovering systems at a recovery site and performing production tasks while the primary site performs normal operations.

- **Full interruption**: In a full interruption test, the primary site's operations are halted, and the team must recover systems at the recovery site. This is the most thorough test of a DRP and also the most disruptive and risky.

Participate in Business Continuity (BC) Planning and Exercises

Additionally, BC planning involves creating and implementing a plan to ensure the continuity of operations during and after a disaster. Exercises can involve testing the plan, training, and performing post-exercise evaluations. This includes

- **Implement and manage physical security**: Physical security involves measures designed to protect physical assets, like buildings and equipment, from harm. This includes perimeter security controls, like fences and surveillance cameras, and internal security controls, like access control systems and secure areas.

- **Address personnel safety and security concerns**: This involves taking steps to ensure the safety and security of personnel. This could involve providing security training and awareness, managing travel security, and implementing emergency management procedures.

- **Emergency management**: Emergency management involves planning and coordinating emergency responses to protect people, property, and the environment. This might include evacuation plans, emergency response teams, and emergency communication systems.

- **Duress**: Duress involves situations where a person is forced to act against their will under threat. In a security context, duress systems can alert security personnel when someone is forced to act, like entering a secure area.

Understanding these topics is vital for the CISSP exam and your future role as a security professional.

Summary

This chapter focused on the essentials of Security Operations, one of the key domains of the CISSP exam. The chapter began with exploring the importance of understanding and complying with investigations, touching upon various investigative techniques and digital forensics tools.

The significance of logging and monitoring activities was then delved into, highlighting the role of intrusion detection systems (IDS), intrusion prevention systems (IPS), security information and event management (SIEM), and user and entity behavior analytics (UEBA).

Further, the chapter discussed the need for effective configuration management (CM) and the application of foundational security operations concepts such as the principle of least privilege, separation of duties, and privileged account management. Resource protection techniques were also addressed, including media management and media protection techniques.

Incident management, encompassing stages from detection to lessons learned, played a crucial role in our discussion. This was followed with an in-depth look at various detective and preventative measures, including firewalls, IDS/IPS, allowlisting/blocklisting, sandboxing, honeypots/honeynets, anti-malware solutions, and the growing role of machine learning and AI in security.

The chapter also covered the importance of implementing and supporting patch and vulnerability management, understanding and participating in change management processes and implementing recovery strategies, including backup storage, recovery site strategies, and maintaining system resilience.

A detailed discussion on disaster recovery processes and the importance of testing disaster recovery plans (DRP) closed the chapter. The need for business continuity planning, implementing and managing physical security, and addressing personnel safety and security concerns rounded off the chapter.

Key Takeaways

- **Security operations** are a critical component of information security, involving the application of security principles and practices to an organization's everyday tasks and functions.

- **Understanding and complying with investigations**, effective logging and monitoring, and strong configuration management practices form the foundation of security operations.

- **Incident management** is a critical skill encompassing detection, response, mitigation, reporting, recovery, remediation, and learning from incidents.

- **Employing various tools and techniques**, including preventative measures like firewalls and IDS/IPS and detective measures like SIEM and UEBA, is crucial to maintaining a robust security posture.

- **Implementing and supporting patch and vulnerability** management, understanding change management processes, and possessing strong recovery strategies are essential for system resilience.

- **Disaster recovery and business continuity planning** are necessary to ensure an organization's continued operation during and after a disaster.

- **Physical security and personnel safety** hold equal importance to digital security.

- **Continuous learning and adaptation** are key in the ever-evolving field of cybersecurity.

Understanding and mastering these concepts will prepare you well for the Security Operations domain of the CISSP exam. The next chapter will expand your knowledge and bring you closer to your certification goal.

Practice Questions

As you conclude your exploration of the complex domain of Security Operations in this chapter, a critical phase of your CISSP exam preparation awaits. This section presents a collection of practice questions meticulously crafted to reinforce your understanding of the multifaceted principles, concepts, and best practices governing this vital information security area.

These questions are not merely a test of your recall but an essential extension of your learning journey. Reflecting the complexity and depth you will face in the actual exam, they encapsulate the profound insights and real-world applications needed for success. Engaging with each question, delving into the explanations, and reflecting on the answers will reveal your strengths and illuminate areas that may require further refinement.

Approach these questions with determination, curiosity, and a readiness to be challenged. Embrace the lessons from correct responses and mistakes, and immerse yourself in critical thinking and analysis. Remember, these practice questions are not just an assessment of your knowledge but a tool to deepen your comprehension and hone your readiness for the CISSP exam.

Take the time you need, ponder each question, and let these practice questions guide your success in the CISSP exam and your continued development as an information security professional. Your exploration of Security Operations has equipped you with the knowledge and skills that are essential for the exam and vital for your cybersecurity career.

1. Which of the following best describes the primary focus of the chain of custody in evidence handling?

    A. Documenting the location of evidence

    B. Taking photographs of the crime scene

    C. Control of evidence to maintain its integrity for court presentation

    D. Sealing off access to the area where a crime may have occurred

2. Which of the following is NOT a type of evidence that might be considered during a computer security investigation?

    A. Corroborative evidence

    B. Hearsay evidence

    C. Secondary evidence

    D. Predictive evidence

3. What is the primary difference between a virus and a worm in terms of malware?

    A. A virus requires human interaction to trigger, while a worm can self-propagate.

    B. A virus can self-propagate, while a worm requires human interaction to trigger.

    C. Both virus and worm require human interaction to trigger.

    D. Both virus and worm can self-propagate without human interaction.

4. Which of the following is a key characteristic of a Trojan horse in the context of malware?

   A. It can self-propagate and spread through a network.

   B. It looks harmless or desirable but contains malicious code.

   C. It changes aspects of itself, like file name or code structure, to evade detection.

   D. It is a piece of malware that makes minimal changes over a long period to evade detection.

5. In the context of backup strategies, what does the term "mirror backup" refer to?

   A. A backup that is an exact copy of a dataset without any compression

   B. A backup that includes only the changes since the last full backup

   C. A backup that includes changes since the last incremental backup

   D. A backup that changes its structure to evade detection

6. Which of the following best describes the concept of "live evidence" in digital forensics?

   A. Evidence that is stored on a hard drive

   B. Evidence that is stored in places like RAM, cache, and buffers of a running system

   C. Evidence that is taken from surveillance footage from security cameras

   D. Evidence that is stored on backup tapes

7. In the context of security operations, what does the term "Service-Level Agreements (SLAs)" primarily refer to?

   A. Agreements that specify the minimum security standards to be maintained

   B. Agreements that denote time frames against the performance of specific operations

   C. Agreements that define the roles and responsibilities of security personnel

   D. Agreements that outline the backup and recovery strategies

8. Which of the following is NOT a step in the incident response process?

   A. Detection

   B. Encryption

   C. Mitigation

   D. Remediation

9. What is the primary purpose of user and entity behavior analytics (UEBA)?

   A. To monitor network traffic and block malicious IPs

   B. To analyze and correlate log data from multiple sources

   C. To monitor the behavior and patterns of users and entities

   D. To provide threat intelligence and analysis of emerging threat trends

10. Which of the following malware types is designed to make minimal changes over a long period to avoid detection?

    A. Ransomware

    B. Rootkit

    C. Data diddler

    D. Logic bomb

11. In the context of malware, which type changes aspects of itself, like file name, file size, and code structure, to evade detection every time it replicates across a network?

    A. Trojan

    B. Rootkit

    C. Polymorphic malware

    D. Logic bomb

12. Which of the following is NOT a type of evidence considered in computer security investigations?

    A. Oral/written statements

    B. Visual/audio evidence

    C. Digital footprints

    D. Hearsay evidence

13. What is the primary goal of the incident response process?

    A. To detect and prevent future attacks

    B. To provide an effective and efficient response to reduce impact to the organization

C. To identify the attackers and prosecute them

D. To restore all compromised systems to their original state

14. Which option is least likely to be employed to mitigate single points of failure?

   A. RAID 0

   B. RAID 1

   C. Utilizing an alternative Internet connection through a distinct ISP

   D. Employing a load-balanced server cluster

15. In a black box penetration test, what level of knowledge is typically granted to the red team regarding the target infrastructure?

   A. The specific targets and the duration of the test

   B. Comprehensive details

   C. No information

   D. The enterprise's IP subnet layout

16. Which terminology pertains to the statistical evaluation of a system or device's operational lifespan?

   A. Maximum tolerable downtime (MTD)

   B. Statistical deviation

   C. Mean time to repair (MTTR)

   D. Mean time between failures (MTBF)

17. How is Hierarchical Storage Management (HSM) best characterized?

    A. The organization of files and directories on a hard drive

    B. The method of transporting tapes to off-site locations using armored vehicles and armed personnel

    C. The process of transitioning files from high-cost, high-speed storage to more affordable, slower storage solutions

    D. The technique of powering down disk drives to conserve energy, reduce heat, and extend disk lifespan when the stored files are not in use

18. During which stage of a targeted assault would a sniffer tool most likely be initially employed?

    A. Active reconnaissance

    B. Passive reconnaissance

    C. Pillaging

    D. Fingerprinting

19. What best defines the reason for collusion and the most effective countermeasure against it?

    A. A comprehensive penetration testing contract

    B. Implementing separation of duties and rotating job responsibilities

    C. Addressing software vulnerabilities through consistent OS and application updates

    D. Employing data redundancy and fault-tolerant technologies

20. Upon Nicole's transfer to a different department and role, why is it essential for an administrator to revoke her previous access rights?

    A. To mitigate single points of failure

    B. To prevent sequential access procedures

    C. To reset the archive attribute

    D. To counteract privilege accumulation

21. Which statement best captures the essence of Hierarchical Storage Management (HSM)?

    A. The structure in which files and directories are saved on a hard drive

    B. The procedure of securely transporting tapes to off-site locations using armored vehicles and security personnel

    C. The strategy of transitioning files from high-speed, high-cost storage to more economical, slower storage media

    D. The practice of deactivating disk drives to conserve energy, diminish heat, and extend their lifespan when the stored files are not being accessed

22. When analyzing a suspicious attachment by running it within a controlled virtual setting, how is this environment best described?

    A. Honeypot

    B. Hyperjacking

    C. Sandbox

    D. Decompiler

23. Which of the following does not provide a security
     or operational justification for enforcing mandatory
     vacations?

     A. The chance for the organization to review an
         employee's work

     B. Ensuring the employee is rejuvenated

     C. Preventing a single individual from easily conducting
         clandestine activities

     D. Making employees aware that unauthorized actions
         might be detected

24. What kind of security measure is represented by an
     audit trail?

     A. Application

     B. Administrative

     C. Preventative

     D. Detective

25. Which option does not represent an advantage of
     RAID (Redundant Array of Independent Disks)?

     A. Enhanced storage capacity

     B. Prolonged recovery time

     C. Performance enhancements

     D. Fault resilience

26. Which concept is closely associated with the principle of separation of duties?

   A. Dual controls

   B. Principle of least privilege

   C. Job rotation

   D. Principle of privilege

27. Which resource is primarily targeted by phreakers?

   A. Mainframes

   B. Networks

   C. PBX systems

   D. Wireless networks

28. After sending an email to an old colleague, it was rejected and you were prompted to resend it. What likely occurred with the message transfer agent?

   A. Allowlist

   B. Graylist

   C. Blocklist

   D. Black hole

29. In the event of a significant disruption, which of the following is designed to assume operational responsibilities when the primary site is inoperative?

   A. BCP (business continuity plan)

   B. Audit

   C. Incident response

   D. COOP (continuity of operations plan)

30. Which RAID configuration offers data striping without any redundancy?

A. RAID 0

B. RAID 1

C. RAID 3

D. RAID 4

31. Which backup method is the quickest to perform but requires the most time to restore?

A. Incremental

B. Differential

C. Full

D. Grandfathered

32. Which type of intrusion detection system primarily differentiates between typical and atypical activities?

A. Pattern based

B. Statistical based

C. Traffic based

D. Protocol based

33. Which process involves replacing data with zeros?

A. Formatting

B. Drive wiping

C. Zeroization

D. Degaussing

34. Which RAID configuration is characterized by a combination of striping and mirroring?

    A. RAID 1

    B. RAID 5

    C. RAID 10

    D. RAID 15

35. Which multi-disk technique allows for the utilization of hard drives of varying sizes, provides no speed benefits, does not mirror, and can be implemented on two or more drives?

    A. RAID 0

    B. RAID 1

    C. RAID 5

    D. JBOD (Just a Bunch of Disks)

36. If you are working on a confidential project that demands an immense amount of computational power, which technique would be most appropriate?

    A. Redundant servers

    B. Clustering

    C. Distributed computing

    D. Cloud computing

37. How would you best describe a business continuity/ disaster recovery plan?

   A. A strategy for preventing disasters

   B. A sanctioned set of preparations and adequate procedures to react to disasters

   C. A set of actions and methods to respond to disasters without needing managerial consent

   D. The necessary preparations and methods to ensure the ongoing operation of all organizational functions

38. Which legal and regulatory requirement is universally applicable across all industries?

   A. Sarbanes-Oxley

   B. HIPAA

   C. Due diligence

   D. BS25999

39. Which statement most accurately captures the scope and focus of business continuity or disaster recovery planning within an organization?

   A. Continuity planning is a paramount organizational concern encompassing all organizational areas or functions.

   B. Continuity planning primarily focuses on technology, emphasizing the recovery of technological assets.

C. Continuity planning is essential only where there's intricate voice and data communication.

D. Continuity planning is a crucial managerial concern, focusing on the main functions as determined by management.

40. The primary objective of a business impact analysis is to

A. Determine the effects of a threat on organizational operations

B. Identify potential loss exposures for the organization

C. Assess the repercussions of a risk on the organization

D. Find the most cost-effective method to eliminate threats

41. During the risk analysis phase of planning, which action is most effective in managing threats or reducing the consequences of an event?

A. Altering the exercise scenario

B. Crafting recovery procedures

C. Increasing dependence on key personnel

D. Instituting procedural controls

42. What is the primary reason for introducing additional controls or safeguards?

A. To discourage or eliminate the risk

B. To detect and remove the threat

C. To minimize the threat's impact

D. To recognize the risk and the threat

43. Which statement most accurately defines a business impact analysis?

A. Risk analysis and organizational impact analysis are synonymous terms describing the same project effort.

B. A business impact analysis measures the likelihood of disruptions within the organization.

C. A business impact analysis is vital for the creation of a business continuity plan.

D. A business impact analysis determines the consequences of disruptions on the organization.

44. The term "disaster recovery" pertains to the restoration of

A. Organizational operations

B. The technological environment

C. The manufacturing environment

D. Personnel environments

45. Which term most accurately describes the effort to understand the potential repercussions of disruptions resulting from a disaster?

A. Business impact analysis

B. Risk analysis

C. Risk assessment

D. Project problem definition

46. What is the primary benefit of utilizing a cold site as a recovery strategy?

   A. It's a more cost-effective recovery option.

   B. It can be set up and made operational for any organizational function.

   C. It's preconfigured for communications and can be tailored for organizational functions.

   D. It's the most readily available option for testing server and communication restorations.

47. Which of the following best describes the components of risk?

   A. Natural and man-made disasters

   B. Threats, assets, and controls to mitigate them

   C. Risk assessment and business impact analysis

   D. Business impact analysis and controls to mitigate risks

48. What does the term "recovery time objective" (RTO) refer to?

   A. The maximum duration a service or system can be down

   B. The duration a disaster recovery process should take

   C. The time needed to transition from a primary to a backup site

   D. The waiting period before initiating a crisis communication plan

49. Which backup type allows for the most efficient restoration from tape backup?

    A. Full backup

    B. Incremental backup

    C. Partial backup

    D. Differential backup

50. What is a primary advantage of a hot site recovery solution?

    A. It's more cost-effective.

    B. It's highly available.

    C. It ensures zero downtime.

    D. It requires no maintenance.

51. Which method is not recommended for testing the business continuity plan?

    A. Tabletop exercise

    B. Call exercise

    C. Simulated exercise

    D. Interrupting a live production application or function

52. What is the main objective of a well-structured business continuity exercise?

    A. To pinpoint the strengths and weaknesses of the plan

    B. To meet managerial requirements

    C. To adhere to an auditor's stipulations

    D. To sustain shareholder trust

53. When is the optimal time to update and maintain a
     business continuity plan?

     A. Yearly or upon an auditor's request

     B. Only when new software versions are rolled out

     C. Exclusively when new hardware is introduced

     D. As part of the configuration and change management
        procedure

54. Which factor is paramount for the success of
     business continuity?

     A. Support from senior leadership

     B. A competent technical support team

     C. A comprehensive Wide Area Network infrastructure

     D. A cohesive incident response team

55. If the recovery time objective for a service is two
     months, which alternate site strategy is most suitable?

     A. Cold site

     B. Reciprocal agreement

     C. Warm site

     D. Hot site

56. If a service's recovery point objective is zero, which
     strategy is best to ensure this requirement is met?

     A. RAID 6 with a hot site alternative

     B. RAID 0 with a warm site alternative

     C. RAID 0 with a cold site alternative

     D. RAID 6 with a reciprocal agreement

57. What is the main role of a physical protection system?

    A. Ascertain, guide, and dispatch

    B. Detect, delay, and respond

    C. Display, develop, initiate, and capture

    D. Evaluate, dispatch, and detain

58. For a successful vulnerability assessment, understanding protection systems is crucial through which of the following?

    A. Threat definition, target identification, and facility characterization

    B. Threat definition, conflict control, and facility characterization

    C. Risk assessment, threat identification, and incident review

    D. Threat identification, vulnerability evaluation, and access review

59. In which scenarios is laminated glass recommended?

    A. All external glass windows

    B. Interior boundary breaches and vital infrastructure facilities

    C. Windows at street level, entrances, and other access points

    D. Capacitance proximity, intrusion detection locations, and boundary breaches

60. What is the strategy called that involves creating multiple layers of protection around a resource or facility?

    A. Secured boundary

    B. Defense in depth

    C. Strengthened barrier deterrent

    D. Reasonable asset defense

61. Which technique is most effective in shaping a physical environment to positively impact human behavior and reduce crime?

    A. Asset protection and vulnerability evaluations

    B. Minimizing vulnerability by safeguarding, compensating, or transferring the risk

    C. Crime prevention through environmental design

    D. Implementing employee screening and programs against workplace violence

62. What is the cornerstone of an effective physical protection system?

    A. Integration of individuals, processes, and equipment

    B. Combination of technology, risk evaluation, and human engagement

    C. Safeguarding, compensating, and risk transfer

    D. Detection, prevention, and reaction

63. What is the main goal of regulating access to a
     facility or zone?

     A. Manage time controls for all staff members

     B. Ensure only authorized individuals gain entry

     C. Prevent potential threats or unauthorized materials that
         could be used for sabotage

     D. For identification purposes

64. What is the recommended lighting level for safety in
     perimeter zones like parking areas or garages?

     A. 3 fc

     B. 5 fc

     C. 7 fc

     D. 10 fc

65. Which interior sensor is most suitable for a structure
     with ground-floor windows?

     A. Infrared glass-break sensor

     B. Ultrasonic glass-break sensors

     C. Acoustic/shock glass-break sensors

     D. Volumetric sensors

66. Which options accurately represent three distinct
     functions of CCTV?

     A. Monitoring, deterrence, and evidence collection

     B. Intrusion detection, containment, and response

     C. Optical scanning, infrared projection, and illumination

     D. Observation, white balancing, and inspection

67. While security technologies aren't a panacea for all organizational security challenges, what benefit do they offer when applied correctly?

   A. Reduction in electricity expenses

   B. Enhancement of the security framework, often leading to cost savings for the organization

   C. Government tax breaks for improved physical security systems

   D. Increased property value due to advanced integrated technologies

68. For what primary reason should a comprehensive evaluation of a facility or structure be conducted?

   A. To identify the locations of all fire exits

   B. In relation to the specified threats and the worth of the organization's assets

   C. To tally the number of staff members inside the facility

   D. To assess the robustness of the boundary walls

69. Which of the following is the optimal example of designing a new facility with security in mind?

   A. Minimizing the number of entrances that need monitoring, staffing, and protection

   B. Cutting down costs related to energy consumption for the physical security system

   C. Providing employees with easy access without them being aware of the security measures monitoring them

   D. Applying blast-resistant film to all external windows

70. Why is it an established protocol for all visitors to sign in and out using a visitor's log when entering a facility?

   A. For detection, responsibility, and the potential need for action

   B. For access control and observation

   C. To record the duration of the visit, the person visited, and to account for everyone in emergencies

   D. For planning evaluation and proper designation requirements

71. What is the most effective method to safeguard the physical components linked to the alarm system?

   A. Tamper protection

   B. Target fortification

   C. Security design

   D. UL 2050 standard

72. When utilizing portable computing devices or media, either within a facility or outside for legitimate business reasons, which protective measures are BEST to ensure their security?

   A. Cable locks, encryption, password safeguards, and heightened awareness

   B. Mitigating vulnerability through protection, risk offset, or risk transfer

   C. Operational readiness, physical security systems, and standard operating procedures

   D. Enhancing awareness, environmental design, and physical security measures

73. Which systems authenticate individuals based on unique physical characteristics like fingerprints, eye patterns, or voice?

   A. Biometric devices

   B. Technological systems

   C. Physiometric devices

   D. Physical analysis devices

74. Physical security is implemented using what kind of approach with protective measures to deter unauthorized access or property damage?

   A. Layers

   B. Methods

   C. Varieties

   D. Types

75. What term describes a thorough review of a facility, encompassing physical security controls, policies, procedures, and employee safety?

   A. Availability assessment

   B. Security survey

   C. Budgetary and financial review

   D. Defense in depth

76. Which security measure is most effective in preventing unauthorized access methods like "piggybacking" or "tailgating"?

   A. Cameras

   B. Turnstiles

   C. Keys

   D. Identification badges

77. From which source does the most significant threat of cybercrime originate?

   A. External actors

   B. State-sponsored actors

   C. Internal actors or employees

   D. Novice hackers or enthusiasts

78. What is the primary obstacle in combating computer-related crimes?

   A. Cybercriminals tend to be more intelligent than cyber investigators.

   B. Insufficient funds to stay ahead of cybercriminals.

   C. The global nature of computer crime activities.

   D. The overwhelming number of cybercriminals compared to investigators.

79. Computer forensics combines computer science, IT, and engineering with which of the following?

   A. Legal principles

   B. Information systems

C. Analytical reasoning

D. Scientific methodology

80. Which principle suggests that a criminal always leaves behind evidence while also taking something from the crime scene?

A. Meyer's principle of legal non-liability

B. Principles of criminalistics

C. IOCE/Group of 8 Nations principles for computer forensics

D. Locard's exchange principle

81. Which combination correctly represents the essential rules of evidence?

A. Be genuine, be duplicated, and be permissible in court.

B. Be exhaustive, be genuine, and be permissible in court.

C. Be exhaustive, be duplicated, and be genuine.

D. Be duplicated, be permissible in court, and be exhaustive.

82. Which of the following is not typically considered a stage in the incident response process?

A. Recordkeeping

B. Legal action

C. Isolation

D. Examination

83. Which legal system primarily focuses on theoretical legal concepts and is influenced by academic writings and scholars?

    A. Criminal law

    B. Civil law

    C. Theocratic law

    D. Regulatory law

84. Which form of intellectual property protection covers the representation of ideas, rather than the ideas themselves?

    A. Brand mark

    B. Invention protection

    C. Literary and artistic works protection

    D. Business confidential information

85. Which intellectual property right safeguards the reputation and brand recognition a business establishes for its products?

    A. Brand mark

    B. Invention protection

    C. Literary and artistic works protection

    D. Business confidential information

86. Which combinations represent recognized guidelines in the field of computer forensics?

    A. IOCE, Method of Operation (MOM), and SWGDE

    B. Method of Operation (MOM), SWGDE, and IOCE

    . C. IOCE, SWGDE, and ACPO

    D. ACPO, Method of Operation (MOM), and IOCE

87. Which of the following options lists types of software licenses?

    A. No-cost software, open source, and paid software

    B. Paid software, educational, and open source

    C. Educational, no-cost software, and open source

    D. No-cost software, paid software, and educational

88. Which term best describes the rights and responsibilities related to the handling of personal data?

    A. Personal rights

    B. Confidentiality

    C. Data accessibility

    D. Data trustworthiness

89. Which of the following best describes the initial stages of responding to an incident?

    A. Gathering, moving, testifying

    B. Tracing, replying, returning

    C. Spotting, recognizing, alerting

    D. Securing, ensuring, providing

90. How can the authenticity of a forensic digital copy be verified?

    A. By comparing digital signatures with the original

    B. Through meticulous recordkeeping

    C. By photographing the process

    D. Using cryptographic keys

91. Regarding digital evidence, the crime scene should

    A. Remain untouched

    B. Be able to be duplicated in court

    C. Be located in a single jurisdiction

    D. Have minimal interference

92. When IT systems are outsourced

    A. All legal and compliance responsibilities are transferred to the service provider.

    B. The outsourcing organization no longer has compliance responsibilities.

    C. The outsourced IT systems are exempt from compliance responsibilities.

    D. The service provider is exempt from compliance responsibilities.

93. How does the ISC2 Code of Ethics address conflicts between its principles?

    A. It states that conflicts between principles are impossible.

    B. It resolves them through a formal adjudication process.

C. It uses the order in which the principles are listed.

D. It refers all conflicts to its board of directors for resolution.

94. To ensure proper forensic procedures are followed when needed, an incident response program should

A. Ensure the organization's legal team is not involved

B. Regularly create digital copies of all computers

C. Only escalate closed incidents to law enforcement

D. Approach every incident as if it might lead to legal action

95. If a hard drive is recovered from a submerged vehicle and is needed for a court case, what is the best method to retrieve data from the drive?

A. Let the drive dry, install it in a computer, and use standard commands to access the data.

B. Dry the drive in a forensic oven, use a degausser to remove humidity, then access the data using a laptop.

C. Make a forensic copy of the drive while it's still wet.

D. Contact a professional data recovery service, explain the situation, and ask them to create a forensic image.

96. Among the listed cloud service models, which one grants an organization the highest degree of administrative control while also necessitating that the organization undertake comprehensive maintenance responsibilities for both the operating systems and applications?

    A. Infrastructure as a Service (IaaS)

    B. Platform as a Service (PaaS)

    C. Software as a Service (SaaS)

    D. Public Cloud Service

97. Which of the following is the most secure method for storing log files?

    A. On the same server as the application

    B. On a dedicated logging server

    C. On removable media

    D. In a public cloud storage service

98. Which of the following IDS types is best suited for detecting zero-day attacks?

    A. Signature-based IDS

    B. Anomaly-based IDS

    C. Stateful protocol analysis IDS

    D. Heuristic-based IDS

Answers

1. Answer: C. Control of evidence to maintain its integrity for court presentation

   Explanation: The primary focus of the chain of custody is to ensure the control and integrity of evidence so that it can be presented in court without any doubts about its authenticity.

2. Answer: D. Predictive evidence

   Explanation: While corroborative, hearsay, and secondary are types of evidence mentioned, predictive evidence is not listed as a type of evidence in the context of a computer security investigation.

3. Answer: A. A virus requires human interaction to trigger, while a worm can self-propagate.

   Explanation: A virus is a type of malware that requires some form of human interaction to be activated, such as opening a file. In contrast, a worm can spread on its own by exploiting vulnerabilities in systems.

4. Answer: B. It looks harmless or desirable but contains malicious code.

   Explanation: A Trojan horse is a type of malware that appears to be something legitimate or desirable but contains hidden malicious code. It tricks users into downloading or running it, thinking it's safe or beneficial.

5. Answer: A. A backup that is an exact copy of a dataset without any compression

    Explanation: A mirror backup creates an exact replica of a dataset. It does not use compression, making it the fastest backup type in terms of both backup and restore, but it requires a significant amount of storage.

6. Answer: B. Evidence that is stored in places like RAM, cache, and buffers of a running system

    Explanation: Live evidence refers to data stored in a running system's volatile memory, such as RAM, cache, and buffers. This type of evidence can change or disappear if the system's state is altered.

7. Answer: B. Agreements that denote time frames against the performance of specific operations

    Explanation: SLAs contain terms that specify related time frames against the performance of certain operations agreed upon within the overall contract.

8. Answer: B. Encryption

    Explanation: While detection, mitigation, and remediation are steps in the incident response process, encryption is not a step in this process. Encryption is a method to secure data.

9. Answer: C. To monitor the behavior and patterns of users and entities

   Explanation: UEBA focuses on analyzing the behavior and patterns of users and entities, logging and correlating the underlying data, analyzing the data, and triggering alerts when necessary.

10. Answer: C. Data diddler

    Explanation: A data diddler is a type of malware that makes minimal changes over a prolonged period to evade detection. Its primary goal is to subtly alter data without being noticed.

11. Answer: C. Polymorphic malware

    Explanation: Polymorphic malware can change aspects of itself to evade detection every time it replicates across a network.

12. Answer: C. Digital footprints

    Explanation: While oral/written statements, visual/audio evidence, and hearsay evidence are considered types of evidence in computer security investigations, "digital footprints" is not specifically mentioned as a type of evidence.

13. Answer: B. To provide an effective and efficient response to reduce impact to the organization

    Explanation: The main goals of incident response are to provide an effective and efficient response to reduce the impact on the organization, maintain or restore business continuity, and defend against future attacks.

14.   Answer: A. RAID 0

Explanation: Single points of failure refer to components or parts of a system that, if they fail, will cause the entire system to fail. To mitigate these vulnerabilities, redundancy is often introduced. Among the options, RAID 0 does not provide redundancy. Instead, it stripes data across multiple disks, which can improve performance but does not eliminate a single point of failure. If one disk in a RAID 0 array fails, all data is lost. On the other hand, RAID 1, having a secondary Internet connection, and using a load-balanced server cluster all introduce redundancy and help in eliminating single points of failure.

15.   Answer: C. No information

Explanation: Black box penetration testing simulates an external attack where the attacker has no prior knowledge of the target system. The red team, in this context, is given no specific details about the infrastructure they are testing. This approach is designed to mimic the perspective of a real-world attacker and identify vulnerabilities that may be exploited by someone with no inside knowledge.

16.   Answer: D. Mean time between failures (MTBF)

Explanation: MTBF (mean time between failures) is a measure used to estimate the time between inherent failures of a system during its operational phase. It provides an average time span between failures and is commonly used in reliability engineering to assess the reliability of a product or system. MTTR, on the other hand, refers to the average time taken to repair a failed component. MTD is the maximum time a service or system can be down without causing significant harm to the business. Statistical deviation is a general term and does not specifically relate to the functional lifetime of a system or device.

17. Answer: C. The process of transitioning files from high-cost, high-speed storage to more affordable, slower storage solutions

    Explanation: Hierarchical Storage Management (HSM) is a data storage technique that automatically moves data between high-cost and low-cost storage media. As data ages and is accessed less frequently, it is moved to slower, more cost-effective storage media. This ensures that critical and frequently accessed data remains on faster storage, while older, less accessed data is moved to cheaper storage.

18. Answer: B. Passive reconnaissance

    Explanation: Passive reconnaissance involves collecting information without directly interacting with the target system. A sniffer, which captures network traffic, is a tool that can be used during this phase to gather valuable information without alerting the target. Active reconnaissance, on the other hand, involves direct interaction with the target, which can raise alarms.

19.   Answer: B. Implementing separation of duties and rotating job responsibilities

Explanation: Collusion refers to the act of two or more individuals working together to commit fraud or other malicious activities. The best defense against collusion is the separation of duties, ensuring that no single individual has control over all aspects of any critical transaction. Job rotation further reduces the risk by regularly changing individuals' responsibilities, making it harder for them to collaborate maliciously over an extended period.

20.   Answer: D. To counteract privilege accumulation

Explanation: Privilege accumulation, often referred to as "authorization creep," occurs when individuals retain old privileges even after changing roles within an organization. Over time, this can lead to users having more access rights than necessary for their current position, increasing the risk of accidental or intentional data misuse. By revoking Nicole's previous privileges upon her transfer, the organization ensures she only has access to what's relevant to her new role, maintaining a principle of least privilege.

21.   Answer: C. The strategy of transitioning files from high-speed, high-cost storage to more economical, slower storage media

Explanation: Hierarchical Storage Management (HSM) is a data storage technique that moves data between high-cost and low-cost storage media based on its age and access frequency. As data becomes older and is accessed less frequently, it is transferred to slower, more economical storage solutions.

22. Answer: C. Sandbox

Explanation: A sandbox is a controlled environment where potentially malicious code can be executed safely, without posing a risk to the host system or network. It is isolated from the main system, ensuring that any malicious actions are contained within the sandbox and do not affect the broader environment.

23. Answer: B. Ensuring the employee is rejuvenated

Explanation: While ensuring an employee is well rested is a good general practice for employee well-being, it is not specifically a security or operational reason related to mandatory vacations. The other options relate directly to security and operational benefits.

24. Answer: D. Detective

Explanation: An audit trail is a record of activities, typically in the context of a computer system, which can be used to detect and investigate unauthorized or anomalous activities. It is a detective control because it helps in identifying issues after they have occurred.

25. Answer: B. Prolonged recovery time

Explanation: RAID is designed to provide
redundancy, improve performance, and increase
storage capacity. One of its primary benefits is fault
tolerance, which means that if one disk fails, data is
not lost. However, prolonged recovery time is not a
benefit; in fact, certain RAID configurations aim to
reduce recovery time.

26. Answer: A. Dual controls

Explanation: Separation of duties and dual
controls are both strategies to ensure that no single
individual has complete control over all aspects of
any critical financial transaction. By requiring two or
more individuals to complete a task or transaction,
the risk of fraud or error is reduced.

27. Answer: C. PBX systems

Explanation: Phreakers are individuals who
manipulate or hack telephone systems, primarily
targeting Private Branch Exchange (PBX) systems.
Their activities often involve making free long-
distance calls or gaining unauthorized access to
telecommunication systems.

28. Answer: B. Graylist

Explanation: Graylisting is an anti-spam technique
where the mail server temporarily rejects emails from
unknown senders and asks the sending server to
resend the message after a certain period. If the email
is legitimate, the sending server will attempt to resend
it, and it will be accepted on the subsequent attempt.

29. Answer: D. COOP (continuity of operations plan)

   Explanation: A continuity of operations plan (COOP) is designed to ensure that essential functions continue during and after a disaster. It focuses on restoring an organization's mission-essential functions at an alternate site and performing those functions for up to 30 days before returning to normal operations.

30. Answer: A. RAID 0

   Explanation: RAID 0 uses data striping, where data is split into blocks and each block is written to a separate disk drive. It improves performance but offers no redundancy. If one drive fails, all data in the RAID 0 array is lost.

31. Answer: A. Incremental

   Explanation: Incremental backups only save the changes made since the last backup, making them faster to perform. However, during a restore, you would need the last full backup and all subsequent incremental backups, making the restoration process longer compared to other backup methods.

32. Answer: B. Statistical based

   Explanation: A statistical-based intrusion detection system (IDS) monitors network traffic and compares it against an established baseline. The baseline will identify what is considered "normal" behavior. When the IDS detects activity that deviates significantly from the baseline, it will trigger an alert.

33. Answer: C. Zeroization

Explanation: Zeroization is the process of erasing sensitive data by overwriting it with zeros. This ensures that the original data is unrecoverable.

34. Answer: C. RAID 10

Explanation: RAID 10, also known as RAID 1+0, combines the features of RAID 1 (mirroring) and RAID 0 (striping). It stripes data across mirrored pairs. As a result, it offers both performance improvements (from striping) and redundancy (from mirroring).

35. Answer: D. JBOD (Just a Bunch of Disks)

Explanation: JBOD stands for "Just a Bunch of Disks" or "Just a Bunch of Drives." It is a method of combining multiple hard drives into one logical unit, but without any RAID features like redundancy or performance improvement. Each drive operates independently, and the total storage is the sum of all drives.

36. Answer: C. Distributed computing

Explanation: Distributed computing involves using multiple computers, often spread across vast distances, to work together on a single task. This approach can harness a massive amount of processing power by breaking down a problem into smaller parts and processing them concurrently across multiple machines. It's particularly useful for tasks that require extensive computational resources.

37. Answer: B. A sanctioned set of preparations and adequate procedures to react to disasters

Explanation: A business continuity/disaster recovery plan is a comprehensive approach that outlines how an organization will continue its operations and recover from unforeseen disasters. It's not just about preventing disasters but having a structured and approved response when they occur.

38. Answer: C. Due diligence

Explanation: Due diligence refers to the care that a reasonable person or organization exercises to avoid harm to others or their property. It's a general principle that applies across industries, ensuring that organizations act responsibly and with caution.

39. Answer: A. Continuity planning is a paramount organizational concern encompassing all organizational areas or functions.

Explanation: Business continuity planning should be holistic, addressing all parts of an organization. While technology recovery is essential, other functions like human resources, operations, and supply chain management are equally crucial.

40. Answer: A. Determine the effects of a threat on organizational operations

Explanation: Business impact analysis (BIA) is conducted to understand the potential effects of disruptions on an organization's operations. It helps in identifying critical functions and the impact if these functions were to be interrupted.

41.   Answer: D. Instituting procedural controls

Explanation: Implementing procedural controls is a proactive approach to manage threats and mitigate the effects of potential events. These controls provide structured guidelines and processes to ensure that risks are minimized and managed effectively.

42.   Answer: A. To discourage or eliminate the risk

Explanation: The main purpose of implementing controls or safeguards is to deter potential threats or to mitigate the associated risks, ensuring that the organization's assets and operations remain secure.

43.   Answer: D. A business impact analysis determines the consequences of disruptions on the organization.

Explanation: Business impact analysis (BIA) is primarily concerned with understanding the potential effects of disruptions on an organization's operations. It helps in identifying critical functions and the impact if these functions were to be interrupted.

44.   Answer: B. The technological environment

Explanation: Disaster recovery primarily focuses on the recovery of IT systems and data after a disaster. It's a subset of business continuity planning and emphasizes the restoration of IT infrastructure, systems, and data.

45. Answer: A. Business impact analysis

    Explanation: Business impact analysis (BIA) is
    the process of determining the potential effects
    of interruptions to an organization's operations.
    It helps organizations understand the potential
    consequences of various disruptions and prioritize
    recovery strategies.

46. Answer: A. It's a more cost-effective recovery option.

    Explanation: A cold site is a backup facility that is
    not immediately ready for use but can be equipped
    and made operational relatively quickly. Its primary
    advantage is that it's typically less expensive than
    other recovery options, such as hot sites, which are
    fully equipped and ready for immediate use.

47. Answer: B. Threats, assets, and controls to
    mitigate them

    Explanation: Risk is typically understood in terms of
    potential threats to assets and the controls in place
    to mitigate those threats. It's a combination of the
    likelihood of an event occurring and the potential
    impact if it does.

48. Answer: A. The maximum duration a service or
    system can be down

    Explanation: RTO, or recovery time objective, refers
    to the target time within which a business process
    or IT system must be restored after a disruption to
    avoid unacceptable consequences.

49. Answer: A. Full backup

Explanation: A full backup captures all the data in an entire system or subsystem. When restoring from a full backup, all the data can be retrieved in one operation, making it the most efficient restore method.

50. Answer: B. It's highly available.

Explanation: A hot site is a fully equipped data center that can take over operations almost immediately after a disaster. Its primary advantage is its high availability, ensuring minimal disruption to operations.

51. Answer: D. Interrupting a live production application or function

Explanation: Halting a live production application or function can have real-world consequences and is not a recommended method for testing a business continuity plan. The other options are controlled exercises designed to test various aspects of the plan without causing disruptions.

52. Answer: A. To pinpoint the strengths and weaknesses of the plan

Explanation: The primary goal of a business continuity exercise is to test the plan in a controlled environment, allowing the organization to identify areas where the plan excels and areas that need improvement.

53.   Answer: D. As part of the configuration and change management procedure

Explanation: Business continuity plans should be updated regularly to reflect changes in the organization's environment, operations, or risk profile. Integrating updates into the configuration and change management process ensures that the plan remains current and relevant.

54.   Answer: A. Support from senior leadership

Explanation: While all the options are important, the support and commitment of senior leadership are crucial for the success of business continuity. Their support ensures that the necessary resources are allocated, and it emphasizes the importance of continuity planning throughout the organization.

55.   Answer: A. Cold site

Explanation: A cold site is a backup facility that is not immediately ready for use but can be equipped and made operational within a certain time frame. Given a recovery time objective of two months, a cold site would be the most cost-effective and suitable option.

56. Answer: A. RAID 6 with a hot site alternative

    Explanation: A recovery point objective (RPO) of zero means no data loss is acceptable. RAID 6 provides fault tolerance and can handle two simultaneous drive failures. Paired with a hot site, which is a fully equipped data center ready for immediate use, this combination ensures both data integrity and rapid recovery. RAID 0, on the other hand, offers no redundancy and is not suitable for scenarios where data loss is unacceptable.

57. Answer: B. Detect, delay, and respond

    Explanation: The primary function of a physical protection system is to detect any unauthorized activities or intrusions, delay the intruder's progress, and respond to the situation, either by alerting security personnel or initiating other security measures.

58. Answer: A. Threat definition, target identification, and facility characterization

    Explanation: A comprehensive vulnerability assessment requires understanding the potential threats, identifying potential targets, and characterizing the facility's features and vulnerabilities.

59. Answer: C. Windows at street level, entrances, and other access points

    Explanation: Laminated glass is designed to remain intact even when shattered, making it ideal for areas vulnerable to break-ins or accidental damage, such as street-level windows and doorways.

60. Answer: B. Defense in depth

    Explanation: Defense in depth is a security strategy
    that employs multiple layers of defense to protect
    assets. This approach ensures that if one layer
    is breached, additional layers remain to provide
    protection.

61. Answer: C. Crime prevention through
    environmental design

    Explanation: Crime prevention through
    environmental design (CPTED) is a
    multidisciplinary approach to deterring criminal
    behavior through environmental design. It focuses
    on designing a physical environment that positively
    influences human behavior, making spaces less
    conducive to crime and more conducive to positive
    social interaction.

62. Answer: A. Integration of individuals, processes, and
    equipment

    Explanation: An effective physical protection system
    relies on the harmonious integration of people (who
    operate and respond to the system), procedures (the
    guidelines and protocols in place), and equipment
    (the physical and technological tools used).

63. Answer: B. Ensure only authorized individuals
    gain entry

    Explanation: The primary purpose of access control
    is to ensure that only those with the appropriate
    permissions or credentials can enter a specific area
    or facility, thereby maintaining security.

64. Answer: B. 5 fc

Explanation: Adequate lighting is essential for safety in perimeter areas. A level of 5 foot-candles (fc) is commonly recommended for such zones to ensure visibility and deter potential threats.

65. Answer: C. Acoustic/shock glass-break sensors

Explanation: Acoustic or shock glass-break sensors detect the specific frequencies or vibrations associated with breaking glass, making them ideal for buildings with accessible windows.

66. Answer: A. Monitoring, deterrence, and evidence collection

Explanation: CCTV systems primarily serve to monitor areas, act as a deterrent to potential intruders or malicious actors, and provide evidence in case of incidents.

67. Answer: B. Enhancement of the security framework, often leading to cost savings for the organization

Explanation: When security technologies are appropriately implemented, they can bolster the organization's security measures. This not only enhances protection but can also lead to operational efficiencies and cost savings in the long run.

68. Answer: B. In relation to the specified threats and the worth of the organization's assets

    Explanation: A meaningful assessment of a facility should be conducted to understand the potential threats against it and to evaluate the security measures in place relative to the value of the assets it houses.

69. Answer: A. Minimizing the number of entrances that need monitoring, staffing, and protection

    Explanation: When designing a facility with security as a priority, it's crucial to limit potential vulnerabilities. By reducing the number of entrances, the facility can more effectively monitor, staff, and secure those points of entry.

70. Answer: C. To record the duration of the visit, the person visited, and to account for everyone in emergencies

    Explanation: A visitor's log serves multiple purposes, but its primary function is to maintain a record of individuals entering and exiting the facility. This ensures that in case of emergencies, there's an accurate account of everyone present, enhancing safety and accountability.

71. Answer: A. Tamper protection

    Explanation: Tamper protection mechanisms are designed to prevent unauthorized access or interference with the physical components of an alarm system. If someone tries to tamper with the system, an alert is typically triggered, ensuring the system's integrity and reliability.

72. Answer: A. Cable locks, encryption, password safeguards, and heightened awareness

Explanation: Portable devices are vulnerable to theft or unauthorized access. Employing physical measures like cable locks, combined with digital security measures like encryption and password protection, and fostering a heightened awareness among users are the best practices to ensure their security.

73. Answer: A. Biometric devices

Explanation: Biometric devices authenticate individuals based on their unique physical or behavioral characteristics. These can include fingerprints, retina or iris patterns, voice recognition, and facial recognition, among others.

74. Answer: A. Layers

Explanation: The layered approach to physical security ensures that multiple levels of protection are in place. If one layer is breached, additional layers remain to provide protection, making it more challenging for unauthorized individuals to gain access or cause damage.

75. Answer: B. Security survey

Explanation: A security survey provides a comprehensive overview of a facility's security posture. It evaluates physical security controls, policies, procedures, and ensures the safety of employees, identifying potential vulnerabilities and areas for improvement.

76. Answer: B. Turnstiles

Explanation: Turnstiles are physical barriers that allow only one person to pass at a time, making it difficult for someone to "piggyback" or "tailgate" behind an authorized individual. They are especially effective in high-security areas or entrances where strict access control is required.

77. Answer: C. Internal actors or employees

Explanation: While all the listed entities pose threats, insiders often have direct access to an organization's systems and data, making them a significant risk. They might exploit their access for malicious purposes, either intentionally or inadvertently.

78. Answer: C. The global nature of computer crime activities

Explanation: Computer crime often transcends borders, making jurisdiction and international cooperation challenging. While all the options present challenges, the international nature of cybercrime complicates investigations, prosecution, and prevention.

79. Answer: A. Legal principles

Explanation: Computer forensics involves the collection, analysis, and preservation of digital evidence in a manner that is legally admissible in a court of law. Thus, it marries technical expertise with legal principles.

80. Answer: D. Locard's exchange principle

Explanation: Dr. Edmond Locard posited that every contact leaves a trace. This means that criminals will always leave some evidence behind at a crime scene and simultaneously take something with them.

81. Answer: B. Be exhaustive, be genuine, and be permissible in court.

Explanation: For evidence to be effective in a legal setting, it must be complete (covering all aspects of the matter), authentic (verifiable and genuine), and admissible (acceptable in a court of law).

82. Answer: B. Legal action

Explanation: While prosecution might be an outcome or follow-up to an incident response, it is not typically considered a phase of the incident response process itself. The primary stages often include preparation, identification, containment, eradication, recovery, and lessons learned/documentation.

83. Answer: B. Civil law

Explanation: Civil law, also known as code-based or codified law, is based on comprehensive statutes and codes that emphasize abstract legal principles. It is influenced by legal scholars and is distinct from common law systems.

84. Answer: C. Literary and artistic works protection (copyright)

    Explanation: Copyrights protect the expression of ideas, such as writings, music, and art. They do not protect the underlying ideas themselves.

85. Answer: A. Brand mark (trademark)

    Explanation: Trademarks protect symbols, names, and slogans used to identify goods or services. They safeguard the goodwill and brand recognition a company has built.

86. Answer: C. IOCE, SWGDE, and ACPO

    Explanation: IOCE (International Organization on Computer Evidence), SWGDE (Scientific Working Group on Digital Evidence), and ACPO (Association of Chief Police Officers) are all recognized entities that provide guidelines and best practices in the field of computer forensics.

87. Answer: A. No-cost software, open source, and paid software (freeware, open source, and commercial)

    Explanation: Freeware is software that is available at no cost. Open source software is software for which the original source code is made freely available and may be redistributed and modified. Commercial software is sold for profit.

88. Answer: A. Personal rights (privacy)

    Explanation: Privacy pertains to the rights and obligations of individuals and organizations concerning the collection, use, retention, and disclosure of personal information.

89.   Answer: C. Spotting, recognizing, alerting
       (detection, identification, notification)

       Explanation: Triage in incident response typically
       involves detecting the incident, identifying its
       nature, and notifying relevant stakeholders.

90.   Answer: A. By comparing digital signatures
       with the original (comparing hash totals to the
       original source)

       Explanation: Hash values (like MD5 or SHA-256) are
       used to verify the integrity of data. If the hash value
       of the original matches the hash value of the copy,
       it indicates that the copy is an exact replica of the
       original.

91.   Answer: D. Have minimal interference (must have
       the least amount of contamination that is possible)

       Explanation: While it's crucial to preserve the
       integrity of a digital crime scene, it's also understood
       that some interaction might be necessary for
       investigation. The goal is to minimize any changes
       or contamination.

92.   Answer: A. All legal and compliance responsibilities
       are transferred to the service provider.

       Explanation: While the service provider has its own
       set of responsibilities, the primary organization
       remains ultimately responsible for ensuring
       compliance. It's essential to ensure that any
       outsourced services meet the required compliance
       standards.

93. Answer: C. It uses the order in which the principles are listed (the order of the canons).

    Explanation: The ISC2 Code of Ethics uses the order of its canons (principles) to prioritize and resolve conflicts.

94. Answer: D. Approach every incident as if it might lead to legal action (treat every incident as though it may be a crime)

    Explanation: By treating every incident as a potential crime, organizations ensure that evidence is preserved and handled correctly from the outset.

95. Answer: D. Contact a professional data recovery service, explain the situation, and ask them to create a forensic image.

    Explanation: Professional data recovery services have the expertise and equipment to handle such situations. They can ensure that the data is retrieved without further damaging the drive or compromising the integrity of the evidence.

96. Answer: A. Infrastructure as a Service (IaaS)

    Explanation: Infrastructure as a Service (IaaS) provides an organization with the most control over its cloud resources, including virtual machines, storage, and networking. However, this level of control comes with the responsibility of managing and maintaining the operating systems and applications. Unlike PaaS and SaaS, where the cloud provider takes on more of the management burden, IaaS requires the organization to handle all aspects of maintenance and administration.

97. Answer: B. On a dedicated logging server

Explanation: Storing log files on a dedicated logging server is generally the most secure method as it isolates the logs from potential compromise of the application or system being monitored.

98. Answer: B. Anomaly-based IDS

Explanation: Anomaly-based IDS systems are effective in detecting zero-day attacks because they identify deviations from established baselines, rather than relying on known signatures.

CHAPTER 10

Software Development Security

Software development security is integral to the CISSP certification exam. This domain, also called Domain 8, focuses on security's role in the Software Development Life Cycle phases, from the initial conception of a software project to its deployment and ongoing maintenance.

The security risks associated with software applications are numerous and continuously evolving. Therefore, it is essential to integrate security principles and practices into the software development process. This involves applying security controls and countermeasures during software design and development, employing secure coding practices, and performing thorough security testing before deployment.

This chapter will delve into the core concepts of Domain 8: Software Development Security. We will explore various development methodologies, examine the role of maturity models, and understand the importance of operation and maintenance in ensuring secure software. Furthermore, we will discuss change management and the significance of Integrated Product Teams (IPTs) in software development projects.

Through this chapter, you will thoroughly understand the information security concepts and best practices outlined in the CISSP CBK for this domain and equip yourself with practical insights and expert strategies to ace this section in the CISSP exam.

Let's dive into the fascinating world of software development security.

© Mohamed Aly Bouke 2023
M. A. Bouke, *CISSP Exam Certification Companion*, Certification Study Companion Series,
https://doi.org/10.1007/979-8-8688-0057-3_10

Understanding and Integrating Security in the SDLC

Integrating security throughout the Software Development Life Cycle (SDLC) is crucial for developing secure and reliable software systems. This approach ensures that security concerns are considered from the earliest design and development stages to ongoing maintenance and operations. The SDLC is a framework that outlines the phases and activities involved in developing and maintaining software systems. Integrating security into the SDLC involves incorporating security considerations, practices, and controls into each process phase.

- **Requirements analysis**: During the requirements analysis phase, security requirements should be identified and documented alongside functional and nonfunctional requirements. This involves understanding the system's purpose, its users, and the potential threats and risks it may face. A thorough analysis of the system's context and regulatory environment is crucial to consider all relevant security requirements. For example, a software system that handles sensitive customer data may have a security requirement to comply with data protection regulations, such as the General Data Protection Regulation (GDPR). This would necessitate implementing data protection measures throughout the SDLC, such as encryption and access controls.

- **Design**: In the design phase, security should be a core consideration in developing the system's architecture and selecting appropriate technologies. Secure design principles, such as least privilege, defense in depth, and separation of duties, should be incorporated to minimize the attack surface and reduce the risk of security vulnerabilities. To illustrate, a web application might implement defense in depth by using multiple layers of security controls, including network firewalls, web application firewalls, and secure coding practices. This ensures that even if one layer of security is compromised, other layers can still provide protection.

- **Implementation:** During the implementation phase, secure coding practices should be followed to minimize the introduction of security vulnerabilities. Developers should be familiar with common security risks, such as those outlined in the OWASP Top Ten, and implement appropriate countermeasures. For instance, developers should use prepared statements or parameterized queries to mitigate the risk of SQL injection attacks when interacting with databases rather than constructing SQL queries using string concatenation. Additionally, conducting regular code reviews focusing on security can help identify potential issues early in development. Automated tools like static and dynamic code analysis can also detect security vulnerabilities.

- **Testing:** Security testing should be an integral part of the testing phase. This can include various types of testing, such as vulnerability assessments, penetration testing, and fuzz testing. Security testing should aim to validate that the implemented security controls are adequate and that no known vulnerabilities are present in the system. For example, penetration testing involves simulating attacks on the system to identify vulnerabilities and assess its ability to withstand real-world threats. This can provide valuable insights into the system's security posture and help identify areas for improvement.

- **Operations and maintenance**: Ensuring the security of software systems involves ongoing operations and maintenance activities, such as monitoring and analyzing system logs for signs of security incidents, applying security patches and updates on time, and conducting periodic security assessments and penetration tests.

Implementing incident response and disaster recovery plans can help organizations respond effectively to security incidents and minimize the impact on the system's availability and integrity.

Development Methodologies

In the demanding field of software development, understanding how to integrate security within various development methodologies is essential for creating robust applications and a critical area of focus for several IT certification exams. This chapter is designed to serve as a comprehensive study guide for students, professionals, and exam takers who aspire to master the integration of security measures within the Software Development Life Cycle (SDLC).

The methodologies explored in this chapter are frequently featured in exams and are vital for anyone seeking to excel in software security. Each section is crafted to provide detailed insights into different development methodologies, emphasizing how they can be leveraged to embed security within the SDLC:

- **Agile:** Agile is an iterative and incremental approach to software development that prioritizes flexibility and collaboration. Security can be integrated into Agile by incorporating security-related user stories and ensuring security is considered during sprint planning, reviews, and retrospectives. Security tasks can be included in the product backlog, and security-related acceptance criteria should be established for each user story. For example, a user story might involve the implementation of secure user authentication for a web application. The acceptance criteria could include using strong password hashing algorithms, implementing multifactor authentication, and enforcing password complexity rules.

- **Waterfall:** The Waterfall model is a linear and sequential approach to software development in which each phase is completed before moving on to the next. Security activities can be included in each phase of the Waterfall model, such as conducting threat modeling during the design phase and performing security testing during the testing phase. This methodical approach allows for a thorough consideration of security concerns throughout the development process.

- **DevOps:** DevOps is an approach that emphasizes collaboration between development and operations teams to streamline software delivery. Integrating security into DevOps can involve incorporating security tools and practices into the continuous integration and continuous delivery (CI/CD) pipeline. This can include using automated security testing tools, vulnerability scanners, and configuration management tools to identify and remediate security issues during development.

- **DevSecOps**: DevSecOps is an extension of DevOps that explicitly integrates security practices and considerations throughout the development and operations processes. DevSecOps involves automating security testing, vulnerability scanning, and risk assessments in the CI/CD pipeline and fostering a culture of security awareness among team members. This approach promotes a "shift-left" mentality, where security concerns are addressed early in the development process, reducing the likelihood of security issues in the final product.

Maturity Models

Maturity models in software development are more than mere theoretical constructs; they are practical tools that guide organizations in assessing and enhancing their development processes, including vital security practices. This chapter offers a unique perspective on these models, focusing on their practical application and relevance to IT certification exams. Some common maturity models include

- **Capability Maturity Model (CMM)**: The Capability Maturity Model (CMM) is a well-known framework that assesses the maturity of an organization's software development processes. It consists of five levels, each representing a different stage of process maturity (Table 10-1).

Table 10-1. *Capability Maturity Model Levels*

Level	Description	Security Example
1	Processes are unpredictable, poorly controlled, and reactive	An organization without formal security policies, reacting to security incidents as they occur
2	Processes are characterized for projects and are often repeatable	An organization that has established basic security guidelines, such as regular password updates
3	Processes are defined and documented across the organization	An organization that has standardized security protocols, such as a uniform encryption method
4	Processes are measured and controlled	An organization that uses metrics to evaluate security measures, such as tracking detected vulnerabilities
5	Focus on continuous process improvement	An organization that continually assesses and improves security practices, learning from previous incidents

Table 10-1 illustrates the progression from ad hoc and reactive processes at Level 1 to optimized and proactive processes at Level 5. The security examples provided in the table highlight how security practices evolve and mature alongside the development processes. For instance, Level 1 represents an organization without formal security policies, while Level 5 depicts an organization that continually assesses and improves its security practices.

- **Software Assurance Maturity Model (SAMM):**
  The Software Assurance Maturity Model (SAMM) is specifically designed to assess and improve an

organization's software security practices. It focuses
on four key aspects of the Software Development Life
Cycle (SDLC): governance, construction, verification,
and deployment (Table 10-2).

Table 10-2. *Software Assurance Maturity Model Aspects*

Aspect	Description	Example
Governance	Establishing and maintaining security governance	Implementing a security policy defining roles, responsibilities, and procedures for managing security
Construction	Building secure software by integrating security practices	Incorporating secure coding guidelines and conducting regular code reviews
Verification	Ensuring that the software meets security requirements	Conducting penetration testing to verify that the application can withstand malicious attacks
Deployment	Managing the security of software once it's deployed	Implementing a patch management process to ensure that security updates are applied promptly

Table 10-2 provides a comprehensive overview of the SAMM's focus on
software security. Each aspect represents a critical phase in the SDLC, with
corresponding examples illustrating practical applications. For example, the
construction aspect emphasizes building secure software through practices
like secure coding guidelines. In contrast, deployment focuses on managing
security once the software is deployed, such as through patch management.

In conclusion, the CMM and the SAMM present structured
methodologies for evaluating and enhancing software development
processes, emphasizing security. The tables elucidate these models,
accentuating their essential characteristics and real-world applications.

Through comprehension and implementation of these models, organizations stand to elevate their software development and security practices, achieving alignment with industry standards and best practices.

Operation and Maintenance

The continuous security of software systems is a multifaceted challenge that requires ongoing attention to operations and maintenance activities. This section delves into the key components and provides detailed examples to illustrate the concepts:

- **Monitoring**: Monitoring is a foundational aspect of maintaining the security of software systems. It involves continuous observation of system logs, network traffic, and user activity. For example, system administrators may set up alerts for multiple failed login attempts within a short time frame, which could indicate a brute-force attack attempt. Monitoring tools can also detect unusual patterns in network traffic, such as a sudden spike in data being sent to an unknown IP address, possibly signaling data exfiltration. Regular review of user activity logs can uncover unauthorized access or suspicious behavior within the system. In essence, monitoring serves as an early warning system, enabling timely response to potential security incidents.

- **Patch management**: Patch management is the process of identifying, acquiring, installing, and verifying patches for products and systems. For instance, when a new vulnerability is discovered in an operating system, the vendor may release a security patch to fix the issue.

Organizations must promptly apply these patches to prevent potential exploitation by attackers. A well-defined patch management process includes regular vulnerability assessments to identify needed patches, risk prioritization to determine the urgency of patching, and timely deployment to ensure that the systems are protected. Failure to promptly apply critical patches can leave systems exposed to known risks, as with the WannaCry ransomware attack, which exploited unpatched Windows systems.

- **Periodic assessments**: Regular security assessments such as penetration testing and vulnerability scanning are vital for maintaining system security. Penetration testing involves ethical hackers attempting to breach the system's defenses, simulating real-world attack scenarios. For example, a penetration test might uncover weak password policies allowing easy access to sensitive data. Vulnerability scanning is an automated process that scans the system for known vulnerabilities, such as outdated software, that could be exploited. These assessments should be conducted regularly, especially after significant system or environmental changes, to ensure new vulnerabilities are discovered and addressed.

- **Incident response plans**: An incident response plan outlines the process to follow when a security incident occurs. It defines the roles and responsibilities of team members, establishes communication protocols, and details the steps for containing, eradicating, and recovering from incidents. For example, if a phishing email leads to a malware infection, the incident response plan would guide the team in isolating the affected system, removing the malware, investigating the breach, and restoring the system to normal operation. A well-crafted incident response plan ensures that the organization can respond effectively and efficiently to security incidents, minimizing potential damage.

- **Disaster recovery plans**: Disaster recovery planning focuses on restoring critical systems and data in the event of a major disruption or failure. This involves identifying essential assets, establishing recovery time objectives (RTOs) and recovery point objectives (RPOs), and implementing backup and recovery strategies. For example, if a natural disaster destroys a data center, the disaster recovery plan would guide restoring critical systems from backups at a secondary location, ensuring business continuity.

- **Change management controls**: Change management controls changes to an organization's software systems to minimize the risk of introducing security vulnerabilities or disrupting the system's functionality. This includes

  - **Change request process**: All proposed changes must be evaluated for potential security risks and impacts. For example, a proposed update to a web application's login mechanism would be documented, and its security implications assessed, such as potential weaknesses in authentication.

- **Change review and testing:** Changes must be thoroughly reviewed and tested. A proposed modification to a firewall rule would undergo security testing to ensure that it does not inadvertently expose internal services to the public Internet.

- **Change rollback and recovery:** If a change introduces unforeseen risks or disrupts functionality, a plan must be in place to revert the change. For instance, if a database update leads to performance issues, the organization would roll back to the previous version, using version control systems or backups.

The continuous security of software systems requires a multifaceted approach, encompassing monitoring, patch management, assessments, planning, and change control. This section thoroughly explores each aspect, offering practical insights and real-world examples. Understanding these concepts is essential for developing secure software systems and preparing for related exam questions.

Essential Tools and Technologies for Secure Software Development

Developing secure software requires a deep understanding of software development tools, technologies, and practices. This section will provide a comprehensive overview of programming languages, libraries, toolsets, and other critical technologies in secure software development. We will also discuss the importance of security orchestration, automation, and response (SOAR), software configuration management (SCM), and various application security testing techniques.

Programming languages are the foundation of software development, and selecting the right language for a project can significantly impact its security. Some popular programming languages for secure software development include

- **C/C++**: C and C++ are widely used for system-level programming and offer high-performance and fine-grained control over system resources. However, they also require careful memory management and can be susceptible to common security issues such as buffer overflows and memory leaks.

- **Java**: Java is a popular, platform-independent language that offers built-in security features such as automatic memory management and type safety. Java's security model, including the Java sandbox and bytecode verification, helps minimize the risk of security vulnerabilities.

- **Python**: Python is a versatile, high-level programming language emphasizing readability and simplicity. It includes an extensive standard library and offers several security-focused libraries, such as cryptography and PyOpenSSL, to facilitate secure software development.

- **Libraries**: Libraries are collections of reusable code and resources that can help developers implement secure functionality more efficiently. Some notable security-focused libraries include

- **OpenSSL**: OpenSSL is a widely used open source library that provides cryptographic functions, SSL/TLS protocols, and a general-purpose cryptographic library for various programming languages.

- **Libsodium**: Libsodium is a modern, easy-to-use software library for encryption, decryption, signatures, password hashing, and more, designed to improve the security of applications.

Moreover, toolsets are collections of software tools designed to support specific tasks and processes in software development. Some common toolsets for secure software development include

- **Static analysis tools**: Static analysis tools analyze source code without executing it, helping developers identify potential security vulnerabilities, such as SQL injection or cross-site scripting, early in the development process.

- **Dynamic analysis tools**: Dynamic analysis tools analyze running applications to detect security vulnerabilities, such as memory leaks or race conditions, which may not be apparent during static analysis.

Additionally, an Integrated Development Environment (IDE) is a software application that provides a comprehensive set of tools for software development, including code editing, debugging, and testing. Many modern IDEs offer security features like vulnerability scanning, code review, and secure coding recommendations. Some popular IDEs for fast software development include

- **Visual Studio**: Visual Studio is a powerful IDE from Microsoft that supports multiple programming languages and platforms. It offers various security features, including static code analysis, runtime analysis, and integration with various security testing tools.

- **IntelliJ IDEA**: IntelliJ IDEA is a versatile IDE from JetBrains that supports Java, Kotlin, and other JVM languages. It provides several built-in security features, such as code inspections and integration with static and dynamic analysis tools.

- **Runtime**: Runtime refers to the environment in which a software application executes. Ensuring a secure runtime environment involves proper configuration, isolation, and monitoring of application components.

Some common runtime security best practices include

- **Process isolation**: Process isolation involves running application components in separate processes to prevent one component from affecting the security or stability of another.

- **Least privilege**: Adhering to the principle of least privilege in the runtime environment ensures that application components only have the minimal permissions necessary to perform their functions, reducing the potential impact of a security breach.

- **Runtime analysis**: Runtime analysis involves monitoring the behavior of a running application to detect and respond to potential security threats. This can include analyzing system logs, network traffic, and application performance data.

- **Continuous integration and continuous delivery (CI/CD)**: Continuous integration (CI) and continuous delivery (CD) are practices in software development where code changes are frequently integrated, tested, and delivered to production. CI/CD pipelines can enhance security by automating code testing, vulnerability scanning, and deployment processes.

- **CI/CD tools:** Tools like Jenkins, Travis CI, and CircleCI facilitate CI/CD by automating the build, test, and deployment processes. They can integrate with other tools for static code analysis, dynamic security testing, and dependency checking, helping to ensure that security checks are a routine part of the development process.

- **Security orchestration, automation, and response (SOAR):** SOAR is a term that describes the convergence of three distinct technology markets: security orchestration and automation, security incident response platforms, and threat intelligence platforms. SOAR tools allow organizations to collect data about security threats from various sources and respond to low-level security events without human assistance.

- **SOAR tools:** Tools like Splunk Phantom, IBM Resilient, and Rapid7 InsightConnect allow teams to automate their threat detection and response procedures, reducing the time it takes to respond to an incident and making the process more efficient.

- **Software configuration management (SCM):** Software configuration management is a process of tracking and controlling changes in the software. SCM practices include revision control, establishment of baselines, and change management. It is crucial for maintaining system stability and traceability and ensuring that all changes to system assets are identifiable, controlled, and auditable.

- **SCM tools**: Tools like Git, Subversion, and Mercurial support SCM by managing changes to a software project, allowing teams to track changes, maintain historical versions, and manage parallel development efforts.

- **Code repositories**: Code repositories are where the codebase is stored and often come with version control systems. They allow developers to work concurrently, maintain previous code versions, and help in rapid recovery in case of a crash. Services like GitHub, GitLab, and Bitbucket are popular choices for hosting code repositories.

Application Security Testing

Application security testing is a vital and multifaceted aspect of secure software development. This section delves into the two primary methods for performing security testing, offering a detailed exploration of their intricacies, applications, and importance:

- **Static Application Security Testing (SAST)**: SAST, or "white box" testing, is a method that involves analyzing an application's source code, bytecode, or binary code to identify security vulnerabilities without executing the application. It provides an in-depth examination of the code's structure, logic, and potential weak points.

Key Focus Areas, Benefits, and Usage

Focus Area	Description	Example	Benefits and Usage
Input Validation Errors	Detects failures in sanitizing user input, leading to vulnerabilities like SQL injection or XSS	Direct user input in a SQL query without validation leads to potential SQL injection	Integrated early in the development life cycle, SAST identifies vulnerabilities at the coding stage, allowing for early remediation
Buffer Overflows	Identifies instances where data might be written outside allocated memory, leading to attacks	Writing data beyond the buffer's boundary, potentially allowing arbitrary code execution by an attacker	SAST's ability to analyze code in detail helps uncover complex vulnerabilities like buffer overflows
Insecure Server Configurations	Uncovers weak or misconfigured security settings within the server	Using outdated encryption algorithms or insecure authentication mechanisms exposes the system to breaches	SAST provides a comprehensive view of server configurations, ensuring alignment with security best practices

- **Dynamic Application Security Testing (DAST):** DAST, or "black box" testing, takes a contrasting approach by analyzing the application's running state. Unlike SAST, DAST does not have access to the underlying code and simulates how an external attacker might perceive and exploit vulnerabilities, providing a real-world perspective on the application's security posture.

Key Focus Areas, Benefits, and Usage

Focus Area	Description	Example	Benefits and Usage
Runtime Errors	Detects errors that occur during actual operation, such as insecure data handling	The transmission of sensitive data like passwords in plaintext exposes them to potential interception	DAST offers a real-world perspective, identifying vulnerabilities that might be missed by static analysis, such as runtime errors
Server Configuration Issues	Uncovers misconfigurations in server security settings that are not apparent in static code analysis	Exposed administrative interfaces or improperly configured firewalls leave the system vulnerable to unauthorized access	DAST provides continuous security assessment in live environments, often employed later in the development process or post-deployment

The synergy between SAST and DAST forms the cornerstone of a robust application security testing strategy. SAST's deep code analysis combined with DAST's real-world attack simulation offers a comprehensive security assessment. Understanding these methods and effectively leveraging the right tools and technologies is paramount for developing secure software. By weaving secure practices throughout the development process, organizations lay the foundation for software that is functionally robust and secure by design.

663

Ensuring Security Through Assessment and Risk Management

Ensuring the security of software is a critical aspect of information security management. It requires assessing the effectiveness of software security measures, maintaining detailed audit logs, conducting risk analysis and mitigation, and understanding the security impact of acquired software. This section will dive into these areas, elucidating how they play an integral role in the overall cybersecurity framework of an organization.

- **Assessing the effectiveness of software security**: Effective software security extends beyond implementing security controls; it requires ongoing evaluation to ensure that the controls are working as expected and adapting to evolving threats.

- **Security testing**: Security testing involves a series of techniques and methodologies to identify vulnerabilities in a software system. This includes static and dynamic analysis, penetration testing, and vulnerability scanning. The results of these tests help in understanding the effectiveness of the implemented security measures.

- **Security metrics**: Security metrics can provide quantifiable data to assess the effectiveness of security controls. These could include metrics on the number of security incidents detected, the time taken to respond to security incidents, and the number of vulnerabilities identified and remediated.

- **Auditing and logging of changes**: An essential aspect of software security is the ability to track and audit changes to the software and its associated systems. This includes maintaining detailed logs of system activities, user actions, and changes to system configurations.

- **Audit trails**: Audit trails provide a chronological record of system activities for detecting and understanding the scope of any potential security incidents. They help identify unauthorized activities or changes that could negatively impact the system's security.

- **Log management**: Log management involves collecting, storing, and analyzing data from various sources. Effective log management can help detect security incidents in real time, facilitate forensic investigations, and comply with regulatory requirements.

- **Risk analysis and mitigation**: Risk analysis involves identifying potential threats, assessing the vulnerabilities that could be exploited, and evaluating the potential impact of such exploits. Based on this analysis, risk mitigation strategies can be developed to reduce, eliminate, or accept the risk.

- **Risk assessment**: Risk assessments involve identifying and evaluating risks to the organization's information assets. It helps prioritize risks based on their potential impact and the likelihood of occurrence.

- **Risk mitigation strategies**: Once risks are identified and assessed, appropriate risk mitigation strategies must be developed. These could include implementing additional security controls, adopting alternative processes, transferring the risk through insurance, or accepting the risk if it's within acceptable thresholds.

- **Assess the security impact of acquired software**:
  When incorporating third-party software, including
  commercial off-the-shelf (COTS), open source, third-
  party managed services, or Software as a Service (SaaS),
  Infrastructure as a Service (IaaS), or Platform as a Service
  (PaaS), it's critical to assess their security impact.

COTS and Open Source Software

In today's diverse technological environment, organizations leverage
various software solutions and services to achieve their goals. This section
explores five key concepts: commercial off-the-shelf (COTS) software,
open source software, Software as a Service (SaaS), Infrastructure as
a Service (IaaS), and Platform as a Service (PaaS). Each offers unique
benefits and poses specific security considerations. Understanding
these aspects is vital for informed decision-making and robust security
management, reflecting the ongoing and integrated nature of software
security in the development and operational life cycle:

- **Commercial off-the-shelf (COTS)**: COTS refers
  to ready-made software products commercially
  available for purchase and use without customization.
  The benefits of COTS include cost-effectiveness,
  standardization of features, and vendor support.
  However, security considerations must be taken into
  account. Ensuring the software doesn't contain known
  vulnerabilities or insecure configurations, aligning
  with organizational security policies, and assessing
  the vendor's reputation and commitment to security
  are vital. An example might be using a COTS antivirus
  solution that provides regular updates and aligns with
  the organization's security requirements.

- **Open source software**: Open source software is software for which the source code is freely available and may be redistributed and modified. The flexibility to customize, community support, and source code transparency are key benefits. Security considerations include conducting a thorough code review for potential security flaws, understanding the community's engagement in maintaining and updating the software, and ensuring compliance with the software's licensing terms to avoid legal issues. An example is using an open source database system that is actively maintained by the community and aligns with the organization's security protocols.

- **Software as a Service (SaaS)**: SaaS involves a provider hosting the software and user data, with users accessing the software over the Internet. Understanding the provider's security measures, data protection protocols, and incident response strategies is essential. Clarity on data ownership, privacy regulations, compliance, and robust access controls are also crucial. An example is using a cloud-based CRM system where the provider manages application-level security, and the organization ensures proper access controls.

- **Infrastructure as a Service (IaaS)**: IaaS involves the provider hosting infrastructure components, including servers, storage, and networking hardware. The division of security responsibilities between the provider and the user must be clear. Key considerations include the provider's commitment to securing the underlying infrastructure and the user's responsibility for security at the operating system, middleware, and application levels. An example is utilizing virtual servers in the cloud, where the provider secures the infrastructure, and the organization secures the operating system and applications.

- **Platform as a Service (PaaS)**: PaaS involves the provider hosting the infrastructure and platform software, such as the operating system and databases. Ensuring the provider's security measures for infrastructure and platform software, implementing security for the applications developed and deployed on the platform, and aligning with regulatory compliance and industry standards are vital. An example is using a cloud-based development environment where the provider secures the underlying platform, and the organization ensures the security of the developed applications.

Maintaining software security is a continuous and multifaceted process. It requires a proactive approach, encompassing evaluation, tracking, risk analysis, and understanding the security impact of third-party software. Regularly reviewing and updating these practices are essential to avoid potential threats and ensure robust security. As we move forward, remember that security is not a one-time activity but an ongoing process that must be integrated into every stage of the software development and operational life cycle.

Establishing Secure Coding Guidelines and Standards

In the evolving cybersecurity landscape, secure coding practices are more important than ever. This section focuses on defining and applying secure coding guidelines and standards, including understanding security weaknesses and vulnerabilities at the source-code level, ensuring the security of Application Programming Interfaces (APIs), and understanding the role of software-defined security.

- **Defining and applying secure coding guidelines and standards**: Secure coding guidelines provide developers with a set of practices to follow when writing code, helping to prevent common security vulnerabilities. They are often based on industry standards such as the OWASP Secure Coding Practices or the CERT Secure Coding Standards.

- **Coding standards**: Coding standards are formalized rules and practices adopted to improve the quality of the source code. They can range from coding style and best practices to more advanced topics like error handling and security.

- **Secure coding guidelines**: Secure coding guidelines are a subset of coding standards focusing on security. They address how to write functional, efficient, and secure code against known vulnerabilities.

- **Security weaknesses and vulnerabilities at the source-code level**: Understanding security weaknesses and vulnerabilities at the source-code level is crucial to secure coding. These could include buffer overflows, injection flaws, insecure direct object references, and cross-site scripting.

669

- **Code review and static analysis**: Code review and static analysis tools can be employed to identify these vulnerabilities. Code reviews involve systematically examining the source code for potential flaws, while static analysis tools automatically analyze code to detect vulnerabilities.

- **Security of Application Programming Interfaces (APIs)**: APIs, which allow different software components to communicate with each other, can introduce security vulnerabilities if not properly secured. This includes improper key management, insufficient data protection, and a lack of robust authentication and authorization mechanisms.

- **API security practices**: To secure APIs, it is necessary to employ practices such as encrypting sensitive data, implementing strong access controls, and regularly auditing and testing the APIs for security vulnerabilities.

- **Secure coding practices**: Secure coding practices follow guidelines designed to avoid common security pitfalls in software development.

- **Input validation**: Input validation is a critical secure coding practice that involves checking any data that the software receives to ensure it is correct and safe.

- **Error handling**: Proper error handling can prevent an application from revealing sensitive information when something goes wrong.

- **Secure dependencies**: Using secure dependencies ensures that any third-party code used in the application does not introduce vulnerabilities.

- **Software-defined security**: Software-defined security is a type of security model in which software implements and manages security controls. It's a vital aspect of modern security practices, particularly in cloud environments, as it allows for flexibility and scalability in managing security controls. Implementing software-defined security involves setting up security controls such as firewalls, intrusion detection systems, and data loss prevention systems in a software-based format, often within virtual environments.

The landscape of secure coding is intricate and multifaceted, encompassing guidelines, standards, practices, and modern methodologies like software-defined security. As we navigate the complexities of cybersecurity, the emphasis on secure coding practices becomes paramount. From understanding vulnerabilities at the source-code level to ensuring the security of APIs and employing software-defined security models, the principles outlined in this section form the bedrock of resilient and trustworthy software development. Embracing these practices is a technical necessity and a strategic imperative in building a secure and sustainable digital ecosystem.

Summary

In this chapter, we have embarked on a comprehensive exploration of secure operations within software development. We've dissected the principles of defining and applying secure coding guidelines and standards, emphasizing the importance of maintaining the source code's integrity and security. The chapter highlighted identifying and mitigating security weaknesses and vulnerabilities at the source-code level, a critical aspect of robust software development.

We further delved into the vital role of Application Programming Interfaces (APIs), elucidating how their security is integral to the overall protection of software applications. The chapter also provided insights into essential secure coding practices, including input validation, error handling, and the utilization of secure dependencies. Concluding the discussion, we explored the innovative concept of software-defined security, highlighting how its strategic implementation can infuse flexibility and scalability into security controls.

Key Takeaways

- **Secure coding guidelines and standards** are foundational to crafting secure, high-quality software. They foster a consistent and disciplined approach to coding across the development team by preventing common security vulnerabilities.

- **Security vulnerabilities at the source-code level**: Understanding and addressing these vulnerabilities is vital. Regular code reviews and static analysis can facilitate early detection and rectification, enhancing overall security.

- **API security**: APIs act as critical conduits in software applications. Their security, ensured through practices like encryption, robust access controls, and continuous auditing, is pivotal in preventing potential breaches.

- **Secure coding practices**: Practices such as input validation, error handling, and selecting secure dependencies are cornerstones in developing secure software.

- **Software-defined security**: This modern approach offers adaptability and scalability in managing security controls, especially in virtual and cloud environments. It allows for dynamic alignment with the ever-changing threat landscape and business needs.

In conclusion, secure coding transcends a mere technical process; it embodies an ongoing commitment and a strategic alignment with the broader cybersecurity landscape. It demands continuous vigilance, adaptation, and enhancement to stay abreast of the evolving challenges and opportunities in software security.

Practice Questions

As you conclude this chapter's comprehensive exploration of software development security, you are poised at a significant milestone in your CISSP exam preparation. This section introduces a series of practice questions to solidify your understanding of the complex principles, methodologies, and practical applications that define this critical cybersecurity domain.

These questions extend beyond mere memory assessment; they are a vital continuation of your learning journey. Echoing the intricacy and subtlety you will face in the actual exam, they encapsulate the deep insights and hands-on expertise essential for success. Engaging with each question, delving into the explanations, and reflecting on the answers will highlight your strengths and identify areas needing further enhancement.

Approach these questions with determination, curiosity, and readiness for intellectual challenge. Embrace the insights from correct and incorrect answers, and immerse yourself in critical thinking and analysis. Remember, these practice questions are not just a measure of your knowledge but a tool to deepen your comprehension and fine-tune your readiness for the CISSP exam.

Take the time you need, ponder each question thoughtfully, and let these practice questions guide your success in the CISSP exam and your continued growth as a software development security professional. Your journey through this chapter has equipped you with the essential knowledge and skills for the exam and laid a robust foundation for your career in the dynamic world of software development security.

1. Which phase of the Software Development Life Cycle (SDLC) emphasizes the importance of risk analysis and threat modeling?

   A. Deployment

   B. Maintenance

   C. Early phases

   D. Decommissioning

2. Which development methodology does not allow revisiting a previous phase?

   A. Agile

   B. Spiral Method

   C. Waterfall

   D. Cleanroom

3. What does DevOps ideally incorporate to make security an integral part of the development process?

   A. DevSecOps

   B. DevTestOps

   C. DevNetOps

   D. DevSysOps

4. Which maturity model is described as "the prime maturity model for software assurance" by OWASP?

   A. Capability Maturity Model (CMM)

   B. Software Assurance Maturity Model (SAMM)

   C. Development Maturity Model (DMM)

   D. Application Maturity Model (AMM)

5. Which type of testing focuses on quick preliminary testing after a change to identify any simple failures of the most important existing functionality?

   A. Regression testing

   B. Canary testing

   C. Smoke testing

   D. Black box testing

6. Which of the following refers to a storage location for software and application source code?

   A. Integrated Development Environment (IDE)

   B. Code repository

   C. Software Development Kit (SDK)

   D. Application Programming Interface (API)

7. What does the term "polyinstantiation" refer to in the context of software development?

   A. Code that can vary based on requirements

   B. Instantiating into multiple separate or independent instances

  C. Code that can be placed inside another

  D. Code that can inherit characteristics of previously created objects

8. Which of the following is a common software vulnerability arising from the use of insecure coding practices?

  A. Buffer overflow

  B. Code encapsulation

  C. Code inheritance

  D. Code polymorphism

9. Which of the following APIs is XML based?

  A. Representational State Transfer (REST)

  B. Simple Object Access Protocol (SOAP)

  C. Code Repository API

  D. Integrated Development Environment (IDE) API

10. In the context of software development, what does the term "encapsulation" refer to?

  A. The ability of an object to inherit characteristics of other objects

  B. Code that can vary based on requirements

  C. The idea that an object can be placed inside another, protecting it by wrapping it in other objects

  D. Hiding or obscuring code to protect it from unauthorized viewing

11. Which of the following best describes "code obfuscation"?

    A. The process of making code more efficient

    B. The practice of writing code in multiple programming languages

    C. Intentionally creating source code that is difficult for humans to understand

    D. The process of documenting code for better readability

12. Which software development approach is risk-driven and follows an iterative model while also including waterfall elements?

    A. Agile

    B. Spiral Method

    C. Waterfall

    D. Cleanroom

13. What is the primary purpose of "software configuration management (SCM)" in the software development process?

    A. To accelerate the development process

    B. To manage changes in software

    C. To integrate security into the development process

    D. To facilitate communication between development teams

14. Which of the following is NOT a characteristic of a Relational Database Management System (RDBMS)?

    A. Allows objects and data to be stored and linked together.

    B. Data is stored in two-dimensional tables composed of rows and columns.

    C. Data is stored hierarchically with parent-child relationships.

    D. Information can be related to other information, driving inference and deeper understanding.

15. Which of the following best describes the term "metadata"?

    A. Data that is encrypted for security purposes

    B. Data that offers insights into other data

    C. Data that is stored in a relational database

    D. Data that is used for backup purposes

16. What does the term "ACID" stand for in the context of an RDBMS environment?

    A. Atomicity, Clarity, Isolation, Durability

    B. Accuracy, Consistency, Integrity, Durability

    C. Atomicity, Consistency, Isolation, Durability

    D. Accuracy, Clarity, Integrity, Durability

17. Which of the following is a primary concern when citizen developers write code?

   A. They often produce highly optimized code.

   B. They typically follow best practices for secure coding.

   C. They often have access to powerful programming tools but may lack secure coding practices.

   D. They always rely on open source software.

18. Which of the following APIs provides a way for applications to communicate using HTTP?

   A. Representational State Transfer (REST)

   B. Simple Object Access Protocol (SOAP)

   C. Code Repository API

   D. Integrated Development Environment (IDE) API

19. In software development, what does "coupling" refer to?

   A. The level of relatedness between units of a codebase

   B. The process of making code more efficient

   C. The practice of writing code in multiple programming languages

   D. The process of documenting code for better readability

20. In the context of software development, what does "cohesion" refer to?

   A. The level of relatedness between different units of a codebase

   B. The level of relatedness between the code that makes up a unit of code

   C. The process of making code more efficient

   D. The practice of writing code in multiple programming languages

21. Which of the following best describes "sandboxing" in software development?

   A. A method to test new code in isolation

   B. The process of documenting code for better readability

   C. A technique to optimize code performance

   D. The practice of writing code in a collaborative environment

22. What is the primary purpose of "code signing" in the software development process?

   A. To optimize the performance of the code

   B. To verify the authenticity and integrity of the code

   C. To document the changes made in the code

   D. To make the code more readable

23. Which of the following is NOT a characteristic of "object-oriented programming (OOP)"?

    A. Polymorphism

    B. Encapsulation

    C. Cohesion

    D. Inheritance

24. Which of the following best describes "race conditions" in software development?

    A. Conditions where two or more threads access shared data simultaneously

    B. Conditions where the software runs faster than expected

    C. Conditions where the software is tested for speed and performance

    D. Conditions where the software is developed in a competitive environment

25. What is the primary concern of "secure coding practices"?

    A. To accelerate the development process

    B. To ensure the code is optimized for performance

    C. To ensure the software is free from vulnerabilities

    D. To make the code more readable and maintainable

26. In the context of databases, what does "normalization" refer to?

    A. The process of optimizing database performance

    B. The process of ensuring data integrity and reducing data redundancy

    C. The process of backing up the database regularly

    D. The process of encrypting the database for security purposes

27. Which of the following is a common method to prevent SQL injection attacks?

    A. Using regular expressions to validate input

    B. Encrypting the database

    C. Using parameterized queries

    D. Increasing the database's storage capacity

28. What is the primary purpose of "version control" in the software development process?

    A. To optimize the performance of the software

    B. To ensure the software is free from vulnerabilities

    C. To track and manage changes to the codebase

    D. To make the code more readable

29. Which of the following best describes "fuzz testing" in software development?

    A. Testing the software's user interface for usability

    B. Testing the software by providing random and unexpected inputs

C. Testing the software for speed and performance

D. Testing the software in a real-world environment

30. Which of the following best describes the "principle of least privilege" in software development?

A. Granting users only the permissions they need to perform their tasks

B. Encrypting sensitive data to prevent unauthorized access

C. Ensuring that software is updated regularly

D. Making the codebase open source for transparency

31. What is the primary goal of "threat modeling" in the software development process?

A. To identify potential threats and vulnerabilities in the software

B. To optimize the performance of the software

C. To document the software development process

D. To ensure code readability and maintainability

32. Which of the following is NOT a type of software testing?

A. Canary testing

B. Waterfall testing

C. Regression testing

D. Penetration testing

33. In the context of software development, what does "refactoring" refer to?

    A. Adding new features to the software

    B. Testing the software for vulnerabilities

    C. Rewriting certain parts of the code to improve its structure without changing its functionality

    D. Changing the user interface of the software

34. Which of the following best describes "static code analysis"?

    A. Analyzing the software's performance during runtime

    B. Reviewing the codebase without executing the program

    C. Testing the software in a production environment

    D. Analyzing user feedback about the software

35. What is the primary purpose of "code reviews" in the software development process?

    A. To optimize the software's performance

    B. To ensure the software is free from vulnerabilities

    C. To ensure the quality and correctness of the code

    D. To make the codebase open source

36. Which of the following is a common method to ensure data confidentiality in software applications?

    A. Data normalization

    B. Data encryption

C. Data refactoring

D. Data versioning

37. In the context of software development, what does "integrity" refer to?

A. Ensuring the software is free from vulnerabilities

B. Ensuring the data is accurate and has not been tampered with

C. Ensuring the software performs optimally

D. Ensuring the software is user-friendly

38. Which of the following best describes "runtime application self-protection (RASP)"?

A. A method to optimize software performance during runtime

B. A tool that detects and prevents real-time application attacks

C. A technique to refactor code during runtime

D. A tool for static code analysis

39. Which of the following is a primary concern when using third-party libraries or components in software development?

A. The size of the library or component

B. The popularity of the library or component

C. Potential vulnerabilities or security risks associated with the library or component

D. The cost of the library or component

40. Which of the following best describes the "security by design" principle in software development?

   A. Implementing security measures after the software is developed

   B. Designing the software with security considerations from the outset

   C. Relying solely on third-party security tools

   D. Focusing only on the user interface security

41. In the context of software development, what is the primary goal of "input validation"?

   A. To optimize the software's performance

   B. To ensure the software's user interface is intuitive

   C. To verify that the input meets the specified criteria before it's processed

   D. To ensure the software is compatible with various devices

42. Which of the following is NOT a type of "authentication" method in software development?

   A. Something you know

   B. Something you have

   C. Something you are

   D. Something you dislike

43. What is the primary purpose of "penetration testing" in the software development process?

    A. To document the software development process

    B. To ensure the software's user interface is user-friendly

    C. To identify vulnerabilities by simulating cyberattacks on the software

    D. To verify the software's compatibility with various operating systems

44. Which of the following best describes "two-factor authentication (2FA)" in software development?

    A. Using two different passwords for authentication

    B. Verifying the user's identity using two different methods or factors

    C. Using biometric authentication twice for added security

    D. Asking the user to input their password at two different stages of login

45. In software development, what does "availability" in the context of the CIA triad refer to?

    A. Ensuring that software is free from vulnerabilities

    B. Ensuring that software is accessible and usable when needed

    C. Ensuring that software data remains confidential

    D. Ensuring that software data is accurate and trustworthy

46. Which of the following is a common method to ensure "data integrity" in software applications?

    A. Data compression

    B. Data encryption

    C. Data hashing

    D. Data visualization

47. What is the primary concern of "defense in depth" in software security?

    A. Relying on a single layer of security

    B. Implementing multiple layers of security measures

    C. Focusing solely on external threats

    D. Prioritizing speed over security

48. In the context of software development, what does "confidentiality" in the CIA triad refer to?

    A. Ensuring that software is free from vulnerabilities

    B. Ensuring that software data remains private and restricted to authorized individuals

    C. Ensuring that software is accessible and usable when needed

    D. Ensuring that software data is accurate and trustworthy

49. Which of the following best describes the "principle of non-repudiation" in software security?

    A. Ensuring that users cannot deny their actions

    B. Ensuring that software is free from vulnerabilities

C. Verifying the user's identity using multiple authentication methods

D. Ensuring that data remains confidential

50. In the context of software security, which of the following best describes "data at rest"?

A. Data that is being transmitted over a network

B. Data that is stored and not actively being used or processed

C. Data that is currently being processed by an application

D. Data that is temporarily stored in memory

51. Which of the following is a primary concern when considering "data in transit" in software security?

A. Ensuring data storage optimization

B. Ensuring data remains confidential while being transmitted

C. Ensuring data is regularly backed up

D. Ensuring data is indexed for faster retrieval

52. What is the main goal of "security patches" in the software development process?

A. To add new features to the software

B. To improve the software's user interface

C. To fix known security vulnerabilities in the software

D. To optimize the software's performance

53. Which of the following best describes "zero-day vulnerabilities" in software security?

A. Vulnerabilities that are discovered and patched within a day

B. Vulnerabilities that have no impact on the software's functionality

C. Vulnerabilities that are unknown to the software developer and have no available patches

D. Vulnerabilities that are discovered during the software's first day of release

54. In the context of software security, what is the primary purpose of "intrusion detection systems (IDS)"?

A. To detect and prevent unauthorized access to the software

B. To back up the software's data

C. To optimize the software's performance

D. To manage user permissions and roles

55. Which of the following is NOT a type of "malware"?

A. Ransomware

B. Adware

C. Debugger

D. Trojan

56. What is the primary goal of "allowlisting" in software security?

    A. To list all known vulnerabilities in the software

    B. To specify which users have administrative privileges

    C. To define a list of approved software or processes that are allowed to run

    D. To list all outdated components of the software

57. Which of the following best describes "phishing" in the context of software security threats?

    A. An attack where the attacker floods the network with excessive requests

    B. An attack where the attacker tricks users into revealing sensitive information

    C. An attack where the attacker exploits a zero-day vulnerability

    D. An attack where the attacker uses brute force to crack passwords

58. In software security, what is the primary purpose of "firewalls"?

    A. To detect software bugs and errors

    B. To manage user permissions and roles

    C. To monitor and control incoming and outgoing network traffic

    D. To back up the software's data

59. Which of the following is a common method to
     ensure "data redundancy" in software applications?

     A. Data encryption

     B. Data compression

     C. Data replication

     D. Data hashing

60. In the context of software security, which of the
     following best describes "heuristic analysis"?

     A. A method of detecting malware based on known
         signatures

     B. A method of analyzing software
         performance metrics

     C. A method of detecting potential threats based on
         behavioral patterns

     D. A method of encrypting data for secure
         transmission

61. Which of the following is a primary concern when
     considering "data disposal" in software security?

     A. Ensuring data is transmitted securely

     B. Ensuring data is stored in an optimized format

     C. Ensuring data is permanently deleted and cannot
         be recovered

     D. Ensuring data is regularly backed up

62. What is the main goal of "security awareness training" in the context of software security?

    A. To teach developers how to write code

    B. To inform users about the latest software features

    C. To educate employees about security threats and best practices

    D. To introduce new security tools and technologies

63. Which of the following best describes "brute-force attacks" in software security?

    A. Exploiting software vulnerabilities using advanced tools

    B. Attempting to guess passwords or encryption keys through trial and error

    C. Sending large volumes of data to crash a system

    D. Tricking users into revealing their credentials

64. In the context of software security, what does "hardening" refer to?

    A. Making the software's user interface more intuitive

    B. Strengthening the software against potential attacks or vulnerabilities

    C. Compressing the software's data for optimized storage

    D. Upgrading the software to the latest version

65. Which of the following is NOT a type of "intrusion detection system (IDS)"?

A. Network-based IDS

B. Host-based IDS

C. Signature-based IDS

D. Encryption-based IDS

66. What is the primary purpose of "role-based access control (RBAC)" in software security?

A. To define user roles based on their job functions

B. To encrypt user data based on their roles

C. To monitor user activities in real time

D. To back up user data based on their roles

67. In software security, which of the following best describes "honeypots"?

A. Software tools to detect vulnerabilities in the code

B. Decoy systems designed to attract potential attackers

C. Systems designed to store sensitive data securely

D. Tools to optimize the performance of the software

68. Which of the following best describes "cross-site scripting (XSS)" in the context of software security threats?

A. An attack where malicious scripts are injected into trusted websites

B. An attack where the attacker floods the network with excessive requests

C. An attack where the attacker gains unauthorized access to the database

D. An attack where the attacker redirects users to a fake website

69. What is the primary goal of "input sanitization" in the software development process?

A. To optimize the software's performance

B. To ensure the software's user interface is user-friendly

C. To clean user input to prevent malicious data from harming the system

D. To compress user input data for optimized storage

70. In the context of software security, which of the following best describes "tokenization"?

A. The process of converting sensitive data into nonsensitive tokens

B. The process of authenticating users based on tokens

C. The process of optimizing software tokens for better performance

D. The process of distributing software tokens to users

71. Which of the following is a primary concern when considering "secure software deployment"?

A. Ensuring the software is compatible with all devices

B. Ensuring the software is free from known vulnerabilities before deployment

   C. Ensuring the software has the latest features

   D. Ensuring the software is available in multiple languages

72. What is the main goal of "digital signatures" in the context of software security?

   A. To optimize the software's performance

   B. To verify the authenticity and integrity of a message or document

   C. To encrypt data for secure storage

   D. To provide a unique identifier for each user

73. In software security, which of the following best describes "cross-site request forgery (CSRF)"?

   A. An attack where the attacker tricks a user into executing unwanted actions on a web application

   B. An attack where the attacker injects malicious scripts into trusted websites

   C. An attack where the attacker gains unauthorized access to user accounts

   D. An attack where the attacker redirects users to malicious websites

74. Which of the following is NOT a primary component of "public key infrastructure (PKI)"?

   A. Digital certificate

   B. Certificate authority (CA)

   C. Key exchange protocol

   D. Private key

75. What is the primary purpose of "secure boot" in the context of software security?

   A. To ensure faster booting of the system

   B. To ensure that only signed and trusted software can run during the system startup

   C. To encrypt data during the boot process

   D. To provide a user-friendly interface during booting

76. In the context of software security, what does "chain of trust" refer to?

   A. A sequence of trusted entities ensuring overall system security

   B. A sequence of software patches applied to the system

   C. A sequence of user authentication methods

   D. A sequence of encryption algorithms used in the system

77. Which of the following best describes "containerization" in software security?

   A. The process of segmenting software into isolated environments

   B. The process of encrypting software containers

   C. The process of optimizing software containers for better performance

   D. The process of distributing software containers to users

78. What is the primary goal of "anomaly-based intrusion detection" in software security?

   A. To detect intrusions based on known attack signatures

   B. To detect intrusions based on deviations from a baseline of normal behavior

   C. To detect intrusions based on user feedback

   D. To detect intrusions based on system performance metrics

79. Which of the following is NOT a type of "access control" in software security?

   A. Mandatory access control (MAC)

   B. Role-based access control (RBAC)

   C. Discretionary access control (DAC)

   D. Performance-based access control (PBAC)

80. In the context of software security, which of the following best describes "sandboxing"?

   A. The process of testing software in a controlled environment

   B. The process of isolating applications in a restricted environment to prevent malicious activities

   C. The process of optimizing software for better performance

   D. The process of backing up software data

81. Which of the following is a primary concern when considering "secure coding practices"?

    A. Ensuring the software has a user-friendly interface

    B. Ensuring the software is developed without introducing vulnerabilities

    C. Ensuring the software is compatible with all devices

    D. Ensuring the software has the latest features

82. What is the main goal of "data loss prevention (DLP)" tools in the context of software security?

    A. To optimize the software's performance

    B. To prevent unauthorized access and data breaches

    C. To prevent the unintentional loss or exposure of sensitive data

    D. To ensure data is stored in an optimized format

83. In software security, which of the following best describes "session management"?

    A. The process of managing user access to software features

    B. The process of managing and maintaining the state of a user's interaction with software

    C. The process of managing software updates

    D. The process of managing software backups

84. Which of the following is NOT a primary component of "Identity and Access Management (IAM)"?

    A. User authentication

    B. User authorization

    C. User profiling

    D. Role-based access

85. What is the primary purpose of "cryptographic hashing" in software security?

    A. To create a unique fixed-size output from input data

    B. To encrypt data for secure transmission

    C. To optimize data storage

    D. To create a backup of data

86. Which of the following best describes "security orchestration, automation, and response (SOAR)" in software security?

    A. A platform for managing and automating security operations

    B. A tool for static code analysis

    C. A method for optimizing software performance

    D. A tool for user authentication

87. In the context of software security, what does "endpoint protection" refer to?

    A. Protecting the software's database endpoints

    B. Protecting the user interface of the software

    C. Protecting devices like computers and mobile devices that connect to the network

    D. Protecting the software's API endpoints

88. Which of the following is a common method to ensure "data authenticity" in software applications?

    A. Data compression

    B. Data encryption

    C. Digital signatures

    D. Data replication

89. What is the primary goal of "security information and event management (SIEM)" systems in software security?

    A. To manage user permissions and roles

    B. To provide real-time analysis of security alerts generated by applications and network hardware

    C. To back up and restore software data

    D. To manage software updates and patches

90. In the context of software security, which of the following best describes "threat modeling"?

    A. The process of designing user-friendly interfaces

    B. The process of predicting software performance under various conditions

    C. The systematic identification and evaluation of potential threats to the software

    D. The process of simulating user interactions with software

91. Which of the following is a primary concern when considering "secure software design"?

    A. Ensuring the software has the latest features

    B. Ensuring the software's user interface is visually appealing

    C. Ensuring the software architecture is designed with security principles in mind

    D. Ensuring the software is compatible with all devices

92. What is the main goal of "application allowlisting" in the context of software security?

    A. To create a list of users authorized to access the application

    B. To specify which applications are allowed to run on a system

    C. To identify and block malicious applications

    D. To optimize the performance of authorized applications

93. In software security, which of the following best describes "security misconfiguration"?

    A. A situation where security settings are left at their default values

    B. A situation where security software is not updated regularly

    C. A situation where security protocols are overly complex

    D. A situation where security measures are redundant

94. Which of the following is NOT a primary component of "incident response" in software security?

    A. Identification of the incident

    B. Containment of the incident

    C. Resolution of the software bug

    D. Recovery and lessons learned

95. What is the primary purpose of "security audits" in software security?

    A. To identify and fix performance issues in the software

    B. To verify that the software meets user requirements

    C. To assess and ensure the software adheres to security standards and policies

    D. To introduce new features to the software

96. In the context of software security, what does "patch management" refer to?

    A. The process of designing user interfaces

    B. The process of regularly updating and managing patches for software vulnerabilities

    C. The process of managing user feedback and reviews

    D. The process of optimizing software code

97. Which of the following best describes "man-in-the-
middle (MITM)" attacks in software security?

A. Attacks where the attacker directly communicates
with the victim

B. Attacks where the attacker intercepts and possibly
alters the communication between two parties

C. Attacks where the attacker impersonates a software
application

D. Attacks where the attacker floods a system
with traffic

98. What is the primary goal of "multifactor
authentication (MFA)" in software security?

A. To provide multiple layers of encryption

B. To verify user identity using multiple methods
or factors

C. To allow multiple users to access the same account

D. To optimize the user login process

99. In the context of software security, which of the
following best describes "risk assessment"?

A. The process of designing secure software
architectures

B. The process of evaluating the potential risks
associated with software vulnerabilities

C. The process of training users on software features

D. The process of updating software to the
latest version

100. What service can integrate an app with a social
     media site that provides software libraries and tools?

   A. Software Development Kit (SDK)

   B. Data Loss Prevention (DLP)

   C. Integrated Development Environment (IDE)

   D. Application Programming Interface (API)

Answers

1. Answer: C. Early phases

   Explanation: Risk analysis and threat modeling
   are critical components of the early phases of the
   SDLC. They continue through to the architecture
   and design phase.

2. Answer: C. Waterfall

   Explanation: The Waterfall model requires the
   completion of each development phase before
   moving to the next. It does not allow revisiting a
   previous phase.

3. Answer: A. DevSecOps

   Explanation: DevOps should ideally be referred to as
   DevSecOps, where security is an integral part of the
   development process.

4. Answer: B. Software Assurance Maturity Model (SAMM)

   Explanation: OWASP's Software Assurance Maturity
   Model (SAMM) is described as the prime maturity
   model for software assurance.

5.   Answer: C. Smoke testing

Explanation: Smoke testing focuses on quick preliminary testing after a change to identify any simple failures of the most important existing functionality that worked before the change was made.

6.   Answer: B. Code repository

Explanation: A code repository is a storage location for software and application source code.

7.   Answer: B. Instantiating into multiple separate or independent instances

Explanation: Polyinstantiation refers to something being instantiated into multiple separate or independent instances.

8.   Answer: A. Buffer overflow

Explanation: Buffer overflow is a common problem with applications and occurs when information sent to a storage buffer exceeds the buffer's capacity.

9.   Answer: B. Simple Object Access Protocol (SOAP)

Explanation: Simple Object Access Protocol (SOAP) is an XML-based API.

10.   Answer: C. The idea that an object can be placed inside another, protecting it by wrapping it in other objects

Explanation: Encapsulation refers to the idea that an object – a piece of code – can be placed inside another. Other objects can be called by doing this, and objects can be protected by encapsulating or wrapping them in other objects.

11. Answer: C. Intentionally creating source code that is difficult for humans to understand

Explanation: Code obfuscation refers to hiding or obscuring code to protect it from unauthorized viewing. It intentionally makes source code difficult for humans to understand.

12. Answer: B. Spiral Method

Explanation: The Spiral Method is a risk-driven development process that follows an iterative model while also including waterfall elements.

13. Answer: B. To manage changes in software

Explanation: Software configuration management focuses explicitly on managing changes in software and is part of the overall configuration/change management.

14. Answer: C. Data is stored hierarchically with parent-child relationships.

Explanation: RDBMS systems store data in tables, not in hierarchical structures.

15. Answer: B. Data that offers insights into other data

Explanation: The term metadata refers to information that offers insights into other data. Essentially, it's data about data.

16. Answer: C. Atomicity, Consistency, Isolation, Durability

Explanation: ACID stands for atomicity, consistency, isolation, and durability and relates to how information and transactions in an RDBMS environment should be treated.

17. Answer: C. They often have access to powerful programming tools but may lack secure coding practices.

Explanation: Citizen developers often have access to powerful programming tools. Still, they're typically self-taught and unskilled regarding secure coding practices, leading to insecure and unreliable application development.

18. Answer: A. Representational State Transfer (REST)

Explanation: Representational State Transfer (REST) is an HTTP-based API.

19. Answer: A. The level of relatedness between units of a codebase

Explanation: Coupling and cohesion are relational terms that indicate the level of relatedness between units of a codebase (coupling) and the level of relatedness between the code that makes up a unit of code (cohesion).

20. Answer: B. The level of relatedness between the code that makes up a unit of code

Explanation: Cohesion refers to the level of relatedness between the code that makes up a unit of code. High cohesion means that the code within a module or class is closely related.

21. Answer: A. A method to test new code in isolation

Explanation: Sandboxing refers to a method where new or untested code is run in a separate environment (a "sandbox") to ensure it doesn't affect the functioning of existing systems.

22. Answer: B. To verify the authenticity and integrity of the code

Explanation: Code signing is a technique used to verify the authenticity and integrity of code. It ensures that the code has not been altered since it was signed.

23. Answer: C. Cohesion

Explanation: While cohesion is an important concept in software design, it is not a specific characteristic of object-oriented programming. OOP is characterized by concepts like polymorphism, encapsulation, and inheritance.

24. Answer: A. Conditions where two or more threads access shared data simultaneously

Explanation: Race conditions occur when two or more threads access shared data at the same time and at least one of them modifies the data, leading to unpredictable outcomes.

25. Answer: C. To ensure the software is free from vulnerabilities

Explanation: Secure coding practices aim to ensure that software is developed in a way that it is free from vulnerabilities that could be exploited by malicious actors.

26. Answer: B. The process of ensuring data integrity and reducing data redundancy

Explanation: Normalization is a process in database design to ensure data integrity and reduce data redundancy by organizing data in tables and establishing relationships between them.

27. Answer: C. Using parameterized queries

Explanation: Parameterized queries ensure that input is always treated as data and not executable code, thus preventing SQL injection attacks.

28. Answer: C. To track and manage changes to the codebase

Explanation: Version control systems track and manage changes to the codebase, allowing developers to revert to previous versions, collaborate, and understand the history of changes.

29. Answer: B. Testing the software by providing random and unexpected inputs

Explanation: Fuzz testing, or fuzzing, involves testing software by providing random and unexpected inputs to identify potential vulnerabilities and crashes.

30. Answer: A. Granting users only the permissions they need to perform their tasks

Explanation: The principle of least privilege emphasizes that users should be granted only the permissions they absolutely need, reducing the risk of unauthorized access or actions.

31. Answer: A. To identify potential threats and vulnerabilities in the software

Explanation: Threat modeling is a structured approach used to identify and evaluate potential threats and vulnerabilities in a software system, helping developers address them proactively.

32. Answer: B. Waterfall testing

Explanation: While "Waterfall" is a software development methodology, there isn't a specific type of testing called "Waterfall testing."

33. Answer: C. Rewriting certain parts of the code to improve its structure without changing its functionality

Explanation: Refactoring involves restructuring existing code without changing its external behavior, aiming to improve the nonfunctional attributes of the software.

34. Answer: B. Reviewing the codebase without executing the program

Explanation: Static code analysis involves examining the code without executing the program, aiming to find vulnerabilities, errors, or areas of improvement.

35. Answer: C. To ensure the quality and correctness of the code

Explanation: Code reviews involve systematically examining the source code of a program with the primary goal of finding and fixing mistakes overlooked during the initial development phase, ensuring the code's quality and correctness.

36. Answer: B. Data encryption

Explanation: Data encryption is a method used to protect data by converting it into a code to prevent unauthorized access, ensuring data confidentiality.

37. Answer: B. Ensuring the data is accurate and has not been tampered with

    Explanation: In software development, integrity refers to the assurance that data is accurate and reliable and has not been tampered with or altered without authorization.

38. Answer: B. A tool that detects and prevents real-time application attacks

    Explanation: Runtime application self-protection (RASP) is a security technology that uses runtime instrumentation to detect and block attacks by taking advantage of information from inside the running software.

39. Answer: C. Potential vulnerabilities or security risks associated with the library or component

    Explanation: When using third-party libraries or components, a primary concern is potential vulnerabilities or security risks that they might introduce into the software.

40. Answer: B. Designing the software with security considerations from the outset

    Explanation: "Security by design" means that the software has been designed from the ground up to be secure, ensuring that security is integrated into every part of the software development process.

41. Answer: C. To verify that the input meets the specified criteria before it's processed

    Explanation: Input validation is a process that ensures an application is rendering the correct data and prevents malicious data from harming the system.

42. Answer: D. Something you dislike

    Explanation: Authentication methods typically revolve around something you know, something you have, or something you are. "Something you dislike" is not a recognized authentication factor.

43. Answer: C. To identify vulnerabilities by simulating cyberattacks on the software

    Explanation: Penetration testing involves simulating cyberattacks on software to identify vulnerabilities that could be exploited in real-world attacks.

44. Answer: B. Verifying the user's identity using two different methods or factors

    Explanation: Two-factor authentication (2FA) requires users to verify their identity using two different methods or factors, enhancing security.

45. Answer: B. Ensuring that software is accessible and usable when needed

    Explanation: In the CIA (confidentiality, integrity, availability) triad, "availability" refers to ensuring that resources are accessible and usable when needed.

46.   Answer: C. Data hashing

Explanation: Data hashing involves creating a fixed-size string of bytes from input data of any size, ensuring data integrity by verifying that data has not been altered.

47.   Answer: B. Implementing multiple layers of security measures

Explanation: "Defense in depth" is a strategy that employs a series of mechanisms to slow the advance of an attack aimed at acquiring unauthorized access to information.

48.   Answer: B. Ensuring that software data remains private and restricted to authorized individuals

Explanation: In the CIA (confidentiality, integrity, availability) triad, "confidentiality" refers to ensuring that data remains private and is only accessible to those with the proper authorization.

49.   Answer: A. Ensuring that users cannot deny their actions

Explanation: Non-repudiation ensures that a user cannot deny having performed a particular action, providing proof of origin or delivery.

50.   Answer: B. Data that is stored and not actively being used or processed

Explanation: "Data at rest" refers to data that is stored in persistent storage (like hard drives) and is not actively being used, processed, or transmitted.

51. Answer: B. Ensuring data remains confidential while being transmitted

    Explanation: "Data in transit" refers to data that is being transferred over a network. The primary concern is to ensure its confidentiality and integrity during transmission.

52. Answer: C. To fix known security vulnerabilities in the software

    Explanation: Security patches are updates released by software developers to address known security vulnerabilities in the software.

53. Answer: C. Vulnerabilities that are unknown to the software developer and have no available patches

    Explanation: Zero-day vulnerabilities refer to software vulnerabilities that are unknown to the vendor. This security risk is called a "zero-day" because the developer has had zero days to fix it.

54. Answer: A. To detect and prevent unauthorized access to the software

    Explanation: Intrusion detection systems (IDS) monitor network traffic or system activities for malicious activities or policy violations and produce reports to a management station.

55. Answer: C. Debugger

    Explanation: While ransomware, adware, and trojans are types of malicious software, a debugger is a tool used by developers to test and debug their code.

56.   Answer: C. To define a list of approved software or processes that are allowed to run

Explanation: Allowlisting is a security approach where a list of approved software applications or processes is created, and only those on the list are allowed to run.

57.   Answer: B. An attack where the attacker tricks users into revealing sensitive information

Explanation: Phishing is a type of social engineering attack where the attacker tricks users into revealing sensitive information, often by masquerading as a trustworthy entity.

58.   Answer: C. To monitor and control incoming and outgoing network traffic

Explanation: Firewalls are network security devices that monitor and filter incoming and outgoing network traffic based on an organization's previously established security policies.

59.   Answer: C. Data replication

Explanation: Data replication involves creating copies of data so that this duplicate data can be used to restore the original data in case of data loss.

60.   Answer: C. A method of detecting potential threats based on behavioral patterns

Explanation: Heuristic analysis involves identifying malicious activities or threats based on behavioral patterns rather than relying on specific signatures.

61. Answer: C. Ensuring data is permanently deleted and cannot be recovered

    Explanation: Proper data disposal ensures that data is not only deleted but also cannot be recovered, preventing unauthorized access or data breaches.

62. Answer: C. To educate employees about security threats and best practices

    Explanation: Security awareness training aims to educate employees about various security threats and the best practices to prevent potential breaches.

63. Answer: B. Attempting to guess passwords or encryption keys through trial and error

    Explanation: A brute-force attack involves trying multiple combinations to guess a password or encryption key, relying on trial and error.

64. Answer: B. Strengthening the software against potential attacks or vulnerabilities

    Explanation: Hardening involves configuring a system to reduce its surface of vulnerability, making it more secure against potential threats.

65. Answer: D. Encryption-based IDS

    Explanation: While network-based, host-based, and signature-based are types of intrusion detection systems, there isn't a specific type called "encryption-based IDS."

66. Answer: A. To define user roles based on their job
     functions

     Explanation: Role-based access control (RBAC)
     is a method where roles are created based on job
     functions, and permissions to access resources are
     assigned to specific roles.

67. Answer: B. Decoy systems designed to attract
     potential attackers

     Explanation: Honeypots are decoy systems set
     up to lure potential attackers, allowing security
     professionals to study their behaviors and tactics.

68. Answer: A. An attack where malicious scripts are
     injected into trusted websites

     Explanation: Cross-site scripting (XSS) is a type
     of attack where malicious scripts are injected into
     otherwise benign and trusted websites.

69. Answer: C. To clean user input to prevent malicious
     data from harming the system

     Explanation: Input sanitization involves cleaning
     or filtering user input to ensure that potentially
     harmful or malicious data doesn't harm or
     compromise the system.

70. Answer: A. The process of converting sensitive data
     into nonsensitive tokens

     Explanation: Tokenization involves replacing
     sensitive data with nonsensitive tokens, which
     can't be reversed to the original data without a
     specific key.

71.   Answer: B. Ensuring the software is free from known vulnerabilities before deployment

Explanation: Secure software deployment focuses on ensuring that the software is free from known vulnerabilities and is securely configured before it's deployed to a live environment.

72.   Answer: B. To verify the authenticity and integrity of a message or document

Explanation: Digital signatures are cryptographic equivalents of handwritten signatures, used to verify the authenticity and integrity of a message or document.

73.   Answer: A. An attack where the attacker tricks a user into executing unwanted actions on a web application

Explanation: CSRF is an attack that tricks the victim into submitting a malicious request, exploiting the trust that a website has in the user's browser.

74.   Answer: C. Key exchange protocol

Explanation: While digital certificate, certificate authority (CA), and private key are components of PKI, a key exchange protocol is not a primary component of PKI.

75.   Answer: B. To ensure that only signed and trusted software can run during the system startup

Explanation: Secure boot is a security standard that ensures that a device boots using only software that is trusted by the manufacturer.

76. Answer: A. A sequence of trusted entities ensuring overall system security

Explanation: The chain of trust refers to a series of trusted entities or components in a system where each component can vouch for the integrity and trustworthiness of the next component.

77. Answer: A. The process of segmenting software into isolated environments

Explanation: Containerization involves encapsulating an application and its dependencies into a "container." This ensures that it runs consistently across various environments.

78. Answer: B. To detect intrusions based on deviations from a baseline of normal behavior

Explanation: Anomaly-based intrusion detection systems monitor network traffic and compare it against an established baseline to detect any deviations, which could indicate a potential intrusion.

79. Answer: D. Performance-based access control (PBAC)

Explanation: While MAC, RBAC, and DAC are recognized types of access control methods, there isn't a specific type called "performance-based access control (PBAC)."

80. Answer: B. The process of isolating applications in a restricted environment to prevent malicious activities

Explanation: Sandboxing involves running applications in a controlled environment to restrict what actions they can perform, preventing potential malicious activities.

81. Answer: B. Ensuring the software is developed without introducing vulnerabilities

Explanation: Secure coding practices focus on writing code in a way that prevents the introduction of vulnerabilities and security flaws.

82. Answer: C. To prevent the unintentional loss or exposure of sensitive data

Explanation: Data loss prevention (DLP) tools are designed to detect and prevent the unauthorized transmission or loss of sensitive data.

83. Answer: B. The process of managing and maintaining the state of a user's interaction with software

Explanation: Session management involves maintaining and tracking a user's state and data as they interact with an application, ensuring that the session remains secure and consistent.

84. Answer: C. User profiling

Explanation: While user authentication, user authorization, and role-based access are components of IAM, user profiling is not a primary component of IAM.

85. Answer: A. To create a unique fixed-size output from input data

    Explanation: Cryptographic hashing functions take input data and produce a fixed-size string of characters, which is typically a sequence of numbers and letters. The output, called the hash value, should be the same length regardless of the length of the input.

86. Answer: A. A platform for managing and automating security operations

    Explanation: SOAR platforms allow organizations to collect data about security threats and respond to low-level security events without human intervention.

87. Answer: C. Protecting devices like computers and mobile devices that connect to the network

    Explanation: Endpoint protection focuses on ensuring that devices such as computers, mobile devices, and other endpoints that connect to a network are secure from potential threats.

88. Answer: C. Digital signatures

    Explanation: Digital signatures are used to verify the authenticity of data, ensuring that it has not been tampered with and comes from a verified source.

89. Answer: B. To provide real-time analysis of security alerts generated by applications and network hardware

Explanation: SIEM systems provide real-time analysis of security alerts generated by various hardware and software resources in an organization.

90. Answer: C. The systematic identification and evaluation of potential threats to the software

Explanation: Threat modeling involves identifying, understanding, and addressing potential threats in the early stages of software development.

91. Answer: C. Ensuring the software architecture is designed with security principles in mind

Explanation: Secure software design focuses on building software that is resilient to threats by incorporating security principles into its architecture.

92. Answer: B. To specify which applications are allowed to run on a system

Explanation: Application allowlisting is a security approach where only specified applications are permitted to run, preventing unauthorized or malicious software from executing.

93. Answer: A. A situation where security settings are left at their default values

Explanation: Security misconfiguration occurs when security settings are not appropriately configured, often left at default, making the system vulnerable.

94.   Answer: C. Resolution of the software bug

Explanation: While identification, containment, and recovery are stages of incident response, the resolution of software bugs is a part of the software development and maintenance process, not specifically incident response.

95.   Answer: C. To assess and ensure the software adheres to security standards and policies

Explanation: Security audits are systematic evaluations of the security of a system or application to ensure compliance with security standards and policies.

96.   Answer: B. The process of regularly updating and managing patches for software vulnerabilities

Explanation: Patch management involves the systematic acquisition, testing, and installation of updates and patches to software to address vulnerabilities and improve security.

97.   Answer: B. Attacks where the attacker intercepts and possibly alters the communication between two parties

Explanation: In a man-in-the-middle attack, the attacker secretly intercepts and potentially alters the communication between two parties without their knowledge.

98. Answer: B. To verify user identity using multiple methods or factors

    Explanation: Multifactor authentication (MFA) enhances security by requiring users to provide multiple forms of identification before granting access.

99. Answer: B. The process of evaluating the potential risks associated with software vulnerabilities

    Explanation: Risk assessment involves identifying, evaluating, and prioritizing risks to determine the potential impact of software vulnerabilities and to decide on mitigation strategies.

100. Answer: A. Software Development Kit (SDK)

    Explanation: A Software Development Kit (SDK) typically includes a set of software libraries, development tools, and documentation that developers can use to create or enhance software. In this case, the social media site provides software libraries and other tools to integrate better applications, characteristic of an SDK.

CHAPTER 11

Tools and Strategies: Study Methods and Exam Techniques

Embarking on the journey to become a CISSP is a significant commitment. This path requires a strategic approach, robust study habits, and a deep understanding of the exam content. The CISSP certification is a prestigious acknowledgment of expertise in information security.

This chapter provides the tools, strategies, and mindset to navigate the CISSP exam preparation process successfully. It will detail essential study methods, exam techniques, and attitudes that will lead to success. Unlike other chapters that may delve into the theoretical aspects of information security, this particular chapter focuses solely on exam preparation.

This chapter includes valuable exam tips and guides to help you confidently approach the CISSP exam. These tips are not generic suggestions; they are tailored to the unique structure and demands of the CISSP exam. From time management strategies to techniques for handling complex scenario-based questions, this chapter offers insights specific to the challenges you will face in the exam.

Additionally, this chapter guides cultivating the right mindset for the exam. It's not just about knowing the material; it's about understanding how to apply that knowledge in the high-pressure environment of the

© Mohamed Aly Bouke 2023
M. A. Bouke, *CISSP Exam Certification Companion*, Certification Study Companion Series,
https://doi.org/10.1007/979-8-8688-0057-3_11

exam room. The guidance here aims to prepare you mentally, helping you think like a security professional and approach the exam calmly and intently.

Effective Preparation

The journey toward CISSP certification begins with effective preparation. This multifaceted process requires careful planning, understanding, practice, and mastery of essential skills.

- **A well-structured study plan**: Crafting a well-structured study plan is the cornerstone of successful exam preparation. This plan must be tailored to your unique situation, considering your work schedule, personal commitments, and the time you can consistently devote to studying. It's not merely about cramming information; it's about creating a balanced routine that includes regular downtime to rest and recharge. Integrating relaxation techniques or hobbies into your study routine can prevent mental exhaustion, which can lead to decreased productivity and retention.

- **Understanding the CISSP exam domains**: The CISSP exam is divided into eight domains, each assigned a different weight. Comprehending the intricacies of each domain is crucial. Focus on those with higher weights, such as the Security and Risk Management domain, which holds 15% weightage. A deep understanding of these domains will guide your study efforts toward areas significantly impacting your overall score.

- **Regular practice tests:** Practice tests are integral to gauging your progress and identifying areas requiring more focus. They familiarize you with the exam format and difficulty and provide an opportunity to assess and improve your understanding of the material. Consistent practice enhances speed and accuracy, building the skills and confidence needed for the actual exam. It's essential to ensure that the practice tests and materials used come from trusted and recognized sources. Utilizing reliable resources prevents the waste of valuable time and protects against inaccurate or misleading information, ensuring that your preparation aligns with the standards and expectations of the CISSP exam.

- **Mastering effective time management:** The CISSP exam, with 125–175 questions to be answered within four hours, demands a calculated approach to time management. Practicing under timed conditions helps you pace yourself during the actual exam. CISSP questions often present scenarios rather than direct questions, requiring careful reading and understanding. This skill is crucial in selecting the correct answer and demonstrates knowledge of the subject matter and the ability to analyze complex information quickly and accurately.

In conclusion, adequate preparation for the CISSP exam is a comprehensive process. It involves strategic planning, an in-depth understanding of the exam structure, regular practice, and effective time management. These elements, when combined, equip you with the knowledge, skills, and confidence needed to succeed in the CISSP exam. Your commitment to this preparation process lays the foundation for passing the exam and a thriving career in information security.

Day of the Exam

The day of the CISSP exam culminates weeks or even months of preparation. It's a day filled with anticipation, excitement, and some anxiety. How you approach this day can have a significant impact on your performance in the exam. Here's a guide to navigating the day of the exam with confidence and focus:

- **Maintaining low-stress levels**: The importance of starting the day with a calm and focused mindset cannot be overstated. Begin the day early, allowing yourself time for a healthy breakfast and a relaxed morning routine. Reach the exam center well ahead of time to avoid any last-minute rush. Avoid studying new topics on the exam day; focus on light revision and remain calm. Deep breathing exercises or a brief walk can also help in calming nerves.

- **Knowing what to bring to the exam**: Preparation for the exam also includes knowing what to bring with you. Essential items include your identification, confirmation email or letter, and other materials required by the testing center. Familiarize yourself with the rules regarding what items you can bring into the testing room to avoid any last-minute stress. Having everything ready the night before can make the morning of the exam go more smoothly.

- **Leveraging multiple resources and gaining practical experience**: While this is more of a long-term strategy, it's worth reflecting on the importance of diversifying your study resources and gaining practical experience in various domains of information security. The CISSP certification is designed for seasoned professionals, so hands-on experience is invaluable. Reflecting on this experience can help you approach the exam with confidence. Additionally, when selecting study resources, choosing those trusted and recognized within the industry is crucial. Utilizing reliable and authoritative materials ensures that your preparation is aligned with the CISSP exam's standards, preventing potential misunderstandings or misconceptions that could arise from inaccurate or outdated information.

- **Dealing with difficult questions:** The CISSP exam is known for its challenging questions. Having strategies in place to tackle these can be beneficial. Techniques like the process of elimination can narrow down your options, increasing your chances of selecting the correct answer. Making educated guesses based on related information can also be a helpful strategy. Remember, every question is an opportunity to demonstrate your knowledge and understanding.

In conclusion, the exam day is not just another day; it's when all your preparation is tested. Approaching it with a calm and focused mindset, knowing what to bring, reflecting on your practice, and having strategies for difficult questions can make the difference between a stressful experience and a successful one. Your performance on the exam is not only a reflection of your knowledge and skills but also of your ability to apply them under pressure. With careful planning and a positive attitude, you can approach the CISSP exam with confidence and poise.

After the Exam

Completing the CISSP exam marks a significant milestone but is not the end of the journey. Whether you pass or need to retake the exam, the experience provides valuable insights that can guide your future learning and career development. Here's a guide to navigating the post-exam period and continuing your growth in cybersecurity:

- **Reviewing your performance**: Once you receive your score, take the time to review your performance. Understand your strengths and identify areas for improvement. This review is not just about analyzing what went right or wrong; it's about understanding your learning process and how you can continue to grow. It can guide your future studies, whether for recertification or for expanding your knowledge in specific areas.

- **Continuing learning and staying updated**: The field of cybersecurity is dynamic and ever-changing. Even after passing the exam, continuing to learn and staying updated on industry trends and changes is essential. Regularly attend webinars, read new cybersecurity research, and participate in discussions on professional platforms like LinkedIn or cybersecurity forums. Engaging with the community and staying informed will keep your skills sharp and your knowledge relevant.

- **Developing a growth mindset**: Cultivating a growth mindset is vital for ongoing success. Believe in your ability to improve and learn with effort and persistence. Engage with the cybersecurity community through

online forums and local ISC2 chapters. Networking
with peers and learning from others' experiences
can provide new perspectives and insights. A
growth mindset encourages you to see challenges as
opportunities and strive for excellence continually.

In conclusion, the journey toward CISSP certification is more than an
exam; it's a continuous learning, growth, and self-care process. Reviewing
your performance, staying updated, and developing a growth mindset
are essential aspects of this journey. The CISSP certification is not just
a validation of your knowledge; it's a commitment to excellence in
information security. Embracing this commitment means recognizing that
learning never stops and that every day offers new opportunities to grow,
connect, and thrive in your career.

Summary

Passing the CISSP exam is a significant achievement that requires a blend
of solid knowledge, practical strategies, and a healthy mindset. It's not
simply about memorizing facts and figures but about understanding
concepts and their practical applications in information security.
Remember to be patient with your progress and consistent in your efforts.
Don't be discouraged by setbacks or difficult topics. Instead, view them
as opportunities to learn and grow. Keep your end goal in sight and
remind yourself why you embarked on this journey. With time, effort, and
persistence, you can join the ranks of CISSP-certified professionals. Good
luck on your CISSP journey!

Exam Questions Sample 1

The journey to CISSP certification is marked with rigorous study, practice, and understanding of complex information security concepts. An essential part of this preparation involves working with sample exam questions. These questions serve as a valuable tool in the learning process, offering insights into the format and complexity of the actual CISSP exam. Sample questions provide a window into the style and substance of the real exam. Working with these questions helps identify areas needing further attention and practice. They also offer a chance to develop essential skills in analyzing, timing, and answering questions effectively.

Strategies for maximum benefit

- **Analyze the questions**: Approach each question analytically. Understand what is being asked, identify key concepts, and recognize underlying principles. This method deepens understanding and enhances the ability to tackle similar questions in the exam.

- **Time yourself**: Practice answering questions under timed conditions. The CISSP exam demands answering many questions within a set time frame. Timing yourself while working with sample questions helps develop a sense of pacing for the exam.

- **Review your answers**: Reflect on your answers after completing the questions. Understand the reasoning behind the correct answers and the flaws in the incorrect ones. This reflection reinforces understanding and highlights areas for further study.

- **Repeat the process**: Consistency in working with sample questions and applying these strategies builds confidence and competence.

Sample exam questions are more than assessment tools; they are opportunities for continuous learning and growth. Approaching them with a strategic and thoughtful mindset maximizes their value in the preparation process. The following section presents a set of carefully crafted sample questions that emulate the CISSP exam's style and substance. Engage with them thoughtfully, diligently, and with a commitment to excellence, and they will serve as valuable guides on your path toward CISSP certification.

1. Which role in data classification is primarily responsible for the technical custody of systems and databases?

   A. Data owner/controller

   B. Data processor

   C. Data custodian

   D. Data steward

2. Which method provides complete confidentiality and anonymity through the use of multiple layers of encryption, making it very difficult to determine the sender and receiver while data is in transit?

   A. End-to-end encryption

   B. Link encryption

   C. Onion network

   D. Homomorphic encryption

3. In which context does data loss prevention (DLP)
    focus on detecting and preventing data breaches
    and potential data exfiltration?

    A. Data in use

    B. Data in motion

    C. Data at rest

    D. All of the above

4. Which of the following best describes the primary
    difference between "labeling" and "marking" in the
    context of asset classification?

    A. Labeling refers to the classification of the asset and is system
       readable, while marking refers to the handling instructions of
       the asset and is human readable.

    B. Labeling is a manual process, while marking is automated.

    C. Labeling is used for tangible assets, while marking is used for
       intangible assets.

    D. Labeling is a temporary classification, while marking is
       permanent.

5. Which obfuscation method involves creating fake
    data to replace real or sensitive data?

    A. Concealing data

    B. Information pruning

    C. Fabricating data

    D. Trimming data

6. Which state of data refers to data that is currently being used in some type of computational activity?

   A. Data at rest

   B. Data in transit

   C. Data in use

   D. Data in archive

7. In the context of access control, which principle emphasizes that access should be granted only to those personnel who absolutely require it to perform their job functions?

   A. Separation of duties

   B. Need to know

   C. Least privilege

   D. Rule-based access control

8. Which metric is used to measure the overall accuracy of a biometric system, representing the intersection between Type 1 (false reject) and Type 2 (false acceptance) errors?

   A. Error acceptance rate

   B. Biometric verification rate

   C. Crossover error rate

   D. Biometric failure rate

9. Which federated access protocol is frequently used in Federated Identity Management (FIM) solutions, providing both authentication and authorization, and has assertions written in XML?

   A. OAuth

   B. OpenID

   C. Kerberos

   D. SAML

10. Which Single Sign-On (SSO) mechanism utilizes tickets and symmetric key cryptography to authenticate users to multiple services without requiring them to reenter their credentials?

   A. OAuth 2.0

   B. SAML

   C. Kerberos

   D. OpenID Connect

11. In which access control model are access decisions based on the user's role within the organization, and users are granted permissions based on their assigned roles?

   A. Discretionary access control (DAC)

   B. Role-based access control (RBAC)

   C. Mandatory access control (MAC)

   D. Attribute-based access control (ABAC)

12. Which password policy aims to prevent attackers from using previously used passwords by maintaining a history of the user's passwords?

    A. Password complexity

    B. Password length

    C. Password history

    D. Password age

13. Which of the following statements best describes the "Zero Trust" design principle in the context of security architecture and engineering?

    A. Systems should automatically trust all internal entities.

    B. Systems should trust entities only after they have been authenticated and authorized.

    C. Systems should trust entities based on their historical behavior.

    D. Systems should trust all external entities but verify their actions continuously.

14. Which security model is primarily focused on preventing conflicts of interest between different departments or entities within an organization?

    A. Bell-LaPadula

    B. Biba

    C. Brewer-Nash (the Chinese Wall)

    D. Clark-Wilson

15. Which of the following is NOT a component of the trusted computing base (TCB)?

    A. Operating systems

    B. Firewall rulesets

    C. Firmware

    D. Processors (CPUs)

16. Which of the following cryptographic mechanisms is primarily designed to provide data integrity without confidentiality?

    A. Symmetric encryption

    B. Asymmetric encryption

    C. Digital signatures

    D. Stream ciphers

17. The Common Criteria (CC) for Information Technology Security Evaluation provides a framework for evaluating the security properties of IT products. Which of the following is NOT a component of the Common Criteria?

    A. Protection Profiles (PP)

    B. Security Target (ST)

    C. Evaluation Assurance Levels (EAL)

    D. Trusted Platform Module (TPM)

18. In the context of system security architecture, which of the following best describes a "reference monitor"?

    A. A tool for monitoring network traffic in real time

    B. A conceptual piece of the system that mediates all access to objects by subjects

    C. A database that stores reference architectures for various systems

    D. A module that references all security patches applied to a system

19. A cybersecurity professional is faced with a situation where they discover a vulnerability in a system that is not under their purview. Which of the following actions aligns best with the ISC2 Code of Professional Ethics?

    A. Exploit the vulnerability to demonstrate its severity to management.

    B. Ignore the vulnerability since it's not within their assigned tasks.

    C. Report the vulnerability to the appropriate team or authority within the organization.

    D. Share the vulnerability on a public forum to raise awareness.

20. Which of the following best describes the primary purpose of the CIA triad in information security?

    A. To define the roles and responsibilities of security personnel

    B. To provide a model for designing, structuring, and implementing security functions

    C. To outline the legal and regulatory requirements for data protection

    D. To establish guidelines for ethical behavior in cybersecurity

21. In the context of risk management, what does the term "threat" specifically refer to?

    A. A weakness in an asset that could be exploited

    B. Any potential danger that can cause damage to an asset

    C. The entity that has the potential to cause damage to an asset

    D. The negative consequences to an asset if a risk is realized

22. Which of the following best describes the primary role of security governance within an organization?

    A. Implementing specific security controls and technologies

    B. Establishing a strategic framework for risk-based decision-making

    C. Conducting day-to-day security operations and incident response

    D. Ensuring compliance with external regulatory requirements

23. An organization is trying to determine the potential loss from a specific threat. They estimate the annual rate of occurrence (ARO) as 5 and the single loss expectancy (SLE) as $10,000. What is the annualized loss expectancy (ALE)?

    A. $2000

    B. $50,000

    C. $15,000

    D. $5000

24. Which of the following is NOT typically a standard data classification level in most organizations?

    A. Confidential

    B. Public

    C. Restricted

    D. Casual

25. Your organization has recently experienced a security breach. The incident response team has been activated and is in the process of assessing the impact of the breach. Which of the following steps should the incident response team prioritize NEXT?

    A. Remediation to prevent similar incidents in the future

    B. Reporting the incident to all relevant stakeholders

    C. Mitigation to contain and minimize the damage or impact from the incident

    D. Recovery to restore operations to normal

26. During a forensic investigation, two identical bit-for-bit copies of the original hard drive are created. What is the primary reason for creating these copies?

    A. To have a backup in case one copy becomes corrupted

    B. To compare the two copies for inconsistencies

    C. To ensure that the original evidence remains uncontaminated

    D. To distribute one copy to law enforcement and retain the other for internal investigations

27. Which of the following is NOT a capability of a security information and event management (SIEM) system?

    A. Aggregation of log data from multiple sources

    B. Normalization of log entries for consistent analysis

    C. Real-time prevention of security breaches

    D. Reporting on analyzed and correlated log entries

28. A security audit of your organization's data center revealed that there are potential vulnerabilities related to physical access. Which of the following measures would be MOST effective in preventing unauthorized physical access?

    A. Implementing biometric authentication at all entry points

    B. Distributing security awareness brochures to all employees

    C. Increasing the frequency of password changes for data center systems

    D. Regularly updating the antivirus software on data center servers

29. Your organization is considering deploying an IDPS solution. Which of the following is a primary advantage of using an intrusion prevention system (IPS) over an intrusion detection system (IDS)?

    A. IPS can detect potential threats in real time.

    B. IPS can take active measures to block or prevent malicious activity.

    C. IPS provides detailed logs and reports for forensic analysis.

    D. IPS requires less maintenance and updates than IDS.

30. Which of the following is the PRIMARY objective of a business impact analysis (BIA) in the context of disaster recovery planning?

A. To identify the organization's vulnerabilities and threats

B. To determine the financial implications of a potential disaster

C. To prioritize the recovery of systems based on their criticality to business operations

D. To ensure compliance with industry regulations and standards

31. In the context of software development, what is the primary purpose of address space layout randomization (ASLR)?

A. To randomize the locations where system executables are loaded into memory

B. To ensure that software is developed using a waterfall model

C. To provide a structured approach for measuring organizational processes

D. To facilitate communication between different software applications

32. Which of the following best describes the Software Assurance Maturity Model (SAMM) as presented by OWASP?

A. A model focused solely on the development phase of software

B. A model that is technology specific and follows a rigid structure

C. A model that provides a way to analyze and improve software security posture throughout the software life cycle

D. A model that emphasizes the importance of code obfuscation in software development

33. In the realm of software development, what does the term "polyinstantiation" refer to?

A. The ability of code to change its behavior to avoid detection

B. The process of hiding or obscuring code to protect it from unauthorized viewing

C. The instantiation of something into multiple separate or independent instances

D. The practice of dividing the development process into multiple rapid iterations

34. Which of the following best describes the primary difference between a static library and a dynamic library in software development?

A. A static library is accessed during program execution, while a dynamic library is accessed during program build.

B. A static library is always larger in size compared to a dynamic library.

C. A static library is accessed during program build, while a dynamic library is accessed during program execution.

D. A static library can be modified by the end user, while a dynamic library cannot.

35. In the context of software development methodologies, which approach divides the development process into multiple rapid iterations with heavy customer interaction throughout the process?

   A. Waterfall

   B. Spiral Method

   C. Agile

   D. Structured Programming Development

36. Which of the following best describes the term "DevOps" in the context of software development?

   A. A software development methodology that emphasizes code obfuscation

   B. A structured approach that allows an organization to measure processes and understand where strengths and room for improvement exist

   C. An integrated approach where team members from development, operations, and other relevant areas collaborate from the beginning of a project

   D. A specific type of software that focuses on defect prevention to produce software with a certifiable level of reliability

37. During a routine security assessment, an organization discovered that a significant number of employees were using weak passwords. The Chief Information Security Officer (CISO) wants to implement a solution to mitigate this risk. Which of the following would be the MOST effective solution?

    A. Conduct regular security awareness training for employees.

    B. Implement a password complexity policy.

    C. Limit the number of login attempts.

    D. Monitor network traffic for suspicious activity.

38. A company is planning to migrate its on-premises data center to a cloud environment. Which of the following is the PRIMARY concern from a security perspective?

    A. Scalability of the cloud environment

    B. Integration with existing applications

    C. Data sovereignty and compliance

    D. Cost-effectiveness of the migration

39. Which of the following cryptographic methods is BEST suited for ensuring the integrity of a message?

    A. Symmetric encryption

    B. Asymmetric encryption

    C. Digital signature

    D. Key exchange

40. An organization is implementing a new security policy where all employees must undergo a background check. This policy is an example of which type of security control?

    A. Technical control

    B. Physical control

    C. Administrative control

    D. Detective control

41. A security analyst is reviewing the organization's continuity plan and notices that there is no mention of the time it would take to recover from a disaster and resume operations. Which of the following should the analyst recommend adding to the plan?

    A. Recovery point objective (RPO)

    B. Recovery time objective (RTO)

    C. Business impact analysis (BIA)

    D. Incident response plan (IRP)

42. Which of the following best describes the principle of "least privilege" in an information security context?

    A. Users should be given only the minimum levels of access necessary to perform their job functions.

    B. Users should be given full access to all systems and data, but their activities should be logged and audited.

    C. Users should be given access based on their seniority within the organization.

    D. Users should be given access to systems and data based on their job title.

43. Which of the following is a primary purpose of using a demilitarized zone (DMZ) in network security?

    A. To provide a secure area for sensitive data storage

    B. To provide an area isolated from the network for incident response

    C. To provide an area where public-facing servers can be placed

    D. To provide an area for the internal network infrastructure

44. A security analyst at a large corporation is reviewing the company's current security posture. The analyst discovers that the company has a robust security infrastructure with firewalls, intrusion detection systems (IDS), and regular patch management. However, there is no formal process for managing and responding to identified security incidents. Which of the following should be the analyst's NEXT step?

    A. Implement a security information and event management (SIEM) system

    B. Develop an incident response (IR) plan

    C. Conduct a penetration testing exercise

    D. Implement an intrusion prevention system (IPS)

45. An organization is planning to migrate its on-premises email server to a cloud-based email service. The Chief Information Security Officer (CISO) is concerned about the potential loss of control over the organization's data and the inability to conduct forensic investigations in case of a security incident. Which of the following should be the CISO's PRIMARY consideration to mitigate these concerns?

   A. Implementing a Cloud Access Security Broker (CASB)

   B. Ensuring the cloud provider offers strong Service-Level Agreements (SLAs)

   C. Conducting regular security audits of the cloud provider

   D. Implementing end-to-end encryption for emails

46. A company is planning to implement a new software system that will handle sensitive customer data. The Chief Information Security Officer (CISO) is concerned about potential security vulnerabilities in the software. Which of the following should be the CISO's PRIMARY consideration to mitigate these concerns?

   A. Implementing a robust intrusion detection system (IDS)

   B. Conducting a thorough software security assessment before deployment

   C. Ensuring the software vendor provides regular security updates

   D. Encrypting all customer data stored by the software

47. An organization has recently suffered a data breach due to an insider threat. The organization wants to implement measures to detect and prevent such threats in the future. Which of the following should be the organization's PRIMARY focus?

    A. Implementing a robust firewall and intrusion prevention system (IPS)

    B. Conducting regular security awareness training for employees

    C. Implementing a User and Entity Behavior Analytics (UEBA) solution

    D. Regularly updating and patching all systems

48. A company is implementing a Bring Your Own Device (BYOD) policy. The Chief Information Security Officer (CISO) is concerned about the potential security risks associated with this policy. Which of the following should be the CISO's PRIMARY consideration to mitigate these risks?

    A. Implementing a Mobile Device Management (MDM) solution

    B. Conducting regular security audits of employee devices

    C. Implementing a strong password policy for all devices

    D. Ensuring all data transmitted to and from the devices is encrypted

49. A company is planning to implement a new cloud-based Customer Relationship Management (CRM) system. The Chief Information Security Officer (CISO) is concerned about the potential privacy risks associated with storing customer data in the cloud. Which of the following should be the CISO's PRIMARY consideration to mitigate these concerns?

   A. Ensuring the cloud provider complies with relevant data protection regulations

   B. Implementing a robust intrusion detection system (IDS) for the cloud environment

   C. Conducting regular security audits of the cloud provider

   D. Encrypting all customer data stored in the cloud

50. An organization has implemented a new security policy that requires multifactor authentication (MFA) for all users. However, the IT department is receiving numerous complaints from users about the inconvenience of MFA. Which of the following should be the organization's PRIMARY response to these complaints?

   A. Disable MFA for users who find it inconvenient

   B. Provide training to users on the importance of MFA

   C. Implement a Single Sign-On (SSO) solution

   D. Review and update the security policy

51. A company has recently suffered a data breach due to a zero-day exploit. The company wants to improve its ability to respond to such threats in the future. Which of the following should be the company's PRIMARY focus?

    A. Implementing a robust patch management process

    B. Conducting regular penetration testing

    C. Implementing an intrusion prevention system (IPS)

    D. Subscribing to a threat intelligence service

52. A company is planning to implement a new Internet of Things (IoT) solution. The Chief Information Security Officer (CISO) is concerned about the potential security risks associated with IoT devices. Which of the following should be the CISO's PRIMARY consideration to mitigate these concerns?

    A. Ensuring the IoT devices support the latest encryption standards

    B. Implementing a robust intrusion detection system (IDS) for the IoT network

    C. Conducting a thorough security assessment of the IoT devices before deployment

    D. Ensuring the IoT devices are included in the company's regular patch management process

53. An organization is implementing a new web application firewall (WAF) to protect its web applications from attacks. The security team is debating whether to place the WAF in blocking mode or monitoring mode. Which of the following should be the organization's PRIMARY consideration in making this decision?

   A. The potential impact on application performance

   B. The ability of the WAF to accurately differentiate between legitimate traffic and attacks

   C. The cost of the WAF solution

   D. The ease of managing and maintaining the WAF

54. A company is implementing a new policy that requires all employees to use a Virtual Private Network (VPN) when accessing the company network from a remote location. Some employees have complained that the VPN is difficult to use. Which of the following should be the company's PRIMARY response to these complaints?

   A. Provide training to employees on how to use the VPN

   B. Implement a simpler security solution that does not require a VPN

   C. Allow employees to opt out of using the VPN if they find it too difficult

   D. Implement a two-factor authentication (2FA) solution in addition to the VPN

55. A company is planning to implement a new policy that requires all employees to use multifactor authentication (MFA) when accessing company resources. The Chief Information Security Officer (CISO) is concerned about potential resistance from employees due to the perceived inconvenience of MFA. Which of the following should be the CISO's PRIMARY strategy to ensure the successful implementation of this policy?

A. Implementing a Single Sign-On (SSO) solution in addition to MFA

B. Providing training and awareness sessions to employees about the importance of MFA

C. Allowing employees to opt out of MFA if they find it too inconvenient

D. Implementing a biometric authentication method as one of the factors in MFA

56. An organization is implementing a new web application. The security team is concerned about potential SQL injection attacks. Which of the following should be the organization's PRIMARY focus to mitigate this risk?

A. Implementing a web application firewall (WAF)

B. Conducting regular security audits of the web application

C. Implementing input validation for all user inputs in the web application

D. Encrypting all data stored by the web application

57. A company is implementing a new policy that requires all employees to encrypt their email communications. Some employees have complained that the encryption process is too complicated. Which of the following should be the company's PRIMARY response to these complaints?

   A. Provide training to employees on how to encrypt their emails

   B. Implement an email client that automatically encrypts emails

   C. Allow employees to opt out of email encryption if they find it too complicated

   D. Implement a two-factor authentication (2FA) solution for email access

58. A financial organization is considering the adoption of a public cloud solution for its data storage needs. The Chief Information Security Officer (CISO) is concerned about the potential risks associated with data residency and sovereignty. Which of the following should be the CISO's PRIMARY consideration to address these concerns?

   A. Ensuring the cloud provider offers data encryption at rest and in transit

   B. Verifying that the cloud provider has data centers in the same jurisdiction as the organization

   C. Implementing a robust data backup and recovery solution

   D. Conducting regular vulnerability assessments of the cloud environment

59. An organization is implementing a new system that will process and store Personally Identifiable Information (PII). The security team wants to ensure that unauthorized access to this data is prevented. Which of the following should be the organization's PRIMARY focus to achieve this goal?

   A. Implementing a strong password policy for system access

   B. Ensuring that data is encrypted both at rest and in transit

   C. Conducting regular security awareness training for employees

   D. Implementing a role-based access control (RBAC) system

60. A company is concerned about the increasing number of phishing attacks targeting its employees. The Chief Information Security Officer (CISO) wants to implement a solution to reduce the risk of employees falling victim to these attacks. Which of the following should be the company's PRIMARY strategy?

   A. Implementing an email filtering solution to block phishing emails

   B. Providing regular training and simulated phishing exercises for employees

   C. Implementing two-factor authentication (2FA) for all company systems

   D. Regularly updating and patching email servers.

61. A healthcare organization is planning to digitize its patient records. The Chief Information Security Officer (CISO) is concerned about the potential risks associated with the confidentiality and integrity of electronic health records (EHR). Which of the following should be the CISO's PRIMARY consideration to mitigate these concerns?

    A. Implementing a robust backup solution for the EHR system

    B. Ensuring that the EHR system is compliant with relevant healthcare regulations

    C. Implementing a strong password policy for EHR system access

    D. Regularly conducting vulnerability assessments of the EHR system

62. An organization is considering the use of a public Wi-Fi network for its remote employees to access company resources. The security team is concerned about the potential risks associated with public Wi-Fi. Which of the following should be the organization's PRIMARY focus to mitigate this risk?

    A. Implementing a Virtual Private Network (VPN) for remote access

    B. Providing training to employees on the risks of public Wi-Fi

    C. Implementing MAC address filtering on company devices

    D. Ensuring all company devices have updated antivirus software

63. A company is deploying a new web portal for its
     customers. The portal will store sensitive financial
     data, and the company wants to ensure the highest
     level of security. Which of the following should
     be the company's PRIMARY strategy to protect
     the data?

     A. Implementing a Content Delivery Network (CDN) to improve
         portal performance

     B. Conducting regular penetration testing on the web portal

     C. Implementing data encryption both at rest and in transit

     D. Implementing a CAPTCHA system to prevent
         automated attacks

64. A multinational corporation is expanding its
     operations to a country with strict data localization
     laws. The Chief Information Security Officer
     (CISO) is concerned about complying with these
     regulations while maintaining data accessibility for
     global operations. Which of the following should
     be the CISO's PRIMARY strategy to address this
     challenge?

     A. Implementing a hybrid cloud solution with data centers
         located in the new country

     B. Encrypting all data transmitted between the company's
         global offices

     C. Conducting a comprehensive risk assessment of the new
         country's IT infrastructure

     D. Implementing a strong access control policy for data
         originating from the new country

65. A company is transitioning its legacy applications to a microservices architecture. The security team wants to ensure that inter-service communications are secure. Which of the following should be the company's PRIMARY strategy to achieve this?

   A. Implementing an API gateway to manage inter-service communications

   B. Encrypting all data stored by the microservices

   C. Conducting regular vulnerability assessments of the microservices

   D. Implementing mutual TLS (mTLS) for inter-service communications

66. A financial institution is considering the adoption of a multi-cloud strategy to enhance resilience and avoid vendor lock-in. The Chief Information Security Officer (CISO) is concerned about the increased complexity and potential security risks. Which of the following should be the CISO's PRIMARY consideration to address these concerns?

   A. Implementing a centralized identity and access management (IAM) solution across all cloud providers

   B. Ensuring all cloud providers are compliant with industry-specific regulations

   C. Conducting regular backups of data across all cloud environments

   D. Implementing a uniform encryption standard across all cloud providers

67. An organization is deploying an Internet of
   Things (IoT) solution for its manufacturing plants.
   The security team is concerned about potential
   unauthorized access to these IoT devices. Which of
   the following should be the organization's PRIMARY
   focus to mitigate this risk?

   A. Implementing network segmentation to isolate IoT devices

   B. Regularly updating the firmware of the IoT devices

   C. Implementing strong authentication mechanisms for IoT
      device access

   D. Conducting regular security awareness training focused on
      IoT threats

68. A company is developing a new web application
   that will handle sensitive customer data. The
   development team wants to ensure that the
   application is resilient against cross-site scripting
   (XSS) attacks. Which of the following should be the
   company's PRIMARY strategy to achieve this?

   A. Implementing input validation for all user inputs in the
      application

   B. Conducting regular penetration testing focused on XSS
      vulnerabilities

   C. Implementing a web application firewall (WAF) with XSS
      filtering capabilities

   D. Providing training to the development team on secure coding
      practices

69. A retail organization is planning to deploy a new Point of Sale (POS) system across all its stores. The Chief Information Security Officer (CISO) is concerned about potential risks associated with credit card data theft. Which of the following should be the CISO's PRIMARY consideration to address these concerns?

   A. Ensuring the POS system is compliant with the Payment Card Industry Data Security Standard (PCI DSS)

   B. Implementing a strong password policy for all POS system users

   C. Regularly updating the firmware and software of the POS devices

   D. Implementing network segmentation to isolate the POS system from other networks

70. An organization is considering the use of containerization for its application deployment. The security team is concerned about potential risks associated with container escape vulnerabilities. Which of the following should be the organization's PRIMARY focus to mitigate this risk?

   A. Implementing a container orchestration platform with strong security features

   B. Regularly scanning container images for known vulnerabilities

   C. Implementing network segmentation between containers

   D. Providing training to the development team on secure container practices

71. A company is deploying a new cloud-based
    Customer Relationship Management (CRM)
    system. The security team wants to ensure that
    unauthorized access to customer data is prevented.
    Which of the following should be the company's
    PRIMARY strategy to achieve this?

    A. Implementing multifactor authentication (MFA) for CRM
       system access

    B. Regularly backing up customer data to a secure location

    C. Conducting regular vulnerability assessments of the
       CRM system

    D. Encrypting all customer data stored in the CRM system

72. A global organization is implementing a new video
    conferencing solution for its remote workforce.
    The Chief Information Security Officer (CISO) is
    concerned about potential eavesdropping and
    data interception during video calls. Which of
    the following should be the CISO's PRIMARY
    consideration to address these concerns?

    A. Ensuring the video conferencing solution supports end-to-
       end encryption

    B. Implementing a strong password policy for video
       conferencing rooms

    C. Regularly updating the video conferencing software to the
       latest version

    D. Implementing network segmentation for devices using the
       video conferencing solution

73. An organization is deploying an intrusion detection system (IDS) to monitor network traffic for malicious activities. The security team is concerned about potential false positives that might disrupt legitimate business operations. Which of the following should be the organization's PRIMARY focus to mitigate this risk?

    A. Regularly updating the IDS signature database

    B. Implementing a robust incident response plan

    C. Conducting regular security awareness training for employees

    D. Fine-tuning the IDS configuration based on the organization's network traffic patterns

74. A company is considering the adoption of a Software as a Service (SaaS) solution for its human resources (HR) department. The security team is concerned about potential data breaches and unauthorized access to employee data. Which of the following should be the company's PRIMARY strategy to address this concern?

    A. Implementing multifactor authentication (MFA) for the SaaS solution

    B. Regularly auditing the SaaS provider's security practices and compliance certifications

    C. Encrypting all data before uploading it to the SaaS platform

    D. Implementing strict access controls based on job roles within the HR department

75. A pharmaceutical company is developing a new cloud-based platform to store and analyze clinical trial data. The Chief Information Security Officer (CISO) is concerned about the potential risks associated with data integrity and unauthorized data manipulation. Which of the following should be the CISO's PRIMARY consideration to address these concerns?

    A. Implementing a digital signature mechanism for all data entries

    B. Conducting regular backups of the clinical trial data

    C. Implementing a strong password policy for all platform users

    D. Regularly updating the cloud platform's software components

76. An organization is planning to deploy a new ecommerce platform. The security team is concerned about potential distributed denial-of-service (DDoS) attacks that might disrupt the platform's availability. Which of the following should be the organization's PRIMARY focus to mitigate this risk?

    A. Implementing a Content Delivery Network (CDN) with DDoS protection capabilities

    B. Regularly scanning the ecommerce platform for vulnerabilities

    C. Implementing strict access controls for the platform's administrative interfaces

    D. Conducting regular security awareness training focused on DDoS threats

77. A company is transitioning its data analytics operations to a Big Data platform. The security team wants to ensure that sensitive data, such as Personally Identifiable Information (PII), is protected. Which of the following should be the company's PRIMARY strategy to achieve this?

    A. Implementing data masking techniques for sensitive data fields

    B. Regularly auditing user access logs for the Big Data platform

    C. Implementing a robust backup solution for the Big Data platform

    D. Conducting regular vulnerability assessments of the Big Data platform

78. A financial institution is implementing a new online banking platform. The Chief Information Security Officer (CISO) is concerned about potential risks associated with phishing attacks targeting their customers. Which of the following should be the CISO's PRIMARY consideration to address these concerns?

    A. Implementing a Secure Socket Layer (SSL) certificate for the online banking website

    B. Conducting regular phishing simulation exercises for customers

    C. Implementing multifactor authentication (MFA) for customer logins

    D. Regularly updating the online banking platform's software components

79. An organization is deploying a new enterprise resource planning (ERP) system. The security team is concerned about potential risks associated with insider threats. Which of the following should be the organization's PRIMARY focus to mitigate this risk?

A. Implementing strict access controls based on the principle of least privilege

B. Regularly scanning the ERP system for vulnerabilities

C. Implementing a robust backup solution for the ERP system

D. Conducting regular security awareness training focused on insider threats

80. A company is considering the adoption of a hybrid cloud infrastructure to support its growing IT needs. The security team wants to ensure that data movement between the on-premises environment and the cloud is secure. Which of the following should be the company's PRIMARY strategy to achieve this?

A. Implementing a Virtual Private Network (VPN) between the on-premises environment and the cloud

B. Regularly auditing the cloud provider's security practices and compliance certifications

C. Encrypting all data at rest in the cloud environment

D. Implementing strict access controls for data stored in the cloud

81. A healthcare institution is implementing a new electronic health record (EHR) system. The Chief Information Security Officer (CISO) is concerned about potential risks associated with unauthorized access to patient records. Which of the following should be the CISO's PRIMARY consideration to address these concerns?

    A. Implementing a robust audit logging mechanism for all access to the EHR system

    B. Regularly updating the EHR system to the latest version

    C. Implementing multifactor authentication (MFA) for EHR system access

    D. Conducting regular security awareness training focused on the importance of patient data privacy

82. An organization is planning to deploy an Internet-facing web application. The security team is concerned about potential risks associated with web application attacks, such as SQL injection and cross-site scripting (XSS). Which of the following should be the organization's PRIMARY focus to mitigate this risk?

    A. Implementing a web application firewall (WAF) with specific rules to detect and block such attacks

    B. Regularly backing up the web application data

    C. Implementing strict access controls for the web application's administrative interfaces

    D. Conducting regular code reviews to identify and fix vulnerabilities in the application code

83. A company is considering the use of a public cloud platform for its data storage needs. The security team wants to ensure that data confidentiality is maintained even if the cloud provider is compromised. Which of the following should be the company's PRIMARY strategy to achieve this?

   A. Implementing encryption for all data before uploading it to the cloud platform

   B. Regularly auditing the cloud provider's security practices and compliance certifications

   C. Implementing a Virtual Private Network (VPN) between the company's network and the cloud platform

   D. Implementing strict access controls for data stored in the cloud based on job roles

84. A manufacturing company is deploying an industrial control system (ICS) to manage its production line. The Chief Information Security Officer (CISO) is concerned about potential risks associated with cyber-physical attacks that could disrupt production. Which of the following should be the CISO's PRIMARY consideration to address these concerns?

   A. Implementing a dedicated network for the ICS, isolated from the corporate network

   B. Regularly updating the ICS software to the latest version

   C. Implementing multifactor authentication (MFA) for ICS system access

   D. Conducting regular security awareness training focused on the importance of ICS security

85. An organization is planning to deploy a Bring Your Own Device (BYOD) policy to allow employees to use their personal devices for work purposes. The security team is concerned about potential risks associated with data leakage. Which of the following should be the organization's PRIMARY focus to mitigate this risk?

   A. Implementing a Mobile Device Management (MDM) solution to control and monitor devices accessing corporate data

   B. Regularly backing up all data stored on employee devices

   C. Implementing a strong password policy for all devices accessing corporate data

   D. Conducting regular security awareness training focused on the risks of using personal devices for work

86. A company is considering migrating its customer database to a cloud-based solution. The security team wants to ensure that the company retains control over the encryption keys used to protect the data. Which of the following should be the company's PRIMARY strategy to achieve this?

   A. Implementing a hybrid cloud solution to keep sensitive data on-premises

   B. Regularly rotating the encryption keys used for data protection

   C. Using a Bring Your Own Key (BYOK) approach for data encryption in the cloud

   D. Implementing strict access controls for data stored in the cloud based on job roles

771

87. A retail company is deploying a new Point of
    Sale (POS) system across its stores. The Chief
    Information Security Officer (CISO) is concerned
    about potential risks associated with credit card
    skimming attacks. Which of the following should be
    the CISO's PRIMARY consideration to address these
    concerns?

    A. Implementing end-to-end encryption for all credit card
       transactions

    B. Regularly updating the POS system software to the
       latest version

    C. Implementing multifactor authentication (MFA) for POS
       system access

    D. Conducting regular security awareness training focused on
       recognizing skimming devices

88. An organization is planning to integrate artificial
    intelligence (AI) into its cybersecurity operations.
    The security team is concerned about potential
    risks associated with adversarial attacks on the
    AI models. Which of the following should be the
    organization's PRIMARY focus to mitigate this risk?

    A. Implementing a robust backup solution for the AI
       system data

    B. Regularly retraining the AI models with updated and diverse
       datasets

    C. Implementing strict access controls for the AI system's
       administrative interfaces

    D. Conducting regular security awareness training focused on
       the risks of AI in cybersecurity

89. A company is considering the use of containerization for its software development and deployment. The security team wants to ensure that container images are free from vulnerabilities. Which of the following should be the company's PRIMARY strategy to achieve this?

   A. Implementing a strict access control policy for the container registry

   B. Regularly scanning container images for vulnerabilities using specialized tools

   C. Implementing a robust backup solution for the container data

   D. Conducting regular security awareness training focused on container security best practices

90. A multinational corporation is expanding its operations to a country with strict data residency laws. The Chief Information Security Officer (CISO) is concerned about potential risks associated with data sovereignty. Which of the following should be the CISO's PRIMARY consideration to address these concerns?

   A. Implementing data encryption for all data transmitted outside the country

   B. Storing and processing data locally within the country's borders

   C. Implementing multifactor authentication (MFA) for accessing data

   D. Conducting regular security awareness training focused on data residency regulations

91. An organization is planning to adopt a Zero Trust security model. The security team is concerned about potential risks associated with lateral movement attacks within the network. Which of the following should be the organization's PRIMARY focus to mitigate this risk?

    A. Implementing network segmentation based on roles and responsibilities

    B. Regularly updating all network devices to the latest firmware version

    C. Implementing a strong password policy for all network devices

    D. Conducting regular security awareness training focused on the principles of Zero Trust

92. A company is deploying a new IoT-based solution for its smart building infrastructure. The security team wants to ensure that the IoT devices cannot be easily compromised. Which of the following should be the company's PRIMARY strategy to achieve this?

    A. Implementing a dedicated network for IoT devices, isolated from the main corporate network

    B. Regularly rotating the passwords used by IoT devices

    C. Implementing a robust backup solution for the IoT system data

    D. Conducting regular security awareness training focused on IoT security best practices

93. A financial institution is deploying a new mobile banking application. The Chief Information Security Officer (CISO) is concerned about potential risks associated with man-in-the-middle (MITM) attacks during transactions. Which of the following should be the CISO's PRIMARY consideration to address these concerns?

A. Implementing SSL pinning for the mobile application

B. Regularly updating the mobile application to the latest version

C. Implementing multifactor authentication (MFA) for user logins

D. Conducting regular security awareness training focused on recognizing phishing attempts

94. An organization is transitioning to a cloud-based infrastructure. The security team is concerned about potential risks associated with shared resources in a multitenant environment. Which of the following should be the organization's PRIMARY focus to mitigate this risk?

A. Implementing a dedicated virtual private cloud (VPC) for the organization's resources

B. Regularly auditing the cloud provider's security practices and compliance certifications

C. Implementing strong password policies for cloud-based applications

D. Conducting regular security awareness training focused on cloud security best practices

775

95. A company is deploying a new web portal for its customers. The security team wants to ensure that user credentials are not exposed even if the database is compromised. Which of the following should be the company's PRIMARY strategy to achieve this?

    A. Implementing encryption for all data in transit and at rest

    B. Regularly rotating the encryption keys used for data protection

    C. Implementing salted hashing for user passwords

    D. Conducting regular security awareness training focused on password best practices

96. A pharmaceutical company is deploying a new research database containing sensitive patient data. The Chief Information Security Officer (CISO) is concerned about potential risks associated with unauthorized data access. Which of the following should be the CISO's PRIMARY consideration to address these concerns?

    A. Implementing strict access controls based on roles and responsibilities

    B. Regularly updating the database software to the latest version

    C. Implementing a robust logging and monitoring solution for all database activities

    D. Conducting regular security awareness training focused on data privacy regulations

97. An organization is planning to deploy a new intranet portal for internal communications. The security team is concerned about potential risks associated with cross-site request forgery (CSRF) attacks. Which of the following should be the organization's PRIMARY focus to mitigate this risk?

   A. Implementing a Content Security Policy (CSP) for the intranet portal

   B. Regularly scanning the intranet portal for vulnerabilities

   C. Implementing anti-CSRF tokens in all intranet portal forms

   D. Conducting regular security awareness training focused on recognizing phishing attempts

98. A company is deploying a new online collaboration platform for its remote workforce. The security team wants to ensure that data shared on the platform remains confidential, even if accessed by unauthorized individuals. Which of the following should be the company's PRIMARY strategy to achieve this?

   A. Implementing end-to-end encryption for all data shared on the platform

   B. Regularly rotating the passwords used by employees to access the platform

   C. Implementing a robust backup solution for the collaboration platform data

   D. Conducting regular security awareness training focused on sharing best practices

Answers

1. Answer: C. Data custodian

   Explanation: The data custodian holds technical responsibility for data and is responsible for the custody of systems and databases. The data owner/controller is accountable for the protection of data, the data processor processes data on behalf of the owner/controller, the data steward holds business responsibility for data, and the data subject is the individual to whom personal data pertains.

2. Answer: C. Onion network

   Explanation: An onion network provides complete confidentiality and anonymity through the use of multiple layers of encryption. By providing confidentiality of data as well as anonymity, an onion network makes it very difficult to determine the sender and receiver while data is in transit. The other options do not provide the same level of anonymity.

3. Answer: D. All of the above

   Explanation: Data loss prevention (DLP) focuses on identifying, monitoring, and protecting data in all three contexts: data in use, data in motion, and data at rest. In each context, DLP tools attempt to detect and prevent data breaches and potential data exfiltration.

4. Answer: A. Labeling refers to the classification of the asset and is system readable, while marking refers to the handling instructions of the asset and is human readable.

    Explanation: In the context of asset classification, labeling pertains to the classification level of the asset and is designed to be read by systems. On the other hand, marking provides handling instructions for the asset and is intended to be read by humans.

5. Answer: C. Fabricating data

    Explanation: Fabricating data involves creating fake data to replace real or sensitive data. This method is used to protect sensitive information by replacing it with fictitious data, making it difficult for unauthorized individuals to discern the real data.

6. Answer: C. Data in use

    Explanation: Data in use refers to data that is actively being used in some type of computational activity, such as processing or computation. It is distinct from data at rest, which is stored somewhere, and data in transit, which is moving across networks.

7. Answer: B. Need to know

    Explanation: The "need-to-know" principle emphasizes that access should be restricted only to those individuals who require the information to perform their job functions. While "least privilege" is about granting only the minimum permissions required, and "separation of duties" ensures that more than one person is needed to complete a task, "rule-based access control" is a type of discretionary access control based on rules.

8. Answer: C. Crossover error rate

Explanation: The crossover error rate (CER) is a metric used to measure the accuracy of a biometric system. It represents the point where Type 1 (false reject) errors intersect with Type 2 (false acceptance) errors. A number closer to zero indicates a more accurate system.

9. Answer: D. SAML

Explanation: Security Assertion Markup Language (SAML) is a key federated access protocol used in Federated Identity Management (FIM) solutions. It provides both authentication and authorization, and its assertions are written in XML. While OAuth provides authorization and OpenID provides authentication, Kerberos is a major SSO authentication protocol but is not primarily used for federated access.

10. Answer: C. Kerberos

Explanation: Kerberos is an authentication protocol that uses tickets and symmetric key cryptography to allow users to authenticate once and gain access to multiple services without the need to reauthenticate. OAuth 2.0 is an authorization framework, SAML is used for both authentication and authorization in Federated Identity systems, and OpenID Connect is an identity layer on top of OAuth 2.0.

11. Answer: B. Role-based access control (RBAC)

    Explanation: Role-based access control (RBAC) is an access control model where access decisions are based on the user's role within the organization. Users are assigned to roles, and permissions are assigned to roles. DAC is based on the discretion of the owner, MAC uses labels to determine access, and ABAC uses attributes of the user, resource, environment, and action.

12. Answer: C. Password history

    Explanation: Password history is a policy that keeps track of a user's previous passwords to ensure they don't reuse them. This prevents attackers from using old passwords that might have been compromised. Password complexity requires a mix of characters, password length specifies a minimum number of characters, and password age determines how often a password must be changed.

13. Answer: B. Systems should trust entities only after they have been authenticated and authorized.

    Explanation: The "Zero Trust" principle is based on the premise that organizations should not automatically trust anything, whether internal or external. Before granting access, entities must be authenticated and authorized.

14. Answer: C. Brewer-Nash (the Chinese Wall)

    Explanation: The Brewer-Nash model, also known as "the Chinese Wall" model, has its primary goal set on preventing conflicts of interest. It ensures that departments or entities, such as development and production, do not influence each other or allow access between them.

15. Answer: B. Firewall rulesets

Explanation: The trusted computing base (TCB) encompasses all the security controls implemented to protect an architecture. It includes components like hardware, firmware, and software processes that make up the security system. While firewalls play a role in security, their specific rulesets are not considered a core component of the TCB.

16. Answer: C. Digital signatures

Explanation: Digital signatures are cryptographic mechanisms that provide data integrity and authentication. They allow the recipient of a message to verify the sender's identity and ensure that the message has not been tampered with. While encryption mechanisms (both symmetric and asymmetric) provide confidentiality, digital signatures focus on integrity without necessarily encrypting the data.

17. Answer: D. Trusted Platform Module (TPM)

Explanation: The Common Criteria (CC) consists of several components, including Protection Profiles (PP), Security Target (ST), and Evaluation Assurance Levels (EAL). The Trusted Platform Module (TPM) is a hardware-based security feature used for secure key storage and cryptographic operations but is not a component of the Common Criteria.

18. Answer: B. A conceptual piece of the system that mediates all access to objects by subjects

Explanation: A reference monitor is an abstract concept in security architecture. It is responsible for mediating all access requests (from subjects) to resources (objects) and ensuring that these requests comply with the system's security policy. It is not a tool, database, or module as described in the other options.

19. Answer: C. Report the vulnerability to the appropriate team or authority within the organization

Explanation: The ISC2 Code of Professional Ethics emphasizes the protection of society, the common good, and the infrastructure. Sharing vulnerabilities publicly or exploiting them can harm the organization and society at large. Ignoring the vulnerability does not align with acting responsibly. Reporting the vulnerability to the appropriate authority ensures that it can be addressed in a controlled and secure manner.

20. Answer: B. To provide a model for designing, structuring, and implementing security functions

Explanation: The CIA triad stands for confidentiality, integrity, and availability. It is a foundational model that helps organizations design, structure, and implement security functions. The other options, while important in the realm of cybersecurity, are not the primary purpose of the CIA triad.

21. Answer: B. Any potential danger that can cause damage to an asset

Explanation: A "threat" refers to any potential danger that can cause damage to an asset. Option A describes a "vulnerability," option C describes a "threat agent," and option D describes "exposure" or "impact."

22. Answer: B. Establishing a strategic framework for risk-based decision-making

Explanation: Security governance pertains to the establishment of a strategic framework that guides the organization's approach to security and risk management. While governance might influence the other options, its primary role is not about the day-to-day operations, specific control implementations, or solely ensuring external compliance.

23. Answer: B. $50,000

Explanation: The annualized loss expectancy (ALE) is calculated by multiplying the annual rate of occurrence (ARO) with the single loss expectancy (SLE). In this case, 5 (ARO) × $10,000 (SLE) = $50,000.

24. Answer: D. Casual

Explanation: Data classification levels are used to categorize information based on its sensitivity and the impact to the organization if it were disclosed, altered, or unavailable. "Confidential," "Public," and "Restricted" are common classification levels. "Casual" is not a standard classification level in most organizational data classification schemes.

25. Answer: C. Mitigation to contain and minimize the damage or impact from the incident

Explanation: The incident response process follows a sequence of steps. After the impact assessment, the next priority is mitigation to contain the damage and prevent further harm. Remediation and recovery come after mitigation, and reporting occurs throughout the process.

26. Answer: C. To ensure that the original evidence remains uncontaminated

Explanation: In digital forensics, it's crucial to work on a copy of the original evidence to ensure that the original data remains uncontaminated. This allows for accurate analysis without compromising the integrity of the original evidence.

27. Answer: C. Real-time prevention of security breaches

Explanation: SIEM systems are designed for log aggregation, normalization, correlation, secure storage, analysis, and reporting. While they can detect and alert on potential security issues, they do not inherently prevent breaches in real time.

28. Answer: A. Implementing biometric authentication at all entry points

Explanation: While all the options might enhance security in various ways, the question specifically addresses physical access. Implementing biometric authentication at all entry points directly addresses this concern by ensuring that only authorized individuals can gain physical access to the data center.

29. Answer: B. IPS can take active measures to block or prevent malicious activity.

    Explanation: Both IPS and IDS can detect potential threats, and both provide logs and reports. The primary distinction between them is that an IPS can take active measures to block or prevent malicious activity, whereas an IDS primarily detects and alerts.

30. Answer: C. To prioritize the recovery of systems based on their criticality to business operations

    Explanation: A business impact analysis (BIA) is primarily concerned with understanding the potential effects of an interruption to the organization's operations. Its main objective is to prioritize the recovery of systems and processes based on their importance to the business. While it might touch on financial implications, vulnerabilities, and compliance, its primary focus is on the criticality of systems.

31. Answer: A. To randomize the locations where system executables are loaded into memory

    Explanation: ASLR is a security technique designed to prevent buffer overflow attacks by randomizing the locations where system executables are loaded into memory. This makes it difficult for an attacker to predict the location of specific functions or buffers that they might try to exploit. Option B is incorrect because ASLR has nothing to do with the waterfall model of software development. Option C refers to the Capability Maturity Model (CMM), not ASLR. Option D describes the function of Application Programming Interfaces (APIs), not ASLR.

32. Answer: C. A model that provides a way to analyze and improve software security posture throughout the software life cycle

   Explanation: The Software Assurance Maturity Model (SAMM) by OWASP is designed to offer a structured approach for organizations to analyze and enhance their software security posture. It supports the complete software life cycle and is both technology and process agnostic. Option A is incorrect because SAMM supports the entire software life cycle, not just the development phase. Option B is incorrect as SAMM is technology and process agnostic. Option D is not the primary focus of SAMM.

33. Answer: C. The instantiation of something into multiple separate or independent instances

   Explanation: Polyinstantiation refers to the creation of multiple separate or independent instances of something. It can be used in databases to prevent unauthorized inference, allowing the same data to exist at different classification levels. Option A describes polymorphism in the context of malicious software. Option B defines code obfuscation. Option D describes the Agile development methodology.

34. Answer: C. A static library is accessed during
     program build, while a dynamic library is accessed
     during program execution.

     Explanation: A static library is incorporated into a
     program during its build phase, resulting in a larger
     executable size. In contrast, a dynamic library is
     loaded and linked during the program's execution,
     allowing multiple programs to share a single copy
     of the library. Option A is the opposite of the correct
     answer. Option B is not always true, as the size
     depends on the content of the library. Option D is
     incorrect because the modifiability of a library is not
     determined by its type (static or dynamic).

35. Answer: C. Agile

     Explanation: The Agile methodology emphasizes
     dividing the development process into multiple
     rapid iterations, often called "sprints." Throughout
     these iterations, there's a strong emphasis on
     customer feedback and interaction to ensure the
     product meets the user's needs. Option A, Waterfall,
     is a phased approach where one phase must be
     completed before moving to the next. Option B,
     Spiral Method, is risk-driven and combines iterative
     development with elements of the waterfall model.
     Option D, Structured Programming Development,
     focuses on improving clarity, quality, and
     development time through a logical programming
     approach.

36. Answer: C. An integrated approach where team members from development, operations, and other relevant areas collaborate from the beginning of a project

Explanation: DevOps is a cultural and professional movement that emphasizes collaboration between software developers (Dev) and IT operations (Ops) teams. The goal is to break down silos, improve communication, and streamline the process from development to deployment. Option A is a description of code obfuscation, not DevOps. Option B describes the Capability Maturity Model (CMM). Option D describes the Cleanroom development process.

37. Answer: B. Implement a password complexity policy.

Explanation: Correct Answer (B) – Implement a password complexity policy:

The question specifically highlights the issue of employees using weak passwords. A password complexity policy directly addresses this issue by enforcing rules on the creation of passwords, such as requiring a mix of uppercase and lowercase letters, numbers, and special characters. This ensures that passwords are strong and not easily guessable or crackable.

Incorrect Answer (A) – Conduct regular security awareness training for employees:

While security awareness training is essential and can educate employees about the importance of strong passwords, it does not enforce any technical controls to prevent the use of weak passwords. Employees might still choose weak passwords despite being aware of the risks.

Incorrect Answer (C) – Limit the number of login attempts:

Limiting login attempts is a measure to prevent brute-force attacks, where attackers try multiple password combinations to gain access. While this is a good security practice, it does not directly address the issue of employees choosing weak passwords in the first place.

Incorrect Answer (D) – Monitor network traffic for suspicious activity:

Monitoring network traffic is a proactive measure to detect potential security threats or breaches. However, it does not prevent the use of weak passwords. Even if suspicious activity is detected, it might be too late if an attacker has already exploited a weak password to gain access.

38. Answer: C. Data sovereignty and compliance

Explanation: Correct Answer (C) – Data sovereignty and compliance:

When migrating to a cloud environment, understanding where the data resides and ensuring it complies with local and international regulations is crucial. Data sovereignty refers to the concept that

data is subject to the laws of the country in which it
is located. Ensuring compliance can be challenging
in cloud environments where data might be stored
in multiple locations or countries.

Incorrect Answer (A) – Scalability of the cloud
environment:

While scalability is a significant advantage of cloud
environments, it is not primarily a security concern.
Scalability refers to the ability of the system to
handle increased workloads.

Incorrect Answer (B) – Integration with existing
applications:

Integration is more of a technical and operational
concern rather than a primary security concern.
While there might be security implications, the
question specifically asks for the primary security
concern.

Incorrect Answer (D) – Cost-effectiveness of the
migration:

Cost-effectiveness is a financial concern and not
directly related to security. While cost can influence
security decisions, it is not the primary security
concern in this context.

39.   Answer: C. Digital signature

Explanation: Correct Answer (C) – Digital signature:

Digital signatures are cryptographic tools specifically designed to ensure the integrity and authenticity of a message. They allow the receiver to verify that the message has not been altered during transit and that it indeed comes from the claimed sender.

Incorrect Answer (A) – Symmetric encryption:

Symmetric encryption is primarily used for confidentiality, ensuring that only authorized parties can read the message.

Incorrect Answer (B) – Asymmetric encryption:

Asymmetric encryption, while it can be used in conjunction with digital signatures, is primarily used for confidentiality and secure key exchange.

Incorrect Answer (D) – Key exchange:

Key exchange methods, like Diffie-Hellman, are used to securely exchange cryptographic keys over an insecure medium. They do not ensure the integrity of a message.

40.   Answer: C. Administrative control

Explanation: Correct Answer (C) – Administrative control:

Administrative controls, also known as procedural controls, are policies and procedures established by an organization's directives. A policy requiring background checks is a procedural measure and falls under administrative controls.

Incorrect Answer (A) – Technical control:

Technical controls involve the use of technology to mitigate vulnerabilities. Examples include firewalls, encryption, and intrusion detection systems.

Incorrect Answer (B) – Physical control:

Physical controls are measures taken to protect physical assets. Examples include locks, fences, and security guards.

Incorrect Answer (D) – Detective control:

Detective controls are designed to detect and respond to incidents or policy violations. Examples include intrusion detection systems and audit trails.

41. Answer: B. Recovery time objective (RTO)

Explanation: Correct Answer (B) – Recovery time objective (RTO):

The RTO is a metric that defines the maximum acceptable length of time that can elapse from when a disruption occurs until when the system must be fully operational again. It directly addresses the concern raised in the question.

Incorrect Answer (A) – Recovery point objective (RPO):

The RPO is a metric that defines the maximum· acceptable amount of data loss measured in time. It does not directly address the time it would take to recover from a disaster.

Incorrect Answer (C) – Business impact analysis (BIA):

A BIA is a process that identifies and evaluates the potential effects of an interruption to critical business operations. While it's an important part of continuity planning, it doesn't directly address the time to recover from a disaster.

Incorrect Answer (D) – Incident response plan (IRP):

An IRP is a plan for responding to a cybersecurity incident methodically. While it's an important part of an organization's overall security posture, it doesn't directly address the time to recover from a disaster.

42. Answer: A. Users should be given only the minimum levels of access necessary to perform their job functions.

Explanation: Correct Answer (A) – Users should be given only the minimum levels of access necessary to perform their job functions:

The principle of least privilege (PoLP) is a computer security concept in which a user is given the minimum levels of access necessary to complete their job functions. This principle is used to reduce the potential damage caused by a user's actions, whether unintentional or malicious.

Incorrect Answer (B) – Users should be given full access to all systems and data, but their activities should be logged and audited:

This approach contradicts the principle of least privilege. While logging and auditing are important, they do not replace the need for access controls.

Incorrect Answer (C) – Users should be given access based on their seniority within the organization:

Access should be based on job function, not seniority. A senior executive might not need access to sensitive systems if it's not part of their job function.

Incorrect Answer (D) – Users should be given access to systems and data based on their job title:

While job title can give an indication of the access a user might need, it's not always accurate. Access should be based on the actual job functions a user performs.

43.   Answer: C. To provide an area where public-facing servers can be placed

Explanation: Correct Answer (C) – To provide an area where public-facing servers can be placed:

A DMZ is a physical or logical subnetwork that contains and exposes an organization's external-facing services to a larger, untrusted network (usually the Internet). The purpose is to add an additional layer of security to an organization's Local Area Network (LAN).

Incorrect Answer (A) – To provide a secure area for sensitive data storage:

A DMZ is not typically used for storing sensitive data. Sensitive data should be stored in a secure area of the network with strong access controls, not in a zone that is exposed to a larger, untrusted network.

Incorrect Answer (B) – To provide an area isolated from the network for incident response:

While isolating affected systems is a common incident response strategy, a DMZ is not designed for this purpose.

Incorrect Answer (D) – To provide an area for the internal network infrastructure:

The DMZ is designed to be a buffer zone between the public Internet and the internal network. It's not typically where the internal network infrastructure is located.

44. Answer: B. Develop an incident response (IR) plan

Explanation: Correct Answer (B) – Develop an incident response (IR) plan:

The question scenario specifically points out that the company lacks a formal process for managing and responding to security incidents. An incident response (IR) plan directly addresses this gap by providing a structured approach for handling and managing security incidents. It includes steps like incident identification, containment, eradication, recovery, and lessons learned.

Incorrect Answer (A) – Implement a security information and event management (SIEM) system:

While a SIEM system can help in identifying and correlating security events, it does not provide a process for responding to these incidents. Without a formal IR plan, the company may not effectively use the SIEM system to its full potential.

Incorrect Answer (C) – Conduct a penetration testing exercise:

Penetration testing is a proactive measure to identify vulnerabilities in the system. However, it does not provide a process for responding to security incidents. Even if vulnerabilities are identified, without an IR plan, the company may not effectively respond to incidents resulting from these vulnerabilities.

Incorrect Answer (D) – Implement an intrusion prevention system (IPS):

An IPS can help in preventing security incidents, but it does not provide a process for managing and responding to incidents that do occur. It is a preventive measure, not a response measure.

45. Answer: A. Implementing a Cloud Access Security Broker (CASB)

Explanation: Correct Answer (A) – Implementing a Cloud Access Security Broker (CASB):

A CASB can provide visibility into cloud applications, enforce security policies, and detect and respond to potential threats. It can also assist with data loss prevention and enable forensic investigations, directly addressing the CISO's concerns.

Incorrect Answer (B) – Ensuring the cloud provider offers strong Service-Level Agreements (SLAs):

While SLAs are important to ensure the cloud provider meets certain standards of service, they do not directly address the CISO's concerns about data control and forensic investigations.

Incorrect Answer (C) – Conducting regular security audits of the cloud provider:

Regular audits can help ensure the cloud provider is adhering to security standards, but they do not provide real-time visibility or control over the organization's data, nor do they enable forensic investigations.

Incorrect Answer (D) – Implementing end-to-end encryption for emails:

While end-to-end encryption can protect the confidentiality of emails, it does not provide control over data or enable forensic investigations.

46. Answer: B. Conducting a thorough software security assessment before deployment

Explanation: Correct Answer (B) – Conducting a thorough software security assessment before deployment:

A software security assessment can identify potential vulnerabilities in the software before it is deployed, directly addressing the CISO's concerns. It is a proactive measure that can help prevent security incidents.

Incorrect Answer (A) – Implementing a robust intrusion detection system (IDS):

While an IDS can help detect potential security incidents, it does not prevent vulnerabilities in the software itself. It is a reactive measure, not a preventive one.

Incorrect Answer (C) – Ensuring the software vendor provides regular security updates:

Regular security updates are important, but they do not guarantee that the software is free of vulnerabilities at the time of deployment. Updates are typically reactive measures to known vulnerabilities.

Incorrect Answer (D) – Encrypting all customer data stored by the software:

While encryption can protect the confidentiality of customer data, it does not prevent vulnerabilities in the software itself.

47. Answer: C. Implementing a User and Entity Behavior Analytics (UEBA) solution

   Explanation: Correct Answer (C) – Implementing a User and Entity Behavior Analytics (UEBA) solution:

UEBA solutions use machine learning and advanced analytics to detect abnormal behavior or use of IT systems and data by users and entities, which can help detect and prevent insider threats.

Incorrect Answer (A) – Implementing a robust firewall and intrusion prevention system (IPS):

While these measures are important for overall network security, they are less effective at detecting and preventing insider threats, as these threats often involve legitimate users misusing their access.

Incorrect Answer (B) – Conducting regular security awareness training for employees:

While security awareness training is important, it may not be sufficient to prevent determined insider threats.

Incorrect Answer (D) – Regularly updating and patching all systems:

While this is a good security practice, it does not directly address the issue of insider threats.

48.   Answer: A. Implementing a Mobile Device Management (MDM) solution

Explanation: Correct Answer (A) – Implementing a Mobile Device Management (MDM) solution:

An MDM solution can provide centralized control and enforcement of security policies on employee devices, directly addressing the CISO's concerns about the BYOD policy.

Incorrect Answer (B) – Conducting regular security audits of employee devices:

While regular audits can help identify security issues, they do not provide real-time control or enforcement of security policies on the devices.

Incorrect Answer (C) – Implementing a strong password policy for all devices:

While a strong password policy is important, it does not address all the potential security risks associated with a BYOD policy, such as data leakage or malware.

Incorrect Answer (D) – Ensuring all data transmitted to and from the devices is encrypted:

While data encryption is important, it does not provide control over the devices or protect against risks such as device loss or theft.

49. Answer: A. Ensuring the cloud provider complies with relevant data protection regulations

Explanation: Correct Answer (A) – Ensuring the cloud provider complies with relevant data protection regulations:

Compliance with data protection regulations directly addresses the CISO's concerns about privacy risks. It ensures that the cloud provider has implemented necessary controls to protect customer data.

Incorrect Answer (B) – Implementing a robust intrusion detection system (IDS) for the cloud environment:

While an IDS can help detect potential security incidents, it does not address privacy concerns related to data protection regulations.

Incorrect Answer (C) – Conducting regular security audits of the cloud provider:

Regular audits can help ensure the cloud provider is adhering to security standards, but they do not guarantee compliance with specific data protection regulations.

Incorrect Answer (D) – Encrypting all customer data stored in the cloud:

While encryption can protect the confidentiality of customer data, it does not ensure compliance with data protection regulations.

50. Answer: B. Provide training to users on the importance of MFA

Explanation: Correct Answer (B) – Provide training to users on the importance of MFA:

Training can help users understand the importance of MFA in protecting their accounts and the organization's data, which may reduce resistance to its use.

Incorrect Answer (A) – Disable MFA for users who find it inconvenient:

Disabling MFA would reduce the organization's security posture and expose it to increased risk.

Incorrect Answer (C) – Implement a Single Sign-On (SSO) solution:

While SSO can improve user convenience, it does not replace the need for MFA. SSO can still be compromised if a user's primary credentials are stolen.

Incorrect Answer (D) – Review and update the security policy:

While it's important to review and update security policies regularly, this does not address the immediate issue of user resistance to MFA.

51. Answer: D. Subscribing to a threat intelligence service

Explanation: Correct Answer (D) – Subscribing to a threat intelligence service:

Threat intelligence services provide real-time information about emerging threats, including zero-day exploits. This can help the company respond more quickly to such threats.

Incorrect Answer (A) – Implementing a robust patch management process:

While important, patch management may not be effective against zero-day exploits, as patches for these vulnerabilities may not be available immediately.

Incorrect Answer (B) – Conducting regular penetration testing:

Penetration testing is a proactive measure to identify vulnerabilities, but it may not identify zero-day exploits.

Incorrect Answer (C) – Implementing an intrusion prevention system (IPS):

While an IPS can help prevent known attacks, it may not be effective against zero-day exploits, which are unknown and unpatched vulnerabilities.

52. Answer: C. Conducting a thorough security assessment of the IoT devices before deployment

Explanation: Correct Answer (C) – Conducting a thorough security assessment of the IoT devices before deployment:

A security assessment can identify potential vulnerabilities in the IoT devices before they are deployed, directly addressing the CISO's concerns. It is a proactive measure that can help prevent security incidents.

Incorrect Answer (A) – Ensuring the IoT devices support the latest encryption standards:

While encryption is important for protecting data, it does not prevent vulnerabilities in the IoT devices themselves.

Incorrect Answer (B) – Implementing a robust intrusion detection system (IDS) for the IoT network:

While an IDS can help detect potential security incidents, it does not prevent vulnerabilities in the IoT devices themselves.

Incorrect Answer (D) – Ensuring the IoT devices are included in the company's regular patch management process:

While regular patching is important, it does not guarantee that the IoT devices are free of vulnerabilities at the time of deployment.

53. Answer: B. The ability of the WAF to accurately differentiate between legitimate traffic and attacks

Explanation: Correct Answer (B) – The ability of the WAF to accurately differentiate between legitimate traffic and attacks:

The effectiveness of a WAF in blocking mode depends on its ability to accurately differentiate between legitimate traffic and attacks. If it cannot do this effectively, it could block legitimate traffic (false positives), disrupting the operation of the web applications.

Incorrect Answer (A) – The potential impact on application performance:

While performance is a consideration, the primary purpose of a WAF is to protect the applications from attacks. If it cannot do this effectively, its impact on performance is a secondary concern.

Incorrect Answer (C) – The cost of the WAF solution:

While cost is always a consideration, the primary decision factor should be the effectiveness of the WAF in protecting the applications.

Incorrect Answer (D) – The ease of managing and maintaining the WAF:

While ease of management is important, the primary decision factor should be the effectiveness of the WAF in protecting the applications.

54. Answer: A. Provide training to employees on how to use the VPN

Explanation: Correct Answer (A) – Provide training to employees on how to use the VPN:

Training can help employees understand how to use the VPN, which may reduce resistance to its use and ensure that it is used correctly and effectively.

Incorrect Answer (B) – Implement a simpler security solution that does not require a VPN:

While simplicity is important, it should not come at the expense of security. A VPN provides a secure connection to the company network, which is especially important when accessing the network from a remote location.

Incorrect Answer (C) – Allow employees to opt out of using the VPN if they find it too difficult:

Allowing employees to opt out of using the VPN would expose the company to increased risk, as it would potentially allow unsecured connections to the company network.

Incorrect Answer (D) – Implement a two-factor authentication (2FA) solution in addition to the VPN:

While 2FA provides an additional layer of security, it does not address the issue of employees finding the VPN difficult to use.

55. Answer: B. Providing training and awareness sessions to employees about the importance of MFA

Explanation: Correct Answer (B) – Providing training and awareness sessions to employees about the importance of MFA:

Training and awareness sessions can help employees understand the importance of MFA in protecting their accounts and the company's data, which may reduce resistance to its use.

Incorrect Answer (A) – Implementing a Single Sign-On (SSO) solution in addition to MFA:

While SSO can improve user convenience, it does not replace the need for MFA. SSO can still be compromised if a user's primary credentials are stolen.

Incorrect Answer (C) – Allowing employees to opt out of MFA if they find it too inconvenient:

Allowing employees to opt out of MFA would reduce the company's security posture and expose it to increased risk.

Incorrect Answer (D) – Implementing a biometric authentication method as one of the factors in MFA:

While biometric authentication can add an additional layer of security, it does not address the issue of employee resistance to MFA.

56.   Answer: C. Implementing input validation for all user inputs in the web application

Explanation: Correct Answer (C) – Implementing input validation for all user inputs in the web application:

Input validation can prevent SQL injection attacks by ensuring that user inputs do not contain SQL code that can manipulate the application's database queries.

Incorrect Answer (A) – Implementing a web application firewall (WAF):

While a WAF can help protect against SQL injection attacks, it does not prevent the root cause of these attacks, which is the lack of input validation in the application.

Incorrect Answer (B) – Conducting regular security audits of the web application:

While regular security audits can help identify security issues, they do not provide real-time protection against SQL injection attacks.

Incorrect Answer (D) – Encrypting all data stored by the web application:

While data encryption can protect the confidentiality of data, it does not prevent SQL injection attacks, which manipulate the application's database queries.

57. Answer: B. Implement an email client that automatically encrypts emails

Explanation: Correct Answer (B) – Implement an email client that automatically encrypts emails:

An email client that automatically encrypts emails can reduce the complexity of the process for employees, increasing the likelihood of compliance with the policy.

Incorrect Answer (A) – Provide training to employees on how to encrypt their emails:

While training is important, it may not be sufficient to overcome the complexity of manual email encryption for all employees.

Incorrect Answer (C) – Allow employees to opt out of email encryption if they find it too complicated:

Allowing employees to opt out of email encryption would expose the company to increased risk, as it would potentially allow sensitive information to be transmitted without encryption.

Incorrect Answer (D) – Implement a two-factor authentication (2FA) solution for email access:

While 2FA provides an additional layer of security, it does not address the issue of employees finding email encryption difficult to use.

58.   Answer: B. Verifying that the cloud provider has data centers in the same jurisdiction as the organization

Explanation: Correct Answer (B) – Verifying that the cloud provider has data centers in the same jurisdiction as the organization:

Data residency and sovereignty concerns arise when data is stored in a different jurisdiction with different data protection laws. Ensuring that the cloud provider has data centers in the same jurisdiction directly addresses these concerns.

Incorrect Answer (A) – Ensuring the cloud provider offers data encryption at rest and in transit:

While data encryption is crucial for data security, it does not address data residency and sovereignty concerns.

Incorrect Answer (C) – Implementing a robust data backup and recovery solution:

While backups are essential for data availability, they do not address data residency and sovereignty concerns.

Incorrect Answer (D) – Conducting regular vulnerability assessments of the cloud environment:

While vulnerability assessments are important for security, they do not address data residency and sovereignty concerns.

59. Answer: D. Implementing a role-based access control (RBAC) system

Explanation: Correct Answer (D) – Implementing a role-based access control (RBAC) system:

RBAC ensures that only authorized individuals, based on their roles within the organization, have access to specific data. This directly addresses the concern of preventing unauthorized access to PII.

Incorrect Answer (A) – Implementing a strong password policy for system access:

While a strong password policy is essential, it does not specifically control which users have access to PII.

Incorrect Answer (B) – Ensuring that data is encrypted both at rest and in transit:

While encryption is crucial for data security, it does not prevent unauthorized access by authenticated users.

Incorrect Answer (C) – Conducting regular security awareness training for employees:

While security awareness training is important, it does not provide technical controls to prevent unauthorized access to PII.

60. Answer: B. Providing regular training and simulated phishing exercises for employees

Explanation: Correct Answer (B) – Providing regular training and simulated phishing exercises for employees:

811

Training and simulated phishing exercises can help employees recognize and respond appropriately to phishing attempts, directly addressing the human element, which is often the target of these attacks.

Incorrect Answer (A) – Implementing an email filtering solution to block phishing emails:

While email filtering can help reduce the number of phishing emails that reach employees, it may not catch all of them. Employees still need to be trained to recognize and respond to any that get through.

Incorrect Answer (C) – Implementing two-factor authentication (2FA) for all company systems:

While 2FA can prevent unauthorized access even if an attacker obtains user credentials, it does not prevent employees from falling victim to phishing attempts in the first place.

Incorrect Answer (D) – Regularly updating and patching email servers:

While this is a good security practice, it does not directly address the issue of employees being targeted by phishing attacks.

61. Answer: B. Ensuring that the EHR system is compliant with relevant healthcare regulations

Explanation: Correct Answer (B) – Ensuring that the EHR system is compliant with relevant healthcare regulations:

Compliance with healthcare regulations ensures that the EHR system has implemented necessary controls to protect patient data, directly addressing the CISO's concerns about confidentiality and integrity.

Incorrect Answer (A) – Implementing a robust backup solution for the EHR system:

While backups are essential for data availability, they do not directly address the confidentiality and integrity of the data.

Incorrect Answer (C) – Implementing a strong password policy for EHR system access:

While a strong password policy is essential, it does not specifically address the unique requirements of protecting electronic health records.

Incorrect Answer (D) – Regularly conducting vulnerability assessments of the EHR system:

While vulnerability assessments are important for security, compliance with healthcare regulations provides a comprehensive framework for protecting patient data.

62. Answer: A. Implementing a Virtual Private Network (VPN) for remote access

Explanation: Correct Answer (A) – Implementing a Virtual Private Network (VPN) for remote access:

A VPN provides a secure, encrypted tunnel for data transmission over public networks, directly addressing the security concerns associated with public Wi-Fi.

Incorrect Answer (B) – Providing training to employees on the risks of public Wi-Fi:

While training is important, it does not provide a technical solution to secure data transmission over public networks.

Incorrect Answer (C) – Implementing MAC address filtering on company devices:

MAC address filtering does not provide security for data transmission over public networks.

Incorrect Answer (D) – Ensuring all company devices have updated antivirus software:

While updated antivirus software is essential for device security, it does not secure data transmission over public networks.

63. Answer: C. Implementing data encryption both at rest and in transit

Explanation: Correct Answer (C) – Implementing data encryption both at rest and in transit:

Data encryption ensures that sensitive financial data remains confidential and is protected from unauthorized access or interception, directly addressing the primary security concern.

Incorrect Answer (A) – Implementing a Content Delivery Network (CDN) to improve portal performance:

While a CDN can improve performance, it does not directly address the security of sensitive financial data.

Incorrect Answer (B) – Conducting regular penetration testing on the web portal:

While penetration testing is crucial for identifying vulnerabilities, the primary concern of protecting sensitive financial data is best addressed by encryption.

Incorrect Answer (D) – Implementing a CAPTCHA system to prevent automated attacks:

While CAPTCHAs can prevent automated attacks like bots, they do not protect the confidentiality and integrity of sensitive financial data.

64. Answer: A. Implementing a hybrid cloud solution with data centers located in the new country

Explanation: Correct Answer (A) – Implementing a hybrid cloud solution with data centers located in the new country:

By having data centers in the new country, the company can ensure compliance with data localization laws while still integrating with its global IT infrastructure, directly addressing the CISO's concerns.

Incorrect Answer (B) – Encrypting all data transmitted between the company's global offices:

While encryption is essential for data security during transmission, it does not address data localization requirements.

Incorrect Answer (C) – Conducting a comprehensive risk assessment of the new country's IT infrastructure:

While risk assessments are crucial for understanding potential threats and vulnerabilities, they do not directly address the data localization challenge.

Incorrect Answer (D) – Implementing a strong access control policy for data originating from the new country:

While access control is important, it does not ensure compliance with data localization laws.

65. Answer: D. Implementing mutual TLS (mTLS) for inter-service communications

Explanation: Correct Answer (D) – Implementing mutual TLS (mTLS) for inter-service communications:

mTLS ensures that both parties in a communication are authenticated and that the communication itself is encrypted, directly addressing the security of inter-service communications in a microservices architecture.

Incorrect Answer (A) – Implementing an API gateway to manage inter-service communications:

While an API gateway can manage and route communications, it does not inherently ensure the security of those communications.

Incorrect Answer (B) – Encrypting all data stored by the microservices:

While data encryption at rest is important, it does not secure inter-service communications.

Incorrect Answer (C) – Conducting regular vulnerability assessments of the microservices:

While vulnerability assessments are important for identifying potential security issues, they do not provide real-time protection for inter-service communications.

66. Answer: A. Implementing a centralized identity and access management (IAM) solution across all cloud providers

Explanation: Correct Answer (A) – Implementing a centralized identity and access management (IAM) solution across all cloud providers:

A centralized IAM solution ensures consistent access controls and authentication mechanisms across multiple cloud environments, directly addressing the concerns of increased complexity and security risks.

Incorrect Answer (B) – Ensuring all cloud providers are compliant with industry-specific regulations:

While compliance is crucial, it does not directly address the challenges of managing security across multiple cloud providers.

Incorrect Answer (C) – Conducting regular backups of data across all cloud environments:

While backups are essential for data availability and integrity, they do not address the security challenges of a multi-cloud strategy directly.

Incorrect Answer (D) – Implementing a uniform encryption standard across all cloud providers:

While a uniform encryption standard is important, it does not provide a comprehensive solution to the challenges of managing access and identity across multiple cloud environments.

67. Answer: C. Implementing strong authentication mechanisms for IoT device access

Explanation: Correct Answer (C) – Implementing strong authentication mechanisms for IoT device access:

Ensuring that only authorized individuals or systems can access and control the IoT devices directly addresses the concern of unauthorized access.

Incorrect Answer (A) – Implementing network segmentation to isolate IoT devices:

While network segmentation can limit the potential impact of a compromised device, it does not prevent unauthorized access to the devices themselves.

Incorrect Answer (B) – Regularly updating the firmware of the IoT devices:

While firmware updates can patch known vulnerabilities, they do not provide real-time protection against unauthorized access attempts.

Incorrect Answer (D) – Conducting regular security awareness training focused on IoT threats:

While training is essential, it does not provide the technical controls necessary to prevent unauthorized access to IoT devices.

68. Answer: A. Implementing input validation for all user inputs in the application

Explanation: Correct Answer (A) – Implementing input validation for all user inputs in the application:

Input validation can prevent XSS attacks by ensuring that user inputs do not contain malicious scripts that can be executed in the context of the application.

Incorrect Answer (B) – Conducting regular penetration testing focused on XSS vulnerabilities:

While penetration testing can identify vulnerabilities, it does not provide a proactive defense against XSS attacks.

Incorrect Answer (C) – Implementing a web application firewall (WAF) with XSS filtering capabilities:

While a WAF can help protect against XSS attacks, it is a reactive measure. Input validation provides a proactive defense by preventing the introduction of malicious scripts in the first place.

Incorrect Answer (D) – Providing training to the development team on secure coding practices:

While training is crucial for building secure applications, it does not provide a specific technical solution to prevent XSS attacks.

69. Answer: A. Ensuring the POS system is compliant with the Payment Card Industry Data Security Standard (PCI DSS)

Explanation: Correct Answer (A) – Ensuring the POS system is compliant with the Payment Card Industry Data Security Standard (PCI DSS):

PCI DSS compliance ensures that credit card data is handled, processed, and stored securely, directly addressing the concerns of credit card data theft.

Incorrect Answer (B) – Implementing a strong password policy for all POS system users:

While a strong password policy is essential, it does not specifically address the unique requirements of protecting credit card data.

Incorrect Answer (C) – Regularly updating the firmware and software of the POS devices:

While regular updates can patch known vulnerabilities, they do not provide a comprehensive framework for protecting credit card data like PCI DSS does.

Incorrect Answer (D) – Implementing network segmentation to isolate the POS system from other networks:

While network segmentation can enhance security, ensuring PCI DSS compliance provides a holistic approach to credit card data protection.

70. Answer: B. Regularly scanning container images for known vulnerabilities

Explanation: Correct Answer (B) – Regularly scanning container images for known vulnerabilities:

Scanning container images for vulnerabilities can identify and address potential risks before deployment, directly mitigating the risk of container escape vulnerabilities.

Incorrect Answer (A) – Implementing a container orchestration platform with strong security features:

While a secure orchestration platform is important, it does not directly address the vulnerabilities within the container images themselves.

Incorrect Answer (C) – Implementing network segmentation between containers:

While network segmentation can limit the potential impact of a compromised container, it does not prevent container escape vulnerabilities.

Incorrect Answer (D) – Providing training to the development team on secure container practices:

While training is essential, it does not provide a real-time technical solution to identify and address container vulnerabilities.

71.   Answer: A. Implementing multifactor authentication (MFA) for CRM system access

Explanation: Correct Answer (A) – Implementing multifactor authentication (MFA) for CRM system access:

MFA ensures that users provide multiple forms of verification before accessing the CRM system, directly addressing the concern of unauthorized access.

Incorrect Answer (B) – Regularly backing up customer data to a secure location:

While backups are essential for data availability and recovery, they do not prevent unauthorized access to the CRM system.

Incorrect Answer (C) – Conducting regular vulnerability assessments of the CRM system:

While vulnerability assessments can identify potential security issues, MFA provides a direct control to prevent unauthorized access.

Incorrect Answer (D) – Encrypting all customer data stored in the CRM system:

While encryption is crucial for data security, it does not prevent unauthorized access by authenticated users.

72. Answer: A. Ensuring the video conferencing solution supports end-to-end encryption

Explanation: Correct Answer (A) – Ensuring the video conferencing solution supports end-to-end encryption:

End-to-end encryption ensures that data (in this case, video and audio streams) is encrypted from the sender's device and only decrypted at the receiver's device, directly addressing the concerns of eavesdropping and data interception.

Incorrect Answer (B) – Implementing a strong password policy for video conferencing rooms:

While a strong password policy can prevent unauthorized access to video conferencing rooms, it does not protect the data transmitted during the call.

Incorrect Answer (C) – Regularly updating the video conferencing software to the latest version:

While regular updates can patch known vulnerabilities, end-to-end encryption provides a direct solution to the CISO's concerns.

Incorrect Answer (D) – Implementing network segmentation for devices using the video conferencing solution:

While network segmentation can enhance security, it does not directly address the potential eavesdropping and data interception during video calls.

73.   Answer: D. Fine-tuning the IDS configuration based on the organization's network traffic patterns

Explanation: Correct Answer (D) – Fine-tuning the IDS configuration based on the organization's network traffic patterns:

By understanding and configuring the IDS based on the organization's typical network traffic, the likelihood of false positives can be reduced, directly addressing the team's concerns.

Incorrect Answer (A) – Regularly updating the IDS signature database:

While keeping the signature database updated is essential for detecting new threats, it does not directly address the issue of false positives.

Incorrect Answer (B) – Implementing a robust incident response plan:

While an incident response plan is crucial for addressing security incidents, it does not prevent the occurrence of false positives.

Incorrect Answer (C) – Conducting regular security awareness training for employees:

While training is essential, it does not provide a technical solution to reduce false positives in an IDS.

74. Answer: B. Regularly auditing the SaaS provider's
security practices and compliance certifications

Explanation: Correct Answer (B) – Regularly
auditing the SaaS provider's security practices and
compliance certifications:

By ensuring that the SaaS provider adheres to robust
security practices and has relevant compliance
certifications, the company can have confidence
in the security of the employee data stored on the
platform.

Incorrect Answer (A) – Implementing multifactor
authentication (MFA) for the SaaS solution:

While MFA is essential for preventing unauthorized
access, it does not provide a comprehensive
understanding of the SaaS provider's overall security
posture.

Incorrect Answer (C) – Encrypting all data before
uploading it to the SaaS platform:

While encryption is crucial, it does not provide
insights into the SaaS provider's internal security
practices and controls.

Incorrect Answer (D) – Implementing strict
access controls based on job roles within the HR
department:

While role-based access controls are important,
they do not address potential vulnerabilities or
weaknesses in the SaaS provider's infrastructure or
practices.

75. Answer: A. Implementing a digital signature mechanism for all data entries

Explanation: Correct Answer (A) – Implementing a digital signature mechanism for all data entries:

Digital signatures ensure the authenticity and integrity of data. By signing data entries, unauthorized modifications can be detected, directly addressing the concerns of data integrity and unauthorized data manipulation.

Incorrect Answer (B) – Conducting regular backups of the clinical trial data:

While backups are essential for data availability, they do not directly address the issue of data integrity and unauthorized manipulation.

Incorrect Answer (C) – Implementing a strong password policy for all platform users:

While a strong password policy can prevent unauthorized access, it does not ensure the integrity of the data once it's entered into the system.

Incorrect Answer (D) – Regularly updating the cloud platform's software components:

While regular updates can patch known vulnerabilities, they do not provide a mechanism to verify the integrity and authenticity of the data.

76. Answer: A. Implementing a Content Delivery Network (CDN) with DDoS protection capabilities

Explanation: Correct Answer (A) – Implementing a Content Delivery Network (CDN) with DDoS protection capabilities:

A CDN with DDoS protection can absorb and mitigate large volumes of malicious traffic, ensuring the availability of the ecommerce platform, directly addressing the concern of potential DDoS attacks.

Incorrect Answer (B) – Regularly scanning the ecommerce platform for vulnerabilities:

While vulnerability scanning is essential, it does not provide real-time defense against DDoS attacks.

Incorrect Answer (C) – Implementing strict access controls for the platform's administrative interfaces:

While access controls are crucial for security, they do not prevent or mitigate DDoS attacks.

Incorrect Answer (D) – Conducting regular security awareness training focused on DDoS threats:

While training is essential, it does not provide a technical solution to defend against DDoS attacks.

77. Answer: A. Implementing data masking techniques for sensitive data fields

Explanation: Correct Answer (A) – Implementing data masking techniques for sensitive data fields:

Data masking ensures that sensitive data is obfuscated, rendering it useless to unauthorized users, while still allowing the data to be used for analytics purposes. This directly addresses the concern of protecting sensitive data like PII.

Incorrect Answer (B) – Regularly auditing user access logs for the Big Data platform:

While auditing is important for detecting potential unauthorized access, it does not proactively protect the data itself.

Incorrect Answer (C) – Implementing a robust backup solution for the Big Data platform:

While backups are essential for data availability, they do not directly protect the confidentiality of sensitive data.

Incorrect Answer (D) – Conducting regular vulnerability assessments of the Big Data platform:

While vulnerability assessments are important for identifying potential security issues, data masking provides a direct solution to protect sensitive data.

78. Answer: C. Implementing multifactor authentication (MFA) for customer logins

Explanation: Correct Answer (C) – Implementing multifactor authentication (MFA) for customer logins:

MFA ensures that even if a customer's credentials are compromised through a phishing attack, an additional layer of authentication is required, directly addressing the concerns of phishing attacks.

Incorrect Answer (A) – Implementing a Secure Socket Layer (SSL) certificate for the online banking website:

While SSL ensures data encryption during transmission, it does not prevent phishing attacks where users are tricked into providing their credentials.

Incorrect Answer (B) – Conducting regular phishing simulation exercises for customers:

While simulations can raise awareness, they do not provide a technical control to prevent unauthorized access in the event of a successful phishing attack.

Incorrect Answer (D) – Regularly updating the online banking platform's software components:

While regular updates can patch known vulnerabilities, they do not directly address the risk of phishing attacks targeting customers.

79.   Answer: A. Implementing strict access controls based on the principle of least privilege

Explanation: Correct Answer (A) – Implementing strict access controls based on the principle of least privilege:

By ensuring that employees have only the access they need to perform their job functions, the risk of insider threats is directly mitigated.

Incorrect Answer (B) – Regularly scanning the ERP system for vulnerabilities:

While vulnerability scanning is essential, it does not specifically address the unique risks associated with insider threats.

Incorrect Answer (C) – Implementing a robust backup solution for the ERP system:

While backups are essential for data availability, they do not directly mitigate the risk of insider threats.

Incorrect Answer (D) – Conducting regular security awareness training focused on insider threats:

While training is crucial, implementing technical controls like strict access controls provides a more direct solution to the risk of insider threats.

80. Answer: A. Implementing a Virtual Private Network (VPN) between the on-premises environment and the cloud

Explanation: Correct Answer (A) – Implementing a Virtual Private Network (VPN) between the on-premises environment and the cloud:

A VPN ensures that data transmitted between the on-premises environment and the cloud is encrypted and secure, directly addressing the concern of secure data movement.

Incorrect Answer (B) – Regularly auditing the cloud provider's security practices and compliance certifications:

While auditing is important for understanding the cloud provider's security posture, it does not directly secure data in transit between the on-premises and cloud environments.

Incorrect Answer (C) – Encrypting all data at rest in the cloud environment:

While encryption at rest is crucial, it does not secure data during transmission between the on-premises environment and the cloud.

Incorrect Answer (D) – Implementing strict access controls for data stored in the cloud:

While access controls are important for data security, they do not address the security of data in transit between the on-premises and cloud environments.

81. Answer: C. Implementing multifactor authentication (MFA) for EHR system access

Explanation: Correct Answer (C) – Implementing multifactor authentication (MFA) for EHR system access:

MFA ensures that users provide multiple forms of verification before accessing the EHR system, directly addressing the concerns of unauthorized access to patient records.

Incorrect Answer (A) – Implementing a robust audit logging mechanism for all access to the EHR system:

While audit logging is essential for accountability and post-incident investigations, it does not proactively prevent unauthorized access.

Incorrect Answer (B) – Regularly updating the EHR system to the latest version:

While regular updates can patch known vulnerabilities, they do not provide a direct control against unauthorized access.

Incorrect Answer (D) – Conducting regular security awareness training focused on the importance of patient data privacy:

While training is crucial, MFA provides a direct technical control to prevent unauthorized access to patient records.

82. Answer: D. Conducting regular code reviews to identify and fix vulnerabilities in the application code

Explanation: Correct Answer (D) – Conducting regular code reviews to identify and fix vulnerabilities in the application code:

By reviewing the application code for vulnerabilities and fixing them, the organization can proactively address potential web application attacks at their source.

Incorrect Answer (A) – Implementing a web application firewall (WAF) with specific rules to detect and block such attacks:

While a WAF can provide an additional layer of defense, it is a reactive measure. Addressing vulnerabilities in the code provides a proactive defense.

Incorrect Answer (B) – Regularly backing up the web application data:

While backups are essential for data availability, they do not directly mitigate the risk of web application attacks.

Incorrect Answer (C) – Implementing strict access controls for the web application's administrative interfaces:

While access controls are crucial, they do not address the specific risks of SQL injection and XSS attacks.

83. Answer: A. Implementing encryption for all data before uploading it to the cloud platform

Explanation: Correct Answer (A) – Implementing encryption for all data before uploading it to the cloud platform:

By encrypting data before it's uploaded, the company ensures that even if the cloud provider is compromised, the data remains confidential as unauthorized parties cannot decrypt it.

Incorrect Answer (B) – Regularly auditing the cloud provider's security practices and compliance certifications:

While auditing is important for understanding the cloud provider's security posture, it does not directly ensure data confidentiality in the event of a compromise.

Incorrect Answer (C) – Implementing a Virtual Private Network (VPN) between the company's network and the cloud platform:

While a VPN ensures secure data transmission, it does not protect the confidentiality of data at rest in the cloud.

Incorrect Answer (D) – Implementing strict access controls for data stored in the cloud based on job roles:

While role-based access controls are important, they do not protect data confidentiality in the event the cloud provider itself is compromised.

84. Answer: A. Implementing a dedicated network for the ICS, isolated from the corporate network

Explanation: Correct Answer (A) – Implementing a dedicated network for the ICS, isolated from the corporate network:

Isolating the ICS from the broader corporate network ensures that potential cyber threats targeting the corporate environment do not impact the ICS, directly addressing the concerns of cyber-physical attacks.

Incorrect Answer (B) – Regularly updating the ICS software to the latest version:

While regular updates can patch known vulnerabilities, they do not provide a barrier against threats originating from the corporate network.

Incorrect Answer (C) – Implementing multifactor authentication (MFA) for ICS system access:

While MFA is essential for preventing unauthorized access, it does not segregate the ICS from potential threats on the corporate network.

Incorrect Answer (D) – Conducting regular security awareness training focused on the importance of ICS security:

While training is crucial, a dedicated and isolated network provides a direct technical control against cyber-physical threats.

85. Answer: A. Implementing a Mobile Device Management (MDM) solution to control and monitor devices accessing corporate data

Explanation: Correct Answer (A) – Implementing a Mobile Device Management (MDM) solution to control and monitor devices accessing corporate data:

An MDM solution allows the organization to enforce security policies, remotely wipe data, and monitor device compliance, directly addressing the concerns of data leakage on personal devices.

Incorrect Answer (B) – Regularly backing up all data stored on employee devices:

While backups are essential for data availability, they do not prevent data leakage from personal devices.

Incorrect Answer (C) – Implementing a strong password policy for all devices accessing corporate data:

While a strong password policy is crucial, it does not provide comprehensive control over data access and storage on personal devices.

Incorrect Answer (D) – Conducting regular security awareness training focused on the risks of using personal devices for work:

While training is essential, an MDM solution provides a direct technical control to mitigate the risk of data leakage on BYOD devices.

86. Answer: C. Using a Bring Your Own Key (BYOK) approach for data encryption in the cloud

Explanation: Correct Answer (C) – Using a Bring Your Own Key (BYOK) approach for data encryption in the cloud:

BYOK allows the company to retain control over the encryption keys, ensuring that only they have access to the keys used to encrypt and decrypt their data, directly addressing the concern of key control.

Incorrect Answer (A) – Implementing a hybrid cloud solution to keep sensitive data on-premises:

While a hybrid solution can provide more control, it does not specifically address the concern of controlling encryption keys for data that is stored in the cloud.

Incorrect Answer (B) – Regularly rotating the encryption keys used for data protection:

While key rotation is a best practice, it does not ensure that the company retains control over the keys if they are managed by the cloud provider.

Incorrect Answer (D) – Implementing strict access controls for data stored in the cloud based on job roles:

While access controls are essential, they do not address the specific concern of controlling the encryption keys used for data protection.

87. Answer: A. Implementing end-to-end encryption for all credit card transactions

Explanation: Correct Answer (A) – Implementing end-to-end encryption for all credit card transactions:

End-to-end encryption ensures that credit card data is encrypted from the point of entry (the POS terminal) until it reaches its destination, reducing the risk of skimming attacks capturing usable data.

Incorrect Answer (B) – Regularly updating the POS system software to the latest version:

While updates can patch known vulnerabilities, they do not directly protect against the physical threat of skimming devices.

Incorrect Answer (C) – Implementing multifactor authentication (MFA) for POS system access:

While MFA is essential for preventing unauthorized system access, it does not protect against the external threat of skimming devices capturing card data.

Incorrect Answer (D) – Conducting regular security awareness training focused on recognizing skimming devices:

While training is crucial, end-to-end encryption provides a direct technical control against the risk of skimming attacks.

88. Answer: B. Regularly retraining the AI models with updated and diverse datasets

Explanation: Correct Answer (B) – Regularly retraining the AI models with updated and diverse datasets:

Adversarial attacks aim to exploit weaknesses in AI models. By regularly retraining the models with diverse datasets, the organization can ensure that the models remain robust against such attacks.

Incorrect Answer (A) – Implementing a robust backup solution for the AI system data:

While backups are essential for data availability, they do not directly mitigate the risk of adversarial attacks on AI models.

Incorrect Answer (C) – Implementing strict access controls for the AI system's administrative interfaces:

While access controls are crucial, they do not address the specific risks of adversarial attacks on AI models.

Incorrect Answer (D) – Conducting regular security awareness training focused on the risks of AI in cybersecurity:

While training is essential, regularly retraining AI models provides a direct technical control to mitigate the risk of adversarial attacks.

89. Answer: B. Regularly scanning container images for vulnerabilities using specialized tools

    Explanation: Correct Answer (B) – Regularly scanning container images for vulnerabilities using specialized tools:

    Scanning container images ensures that they are free from known vulnerabilities, directly addressing the concern of deploying vulnerable containers.

    Incorrect Answer (A) – Implementing a strict access control policy for the container registry:

    While access controls are essential, they do not ensure that the container images themselves are free from vulnerabilities.

    Incorrect Answer (C) – Implementing a robust backup solution for the container data:

    While backups are essential for data availability, they do not directly ensure the security of container images.

    Incorrect Answer (D) – Conducting regular security awareness training focused on container security best practices:

    While training is crucial, scanning container images provides a direct technical control to ensure they are free from vulnerabilities.

90. Answer: B. Storing and processing data locally within the country's borders

Explanation: Correct Answer (B) – Storing and processing data locally within the country's borders:

To comply with data residency laws and address concerns about data sovereignty, data should be stored and processed locally, ensuring that it doesn't leave the country's jurisdiction.

Incorrect Answer (A) – Implementing data encryption for all data transmitted outside the country:

While encryption is essential for data security during transmission, it does not address data residency laws that require data to remain within specific geographical boundaries.

Incorrect Answer (C) – Implementing multifactor authentication (MFA) for accessing data:

While MFA is crucial for data access security, it does not address the specific requirements of data residency laws.

Incorrect Answer (D) – Conducting regular security awareness training focused on data residency regulations:

While training is essential to ensure employees are aware of regulations, storing and processing data locally provides a direct solution to data sovereignty concerns.

91. Answer: A. Implementing network segmentation based on roles and responsibilities

    Explanation: Correct Answer (A) – Implementing network segmentation based on roles and responsibilities:

    Network segmentation restricts access to only necessary resources based on roles, reducing the potential for lateral movement attacks within the network.

    Incorrect Answer (B) – Regularly updating all network devices to the latest firmware version:

    While firmware updates can patch known vulnerabilities, they do not directly prevent lateral movement within the network.

    Incorrect Answer (C) – Implementing a strong password policy for all network devices:

    While a strong password policy is crucial, it does not directly address the risk of lateral movement once an attacker gains initial access.

    Incorrect Answer (D) – Conducting regular security awareness training focused on the principles of Zero Trust:

    While training is essential, network segmentation provides a direct technical control against lateral movement attacks.

92.   Answer: A. Implementing a dedicated network for IoT devices, isolated from the main corporate network

Explanation: Correct Answer (A) – Implementing a dedicated network for IoT devices, isolated from the main corporate network:

By isolating IoT devices on a separate network, the company can reduce the risk of potential threats on the main corporate network affecting the IoT devices.

Incorrect Answer (B) – Regularly rotating the passwords used by IoT devices:

While password rotation is a best practice, it does not provide comprehensive protection against all potential threats targeting IoT devices.

Incorrect Answer (C) – Implementing a robust backup solution for the IoT system data:

While backups are essential for data availability, they do not directly protect IoT devices from being compromised.

Incorrect Answer (D) – Conducting regular security awareness training focused on IoT security best practices:

While training is crucial, isolating IoT devices on a dedicated network provides a direct technical control against potential threats.

93. Answer: A. Implementing SSL pinning for the mobile application

Explanation: Correct Answer (A) – Implementing SSL pinning for the mobile application:

SSL pinning ensures that the mobile application communicates only with the designated server, thereby reducing the risk of MITM attacks where attackers present fake certificates.

Incorrect Answer (B) – Regularly updating the mobile application to the latest version:

While regular updates can patch known vulnerabilities, they do not directly protect against MITM attacks that exploit certificate trust.

Incorrect Answer (C) – Implementing multifactor authentication (MFA) for user logins:

While MFA is essential for authentication security, it does not prevent MITM attacks that intercept and alter communication.

Incorrect Answer (D) – Conducting regular security awareness training focused on recognizing phishing attempts:

While training is crucial, SSL pinning provides a direct technical control against MITM attacks.

94. Answer: A. Implementing a dedicated virtual private cloud (VPC) for the organization's resources

Explanation: Correct Answer (A) – Implementing a dedicated virtual private cloud (VPC) for the organization's resources:

A VPC provides an isolated environment within the cloud, ensuring that the organization's resources are segregated from other tenants, directly addressing concerns of shared resource risks.

Incorrect Answer (B) – Regularly auditing the cloud provider's security practices and compliance certifications:

While auditing is important for understanding the cloud provider's security posture, it does not directly ensure resource isolation.

Incorrect Answer (C) – Implementing strong password policies for cloud-based applications:

While strong password policies are crucial, they do not address the specific risks associated with shared resources in a multitenant environment.

Incorrect Answer (D) – Conducting regular security awareness training focused on cloud security best practices:

While training is essential, a VPC provides a direct technical control to ensure resource isolation.

95. Answer: C. Implementing salted hashing for user passwords

Explanation: Correct Answer (C) – Implementing salted hashing for user passwords:

Salted hashing ensures that even if the database is compromised, attackers cannot easily reverse-engineer the original passwords, directly addressing the concern of credential exposure.

Incorrect Answer (A) – Implementing encryption for all data in transit and at rest:

While encryption is essential for data security, hashed passwords provide an additional layer of protection against reverse engineering.

Incorrect Answer (B) – Regularly rotating the encryption keys used for data protection:

While key rotation is a best practice, it does not provide protection against the exposure of user credentials in the event of a database compromise.

Incorrect Answer (D) – Conducting regular security awareness training focused on password best practices:

While training is crucial, salted hashing provides a direct technical control to protect user credentials.

96. Answer: A. Implementing strict access controls based on roles and responsibilities

Explanation: Correct Answer (A) – Implementing strict access controls based on roles and responsibilities:

Role-based access controls ensure that only authorized personnel can access sensitive patient data, directly addressing the concerns of unauthorized data access.

Incorrect Answer (B) – Regularly updating the database software to the latest version:

While regular updates can patch known vulnerabilities, they do not directly control who can access the data.

845

Incorrect Answer (C) – Implementing a robust logging and monitoring solution for all database activities:

While logging and monitoring are essential for accountability and post-incident investigations, they do not proactively prevent unauthorized access.

Incorrect Answer (D) – Conducting regular security awareness training focused on data privacy regulations:

While training is crucial, role-based access controls provide a direct technical control against unauthorized data access.

97. Answer: C. Implementing anti-CSRF tokens in all intranet portal forms

Explanation: Correct Answer (C) – Implementing anti-CSRF tokens in all intranet portal forms:

Anti-CSRF tokens ensure that requests made to the intranet portal are legitimate and not forged, directly addressing the concerns of CSRF attacks.

Incorrect Answer (A) – Implementing a Content Security Policy (CSP) for the intranet portal:

While a CSP can help prevent certain types of attacks, such as cross-site scripting (XSS), it does not directly protect against CSRF attacks.

Incorrect Answer (B) – Regularly scanning the intranet portal for vulnerabilities:

While vulnerability scanning is essential, anti-CSRF tokens provide a specific technical control against CSRF attacks.

Incorrect Answer (D) – Conducting regular security awareness training focused on recognizing phishing attempts:

While training is crucial, anti-CSRF tokens provide a direct technical control against CSRF attacks.

98. Answer: A. Implementing end-to-end encryption for all data shared on the platform

Explanation: Correct Answer (A) – Implementing end-to-end encryption for all data shared on the platform:

End-to-end encryption ensures that data remains encrypted from the sender to the recipient, ensuring its confidentiality even if intercepted by unauthorized individuals.

Incorrect Answer (B) – Regularly rotating the passwords used by employees to access the platform:

While password rotation is a best practice, it does not ensure the confidentiality of data shared on the platform.

Incorrect Answer (C) – Implementing a robust backup solution for the collaboration platform data:

While backups are essential for data availability, they do not directly ensure the confidentiality of shared data.

Incorrect Answer (D) – Conducting regular security awareness training focused on sharing best practices:

While training is crucial, end-to-end encryption provides a direct technical control to ensure data confidentiality.

CHAPTER 12

Final Lap: Comprehensive Exam and Preparation Approach

As this comprehensive guide nears its conclusion, it is both timely and prudent to engage in a reflective analysis of the extensive intellectual terrain traversed. The journey toward becoming a CISSP is a monumental undertaking, necessitating a considerable investment of time, effort, and intellectual rigor. This guide, *CISSP Exam Certification Companion: 1000+ Practice Questions and Expert Strategies for Passing the CISSP Exam*, has been your steadfast academic companion, offering an exhaustive exploration of CISSP domains, coupled with strategic exam preparation techniques and an extensive array of practice questions.

Your arrival at this terminal chapter is a testament to your unwavering commitment to professional excellence in the realm of information security. This guide was meticulously constructed to serve as a comprehensive road map through the multifaceted domains that constitute the CISSP certification. Each domain was dissected to provide you with a balanced blend of theoretical understanding, practical

© Mohamed Aly Bouke 2023   849
M. A. Bouke, *CISSP Exam Certification Companion*, Certification Study Companion Series,
https://doi.org/10.1007/979-8-8688-0057-3_12

application, and evaluative practice questions. From the intricacies of Security and Risk Management to the complexities of Software Development Security, each domain was designed to equip you with the requisite knowledge and skills to excel in the CISSP exam and beyond.

Reflecting on the Journey

Congratulations on reaching the final chapter of *CISSP Exam Certification Companion: 1000+ Practice Questions and Expert Strategies for Passing the CISSP Exam*. It is no small feat to cover such a vast body of knowledge, and by making it to this point, you have demonstrated a commendable commitment to your professional growth in the field of information security. Let's take a moment to look back at the ground we've covered:

- **Security and Risk Management**: In this crucial section, we delved into the world of security governance and compliance. We explored risk management concepts, learned about business continuity requirements, and discussed professional ethics in information security.

- **Asset Security**: This domain emphasized the importance of classifying and securing organizational assets. We discussed privacy considerations, retention requirements, and secure data handling requirements.

- **Security Architecture and Engineering**: Here, we focused on the design, implementation, and management of secure network architectures. We unpacked various cryptographic methods, looked at system security models, and delved into system vulnerability analysis.

- **Communications and Network Security**: This section was all about the secure design and protection of networks. We covered network architectures, end-to-end data communications, network attacks, and secure network components.

- **Identity and Access Management**: We examined identity and access services, scrutinized the identity and access provisioning life cycle, and investigated various access control models and techniques.

- **Security Assessment and Testing**: This chapter provided insights into the design and validation of test strategies. We explored the importance of security control testing, data collection methods, and the role of internal and third-party audits.

- **Security Operations**: Here, we dived into the operational aspects of information security. We discussed investigation techniques, incident management, and securing the provision of resources.

- **Software Development Security**: This final domain was dedicated to the integration of security in the Software Development Life Cycle. We explored security controls in development environments, the impact of software security vulnerabilities, and how to apply secure coding guidelines.

Concluding Remarks

The guide you hold, *CISSP Exam Certification Companion: 1000+ Practice Questions and Expert Strategies for Passing the CISSP Exam*, sets itself apart with an exhaustive array of practice questions. These questions are crafted with meticulous attention to mirror the structure and depth of the CISSP exam. They act as indispensable instruments for assessing your preparedness and understanding of each domain. To augment this, an entire chapter is dedicated to strategies for test-taking. This chapter provides crucial guidance on aspects such as time management, stress mitigation, and techniques for making educated guesses. Together, these components form the bedrock of your exam preparation.

Transitioning from exam preparation to long-term career development, it is important to note that earning the CISSP certification is a laudable milestone, yet it merely inaugurates your odyssey in the ever-evolving realm of information security. To maintain your edge, a commitment to perpetual learning is imperative. This can be achieved through various means – subscribing to industry news feeds, attending seminars, and participating in webinars, to name a few. Such activities not only deepen your domain knowledge but also offer opportunities for professional networking.

In the broader context, the CISSP certification stands as a powerful endorsement of your expertise and commitment to the field of information security. This globally acknowledged credential has the potential to substantially elevate your career, boosting both your earning prospects and job satisfaction. It attests to your ability to architect, enact, and oversee a resilient cybersecurity program, thereby establishing you as an invaluable resource in the field.

As you embark on this rigorous path toward CISSP certification, it is essential to recognize that the journey, albeit demanding, is replete with rewards. The certification equips you with the requisite skills to protect organizations from an array of security threats. Moreover, it inducts you into a community of like-minded professionals dedicated to maintaining the integrity of information systems. Throughout this endeavor, it is beneficial to perceive challenges as avenues for personal and professional growth. After all, the pursuit of mastery is more akin to a marathon than a sprint.

In conclusion, we extend our heartfelt gratitude for choosing *CISSP Exam Certification Companion: 1000+ Practice Questions and Expert Strategies for Passing the CISSP Exam* as your study companion. Your journey toward excellence in information security has already set sail. With continued diligence and focus, you are well on your way to achieving your career objectives.

Exam Questions Sample 2

As you continue your rigorous journey toward CISSP certification, the significance of diverse and challenging practice questions cannot be overstated. This second set of sample exam questions aims to further deepen your understanding of the intricate facets of information security. Designed to complement the first set, these questions introduce new scenarios and complexities that you may encounter on the actual CISSP exam. Engaging with this set will not only help you pinpoint areas that may require additional focus but also enhance your skills in critical thinking, time management, and effective question-answering. Consider this set as another stepping stone in your comprehensive preparation strategy.

1. Which of the following is generally NOT considered a key element in the context of a secure Software Development Life Cycle (SDLC)?

    A. Security requirements gathering

    B. Threat modeling

    C. Code review for security flaws

    D. User interface design

2. Which of the following is NOT generally considered a characteristic of a strong password?

   A. It includes both uppercase and lowercase letters.

   B. It is at least 12 characters long.

   C. It is updated regularly.

   D. It is based on a dictionary word.

3. Which of the following is generally NOT considered a key element in the context of a standard risk assessment?

   A. Threat identification

   B. Vulnerability assessment

   C. Asset valuation

   D. Cost-benefit analysis

4. Which of the following is generally NOT considered a primary function of an Identity and Access Management (IAM) system?

   A. Managing user accounts and permissions

   B. Providing Single Sign-On (SSO) capability

   C. Enforcing access control policies

   D. Data backup and recovery

5. Which of the following is generally NOT considered
    a key principle of security governance?

    A. Developing and implementing policies and procedures

    B. Ensuring compliance with laws and regulations

    C. Defining roles and responsibilities

    D. Incident response time optimization

6. Which of the following is generally NOT considered
    a type of security assessment?

    A. Threat assessment

    B. Vulnerability assessment

    C. Penetration test

    D. Software development assessment

7. Which of the following is NOT a key component of a
    risk assessment?

    A. Threat identification

    B. Vulnerability identification

    C. Asset identification

    D. Risk acceptance

8. Which of the following is NOT a function of a
    security information and event management
    (SIEM) system?

    A. Collecting and analyzing security-related data

    B. Providing real-time monitoring and alerting

    C. Generating reports on security-related events

    D. Encrypting data

9. Which of the following is NOT a type of encryption?

    A. Symmetric encryption

    B. Asymmetric encryption

    C. Hash encryption

    D. Keyless encryption

10. Which of the following is NOT a key principle of secure software development?

    A. Minimizing the attack surface

    B. Secure coding practices

    C. Regular software updates

    D. Outsourcing development

11. Which of the following is NOT a type of security assessment?

    A. Penetration testing

    B. Vulnerability assessment

    C. Risk assessment

    D. Social engineering assessment

12. Which of the following is NOT a factor that should be considered when developing a disaster recovery plan?

    A. The impact of a disaster on the organization

    B. The likelihood of a disaster occurring

    C. The availability of resources for recovery

    D. The budget of the organization

13. Which of the following is NOT a key component of a security incident response plan?

    A. Identification of the incident

    B. Containment of the incident

    C. Prevention of future incidents

    D. Provision of legal assistance

14. Which of the following is NOT a key principle of asset management?

    A. Identifying and classifying assets

    B. Establishing ownership and responsibility for assets

    C. Protecting assets from unauthorized access or tampering

    D. Ensuring that assets are used efficiently

15. Which of the following is NOT a key consideration when designing a secure system?

    A. Confidentiality

    B. Integrity

    C. Availability

    D. Usability

16. Which of the following is NOT a type of network attack?

    A. Denial-of-service (DoS) attack

    B. Man-in-the-middle (MITM) attack

    C. Phishing attack

    D. Router attack

17. Which of the following is NOT a function of an Identity and Access Management (IAM) system?

    A. Managing user accounts and permissions

    B. Providing Single Sign-On (SSO) capability

    C. Enforcing access control policies

    D. Monitoring and auditing user activity

18. Which of the following is NOT a common type of security control?

    A. Physical controls

    B. Technical controls

    C. Administrative controls

    D. Legal controls

19. Which of the following is NOT a key element of a business impact analysis (BIA)?

    A. Identifying the critical functions of the organization

    B. Estimating the potential impact of a disruption on the organization

    C. Developing a recovery plan

    D. Establishing a budget for recovery efforts

20. Which of the following is NOT a key principle of compliance?

    A. Adhering to laws and regulations

    B. Ensuring that security policies and procedures are followed

    C. Providing regular reports to regulatory bodies

    D. Outsourcing security functions

21. Which of the following is the MOST important reason to implement a password policy?

    A. To protect against unauthorized access

    B. To prevent data loss

    C. To ensure compliance with industry regulations

    D. To improve system performance

22. Which of the following is the MOST important reason to conduct regular backups of data?

    A. To protect against data loss

    B. To ensure compliance with industry regulations

    C. To improve system performance

    D. To prevent unauthorized access

23. Which of the following is the MOST important reason to implement access controls on a computer system?

    A. To protect against unauthorized access

    B. To ensure compliance with industry regulations

    C. To improve system performance

    D. To prevent data loss

24. Which of the following is the MOST important reason to conduct a risk assessment?

    A. To determine the likelihood of a risk occurring

    B. To assess the impact of a risk on the organization

    C. To prioritize risks based on their likelihood and impact

    D. To identify potential risks to the organization

25. Which of the following is the PRIMARY reason for creating a business continuity plan?

    A. To ensure the safety of employees

    B. To comply with industry regulations

    C. To reduce insurance costs

    D. To minimize the impact of a disaster on the business

26. What is the BEST description of a risk assessment?

    A. The process of managing security policies to influence behavior

    B. The security of an organization within a company

    C. The process of how an organization is managed

    D. The process of identifying and evaluating potential risks to an organization

27. What is the BEST description of a business continuity plan?

    A. The process of managing security policies to influence behavior

    B. The security of an organization within a company

    C. The process of how an organization is managed

    D. A document outlining the steps an organization should take to continue operating in the event of a disaster or other disruptions

28. What is the BEST description of a password policy?

    A. The process of managing security policies to influence behavior

    B. The security of an organization within a company

C. The process of how an organization is managed

D. A set of guidelines for creating and managing passwords

29. What is the BEST description of access controls?

A. The process of managing security policies to influence behavior

B. The security of an organization within a company

C. The process of how an organization is managed

D. Measures that restrict access to resources or information

30. What is the BEST description of data backup?

A. The process of managing security policies to influence behavior

B. The security of an organization within a company

C. The process of how an organization is managed

D. The process of creating copies of data for storage in a separate location

31. Which of the following BEST describes data sensitivity?

A. Data with a high level of criticality

B. Data classified as Top Secret

C. Data classified as public

D. Data classified according to the organization's data classification policy

32. Which of the following is the MOST accurate description of access controls?

   A. Access controls are a collection of technical controls that allow authorized users, systems, and applications to access resources or information.

   B. Access controls involve the use of encryption solutions to secure authentication information during log-on.

   C. Access controls help to protect against vulnerabilities by restricting unauthorized access to systems and information by employees, partners, and customers.

   D. Access controls reduce the risk of threats and vulnerabilities by limiting exposure to unauthorized activities and providing access to information and systems only to those who have been approved.

33. Which of the following is NOT a method used to conduct a vulnerability assessment?

   A. Network scanning

   B. Code review

   C. Social engineering

   D. Patch management

34. Which of the following is NOT a common goal of a penetration test?

   A. To identify vulnerabilities in an organization's systems, networks, and data

   B. To determine the likelihood of a successful cyberattack

    C. To evaluate the effectiveness of an organization's
       security controls

    D. To ensure compliance with industry regulations

35. In the context of information security, who is primarily
    responsible for protecting the data?

    A. The individual who owns the data

    B. The individual who uses the data

    C. The individual who is responsible for maintaining
       the data

    D. The individual who audits the data security measures

36. Which type of firewall is best suited for making
    decisions based on the IP address of the
    incoming packet?

    A. Circuit-level gateway

    B. Application-level gateway

    C. Packet filtering firewall

    D. Stateful inspection firewall

37. What is the primary benefit of using a Virtual Private
    Network (VPN)?

    A. To provide a secure communication channel over an
       untrusted network

    B. To increase the speed of data transmission

    C. To bypass network access controls

    D. To monitor network traffic

38. Which of the following best describes the principle of "least privilege"?

   A. Users should be given the minimum levels of access necessary to perform their duties.

   B. Users should be given only the access necessary to perform their duties.

   C. Users should be given temporary access that expires after a certain period.

   D. Users should be given access based on their seniority in the organization.

39. What is the primary goal of penetration testing?

   A. To identify vulnerabilities in a system before an attacker does

   B. To demonstrate the potential impact of a successful attack

   C. To test the effectiveness of security controls

   D. To comply with regulatory requirements

40. Which of the following is a key component of an incident response plan (IRP)?

   A. A list of potential vulnerabilities in the system

   B. A step-by-step guide for mitigating an incident

   C. A plan for communicating during and after an incident

   D. A list of approved software for the organization

41. What is the primary purpose of input validation in software development?

    A. To improve the user experience

    B. To prevent injection attacks

    C. To ensure the accuracy of the data

    D. To reduce the size of the software

42. Which of the following is the most effective strategy for managing risk?

    A. Accepting all risks

    B. Transferring all risks

    C. Mitigating risks to an acceptable level

    D. Avoiding all risks

43. What is the primary purpose of data classification?

    A. To determine the value of the data

    B. To determine the sensitivity of the data

    C. To determine the age of the data

    D. To determine the owner of the data

44. Which of the following is a key principle of secure system design?

    A. Complexity

    B. Open design

    C. Minimalism

    D. Obscurity

45. Which of the following is a common method for securing wireless networks?

    A. MAC address filtering

    B. Port scanning

    C. Packet sniffing

    D. IP spoofing

46. What is the primary purpose of multifactor authentication?

    A. To simplify the authentication process

    B. To increase the security of the authentication process

    C. To reduce the cost of the authentication process

    D. To speed up the authentication process

47. What is the primary difference between a vulnerability scan and a penetration test?

    A. A vulnerability scan is automated, while a penetration test is manual.

    B. A vulnerability scan is manual, while a penetration test is automated.

    C. A vulnerability scan identifies weaknesses, while a penetration test exploits them.

    D. A vulnerability scan exploits weaknesses, while a penetration test identifies them.

48. Which of the following is a common component of a business continuity plan (BCP)?

    A. A list of potential vulnerabilities in the system

    B. A step-by-step guide for mitigating an incident

C. A plan for maintaining operations during a disruption

D. A list of approved software for the organization

49. Which of the following is a common method for preventing SQL injection attacks?

A. Input validation

B. Code obfuscation

C. Code minification

D. Code refactoring

50. Which of the following best describes the term "due care" in the context of information security?

A. The legal obligation to implement reasonable security measures

B. The process of identifying potential threats

C. The act of transferring risk to another party

D. The process of accepting a certain level of risk

51. Which of the following is the primary purpose of data encryption?

A. To increase data storage efficiency

B. To ensure data integrity

C. To ensure data confidentiality

D. To ensure data availability

52. What is the primary purpose of a security policy?

A. To provide step-by-step instructions for security tasks

B. To define an organization's guiding security principles

C. To detail the technical controls in place

D. To outline the penalties for security violations

53. Which of the following best describes a demilitarized zone (DMZ) in network security?

A. A network segment that is isolated from all other networks

B. A network segment that is exposed to an untrusted network, usually the Internet

C. A network segment that contains only noncritical assets

D. A network segment that is heavily fortified with security controls

54. What is the primary purpose of role-based access control (RBAC)?

A. To grant permissions based on job functions

B. To grant permissions based on user attributes

C. To grant permissions based on security clearances

D. To grant permissions based on request

55. What is the primary goal of a security audit?

A. To identify vulnerabilities in a system

B. To test the effectiveness of security controls

C. To demonstrate compliance with regulations

D. To investigate a security incident

56. Which of the following is a key component of a disaster recovery plan (DRP)?

    A. A list of potential vulnerabilities in the system

    B. A step-by-step guide for resuming operations after a disaster

    C. A plan for maintaining operations during a disruption

    D. A list of approved software for the organization

57. What is the primary purpose of a secure coding standard?

    A. To ensure that the software is free of bugs

    B. To ensure that the software is developed on time

    C. To ensure that the software is developed within budget

    D. To ensure that the software is developed in a way that minimizes security risks

58. Which of the following best describes the concept of "defense in depth"?

    A. Implementing multiple layers of security controls throughout an IT system

    B. Defending against all possible threats

    C. Implementing the strongest possible security controls

    D. Defending against the most likely threats

59. What is the primary purpose of a data retention policy?

   A. To determine how long data should be retained before it is destroyed

   B. To determine who has access to the data

   C. To determine where the data is stored

   D. To determine how the data is used

60. What is the primary purpose of a proxy server?

   A. To provide a separate network segment for public-facing services

   B. To provide a layer of abstraction and control over the data flow between networks

   C. To provide a secure connection between a client and a server

   D. To provide a method for hiding the client's IP address from the server

61. Which of the following is a primary characteristic of a zero-trust network architecture?

   A. Trust is always extended based on network location.

   B. Trust is never extended automatically and must be earned.

   C. Trust is always extended to internal network devices.

   D. Trust is never extended under any circumstances.

62. What is the primary purpose of Single Sign-On (SSO)?

    A. To reduce the number of passwords a user must remember

    B. To increase the complexity of authentication

    C. To provide multiple factors of authentication

    D. To provide a backup authentication method

63. What is the primary purpose of a red team exercise?

    A. To identify vulnerabilities in a system before an attacker does

    B. To test the effectiveness of blue team defenses

    C. To demonstrate compliance with regulations

    D. To investigate a security incident

64. What is the primary purpose of change management in IT operations?

    A. To ensure that changes do not introduce new security risks

    B. To ensure that changes are made as quickly as possible

    C. To ensure that changes are made without approval

    D. To ensure that changes are made without documentation

65. What is the primary purpose of fuzz testing in software development?

    A. To ensure that the software meets its requirements

    B. To ensure that the software does not have any security vulnerabilities

    C. To ensure that the software can handle unexpected input

    D. To ensure that the software is free of bugs

66. Which of the following best describes the concept of "separation of duties"?

    A. Assigning all tasks to a single individual to maintain consistency

    B. Assigning different tasks to different individuals to reduce the risk of fraud

    C. Assigning all tasks to multiple individuals to ensure redundancy

    D. Assigning different tasks to different systems to ensure system performance

67. What is the primary purpose of a data loss prevention (DLP) system?

    A. To prevent data from being deleted

    B. To prevent data from being modified

    C. To prevent data from being exfiltrated

    D. To prevent data from being accessed

68. What is the primary purpose of a public key infrastructure (PKI)?

    A. To manage digital certificates

    B. To manage user passwords

    C. To manage network access controls

    D. To manage firewall rules

69. Which of the following is a primary characteristic of a honeypot?

   A. A system designed to attract attackers to divert them from legitimate targets

   B. A system designed to prevent attackers from accessing the network

   C. A system designed to detect attackers once they have accessed the network

   D. A system designed to eliminate vulnerabilities in the network

70. What is the primary purpose of two-factor authentication (2FA)?

   A. To provide two methods of identification from separate categories of credentials

   B. To provide two methods of identification from the same category of credentials

   C. To provide two methods of identification from any category of credentials

   D. To provide two methods of identification from the user's memory

71. What is the primary purpose of a vulnerability assessment?

   A. To exploit vulnerabilities in a system

   B. To identify vulnerabilities in a system

   C. To eliminate vulnerabilities in a system

   D. To ignore vulnerabilities in a system

72. What is the primary purpose of an intrusion detection system (IDS)?

    A. To prevent attacks from occurring

    B. To detect attacks that are occurring

    C. To recover from attacks that have occurred

    D. To ignore attacks that are occurring

73. Which of the following best describes the concept of "risk appetite"?

    A. The total elimination of risk

    B. The level of risk that an organization is willing to accept

    C. The transfer of risk to another party

    D. The process of identifying potential threats

74. What is the primary purpose of data masking?

    A. To protect data in transit

    B. To protect data at rest

    C. To protect data in use

    D. To protect data from deletion

75. What is the primary purpose of a firewall in a network?

    A. To manage digital certificates

    B. To manage user passwords

    C. To manage network access controls

    D. To manage firewall rules

76. Which of the following is a primary characteristic of a VPN?

   A. A system designed to provide secure remote access over an untrusted network

   B. A system designed to prevent attackers from accessing the network

   C. A system designed to detect attackers once they have accessed the network

   D. A system designed to eliminate vulnerabilities in the network

77. What is the primary purpose of a password policy?

   A. To provide guidelines for creating strong passwords

   B. To provide guidelines for storing user data

   C. To provide guidelines for network access

   D. To provide guidelines for user behavior

78. What is the primary purpose of an incident response plan?

   A. To prevent security incidents from occurring

   B. To detect security incidents that are occurring

   C. To respond to security incidents that have occurred

   D. To ignore security incidents that are occurring

79. Which of the following best describes the concept of "risk transference"?

   A. The process of eliminating all risks

   B. The process of accepting the potential risk and continuing operating the business

    C. The process of shifting the risk to a third party

    D. The process of reducing the impact of the risk

80. What is the primary purpose of a security information and event management (SIEM) system?

    A. To provide real-time analysis of security alerts generated by applications and network hardware

    B. To manage user identities and access controls

    C. To manage network infrastructure

    D. To manage software development processes

81. Which of the following is a primary characteristic of a stateful firewall?

    A. A firewall that only examines the header information in each packet

    B. A firewall that keeps track of the state of network connections

    C. A firewall that only blocks or allows traffic based on the source and destination addresses

    D. A firewall that operates on the application layer of the OSI model

82. What is the primary purpose of a directory service like LDAP?

    A. To provide a method for distributing software updates

    B. To provide a method for storing and accessing user account information and network resources

    C. To provide a method for monitoring network traffic

    D. To provide a method for encrypting network traffic

83. What is the primary purpose of a business continuity plan (BCP)?

    A. To prevent security incidents from occurring

    B. To detect security incidents that are occurring

    C. To respond to security incidents that have occurred

    D. To ensure critical business functions continue during and after a disaster

84. What is the primary purpose of a secure Software Development Life Cycle (SDLC)?

    A. To ensure that the software meets its requirements

    B. To ensure that security is considered throughout the software development process

    C. To ensure that the software can handle unexpected input

    D. To ensure that the software is free of bugs

85. What is the primary purpose of a demilitarized zone (DMZ) in a network?

    A. To provide a secure area for the organization's most sensitive data

    B. To provide an area isolated from the Internet where internal users can work

    C. To provide an area that can safely host public-facing services

    D. To provide an area where all network traffic is blocked

86. What is the primary purpose of a security control self-assessment?

    A. To provide an independent assessment of security controls

    B. To provide a vendor's assessment of security controls

    C. To provide a regulatory body's assessment of security controls

    D. To provide an organization's own assessment of its security controls

87. What is the primary purpose of a security operations center (SOC)?

    A. To provide a location for the organization's servers

    B. To provide a location for the organization's security staff

    C. To provide a centralized unit to deal with security issues

    D. To provide a location for the organization's network equipment

88. What is the primary purpose of code obfuscation?

    A. To make the code run faster

    B. To make the code easier to read

    C. To make the code harder to reverse engineer

    D. To make the code easier to write

89. Which of the following best describes the concept of "risk mitigation"?

    A. The process of accepting the potential risk and continuing operating the business

    B. The process of reducing the impact of a risk

C. The process of transferring the risk to a third party

D. The process of avoiding the risk

90. What is the primary purpose of a security model?

A. To provide a blueprint for implementing security controls

B. To provide a blueprint for network infrastructure

C. To provide a blueprint for software development

D. To provide a blueprint for business operations

91. Which of the following is a primary characteristic of a network intrusion detection system (NIDS)?

A. A system that prevents unauthorized access to the network

B. A system that detects unauthorized access to the network

C. A system that recovers from unauthorized access to the network

D. A system that ignores unauthorized access to the network

92. What is the primary purpose of a disaster recovery plan (DRP)?

A. To prevent disasters from occurring

B. To detect disasters that are occurring

C. To respond to disasters that have occurred

D. To recover from a disaster and resume normal business operations

93. What is the primary purpose of a software patch?

A. To add new features to the software

B. To improve the performance of the software

C. To fix bugs or vulnerabilities in the software

D. To change the user interface of the software

94. What is the primary purpose of a change management process?

A. To prevent unauthorized changes to systems

B. To document all changes to systems

C. To approve all changes to systems

D. To ignore all changes to systems

95. What is the primary purpose of a data destruction policy?

A. To determine how long data should be preserved

B. To determine who has access to the data

C. To determine how data should be securely disposed of when no longer needed

D. To determine when the data should be used

96. What is the primary purpose of a Trusted Platform Module (TPM)?

A. To provide a secure cryptographic processor on a device

B. To provide a secure network connection

C. To provide secure software development processes

D. To provide secure business operations

97. Which of the following is a primary characteristic of a proxy server?

   A. A server that provides secure connections between clients and servers

   B. A server that provides storage for network data

   C. A server that provides a gateway between users and the Internet

   D. A server that provides computational resources for network devices

98. What is the primary purpose of a firewall in a network?

   A. To provide a secure area for the organization's most sensitive data

   B. To provide an area isolated from the Internet where internal users can work

   C. To provide a barrier or shield to prevent unauthorized access to a network

   D. To provide an area where all network traffic is blocked

99. Which of the following is a primary characteristic of a Virtual Local Area Network (VLAN)?

   A. A network that allows public access to internal resources

   B. A network that allows no access to resources

   C. A network that provides secure access to internal resources over a public network

   D. A network that allows a single physical network to be partitioned into multiple logical networks

881

100. What is the primary purpose of a black box testing?

   A. To identify vulnerabilities in a system

   B. To test the functionality of a system without knowledge of its internal structure

   C. To verify that security policies and procedures are being followed

   D. To ignore vulnerabilities in a system

101. What is the primary purpose of a code review in software development?

   A. To ensure that the software meets its requirements

   B. To check the software code for errors or vulnerabilities

   C. To ensure that the software can handle unexpected input

   D. To ensure that the software is free of bugs

Answers

1. Answer: D. User interface design

   Explanation: User interface design is generally not considered a key element of a secure Software Development Life Cycle (SDLC). While it is an important aspect of software development, it does not directly focus on security measures or protocols. Key elements of a secure SDLC include security requirements gathering, threat modeling, and code review for security flaws, all of which are aimed at ensuring the security of the software throughout its development and deployment.

2. Answer: D. It is based on a dictionary word.

   Explanation: Utilizing a dictionary word as the basis for a password is generally not considered a characteristic of a strong password. Strong passwords are typically at least 12 characters long, include a mix of uppercase and lowercase letters, and are updated regularly to enhance security. Using a dictionary word can make the password more susceptible to dictionary attacks, thereby weakening its strength.

3. Answer: D. Cost-benefit analysis

   Explanation: Cost-benefit analysis is generally not considered a key element of a standard risk assessment. While it may be a part of the broader risk management process, it is not a component of the risk assessment itself. Key elements of a risk assessment typically include threat identification, vulnerability assessment, and sometimes asset valuation, all aimed at understanding and evaluating the risks that could adversely affect an organization's assets and operations.

4. Answer: D. Data backup and recovery

   Explanation: Data backup and recovery is generally not considered a primary function of an Identity and Access Management (IAM) system. While backup and recovery are important aspects of overall IT security and management, they are not the focus of IAM systems. IAM systems are primarily concerned with managing digital identities, providing Single Sign-On capabilities, enforcing access control policies, and monitoring and auditing user activity. Therefore, data backup and recovery would be the most appropriate answer as NOT being a primary function of an IAM system.

5. Answer: D. Incident response time optimization

Explanation: Incident response time optimization is generally not considered a key principle of security governance. While it is an important aspect of incident management and overall security, it is not a foundational principle of governance. Security governance primarily focuses on developing and implementing policies and procedures, ensuring compliance with laws and regulations, and defining roles and responsibilities within the organization. Therefore, incident response time optimization would be the most appropriate answer as NOT being a key principle of security governance.

6. Answer: D. Software development assessment

Explanation: Software development assessment is generally not considered a type of security assessment. While it may include security-related evaluations, its primary focus is on the overall quality and functionality of software development processes. On the other hand, threat assessment, vulnerability assessment, and penetration tests are specialized types of security assessments aimed at identifying and evaluating potential security risks. Therefore, software development assessment would be the most appropriate answer as NOT being a type of security assessment.

7. Answer: D. Risk acceptance

   Explanation: Risk acceptance is not a key component of a risk assessment. A risk assessment is a process for identifying and evaluating potential risks to an organization. It typically includes identification of threats, vulnerabilities, and assets, as well as the assessment of the likelihood and impact of risks. Risk acceptance is a decision that may be made after a risk assessment has been completed, but it is not a key component of the assessment itself.

8. Answer: D. Encrypting data

   Explanation: Encrypting data is not a function of a security information and event management (SIEM) system. A SIEM system is a security tool that is used to collect, analyze, and report on security-related data. It provides real-time monitoring and alerting and can generate reports on security-related events, but it does not perform data encryption.

9. Answer: D. Keyless encryption

   Explanation: Keyless encryption is not a type of encryption. Symmetric encryption, asymmetric encryption, and hash encryption are all types of encryption that are used to secure data in different ways.

10. Answer: D. Outsourcing development

   Explanation: Outsourcing development is not a key principle of secure software development. Key principles of secure software development include minimizing the attack surface, using secure coding practices, and implementing regular software updates.

11. Answer: D. Social engineering assessment

    Explanation: Social engineering assessment is not a type of security assessment. Penetration testing, vulnerability assessment, and risk assessment are all types of security assessments that are designed to identify weaknesses and vulnerabilities in an organization's security posture.

12. Answer: D. The budget of the organization

    Explanation: The budget of the organization is not a factor that should be considered when developing a disaster recovery plan. A disaster recovery plan should be based on the impact of a disaster on the organization, the likelihood of a disaster occurring, and the availability of resources for recovery, among other factors.

13. Answer: D. Provision of legal assistance

    Explanation: Provision of legal assistance is not a key component of a security incident response plan. The key components of a security incident response plan typically include identification of the incident, containment of the incident, and prevention of future incidents.

14. Answer: D. Ensuring that assets are used efficiently

    Explanation: Ensuring that assets are used efficiently is not a key principle of asset management. Key principles of asset management include identifying and classifying assets, establishing ownership and responsibility for assets, and protecting assets from unauthorized access or tampering.

15. Answer: D. Usability

    Explanation: Usability is not a key consideration when designing a secure system. Key considerations when designing a secure system include confidentiality, integrity, and availability.

16. Answer: C. Phishing attack

    Explanation: In this question, option C, "phishing attack," is generally not considered a type of network attack in the strictest sense. While phishing attacks often utilize network communications, they primarily target individuals through social engineering tactics rather than exploiting network vulnerabilities. Therefore, "phishing attack" would be the most appropriate answer as NOT being a type of network attack.

17. Answer: D. Monitoring and auditing user activity

    Explanation: While IAM systems are primarily focused on managing user accounts and permissions, providing Single Sign-On (SSO) capabilities, and enforcing access control policies, they are not typically responsible for monitoring and auditing user activity. Monitoring and auditing are generally handled by other specialized systems, such as Security Information and Event Management (SIEM) systems, which are designed to provide comprehensive monitoring, logging, and analysis of security events and user activities.

18. Answer: D. Legal controls

Explanation: Legal controls are not a common type of security control. Physical controls, technical controls, and administrative controls are all common types of security controls that are used to protect assets and prevent unauthorized access or misuse.

19. Answer: D. Establishing a budget for recovery efforts

Explanation: Establishing a budget for recovery efforts is not a key element of a business impact analysis (BIA). A BIA typically includes an identification of the critical functions of the organization, an estimation of the potential impact of a disruption on the organization, and the development of a recovery plan.

20. Answer: D. Outsourcing security functions

Explanation: Outsourcing security functions is not a key principle of compliance. Key principles of compliance include adhering to laws and regulations, ensuring that security policies and procedures are followed, and providing regular reports to regulatory bodies.

21. Answer: A. To protect against unauthorized access

Explanation: Implementing a password policy is an important security measure that helps to prevent unauthorized access to sensitive or confidential information. Ensuring compliance with industry regulations, improving system performance, and preventing data loss are all important considerations, but they are not as critical as protecting against unauthorized access.

22. Answer: A. To protect against data loss

    Explanation: Conducting regular backups of data is an important measure to ensure the availability and integrity of critical information. Ensuring compliance with industry regulations, improving system performance, and preventing unauthorized access are all important considerations, but they are not as critical as protecting against data loss.

23. Answer: A. To protect against unauthorized access

    Explanation: Implementing access controls on a computer system is an important security measure that helps to prevent unauthorized access to sensitive or confidential information. Ensuring compliance with industry regulations, improving system performance, and preventing data loss are all important considerations, but they are not as critical as protecting against unauthorized access.

24. Answer: D. To identify potential risks to the organization

    Explanation: Conducting a risk assessment is an important step in the risk management process that helps to identify potential risks that could impact the organization. Determining the likelihood of a risk occurring, assessing the impact of a risk, and prioritizing risks based on their likelihood and impact are all important considerations, but they are not as critical as identifying potential risks in the first place.

25. Answer: D. To minimize the impact of a disaster on the business

    Explanation: A business continuity plan is a document that outlines the steps an organization should take to continue operating in the event of a disaster or other disruption. Ensuring the safety of employees, complying with industry regulations, and reducing insurance costs are all important considerations, but they are not as critical as minimizing the impact of a disaster on the business.

26. Answer: D. The process of identifying and evaluating potential risks to an organization

    Explanation: A risk assessment is a systematic process of identifying and evaluating potential risks to an organization, with the goal of minimizing the impact of those risks. Managing security policies to influence behavior, the security of an organization within a company, and the process of how an organization is managed are all important considerations, but they are not the best description of a risk assessment.

27. Answer: D. A document outlining the steps an organization should take to continue operating in the event of a disaster or other disruptions

    Explanation: A business continuity plan is a document that outlines the steps an organization should take to continue operating in the event of a disaster or other disruptions. Managing security policies to influence behavior, the security of an organization within a company, and the process of how an organization is managed are all important considerations, but they are not the best description of a business continuity plan.

28.   Answer: D. A set of guidelines for creating and managing passwords

Explanation: A password policy is a set of guidelines that outlines the requirements for creating and managing passwords within an organization. Managing security policies to influence behavior, the security of an organization within a company, and the process of how an organization is managed are all important considerations, but they are not the best description of a password policy.

29.   Answer: D. Measures that restrict access to resources or information

Explanation: Access controls are measures that are put in place to restrict access to resources or information based on predetermined criteria, such as user permissions or roles. Managing security policies to influence behavior, the security of an organization within a company, and the process of how an organization is managed are all important considerations, but they are not the best description of access controls.

30.   Answer: D. The process of creating copies of data for storage in a separate location

Explanation: The best description of data backup is the process of creating copies of data for storage in a separate location. Data backup is the practice of creating copies of important data and storing them in a separate location for safekeeping. This can be done for a variety of reasons, including to protect against data loss due to hardware failures, software errors, or other types of disasters. Data backups can be stored locally, on external hard drives or other storage devices, or in the cloud. They can be used to restore data in the event of a problem or to access historical versions of data for a variety of purposes.

31. Answer: D. Data classified according to the organization's data classification policy

Explanation: Data sensitivity refers to the classification of data according to its importance or value to the organization. An organization's data classification policy typically outlines the different categories of data sensitivity, such as public, internal, confidential, and sensitive, and specifies the appropriate handling and protection measures for each category. Data with a high level of criticality, data classified as Top Secret, and data classified as public are all important considerations, but they are not the best description of data sensitivity.

32. Answer: D. Access controls reduce the risk of threats and vulnerabilities by limiting exposure to unauthorized activities and providing access to information and systems only to those who have been approved.

Explanation: Access controls are a set of mechanisms that work together to protect the assets of the enterprise. They help to reduce the risk of threats and vulnerabilities by limiting exposure to unauthorized activities and granting access to information and systems only to those who have been approved.

33. Answer: D. Patch management

Explanation: Patch management is the process of identifying and installing software updates or patches in order to fix vulnerabilities in software or operating systems. Network scanning, code review, and social engineering are all methods that can be used to conduct a vulnerability assessment, which involves evaluating the security of an organization's systems, networks, and data in order to identify potential risks and vulnerabilities.

34. Answer: D. To ensure compliance with industry regulations

Explanation: A penetration test, also known as a "pen test," is a simulated cyberattack that is conducted by security professionals in order to identify vulnerabilities in an organization's systems, networks, and data. The goals of a pen test include identifying vulnerabilities, determining the likelihood of a successful cyberattack, and evaluating the effectiveness of an organization's security controls. Ensuring compliance with industry regulations is not a common goal of a pen test.

35. Answer: C. The individual who is responsible for maintaining the data

Explanation: While all of these roles have some responsibility for data protection, the primary responsibility lies with the individual maintaining the data (option C), often referred to as the data custodian. The data owner (option A) defines the controls and procedures, but the custodian implements them. The data user (option B) must follow security procedures but is not primarily responsible for data protection. The auditor (option D) checks the effectiveness of security measures but does not directly protect the data.

36. Answer: C. Packet filtering firewall

Explanation: All these firewalls can make decisions based on the IP address, but a packet filtering firewall (option C) is specifically designed to operate at the network layer and make decisions based on the IP address, protocol, and port number in the packet header. Circuit-level gateways (option A) and application-level gateways (option B) operate at higher layers and make decisions based on more complex criteria. Stateful inspection firewalls (option D) operate at the network layer but keep track of the state of network connections and make decisions based on the state and context.

37. Answer: A. To provide a secure communication channel over an untrusted network

Explanation: All these options could be seen as benefits of using a VPN, but the primary benefit is to provide a secure communication channel over an untrusted network (option A). While a well-optimized VPN may improve data transmission speed in some cases (option B), it is not its primary purpose. Bypassing network access controls (option

C) is generally considered a misuse of VPNs and not their intended function. Monitoring network traffic (option D) is a function of network monitoring tools, not VPNs.

38. Answer: A. Users should be given the minimum levels of access necessary to perform their duties.

    Explanation: Options A and B are similar, but the principle of least privilege specifically states that users should be given the minimum levels of access necessary to perform their duties (option A). This minimizes the potential damage that can be caused if their accounts are compromised. Option C describes a temporary privilege escalation, which is a different concept. Option D is incorrect as access should be based on job function, not seniority.

39. Answer: A. To identify vulnerabilities in a system before an attacker does

    Explanation: All these options could be seen as goals of penetration testing, but the primary goal is to identify vulnerabilities in a system before an attacker does (option A). Demonstrating the potential impact of a successful attack (option B), testing the effectiveness of security controls (option C), and complying with regulatory requirements (option D) are all secondary goals.

40. Answer: B. A step-by-step guide for mitigating an incident

    Explanation: All these options could be seen as components of an IRP, but the key component is a step-by-step guide for mitigating an incident

895

(option B). A list of potential vulnerabilities (option A) is important for proactive security, but it is not a component of an IRP. A plan for communicating during and after an incident (option C) is also important, but it is not the key component. A list of approved software (option D) is typically a part of an organization's IT policy, not an IRP.

41. Answer: B. To prevent injection attacks

Explanation: All these options could be seen as benefits of input validation, but the primary purpose is to prevent injection attacks by ensuring that the data entered by a user is safe and valid (option B). Improving the user experience (option A) and ensuring the accuracy of the data (option C) are secondary benefits. Reducing the size of the software (option D) is not a direct benefit of input validation.

42. Answer: C. Mitigating risks to an acceptable level

Explanation: While all these options are strategies for managing risk, the most effective strategy is typically to mitigate risks to an acceptable level (option C). Accepting all risks (option A) might not be feasible if the risks are too high. Transferring all risks (option B) might not be possible or cost-effective. Avoiding all risks (option D) might not be possible without ceasing operations.

43. Answer: B. To determine the sensitivity of the data

Explanation: The primary purpose of data classification is to determine the sensitivity of the data (option B), which helps in applying appropriate security controls. While data classification might indirectly help determine the value of the data (option A), it is not its primary purpose. The age of the data (option C) and the owner of the data (option D) are typically determined through other means.

44. Answer: C. Minimalism

    Explanation: Minimalism (option C) is a key principle of secure system design, which states that the simpler the system, the easier it is to secure. Complexity (option A) often leads to increased security risks. Open design (option B) is a principle that states that the security of a system should not depend on the secrecy of its design. Obscurity (option D) is generally not a recommended principle as it relies on secrecy rather than proven security measures.

45. Answer: A. MAC address filtering

    Explanation: MAC address filtering (option A) is a common method for securing wireless networks by only allowing devices with specific MAC addresses to connect. Port scanning (option B), packet sniffing (option C), and IP spoofing (option D) are techniques often used in network attacks, not for securing networks.

46. Answer: B. To increase the security of the authentication process

    Explanation: The primary purpose of multifactor authentication is to increase the security of the authentication process (option B) by requiring the user to provide two or more forms of identification. While it might increase complexity and cost (options A and C), and it might slow down the process (option D), the increased security is typically worth the trade-offs.

47. Answer: C. A vulnerability scan identifies weaknesses, while a penetration test exploits them.

   Explanation: A vulnerability scan is typically automated and identifies weaknesses in a system (option A), while a penetration test is often manual and goes a step further by attempting to exploit the identified weaknesses (option C). While there can be manual elements in a vulnerability scan and automated elements in a penetration test, the key difference is in the identification vs. exploitation of weaknesses.

48. Answer: C. A plan for maintaining operations during a disruption

   Explanation: A business continuity plan (BCP) typically includes a plan for maintaining operations during a disruption (option C). A list of potential vulnerabilities (option A) is typically part of a risk assessment, not a BCP. A step-by-step guide for mitigating an incident (option B) is part of an incident response plan (IRP), not a BCP. A list of approved software (option D) is typically part of an organization's IT policy, not a BCP.

49. Answer: A. Input validation

Explanation: Input validation (option A) is a common method for preventing SQL injection attacks by ensuring that the data entered by a user is safe and valid. Code obfuscation (option B) makes the code harder to understand but does not prevent SQL injection. Code minification (option C) reduces the size of the code but does not prevent SQL injection. Code refactoring (option D) improves the code's structure but does not prevent SQL injection.

50. Answer: A. The legal obligation to implement reasonable security measures

Explanation: "Due care" refers to the reasonable measures or steps taken to show that an organization has responsibly managed its risk. It's a legal term that implies an organization is operating according to established standards and is taking the necessary steps to protect its resources and employees. The other options, while related to risk management, do not accurately define "due care."

51. Answer: C. To ensure data confidentiality

Explanation: The primary purpose of data encryption is to ensure data confidentiality by transforming readable data into unreadable data to prevent unauthorized access. While encryption can also help with data integrity (option B), it's not its primary purpose. Encryption does not directly contribute to data storage efficiency (option A) or data availability (option D).

52. Answer: B. To define an organization's guiding security principles

    Explanation: The primary purpose of a security policy is to define an organization's guiding security principles and establish the general approach to security. It provides a framework for making specific decisions, such as choosing security solutions or responding to incidents. The other options describe procedures (option A), technical specifications (option C), and possibly elements of a policy, but they do not capture the primary purpose of a security policy.

53. Answer: B. A network segment that is exposed to an untrusted network, usually the Internet

    Explanation: A DMZ is a physical or logical subnetwork that contains and exposes an organization's external-facing services to an untrusted network, usually the Internet. The idea is to provide a layer of protection for the rest of the network by isolating services that might be vulnerable to attack. The other options do not accurately describe a DMZ.

54. Answer: A. To grant permissions based on job functions

    Explanation: The primary purpose of role-based access control (RBAC) is to grant permissions based on job functions. Each role is assigned the permissions necessary to perform associated job functions. The other options describe attribute-based access control (option B), mandatory access control (option C), and discretionary access control (option D), respectively.

55. Answer: C. To demonstrate compliance with regulations

Explanation: The primary goal of a security audit is to demonstrate compliance with regulations by examining and verifying an organization's security policies, procedures, and controls. While a security audit might identify vulnerabilities (option A), test the effectiveness of controls (option B), or be part of an incident investigation (option D), these are not its primary goal.

56. Answer: B. A step-by-step guide for resuming operations after a disaster

Explanation: A disaster recovery plan (DRP) typically includes a step-by-step guide for resuming operations after a disaster, including roles and responsibilities, priorities, and recovery strategies. A list of potential vulnerabilities (option A) is typically part of a risk assessment, not a DRP. A plan for maintaining operations during a disruption (option C) is part of a business continuity plan (BCP), not a DRP. A list of approved software (option D) is typically part of an organization's IT policy, not a DRP.

57. Answer: D. To ensure that the software is developed in a way that minimizes security risks

Explanation: The primary purpose of a secure coding standard is to guide developers in creating software in a way that minimizes security risks.

While a secure coding standard might indirectly help reduce bugs (option A), improve development time (option B), or control development costs (option C), its primary purpose is to improve security.

58. Answer: A. Implementing multiple layers of security controls throughout an IT system

Explanation: "Defense in depth" is a strategy that employs a series of security mechanisms to protect the integrity of the information assets in an enterprise. The idea behind this strategy is to manage risk with diverse defensive strategies, so if one layer of defense turns out to be inadequate, another layer of defense will hopefully prevent a full breach.

59. Answer: A. To determine how long data should be retained before it is destroyed

Explanation: A data retention policy is a guideline about keeping or deleting data. A data retention policy is important for any company that deals with data collection, storage, and retrieval. While it may touch on aspects of access, storage, and usage, its primary purpose is to define how long data should be kept.

60. Answer: B. To provide a layer of abstraction and control over the data flow between networks

Explanation: A proxy server acts as a gateway between users and the Internet. It's an intermediary server separating end-user clients from the websites they browse. Proxy servers provide varying levels of functionality, security, and privacy depending on use case, needs, or company policy.

61. Answer: B. Trust is never extended automatically and must be earned.

    Explanation: Zero Trust is a security concept centered on the belief that organizations should not automatically trust anything inside or outside its perimeters and instead must verify anything and everything trying to connect to its systems before granting access.

62. Answer: A. To reduce the number of passwords a user must remember

    Explanation: Single Sign-On (SSO) is a session and user authentication service that permits a user to use one set of login credentials (e.g., name and password) to access multiple applications. The service authenticates the end user for all the applications the user has been given rights to and eliminates further prompts when the user switches applications during the same session.

63. Answer: B. To test the effectiveness of blue team defenses

    Explanation: A red team exercise is a full-scope, multilayered attack simulation designed to measure how well a company's people and networks, applications, and physical security controls can withstand an attack from a real-life adversary.

64. Answer: A. To ensure that changes do not introduce new security risks

Explanation: Change management is a systematic approach to dealing with the transition or transformation of an organization's goals, processes, or technologies. The purpose of change management is to implement strategies for effecting change, controlling change, and helping people to adapt to change.

65. Answer: C. To ensure that the software can handle unexpected input

Explanation: Fuzzing or fuzz testing is an automated software testing technique that involves providing invalid, unexpected, or random data as inputs to a computer program. The program is then monitored for exceptions such as crashes, failing built-in code assertions, or potential memory leaks.

66. Answer: B. Assigning different tasks to different individuals to reduce the risk of fraud

Explanation: Separation of duties is a key concept of internal controls and is the basis for many of the control activities established in organizations. The principle of separation of duties is that no employee or group should be in a position both to perpetrate and to conceal errors or fraud in the normal course of their duties.

67. Answer: C. To prevent data from being exfiltrated

Explanation: Data loss prevention (DLP) is a strategy for making sure that end users do not send sensitive or critical information outside the corporate network. The term is also used to describe software products that help a network administrator control what data end users can transfer.

68. Answer: A. To manage digital certificates

    Explanation: A public key infrastructure (PKI) is a set of roles, policies, hardware, software, and procedures needed to create, manage, distribute, use, store, and revoke digital certificates and manage public key encryption.

69. Answer: A. A system designed to attract attackers to divert them from legitimate targets

    Explanation: A honeypot is a computer security mechanism set to detect, deflect, or, in some manner, counteract attempts at unauthorized use of information systems. Generally, a honeypot consists of data that appears to be a legitimate part of the site, but is actually isolated and monitored, and that seems to contain information or a resource of value to attackers, who are then blocked.

70. Answer: A. To provide two methods of identification from separate categories of credentials

    Explanation: Two-factor authentication (2FA) is a type of multifactor authentication. It is a method of confirming users' claimed identities by using a combination of two different factors: something they know, something they have, or something they are.

71. Answer: B. To identify vulnerabilities in a system

Explanation: A vulnerability assessment is the process of identifying, quantifying, and prioritizing (or ranking) the vulnerabilities in a system.

72. Answer: B. To detect attacks that are occurring

Explanation: An intrusion detection system (IDS) is a device or software application that monitors a network or systems for malicious activity or policy violations.

73. Answer: B. The level of risk that an organization is willing to accept

Explanation: Risk appetite is the level of risk that an organization is prepared to accept in pursuit of its objectives, before action is deemed necessary to reduce the risk. It represents a balance between the potential benefits of innovation and the threats that change inevitably brings.

74. Answer: C. To protect data in use

Explanation: Data masking is a method of creating a structurally similar but inauthentic version of an organization's data that can be used for purposes such as software testing and user training. The purpose is to protect the actual data while having a functional substitute for occasions when the real data is not required.

75. Answer: C. To manage network access controls

Explanation: A firewall is a network security device that monitors incoming and outgoing network traffic and decides whether to allow or block specific traffic based on a defined set of security rules.

76. Answer: A. A system designed to provide secure remote access over an untrusted network

Explanation: A Virtual Private Network (VPN) extends a private network across a public network and enables users to send and receive data across shared or public networks as if their computing devices were directly connected to the private network.

77. Answer: A. To provide guidelines for creating strong passwords

Explanation: A password policy is a set of rules designed to enhance computer security by encouraging users to employ strong passwords and use them properly.

78. Answer: C. To respond to security incidents that have occurred

Explanation: An incident response plan is a set of instructions to help IT staff detect, respond to, and recover from network security incidents. These types of plans address issues like cybercrime, data loss, and service outages that threaten daily work.

79. Answer: C. The process of shifting the risk to a third party

Explanation: Risk transference is a risk management and control strategy that involves the contractual shifting of a pure risk from one party to another. One example is the purchase of an insurance policy, by which a specified risk of loss is passed from the policyholder to the insurer. It does not eliminate the risk or reduce the impact of the risk, but it does shift the financial burden of the risk to another party.

80. Answer: A. To provide real-time analysis of security alerts generated by applications and network hardware

Explanation: Security information and event management (SIEM) is a set of integrated log management and security event management tools that provide real-time analysis of security alerts generated by applications and network hardware. It collects security data from network devices, servers, domain controllers, and more. SIEM stores, normalizes, aggregates, applies intelligence to, and reports on that data. It's not primarily used for managing identities, network infrastructure, or software development processes.

81. Answer: B. A firewall that keeps track of the state of network connections

Explanation: A stateful firewall is a network firewall that tracks the operating state and characteristics of network connections traversing it. The firewall is configured to distinguish legitimate packets for different types of connections. Only packets matching a known active connection are allowed by the firewall; others are rejected. It does not only examine header information or only block/allow traffic based on addresses, and while it can operate on various layers of the OSI model, that is not its defining characteristic.

82. Answer: B. To provide a method for storing and accessing user account information and network resources

Explanation: LDAP (Lightweight Directory Access Protocol) is a software protocol for enabling anyone to locate organizations, individuals, and other resources such as files and devices in a network, whether on the public Internet or on a corporate intranet. It is primarily used for providing a "phone book" service for email clients, but it also stores and organizes other types of information.

83. Answer: D. To ensure critical business functions continue during and after a disaster

Explanation: A business continuity plan (BCP) is a document that outlines how a business will continue operating during an unplanned disruption in service. It's more comprehensive than a disaster recovery plan and contains contingencies for business processes, assets, human resources, and business partners – every aspect of the business that might be affected.

84. Answer: B. To ensure that security is considered throughout the software development process

Explanation: A secure SDLC process ensures that security assurance activities such as penetration testing, code review, and architecture analysis are an integral part of the development effort. The primary goal of a secure SDLC is to help define and implement appropriate security controls for each phase of the software development process.

This includes the initial concept phase of a project, the requirements phase, design, implementation, testing, and even the retirement phase.

85. Answer: C. To provide an area that can safely host public-facing services

    Explanation: In computer security, a DMZ or demilitarized zone (sometimes referred to as a perimeter network or screened subnet) is a physical or logical subnetwork that contains and exposes an organization's external-facing services to an untrusted network, usually a larger network such as the Internet. The purpose of a DMZ is to add an additional layer of security to an organization's Local Area Network (LAN).

86. Answer: D. To provide an organization's own assessment of its security controls

    Explanation: A self-assessment is a systematic process where staff at all levels in an organization identify and assess risks that might prevent their program, project, or organization from achieving its objectives. It provides an internal review of an organization's capacity, performance, and risks.

87. Answer: C. To provide a centralized unit to deal with security issues

    Explanation: A security operations center (SOC) is a centralized unit in an organization that deals with security issues on an organizational and technical level. A SOC team's primary function is to continuously monitor and improve an organization's security posture while preventing, detecting, analyzing, and responding to cybersecurity incidents.

88. Answer: C. To make the code harder to reverse engineer

   Explanation: Code obfuscation is the act of intentionally creating obfuscated code, that is, source or machine code that is difficult for humans to understand. This can be done for the purpose of intellectual property protection, in order to prevent reverse engineering, or as a form of amusement for the programmer.

89. Answer: B. The process of reducing the impact of a risk

   Explanation: Risk mitigation involves the development of actions and options to enhance opportunities and reduce threats to the project's objectives. It includes risk reduction and risk contingency actions and implementing the risk mitigation plan.

90. Answer: A. To provide a blueprint for implementing security controls

   Explanation: A security model is a design artifact that delineates the security architecture for a system or subsystem. It provides a high-level description of the solution to be implemented and includes the security principles and concepts that guide the design.

91. Answer: B. A system that detects unauthorized access to the network

Explanation: A network intrusion detection system (NIDS) is a system that monitors the traffic on your network to detect malicious activity such as denial-of-service attacks, port scans, or even attempts to crack into computers.

92. Answer: D. To recover from a disaster and resume normal business operations

Explanation: A disaster recovery plan (DRP) is a documented process or set of procedures to execute an organization's disaster recovery processes and recover and protect a business IT infrastructure in the event of a disaster. It is "a comprehensive statement of consistent actions to be taken before, during and after a disaster."

93. Answer: C. To fix bugs or vulnerabilities in the software

Explanation: A patch is a software update comprised of code inserted (or patched) into the code of an executable program. Typically, a patch is installed into an existing software program. Patches are often temporary fixes between full releases of a software package. Patches may do many things, including fixing a software bug, replacing graphics, or improving the usability or performance of a previous version of software.

94. Answer: B. To document all changes to systems

Explanation: Change management is a systematic approach to dealing with the transition or transformation of an organization's goals, processes or technologies. The purpose of change management is to implement strategies for effecting change, controlling change, and helping people to adapt to change. These strategies can be applied to any instance where change is introduced to an organization.

95. Answer: C. To determine how data should be securely disposed of when no longer needed

Explanation: A data destruction policy outlines how to responsibly dispose of data when it is no longer needed. This is important because data that is not disposed of properly can be accessed by unauthorized individuals, leading to data breaches.

96. Answer: A. To provide a secure cryptographic processor on a device

Explanation: A Trusted Platform Module (TPM) is a specialized chip on an endpoint device that stores RSA encryption keys specific to the host system for hardware authentication. The TPM helps to limit the impact of attacks such as software bugs and malware.

97. Answer: C. A server that provides a gateway between users and the Internet

Explanation: A proxy server acts as a gateway between you and the Internet. It's an intermediary server separating end users from the websites they browse. Proxy servers provide varying levels of functionality, security, and privacy depending on your use case, needs, or company policy.

98. Answer: C. To provide a barrier or shield to prevent unauthorized access to a network

Explanation: A firewall is a network security device that monitors incoming and outgoing network traffic and decides whether to allow or block specific traffic based on a defined set of security rules. Firewalls have been a first line of defense in network security for over 25 years.

99. Answer: D. A network that allows a single physical network to be partitioned into multiple logical networks

Explanation: A Virtual LAN (VLAN) is any broadcast domain that is partitioned and isolated in a computer network at the Data Link Layer (OSI Layer 2). LAN is the abbreviation for Local Area Network, and in this context, virtual refers to a physical object recreated and altered by additional logic.

100. Answer: B. To test the functionality of a system without knowledge of its internal structure

Explanation: Black box testing is a method of software testing where the functionality of an application is examined without the knowledge of its internal structures or workings. Specific knowledge of the application's code/internal structure and programming knowledge in general are not required. The tester is aware of what the software is supposed to do but is not aware of how it does it.

101. Answer: B. To check the software code for errors or vulnerabilities

Explanation: Code review is a software quality assurance activity in which one or several people check a program mainly by viewing and reading parts of its source code, and they do so after implementation or as an interruption of implementation. At least one of the persons must not be the code's author. The persons performing the checking, excluding the author, are called "reviewers."

Index

A

Acceptable level, 47, 149, 167, 896

Access control, 33, 39, 47, 265, 469, 737, 816, 825, 827, 831, 833, 837–839

Access control lists (ACLs), 50, 431, 465

Access control matrix, 240, 241

Access control mechanisms, 171, 423

Access control models, 36, 40, 44, 50, 54, 402, 418, 738

Access control policies, 53, 95, 481, 887

Access controls, 459
  description, 861, 891
  most accurate description, 862, 892

Access Control Services, 470, 474, 475

Access Management domain, 418–420

Accountability, 53, 406, 408, 409, 419, 442, 445, 474, 476
  access controls, 407
  audit trails, 407
  FIM, 407
  JIT, 408
  MFA, 407
  monitoring, 407
  multifaceted concept, 406

Account management data, 494

Acoustic/shock glass-break sensors, 608, 636

Adaptability, 314, 673

Address Resolution Protocol (ARP), 333, 358, 372, 386

Address space layout randomization (ASLR), 745, 786, 787

Administrative controls, 77, 459, 792, 793

Administrative processes, 184

Advanced Encryption Standard (AES), 47, 197, 225, 242

Adversarial attacks, 772, 838

Agile methodology, 649, 788

Alice's private key, 318

Allowlisting, 579, 586, 691, 716, 723

Amazon Web Services (AWS), 256, 414

© Mohamad Aly Bouke 2023
M. A. Bouke, *CISSP Exam Certification Companion*, Certification Study Companion Series,
https://doi.org/10.1007/979-8-8688-0057-3

C

Q

X, Y

Z

Printed in the United States
by Baker & Taylor Publisher Services

Printed in the United States
by Baker & Taylor Publisher Services